Lacan in Contexts

Lacan in Contexts

DAVID MACEY

VERSO

London · New York

This edition published by Verso 1988
© 1988 Verso
All rights reserved

Verso
UK: 6 Meard Street, London W1V 3HR
USA: 29 West 35th Street, New York, NY 10001 2291

Verso is the imprint of New Left Books

British Library Cataloguing in Publication Data
Macey, David, *1949–*
    Lacan in contexts.
    1. Psychoanalysis. Lacan, Jacques, 1901–1981.
    Critical studies
    I. Title
    150.19′5
    ISBN 0-86091-215-9
    ISBN 0-86091-942-0 Pbk

US Library of Congress Cataloguing in Publication Data
Macey, David, 1949–
    Lacan in contexts / David Macey.
        p.   cm.
    Bibliography: p.
    Includes index.
    ISBN 0-86091-215-9: $65.00. ISBN 0-86091-942-0 (pbk.): $18.95
    1. Psychoanalysis. 2. Lacan, Jacques, 1901–
3. Psychoanalysis—France—History. 4. Freud, Sigmund, 1865–1939—
Influence. 5. Feminism. I. Title.
BF173.M356 1988
150.19′5—dc19   88-17288
                                                            CIP

Printed in Great Britain by Bookcraft (Bath) Ltd, Midsomer Norton, Avon
Typeset by Leaper & Gard Ltd, Bristol

Contents

Abbreviations

E   Jacques Lacan, *Ecrits*; Paris: Seuil, 1966.

ES   Jacques Lacan, *Ecrits: A Selection*, trans. Alan Sheridan, London: Tavistock, 1977.

PP   Jacques Lacan, *De la Psychose paranoïaque dans ses rapports avec la personnalité, suivi de Premiers Ecrits sur la paranoïa*, Paris: Seuil, 1975.

S I   Jacques Lacan, *Le Séminaire. Livre I: Les Ecrits techniques de Freud*, texte établi par Jacques-Alain Miller, Paris: Seuil, 1975.

S II   Jacques Lacan, *Le Séminaire. Livre II: Le Moi dans la théorie de Freud et dans la technique de la psychanalyse*, texte établi par Jacques-Alain Miller, Paris: Seuil, 1978.

S III   Jacques Lacan, *Le Séminaire. Livre III: Les Psychoses*, texte établi par Jacques-Alain Miller, Paris: Seuil, 1981.

S VII   *Jacques Lacan, Le Séminaire. Livre VII: L'Ethique de la psychanalyse*, texte établi par Jacques-Alain Miller, Paris: 1986.

S XI   Jacques Lacan, *Le Séminaire. Livre XI: Les Quatre Concepts Fondamentaux de la psychanalyse*, texte établi par Jacques-Alain-Miller, Paris: Seuil, 1973.

FFC   Jacques Lacan, *The Four Fundamental Concepts of Psycho-*

analysis, trans. Alan Sheridan, London: The Hogarth Press and The Institute of Psycho-Analysis, 1977

S XX   Jacques Lacan, *Le Séminaire. Livre XX: Encore*, texte établi par Jacques-Alain Miller, Paris: Seuil, 1975.

FS   Jacques Lacan and the Ecole Freudienne, *Feminine Sexuality*, ed. Juliet Mitchell and Jacqueline Rose, trans. Jacqueline Rose, London: Macmillan, 1982.

SE   *The Standard Edition of the Complete Psychological Works of Sigmund Freud*, ed. James Strachey, London: The Hogarth Press and The Institute of Psycho-Analysis, 1953–74, 24 vols.

IJPA   *International Journal of Psycho-Analysis.*

RFP   *Revue Française de Psychanalyse.*

SPP   Société Psychanalytique de Paris.

SFP   Société Française de Psychanalyse.

EFP   Ecole Freudienne de Paris.

IPA   International Psychoanalytical Association

Preface

In Scotland, an isolated peak of over three thousand feet in height is known as a Munro. Climbing Munros is a popular, if potentially hazardous, pastime and can easily become an obsession if one develops the ambition to scale them all. The view from the summit is inevitably spectacular, but it induces a certain loss of perspective, as distances become foreshortened and as the lower ground appears to flatten out. In many respects, the intellectual climate of the early 1970s was conducive to the theoretical equivalent of an obsession with climbing Munros. The study groups of the period oriented themselves with reading lists or maps which suggested that theorists were mountains, and that Lacan was one of the highest. It seemed that, once one had scaled Althusser, it was possible to make the high traverse across Saussure to Lacan; Freud was little more than a col to be scrambled across during the traverse, and there was certainly no need to descend to the marshy ground inhabited by prehistoric creatures such as Edouard Pichon or René Laforgue. It was also deceptively easy to regard the scree on the lower slopes of Lacan (fragments of surrealism, splinters of phenomenology, slivers of Hegel) as so much dross which had been cast up as the peak was thrust upwards by its internal volcanic dynamic. At best it was a minor scenic feature; at worst an obstacle to reaching the summit. It may now be time to abandon the rush for the summit in favour of a more patient exploration, to look at some geological formations rather than at contour lines.

For a long time, the reader of Lacan has been faced with a stark dilemma: total acceptance or total rejection. In one sense this is a reflection of the fierce loyalties and hatreds inspired by a redoubtable individual, and of the sectarian affections that are so often inspired by psychoanalysis. But it is also an effect of the illusion that Lacan's work is a whole which is entire unto itself, that it has no basis in five decades of French intellectual life, that it is the result of some immaculate theoretical conception. If his work is to be evaluated critically, rather than being rejected out of hand or reproduced with filial piety, that illusion must be dispelled. The Munro must be related to the surrounding terrain and the underlying strata.

A number of contexts in which Lacan can be read are proposed here in an attempt to go beyond the dilemma of acceptance or rejection. 'The Final State' looks at the production of the theoretical monolith known as 'Lacan' and relates it to the hero myths which have plagued psychoanalytic historiography ever since Freud confessed to Fliess that he hoped the house in which he discovered the secret of dreams would one day be marked by a marble plaque. 'Retrospective' and 'Baltimore in the Early Morning' introduce a double historical perspective by examining Lacan's relations with an earlier generation of French psychoanalysts and with the classical psychiatric tradition in which he was originally trained, and by looking at his debts to surrealism, a discourse which influences both his views on language and his iconography of the feminine. Lacan does not simply return to Freud; he also returns at significant moments to the distinctive traditions he inherits from almost forgotten figures like Pichon and Clérambault, his 'only master in psychiatry', and he never denies that he has an affinity with the surrealists who manipulated signs and symbols in such a curiously effective manner. The artistic and poetic practices they use contribute almost as much to Lacan's understanding of language as do Saussure and the linguists he begins to refer to so often in the 1950s, while at least one of his psychoanalytic innovations represents a return to the earliest traditions of French psychoanalysis and to a dispute with Freud. In terms of linguistics, Lacan's debt to Saussure has been overstated, both in his own writings and in those of his commentators, and a lasting fascination with certain experiences of language has all too often been mistaken for a serious engagement with any rigorous linguistics. Lacan frequently departs from the orthodoxies of linguistics, constructing a vision of language in which ontology mingles with etymology, primal symbols with phonemes. Levels of analysis are conflated and confused, and linguistics finally gives way to *linguisterie* as the charms of positive linguistics fade in the face of those of psychotic language.

'Philosophy and Post-Philosophy', in the meantime, looks at Lacan's contradictory use of philosophy, which he views in surprisingly conventional terms, which he exploits as a source of conceptual in-puts and guarantees, and against which he hopes to lead a revolution that never materializes. Finally, and no doubt more controversially, the thesis that Lacan has something to offer feminism and can contribute to a theory of the gendering of the subject is challenged by a reading of Lacanian pronouncements upon femininity and by an examination of the metaphors and the iconography with which Lacan himself approached Freud's 'dark continent'.

This is of necessity a partial and limited study. At one level, its limitations reflect the fragmentary nature of the corpus available for research. It is improbable that any full account of Lacan will be written until the Seminar is available in something approaching its entirety, and as only six of the promised twenty-six volumes have been published, it is unlikely that that account will be written in the near future. Other limitations will also be apparent. The precise nature of Lacan's debt to the French psychiatric tradition is no more than touched upon here, and a full excavation must await the services of a more competent archaeologist. The existence of a definite theological strand in Lacan, and particularly in his writings on language, is merely noted here and requires much fuller treatment in future work. Remarks about psychoanalytic practice are general and indicative rather than specific or clinical; it would be somewhat unseemly for a non-analyst (and non-analysand) to venture too far into the clinical field.

Intellectual work is always a collective undertaking and, like anyone else writing on Lacan, I owe a great deal to all those who have written on him before me. Whatever criticisms I may voice of their work, and whatever reservations I may express, that debt is hereby acknowledged. Coming rather closer to home, my thanks are due to Margaret Atack for her solidarity during what feels to have been a long struggle.

Regrettably, the translations of the first two volumes of Lacan's *Seminar* (by John Forrester and Sylvana Tomaselli) were not available for consultation at the time of writing.

David Macey, Leeds, March 1988

1
The Final State

On two separate occasions – in 1885 and 1907 – Freud deliberately destroyed his manuscripts, correspondence and private diaries. In 1885 he explained his motives to his then fiancée, Martha Bernays: 'As for the biographers, let them worry, we have no desire to make it too easy for them. Each of them will be right in his opinion of "The Development of the Hero" and I am already looking forward to seeing them go astray.'[1] Freud obliterates his past. This might be thought a strange action on the part of a man who worked surrounded by a prized collection of antique curios, an unexpected attitude on the part of the founder of a discipline which places such emphasis on the importance of the past, on the recovery of memories. Yet Freud's repeated gesture typifies or anticipates one of the more curious features of the psychoanalytic movement as a whole: its marked tendency to forget or repress its own history. And as psychoanalysis itself teaches us, forgetting is rarely accidental and never innocent.

The tendency to forget takes a variety of forms: the repression of the story of Tausk;[2] the long-standing reluctance to publish the Freud–Jung correspondence; the tendentious editing or even censorship of Freud's letters; the transformation of history into hagiography; the secrecy that surrounds the archives. Whatever one may think of the implications of Masson's recent assault on the Freud heritage, it provides irrefutable evidence that the history of psychoanalysis is befogged by an induced amnesia.[3] Authorized versions of its history tend to centre on what has aptly been termed 'the myth of the hero in psychoanalysis',[4] on a myth in which a culture-hero struggles alone against overwhelming odds, betrayal and prejudice. In Freud's case the struggle was, so the legend goes, a battle against anti-Semitism, the hostility of the academic and medical establishement, and the supposedly Victorian morality of *fin-de-siècle* Vienna.

1

There is something improbable about the latter notion, as Freud's Vienna was also that of Klimt and Schiele, but it persists and generates the image of Freud as 'Victorian physician'.[5] It provides an entertaining counterpart to the myths which hampered the first attempts to import psychoanalysis into France, myths which suggested that Vienna was a hotbed of untrammelled sexuality, but it does little to promote any historical understanding. And who would describe Darwin as a 'Hapsburg biologist'? Freud himself promotes the hero myth by identifying with conquistadores and classical heroes such as Hannibal, and thus contributes to a second and more important aspect of the legend:

> the blotting out of the greatest part of the scientific and cultural context in which psychoanalysis developed, hence the theme of the absolute originality of the achievements, in which the hero is credited with the achievements of his predecessors, associates, disciples, rivals, and contemporaries.[6]

Lacan too has become a culture-hero, and he too contributes to the promotion of his own legend. Like Freud before him, he is reported to have destroyed at least something of his own past and to have told his seminar that he had spent a weekend destroying papers, 'because God knows what use might have been made of them after my death.'[7] Like Freud before him he identifies with the heroes of classical literature, casting his son-in-law Jacques-Alain Miller in the role of *fides Achates*, his step-daughter Laurence Bataille in that of his faithful Antigone and, by implication, himself in the roles of the empire-building Aeneas and the aged Oedipus at Colonnus.[8] The difficulties caused by the obliteration of the past and by the construction of heroic myths are compounded by the conflict between the flamboyant public persona and the surprisingly private individual whose work, unlike that of Freud, contains almost no autobiographical revelations: the outburst against his paternal grandfather in the 1961 Seminar is so uncharacteristic as to be shocking.[9]

Until very recently there was not even a rudimentary biography of Lacan and, in the absence of more objective information, rumours, anecdotes and legends flourished. There are countless anecdotes about the legendary bad manners, the elegant sartorial eccentricities, the alleged promiscuity, and so on. Rumours abound about suicides among Lacan's analysands; the extraordinary tale that he smuggled Daniel Cohn-Bendit across the West German border in the boot of his Jaguar in May 1968 even surfaced in the pages of *The New Yorker*.[10] Certain of these anecdotes have something of the force of the *hadiths* of Islamic tradition – the deeds and words which are attributed to the Prophet, authenticated by chains of authority, and embellished by oral traditions, but for which there is no Koranic authority. A certain obscurity still surrounds Lacan's activities during the Second World War, for example, but they have given rise to a classic *hadith* tradition.

In her highly impressionistic survey of the lives and legends of Lacan, Catherine Clément reports that his second wife Sylvia was imprudent enough to declare her Jewish identity to the French authorities. Lacan ventured into Gestapo headquarters and somehow obtained the compromising file, which was presumably then destroyed. The source for this story is 'someone close to the family'. In his *Jacques Lacan*, Stuart Schneiderman repeats the story but, in true oral style, embellishes it. Sylvia did not declare herself to the French authorities; she was denounced to the Gestapo. Lacan's action in retrieving the file becomes proof that we should recognize him as 'a man whose personal ethical conduct was unimpeachable'. Clément is acknowledged as the source for the original story, but no authority is produced for the denunciation motif. Schneiderman also has the couple escaping from the Occupied Zone by rowing across the Loire at dead of night and spending most of the occupation in Saint-Laurent-du-Var, near Antibes. His sources remain unidentified.

Attractive as it may be, this particular legend has a number of fatal flaws. It is a matter of record that Lacan did not actually marry Sylvia Bataille until 17 July 1953; although separated from Bataille, she had not divorced him at the time of the reported incident. That may be a minor and legalistic detail, but it is indicative of how legends spread. The more measured account given by a historian of French psychoanalysis – and based on a conversation with Sylvia Lacan – confirms the basis of the story, but alters the details considerably. In 1940 Sylvia Bataille was living in Cagnes-sur-Mer, in the Free Zone. There is therefore no possibility of Gestapo involvement. The recovery and destruction of her file allowed the couple to obtain papers permitting them to return to Paris. Lacan did obtain false papers for Jewish friends,[11] but it seems highly unlikely that he ever rowed across the Loire. More prosaically, a photograph taken by Brassaï shows Lacan at a performance of Picasso's *Le Désir attrapé par la queue* in Michel Leiris's home in Paris in January 1944.[12] More prosaically still, in his 1945 report to the International Psychoanalytical Association Jean Leuba states that Lacan continued to work in private practice during the Occupation, and that he also did some teaching.[13] Prosaic perhaps, but indicative of Lacan's undoubted tenacity and loyalty to the Freudian cause. Freud's writings were banned in France and whilst neither the teaching nor the practice of psychoanalysis was illegal, they were rather less than acceptable activities.

If the wartime anecdotes are ultimately of little significance, the same cannot be said of the theoretical myths surrounding Lacan. They are real

obstacles to reading his work and, *a fortiori*, to formulating any judgement of its value. The suppression of a context is always dangerous, as it
leaves us nothing to read with. We are simply faced by an intimidating
monolith and a stark choice between complete and unconditional
acceptance or unthinking rejection. The dilemma is heightened by the
common tendency to represent Lacan as always having been alone:
alone in his battles against ego psychology, alone against the bureau-
cracy of the IPA, alone when he founds the Ecole Freudienne de Paris
('As alone as I always have been in my relations with the psychoanalytic
cause'[14]), alone when its members begin to betray him. Like Freud,
Lacan is always alone. Schneiderman, for instance, seriously believes
that: 'The theory of dreams is contained within one book by one man. In
Lacan's France, all of the great constructions were also the work of one
man.'[15] This is not only a hero myth; it is a masculinist myth. Psychoanalysis owes an incalculable debt to women such as Emmy von N., Lucy
R., Anna O., and Dora. Lacan never denies that it was a woman patient
who brought him to the threshold of psychoanalysis. But the major
effect of the received image of Lacan's isolation is that the contributions
of others are ascribed to him, just as they were to Freud. Thus, it is
common knowledge that Lacan 'introduced' the theory of the mirror
stage at the 1936 Marienbad Conference like a conjuror. The contributions of Wallon are simply forgotten, not to mention those of Hegel and
Kojève. Lacan 'introduces' the concept of foreclosure, the key, so it is
claimed, to the understanding of psychosis, and a debate going back
almost to the beginnings of psychoanalysis in France, a debate in which
Freud himself participated, is simply erased from the record. When Luce
Irigaray reports that some members of the Départment de Psychanalyse
at Vincennes literally believed that the master–slave dialectic was
Lacan's invention, we can only assume that she is not joking.[16]

To begin, then, with a date: 1966, the year of the publication of *Ecrits*
and the birth of the unlikely phenomenon of a psychoanalytic best-
seller. 1966 was something of an *annus mirabilis* in French publishing:
Barthes, *Critique et vérité*; Benveniste, *Problèmes de la linguistique
générale*; Doubrovsky, *Pourquoi la nouvelle critique?*; Foucault, *Les
Mots et les choses*; Genette, *Figures*; Greimas, *Sémantique structurale*;
Lévi-Strauss, *Du Miel aux cendres*; the celebrated issue of *Communications* devoted to the structural analysis of narrative, the first issue of
Cahiers pour l'analyse. ... And *Ecrits*. The previous year had seen the
appearance of Althusser's *Pour Marx* and *Lire 'Le Capital'*; the next
would see that of Derrida's *De La Grammatologie* and *L'Ecriture et la
différence*. In the circumstances, it was probably inevitable that Lacan
would be recruited under the structuralist banner, and the first English

translation of one of the *écrits* duly appeared in *Yale French Studies* 'structuralism' issue.[17]

The ready assumption that he was a 'structuralist' was no doubt overdetermined to some degree by the fact that he was published by Editions du Seuil, the publishing house most closely associated with the new avant-garde: of the above authors, Barthes, Greimas and Derrida (*L'Ecriture*) were all published by Seuil, who were also the distributors for *Communications* and *Cahiers pour l'analyse*. In the 1950s, the inclusion of a novel of Minuit's list was an almost certain guarantee that the author belonged to the *nouveau roman* school. A decade later, publication in Maspero's *Théorie* series (edited by Althusser) had unmistakable political connotations. In 1966, publication by Seuil seemed at least to imply adherence to the tenets of structuralism. Lacan was by definition part of the avant-garde, to be discussed in the same breath as Althusser's epistemological breaks, Foucault's *episteme* and Derrida's *différance.*

Predictably, the structuralist references in Lacan come to dominate everything else: the debts to surrealism, to phenomenology, to Bataille, Kojève and Queneau simply disappear beneath the waves on which the signifier floats. In 1962 Jean Reboul reviews the six issues of *La Psychanalyse* published by the Société Française de Psychanalyse between 1956 and 1961, and makes Lacan's debt to Heidegger, Hegel and Bataille patently obvious; in 1968 Catherine Backès [Clément] reviews *Ecrits* and effectively obscures Reboul's findings beneath a welter of references to linguistics and structural anthropology.[18] Knowledge of the past is forgotten or repressed.

The same process can be observed in English-Language presentations of Lacan. The first extensive study appears in 1968 in the form of Anthony Wilden's *Language of the Self*, an annotated translation of the 'Rome Discourse' of 1953 accompanied by an extended and at times overwhelmingly erudite essay on 'Lacan and the Language of the Self'.[19] As in Reboul's article, it is more than obvious that Lacan is not the son of some mystical marriage between Freud and Saussure. Many of the later presentations do not even mention Wilden, although it is very difficult to imagine anyone who began to read Lacan in the late 1960s or early 1970s not knowing his work. In a review of *Returning to Freud*, the selection of essays edited and translated by Schneiderman, M. Masud R. Khan notes his apparent ignorance of Wilden's work and comments that 'Lacan had differences with Wilden and stopped the sale and publication of the book.'[20]

The precise nature of relations between Lacan and Wilden must remain a matter for speculation, but the implications of the eclipse of *The Language of the Self* are clear. Past knowledge and knowledge of the past have again been abolished. In many respects, Anika Lemaire's *Jacques Lacan* is a typical study from this period: the systematicity of Lacan's work is taken for granted and Lemaire reads it in purely synchronic terms.[21] Being based on the first doctoral thesis to be devoted to Lacan, it is clearly something of a landmark and, as a guide to the supposed system, it is still extremely useful. But there would be something curious about a guidebook to Rome which assumed that all the buildings and ruins in the city were constructed at exactly the same time.

The all-pervading belief that Lacan was part of the 1960s avant-garde now looks increasingly untenable. He was certainly adopted by the literary theorists and experimental novelists of the day, but the enthusiasm was not reciprocated. In a major paper read to the 1971 Colloque de Cérisy, the novelist Claude Simon introduces a discussion of his working methods by citing Lacan's dictum that the word is not a sign but a knot of signification; the compliment is never returned.[22] Lacan rarely alludes to the contemporary avant-garde, even in his later work. Passing references to Joyce, occasionally to such figures as Sollers, and once to Duras aside, he prefers to allude to the French avant-garde of the 1930s, his own formative period, and refers scornfully in 1962 to the 'pedantic invasion' which cast its shadow over French literature in the years following the Second World War.[23] Of the French (literary) authors mentioned in the name index to *Ecrits*, more than half belonged at some point to the surrealist group or were claimed by the surrealists as their forerunners. The philosopher who is cited most frequently is Hegel. These were scarcely the orthodox avant-garde references of 1966.

Nor does Lacan display any discernible interest in contemporary literary theory, and admits in 1973 that the fact that psychoanalysis is 'Appended to the Oedipus' does not mean that it has anything of value to say about Sophocles.[24] His own readings of *Hamlet*, Poe, *Athalie* and *Antigone* are essentially thematic and are subordinated to a search for supports for or illustrations of psychoanalytic theory. The examination of courtly love in the Seminar on Ethics (S VII) is concerned with the theory of sublimation rather than with the poetics of medieval literature. There is no indication that Lacan has learned anything from, say, Barthes, or from the formal debates that accompanied the rise and fall of structuralist theory and criticism. Still less is there any indication that he can be unproblematically incorporated into the post-structuralist vulgate promulgated by the followers of De Man or Derrida.[25]

The abolition of the past and the incorporation of Lacan into the avant-garde of 1966 and afterwards are by no means the only obstacles to reading *Ecrits*. That volume is far from being Lacan's 'Collected Works', even though it does bring together many pieces that were previously all but unobtainable, and even though it does give a forbidding impression of completeness. As will be demonstrated, the collection is not theoretically or epistemologically homogeneous, appearances to the contrary notwithstanding. For the moment it is enough to note that the texts simply do not all have the same status: some are conference papers modified for publication, others are prefaces to books, still others are based on seminars. Chronologically, they span a period of thirty years. A variety of notes were added for publication in book form, and some sections were heavily rewritten. Even at this most basic level, it is difficult to argue that the collection is all of one piece and that all texts are equal.

With the published volumes of the Seminar, matters become even more complex. Some sections are formal lectures; others are improvised addresses to seminar groups. It is not clear from the text which were taped and which were taken down by stenographers. On occasion whole sessions are missing, and the chronology becomes difficult to follow. In some cases Lacan's answers to questions from the floor are reproduced, but not the questions themselves. Speakers from the floor are not always identified and interventions are not always attributed to anyone specific. It is sometimes possible to read Lacan's comments on a paper presented to the Seminar, but not the paper itself. The Seminar poses all the classic problems of the transmission of knowledge, beginning with the question of the status of the text which conveys it.

For twenty years Lacan refused to allow the Seminar to be published, although summaries of parts of it were published by Pontalis with Lacan's consent. It was only in 1973 that he agreed to allow Miller to begin the laborious task of establishing a text on the basis of stenographic transcripts and tape-recordings. The resultant text is as much Miller's as it is Lacan's. Chapter titles, headings and punctuation are all Miller's; he is a joint signatory of the publisher's contract and has the legal status of a co-author.[26] Even though Miller claims that as an individual he counted for nothing in the establishment of the text, he admits that it 'could have been different'.[27]

Just how different it could have been has been a matter for controversy and even litigation. In 1981 a group of former members of the EFP formed an association known as Après and began to publish a bulletin entitled *Stécriture* (a phonetic condensation of *cette écriture* – this writing – occasionally used by Lacan). Their project was to publish a critical edition of the Seminar, beginning with the 1960–61 session on transference. More controversially, they claimed that Miller's text was in fact a rewriting and therefore an interpretation of the original. In 1985 the matter came to court, with Après's lawyer arguing that Lacan's

Seminars did not come within the terms of the 1957 law on literary property; that he had merely transmitted a 'thought' which immediately became his audience's property and which effectively lay within the public domain.[28] Miller's position, expressed in a letter to *Le Monde*, was that his text was based on principles established by Lacan and that, as his literary executor, he had a moral duty to ensure that the transmission of Lacan's doctrine proceeded in accordance with his will.[29] In July 1985 a court ruled against Miller, but its decision was overturned in December and Après was found guilty of infringement of copyright. *Le Monde*'s report on the final decision was titled 'Jacques Lacan "Belongs to" his son-in-law'.[30] The court's ruling means that the only text available is that established by Miller, although pirate editions will no doubt continue to circulate. Whilst neither his probity nor his editorial talent is in dispute, it is greatly to be regretted that no 'original' is available for comparative study. It is also to be regretted that no critical apparatus is provided, as the text is already unwieldy and will become more so as further volumes appear.[31]

To return, however, to *Ecrits*: almost one thousand pages in the original French, the product of some thirty years of research, hesitations and theorization, somehow transformed into a monolith.[32] The texts themselves are notoriously difficult and opaque, giving the impression that one has strayed into the endless labyrinth of some Borgesian library. Many of the allusions are obscure, particularly as few references are given. In mitigation, it has to be said that Lacan is by no means the only French author to give inadequate references for quotations and allusions; Sartre is another obvious example. On the contrary, this is a traditional failing of French scholarship and publishing, and Lacan merely takes it to new heights. The style poses legendary difficulties, and has been interpreted in a variety of ways. Lacan shows no objection to being described as 'the Gongora of psychoanalysis', but he also claims in more pragmatic terms that his style is designed to be a barrier to 'aberrant interpretations' and that his texts are so organized as to prevent skim-reading.[33]

Sometimes dismissed as mere provocation or as obscurantism, sometimes seen as 'a language of the unconscious in its own right', and described by Althusser, in a pleasing variation on the hero theme, as 'the language of a man of the besieged vanguard', Lacan's style is often assumed to be an idiolect.[34] But what if he were to some extent working within or exploiting a tradition, a quasi-literary discourse? He expresses his admiration for the English metaphysical poets,[35] and French literature has its hermetic traditions ranging from Baroque poems which form anagrams or acrostics, to Roussel's extremely methodical explorations of random associations and the word games of the surrealists. The realization that the line [*barre*] which separates signifier from signified in his 'algorithm' is an anagram of the tree [*arbre*] which Saussure uses to illustrate the point that the sign is arbitrary is a source of some fascination to Lacan, but it would also have delighted many a writer who had nothing to do with the return to Freud, Roussel, Perec and certain of the surrealists being obvious examples. The debt to surrealism is particularly conspicuous; Lacan himself points out that the description of the word as being a 'knot of signification' derives directly from Leiris. It has also been convincingly suggested that Lacan's style owes much to André Breton, the high priest of surrealism, who was as talented as Lacan in combining an extremely precious and at times bewildering syntax with violent *ad hominem* attacks on opponents and rivals.[36]

Style is further convoluted by the use of extravagant, even outrageous punning. The 1973–74 Seminar, for instance, is entitled *Les Non-Dupes errent*, literally meaning 'the non-dupes err' (or wander), but phonetically indistinguishable from *les noms du père* (the names of the father). Not all Lacan's puns are gratuitous or ornamental, and they can become an integral part of his discourse. Thus, the letter *s* (as in subject and signifier) is a homonym of the German *Es* (as pronounced in French). It becomes, that is, the id. Other examples do seem to be designed primarily to provoke, or to amuse. In 'La Chose freudienne' (1955) Lacan compares Freud to an Actaeon who has been turned on by the dogs, and then observes: '*Diane à ce qu'ils vaudront reconnaîtra les siens*' (Diane will recognize the hounds for what they are).[37] This would appear to be a punning allusion to the Bishop of Citreaux's legendary reply when he was asked what should be done with the citizens of Béziers, some of whom had been infected by the Catharist heresy: '*Tuez-les tous, Dieu en reconnaîtra les siens*' (Kill them all, God will recognize his own). Forbidding or infuriating as they may be, Lacan's puns also relate to a widespread verbal practice, banal examples of which would include the excruciating wordplay of *Le Canard enchainé*, a popular satirical paper which is not to be read by the faint-hearted.

It would be absurd to suggest that a reader of *Le Canard* would find *Ecrits* an open book, but it is not unreasonable to argue that Lacan's use of puns is not as unique as it sometimes seems. A minor example may help to illustrate the extent to which it can overlap with a distinctly popular exploitation of phonetics. In *Encore*, Lacan remarks: '*On la dit-femme, on la difâme*' (They call her a woman, they defame her). Godard's 1961 film *Une Femme est une femme* ends with this exchange between the main protagonists: '*Angéla, tu es infâme*' ... '*Non*', répond-elle, '*Je suis une femme*' ('Angela, you are infamous' ... 'No,' she replies, 'I am a woman').[38] The play on the syllable *femme/fâme* is almost identical, but Godard's pun is perhaps the more successful as it involves a play on gender as it shifts from *in* (which is very close to *un*) to *une*. Psychoanalytic training is not a requirement for the ability to use – or abuse – French in this manner.

To turn to more weighty matters. The architecture of *Ecrits* is such that it is almost impossible to trace the development or history of the concepts deployed: chronology is in effect abolished. The collection opens with the enigmatic 'Ouverture de ce recueil' (1966), followed by an edited and revised version of the 1955 Seminar on Poe's 'Purloined Letter'. A survey of Lacan's antecedents, written for *Ecrits*, is immediately followed by 'Au-delà du "Principe de réalité"', a paper written in 1936. Needless to say, the reader is not advised as to the order in which the texts are most easily approached. A bibliographical note is appended, but it is overridden by the order of exposition and by the overall architecture.

The armature of *Ecrits* is completed by the formidable *Index raisonné* compiled by Miller. It can be safely assumed that the phrase is modelled on the classic art term *catalogue raisonné*, which has been defined as follows: 'The collection of the complete *œuvre* of the artist, whose coherence as an individual creator is produced by assembling all his (or rarely her) work into an expressive totality.'[39] A *catalogue raisonné* is no innocent or neutral list of titles or dates. One of its primary functions is to establish the provenance of a given work, and thereby to determine its exchange value in the auction room. In a sense it produces the work of the artist: a Goya may not be a Goya until it is authenticated by the catalogue – it is merely 'attributed to Goya'. The function of the index to *Ecrits* is analogous: it guarantees the provenance and theoretical value of concepts, and contributes in no small measure to the production of the systematic theoretical entity known as 'Lacan'. The user is instructed to look, not for words, but for concepts, the implication being that they remain theoretically and epistemologically stable from 1936 to 1966. Miller explicitly states that *Ecrits* is to be read as forming a system. Lacan seems less convinced by his own supposed systematicity. Discussing a detailed and valuable study of his 'Instance de la lettre', he remarks in *Encore*: 'This book ... presupposes that I have an ontology or, which amounts to the same thing, a system',[40] thereby effectively denying that he has either.

In an introductory note to his index, Miller explains that it is based upon '*le dernier état de la théorie*', which Sheridan renders as 'the latest stage in the development of the theory'.[41] There is, however, an intriguing alternative translation. In art history and criticism *le dernier état* is normally translated as 'the final state', a 'state' in this context being an impression taken from a plate at a given stage in its production. A final state is a definitive version arrived at by a process of reworking. It is certainly entertaining and instructive to contemplate the final state of, say, a Goya *capricho*, but it can also be a misleading exercise. Examination of earlier states may reveal that the acids and the burin have altered the plate considerably. Details may have been altered; areas of light and shade may have been inverted. An epigraph may have been added or removed. In short, the whole inscription of the plate may have changed, but it is impossible to tell that from the final state alone.

Having established his final state, Miller then proceeds to index it 'by retroaction', effectively projecting the final state backwards across the years in such a way that the concepts of the 1960s appear to exist in texts written before the Second World War, and forcing Lacan to exist within an ideal time-space. Thus: 'There is a single ideology of which Lacan provides the theory: that of the "modern ego", that is to say, the paranoiac subject of scientific civilization, of which a warped psychology theorizes the imaginary, at the service of free enterprise.'[42] It is true that much of Lacan's theorization concerns the development and function of the ego. It is true that he is an implacable enemy of 'ego psychology', regarding it as little more than a variation on behaviourism. It is, however, an anachronism to suggest that 'The Mirror Stage', perhaps the key text for Lacan's theory of the ego, participates in the polemics of the 1950s and 1960s. On the contrary, that text deals not with the construction of an ego which is at the service of free enterprise but with the constitution of the human subject as such. This description of the 'ideology of the modern ego' probably owes as much to Miller's own position in 1966 as to the history of a concept: he is the editor of *Cahiers pour l'analyse*, one of the cradles of Althusserian Maoism, perhaps the most exquisite political discourse of the period. As Freud remarks in his *Leonardo*, 'history' is often 'an expression of present beliefs and wishes rather than a true picture of the past'.[43]

Ego psychology may well have been a minor input into the industrial psychology associated with Fordism, but it did not roll off the assembly line at the Rouge River plant. It has a perfectly good European pedigree; Hartmann's 'conflict-free ego sphere' first appears in a paper read to the Vienna Society in 1937,[44] and the notion of 'strong and weak ego' was discussed at the 1938 Paris Conference of the IPA. Even Althusserian Maoism would surely have difficulty in sustaining the view that the Vienna of 1937 (or even the Paris of 1938) was the capital of 'scientific civilization' or the homeland of 'free enterprise'. The foregrounding of the polemic against ego psychology also induces amnesia by obscuring the fact that a younger Lacan was by no means averse to attempting to use psychoanalytic models for purposes of social engineering, as is apparent from his remarks on the wartime work of

Bion and even from his 1951 paper on the functions of psychoanalysis in criminology.[45]

Arguments from a final state also typify both the anthologies of Lacanian material currently available in English translation. Schneiderman's *Returning to Freud* contains sixteen texts written by eleven authors over a period of almost twenty years, the earliest dating from 1956. They are collectively ascribed to 'The School of Jacques Lacan', even though no such entity has ever existed. Only one of the texts is by Lacan himself. Significantly, it is the only one not to be dated: Lacan, we must assume, exists outside time and space.[46] The papers included in Mitchell and Rose's *Feminine Sexuality* are said to be by 'Jacques Lacan and the Ecole Freudienne'; of the five papers by Lacan himself, three were written long before the foundation of the Ecole Freudienne de Paris in 1964. In purely historical terms, the collection could equally well be ascribed to 'Jacques Lacan and the Société Française de Psychanalyse'. In both these cases, a new final state has been created in the form of writings by an imaginary collective author. To argue that the use of 'school' in these titles is merely a convention or that it is modelled on such hallowed phrases as 'Paintings of the Impressionist School' is surely disingenuous, as it cannot but be overdetermined by an implied reference to the EFP, almost the final institutional state of Lacanian psychoanalysis ('almost' in that it was dissolved by Lacan in 1980).

In *Feminine Sexuality*, a more interesting example of retroaction on the basis of a final state appears at the level of translation practice. Commenting on the length of time over which the texts were written, Jacqueline Rose remarks: 'I have made no attempt to give a false homogeneity to the very different styles which follow from this deliberate selection.'[47] There is one fascinating exception to this self-imposed rule. The collection contains extracts from *Encore*, the transcript of the 1972–73 Seminar (S XX) in which Lacan makes the notorious pronouncement that '*La femme n'existe pas*', crossing out or 'barring' the definite article to make his point. As the translator explains: 'It is the central tenet of these chapters that "The Woman" does not exist, in that phallic sexuality assigns her to a position of phantasy. Lacan argues that the sexual relation hangs on a fantasy of oneness, which the woman has classically come to support.'[48] In the *Encore* extract, Rose follows Lacan by 'barring' the definite article ('the Woman') or italicizing it; in her general introduction, she alternates between 'Woman' and 'The Woman' without explaining the shift in usage. Regrettably, this translation is then back-projected into contexts in which Lacan's use of the definite article is indicative of nothing more than obedience to French grammatical norms. Thus, in 'The Meaning of the Phallus', a paper read to the Max Planck Institute in 1958, we find 'The masculine unconscious

... the unconscious of the woman', the latter being a translation of the banal *l'inconscient de la femme*, which Sheridan renders more prosaically, but so much more acceptably, as 'the unconscious of women'.[49] At the level of translation practice, the retroactive use of a final state results in an unnecessary infelicity of syntax. At the level of theory, it produces a degree of mystification by suggesting that a notion elaborated in 1972–73 was already current in 1958. It is surely significant that in Rose's version, Lacan's *par hypothèse* becomes 'by definition'.[50]

The timeless atmosphere created by the ascription of texts to an imaginary collective author and by the retroactive use of a final state is heightened by slips in textual dating. In both the bibliography and the body of the text, 'The Mirror Stage' is dated '1936'. True, a version of that paper was read to the Marienbad Conference in 1936,[51] but no transcript survives, and the version included in *Ecrits* is quite clearly stated to have been read to the 1949 Zurich Conference of the IPA. That it does not date from 1936 is also obvious from internal textual evidence; the transparent allusions to Sartre's *L'Etre et le néant* (1943) could not have been made in that year.[52] This is not merely a pedantic point; the inaccurate dating is quite consonant with the anachronisms of the translation and with the construction and reproduction of a final state.

Imaginary constructs typify many English-language presentations of Lacan, as a fundamental assumption of unity and systematicity transforms *Ecrits* into a conceptually homogeneous text rather than a collection of papers written over a considerable period of time, with all the shifts and modifications that implies. Thus, the alleged importance of structural linguistics – as opposed to an interest in language – constructs Lacan into the child of Freud and Saussure. The irony is that the construction of the imaginary unity of 'Lacan' is contemporaneous with the strenuous effort to demonstrate that 'Marx' is not a unified body of theory, and that there are considerable differences between the 'Young Marx' and the 'Mature Marx'. Indeed, many of the agents involved in the construction of 'Lacan' also worked as reading *Capital* in great epistemological detail and at deconstructing the assumed unity of Marx. The paradox is apparent at the most basic level. References to *Ecrits* were – and are – often given simply at '*Ecrits*, Paris, 1966', followed by a page number, but with no indication as to which particular *écrit* was meant. It is not difficult to imagine the howls of outrage that would have been heard in the same circles had an author been so crass as to supply a reference to 'Lenin, *Selected Works*, Moscow, 1966' without specifying whether the text in question dated from 1905 or 1917.

The illusion of unity was no doubt partly fostered by the fact that until 1977, when Sheridan's *Selection* appeared, few texts were available in translation. It was perhaps therefore not entirely unreasonable to assume that they were representative fragments of a larger whole. But the same illusion was enhanced by the process whereby Lacan was imported. That process is visible in almost caricatural form in Mehlman's 'The Floating Signifier', an essay in the influential 'French Freud' issue of *Yale French Studies*. The final section consists of fragments from 'Radiophonie' which are glossed and commented upon at some length. The fragments are not translated, and the commentary is in English. The reader thus has a commentary on a text which is deliberately withheld. The author describes this peculiar exercise as being 'somewhere between an intellectual prose poem and a crossword puzzle'.[53] 'French Freud' also contains a translation of the 'Purloined Letter' Seminar, Derrida's 'Freud and the Scene of Writing' and extracts from Laplanche and Pontalis's invaluable dictionary of psychoanalysis, and the whole issue is clearly designed to serve an introductory or pedagogic strategy. Yet Mehlman's intellectual hybrid is quite at odds with any such strategy. On the one hand, the reader is offered knowledge in the form of a commentary; on the other, the reader is refused direct access to the text to which the commentary refers. The reader is thus placed in a totally contradictory position and is subjected to the intellectual terrorism characteristic of so many presentations of Lacan.

In her *Psychoanalytic Politics*, Sherry Turkle begins to remedy this situation by outlining at least some context in which to read Lacan and by supplying a great deal of empirical information, a commodity in regrettably short supply in many studies. The book is, however, marred by the author's evident nostalgia for May 68 and by her apparent belief that Lacan is in some sense an anti-authoritarian figure: the subtitle 'Jacques Lacan and Freud's French Revolution' says a great deal about the assumptions that inform it. The belief that the May events represented a quasi-revolution now looks woefully dated, but the assumption that Lacan is a revolutionary lingers on in some quarters. It masks some curious contradictions.

Lacan is often presented as the opponent of the medicalization of psychoanalysis and as the proponent of a revolutionary return to Freud. It is forgotten that he retains to the very end one of the classic practices of French psychiatry: *la présentation des malades*. The patient who is 'presented' is interviewed by Lacan before an audience of doctors and aspiring analysts in a ritual which is part diagnostic and part pedagogic. Lacan refers quite frequently to his 'presentations' in the Seminar – and such references are the nearest thing we get to a case-history – but there appears to be only one transcript of the ritual itself.[54] At the end of the *présentation* Lacan remarks: 'Today we have seen a "Lacanian" psychosis', and in his discussion of its lessons Miller refers to it as a case of 'pure mental automatism', adding: 'The subject had in fact read the *Ecrits*, but this took nothing away from the authenticity of his experience.'[55] One is irresistibly and irreverently reminded of the importance of suggestion in Charcot's successful demonstrations of hysterical symptoms during his celebrated lectures at the Salpêtrière. The association may be irreverent, but it is not inappropriate to bring Charcot and his heirs into a discussion of Lacan. His adherence to the ritual *présentation* is an index of his debt to classical French psychiatry. The term 'mental automatism' is associated with Janet rather than Freud and therefore provides a link with Lacan's background in psychiatry, trace elements of which survive in many of his writings, as the brief retrospective provided in the next chapter will demonstrate.

A variety of agencies ranging from *New Left Review* to *Yale French Studies* were involved in the initial importation of Lacan, the one thing they all have in common being that they are far removed from the psychoanalytic community and from any clinical practice. Indeed, *New Left Review* implies that it is *because* 'Lacan's work is widely influential outside his own discipline' that 'it is time it received its due international recognition.'[56] *Ecrits* received the accolade of a three-page review in *The Times Literary Supplement* ... and two short paragraphs in the *International Journal of Psycho-Analysis*, the burden of which is: 'That Dr Lacan has a devout passion for Freud's writing cannot be gainsaid, but it is difficult to determine the nature of his use of Freud's researches, especially in their clinical aspects.'[57] To date, the *IJPA* has published only one paper by Lacan, namely 'Some Reflections on the Ego', which was read to the British Society in May 1951.[58] It gives no indication as to the paper's reception, but one American analyst succinctly, if brutally, described it as an example of 'neo-confusionism'.[59] More generally, hostility or indifference to Lacan was expressed by silence. There are indications that the climate is changing, as Lacan is discussed more frequently in the IJPA and as more or less overtly Lacanian works are reviewed with increasing sympathy. This is unlikely to signal a mass conversion to the Lacanian cause but it does mean that Lacan can be discussed as an analyst among other analysts, and that in itself may help to resolve the dilemma between total acceptance and unthinking rejection.

The Lacan who was imported into Britain in the early 1970s was not, however, the intellectual property of the psychoanalysts, and perhaps the most important import agency was *Screen*, the journal of the Society for Education in Film and Television. The *Screen* version of Lacan is of major importance in that it largely determines the nature of other appropriations of his work and in that the assumptions that underlie it continue to inform the dominant image of Lacanian psychoanalysis. *Screen* was without any doubt one of the most influential theoretical journals of the decade 1971–81 and was a major channel for a variety of imports ranging from structuralism, semiology, Russian formalism and Althusserian Marxism (in association with *Theoretical Practice*[60]) to Lacan. To trace the process whereby it imported Lacan is therefore not merely a historical or bibliographical exercise; it is a means of identifying certain assumptions which still inform presentations of his work and the use made of it.

Screen's approach to Lacan is from the outset strikingly instrumental. The point is never to read Lacan as such, or to situate him within the history of psychoanalysis, but to use him to consolidate the theoretical project of elaborating a theory of the subject and of ideology that can supplement Marxism. To that extent, Lacan is regarded as a pre-given theoretical entity whose concepts can be appropriated, deployed and applied quite unproblematically. The fact that Lacan displays no enthusiasm for being articulated with Marxism and has little of interest to say on that subject is simply ignored. The stated intentionality of a theorist is obviously not the sole criterion by which the adaptability of his or her work is to be judged, but the very ease with which Lacan is appropriated is disturbing, not least in that his 'subject' is a universal which it is difficult to reconcile with the central Marxist concept of class (a concept not greatly in evidence in *Screen*'s analyses). *Screen*'s project is predicated on a move away from what it decries as 'subjective taste-ridden criticism' and therefore on a 'crucial' emphasis on theory.[61] Lacan is present from the beginning of the project, initially cast in the role of one of many 'structuralists'[62] but rapidly moving to the centre of the theoretical-epistemological stage, notably with the translation of *Cahiers du cinéma*'s analysis of Ford's *Young Mister Lincoln* in the Autumn 1972 issue.

According to the Editorial, there is nothing problematic about this sudden foregrounding of an author who must still have been relatively unfamiliar to much of the journal's readership: 'The deployment of psychoanalytic categories by the *Cahiers* writers, derived from the work of Lacan, is justified by their search for what is repressed in the film (politics, eroticism, violence) and the signs which indicate the effort involved in that repression.'[63] Lacan's work consists, it is implied, of categories which may be deployed and derived at will: its theoretical use-value is pre-given. The use of psychoanalysis does not have to be justified either politically or historically. Not all the editorial board appear to have been in agreement with this position, and three years later four of them resigned (Edward Buscombe, Christine Gledhill, Alan Lovell and Christopher Williams), giving *Screen*'s 'unproblematic acceptance of psychoanalysis' as one of the reasons for their departure.[64] Even in translation, Lacan's uncanny ability to provoke schisms remains unimpaired. In retrospect, it is difficult not to agree with the dissidents: *Screen*'s acceptance of psychoanalysis is indeed unproblematic. It is also terroristic: the reader is simply assumed to know and understand the importance of Lacan.

Yale French Studies introduces an element of intellectual terrorism in its 'French Freud' issue, and *Screen* refines the climate of terror by failing to resolve the contradiction between its supposed pedagogic aims and its reliance upon decontextualized theories for the furthering of its theoretical project. In so doing it establishes an unfortunate precedent. Thus, the feminist journal *m/f* can suddenly publish a 'dossier on motherhood' from *L'Ane* without informing the reader what *L'Ane* is: a self-styled 'Freudian magazine' which began publication in 1981 (the title, literally meaning 'the donkey', derives from an acronym for the publishing group: Analyse Nouvelle Expérience).[65] The reader is simply presumed to know; to parody the title of *Scilicet*, the journal of the EFP, you may know, provided that you understand the Latin in the first place. A similar note is struck in *Feminine Sexuality*, where, in an introductory note to the *Encore* extract, Rose comments: 'The cultural references in this text are especially dense. But rather than weigh down the text with references, we have chosen to leave the various allusions to work in terms of how they are used in the course of Lacan's argument.'[66] If the various allusions fail to 'work', the responsibility presumably lies with the reader rather than the editor or translator.

At a literal level, such statements suggest either a disavowal of non-knowledge or a refusal to impart and share knowledge. At a more theoretical level, they are of course consonant with the decision to leave terms such as *jouissance* and *signifiance* in the original French, as as 'to allow the meaning to emerge from the way in which they operate'.[67] That the terms border on the untranslatable is not in dispute, but this implies a very curious view of translation. As will be obvious to any non-French-speaker who has struggled with an English translation of a nineteenth-century Russian novel which insists on retaining fragments of French dialogue, the meaning of signifiers from a foreign language does not simply 'emerge'; they come to connote 'otherness'. As with *la femme*, Rose in fact breaks with her stated convention and occasionally translates *jouissance* as 'orgasm' or 'enjoyment'. The departures from the norm are not signalled. The terrorism which has so often accompanied theoretical imports is still sadly in evidence.

Lacan finally emerges as a major figure in *Screen*'s pantheon with the double issue on 'Cinema, Semiotics and the Work of Christian Metz' (Spring–Summer 1973). In a rare gesture towards the uninitiated, a glossary and some notes are supplied. For the first time some concrete information about Lacan is forthcoming:

> JACQUES LACAN: French psychoanalyst, born in 1901. Lacan demon-strated that Freud founded a new science: the science of the unconscious. The scientific study of the unconscious is made possible by returning to 'the theory established, fixed and founded firmly in Freud himself' (Althusser's phrase) with the help of structural linguistics, because 'the discourse of the uncon-scious is structured like a language'.[68]

The connection between Althusser and Lacan is also made in the Edito-rial, which quotes approvingly from 'Freud and Lacan', one of the most influential early presentations of Lacan to have made its way across the Channel. *Screen* has silently moved from an unargued assertion of Lacan's importance to a classic appeal to authority.

Althusser's short article argues that the 'darkness' cast over Freud's work by his recourse to a thermodynamic model has at last been dispelled by the light of structural linguistics: 'Lacan would be the first to admit that his attempted theorization would have been impossible but for the emergence of a new science: *Linguistics*.'[69] The theoretical model operating here is that elaborated in 'On The Materialist Dialec-tic': the model of the generalities.[70] To put it crudely, linguistics 'works upon' Freud to produce Lacan. Rereading 'Freud and Lacan', one is inevitably struck by the purity of the supposed relationship between the two psychoanalysts: 'Lacan thinks but nothing but Freud's concepts, giving them the form of our scientificity.'[71] As it happens – and as will become increasingly obvious – Lacan 'thinks' many other things too. For the moment, it is more relevant simply to note the extraordinarily abstract and remote quality of an article which supposedly has an expos-itory role and which is intended to woo the Parti Communiste Français away from its secular hostility to psychoanalysis, which was officially anathematized as a 'reactionary ideology' in a collective article published by *La Nouvelle Critique* in June 1949.[72] There are no specific references to individual texts by Lacan, merely a bibliographical 'study guide' listing articles which were for the most part singularly difficult of access when Althusser's piece first appeared in 1964.

And for all his insistence on the need to read *Capital*, Althusser shows little sign of having read Lacan in any great detail. He is in fact not concerned with doing so, but primarily with appropriating concepts in an attempt to construct a general theory of ideology and of the subject as founded by the 'misrecognition' of the mirror stage. The structure of misrecognition provides the underpinnings for a definition of ideology as being 'a "representation" of the imaginary relationship to their real conditions of existence'.[73] This definition, which was to acquire an almost canonical force, in fact betrays Lacan's conceptual specificity. Althusser effectively equates 'real conditions of existence' with actual existing social conditions; for Lacan, the real is a dimension beyond symbolization and resistant to symbolism, and it is not to be ameliorated by any class struggle. The primary connotations of 'imaginary' relate to the construction of images, not to a duality between real and imaginary or science and ideology. Finally, there is little room in Althusser's dualism for the crucial dimension of the symbolic.

Secure in its reliance on the unproblematic value of Lacan and on the appeal to authority, *Screen* does not in fact define what it understands by psychoanalysis until 1975. A preliminary definition is supplied in an editorial signed by Ben Brewster: 'A theory of the symbolic system as imposed on the human subject, and the dynamics and economics that imposition and construction imply.'[74] It is further specified by Colin MacCabe in an article on realism:

Freud's theory is a theory of the construction of the subject: the entry of the small infant into language and society and the methods whereby it learns what positions, as subject, it can take up. This entry into the symbolic (the whole cultural space which is structured, like a language, through a set of differences and oppositions) is most easily traced in the analytic situation through that entry which is finally determining for the infant, the problem of sexual difference.[75]

Quite apart from the fact that this definition elides the hazardous issue of what Freud's theory 'is' at any given moment of its development, the sleight of concept is astonishing: the theory ascribed to Freud is Lacan, pure and complicated. Freud never uses the consecrated phrase 'like a language', the whole point of Lacanian orthodoxy being that he could not do so precisely because the science of 'modern linguistics' was not available to him. Nor does he use 'the symbolic' in its Lacanian or Lévi-Straussean sense. As Laplanche and Pontalis note, '*die Symbolik*' is used in *The Interpretation of Dreams*, but Freud understands it as referring simply to 'all the symbols having a constant meaning that are to be met with in various products of the unconscious'.[76] *Screen* is now projecting the final state back to Vienna itself.

Throughout the elaboration of its 'project' *Screen* assumes, but never demonstrates, that psychoanalysis can and must be articulated with historical materialism, that it is 'a science whose specific object is the unconscious and its formations and which, *as such*, is a necessary component of historical materialism in the knowledge it produces of the constitution of the subject.'[77] The argument hinges upon a rhetorical 'as

such', and the scientificity of psychoanalysis is established by connotation rather than by demonstration. Thus, it is claimed that any knowledge produced by the psychoanalytic study of film will 'depend for its
authority on a practice outside film study itself, i.e. on clinical analysis'.[78]
The authority of clinical analysis is taken as axiomatic, even though it
remains undefined and even though Lacan's writings are notoriously
devoid of specific references to the clinical. Psychoanalysis is a practice,
and that term functions here as what Freud might have defined as a
switch-word. It permits, that is, a slippage from the clinical practice of
an analyst to the Althusserian definition of practice, and specifically
theoretical practice, as a constituent moment in the production of scientific knowledge. No doubt it also spares *Screen* the epistemological
embarrassment of having to stoop to an empiricist reference to therapeutic practice.

Screen's appropriation of Lacan rests, then, upon a series of
unproven assertions and unfounded assumptions. Lacan represents a
body of categories, a theory which requires no contextualization or
explanation. At no point does *Screen* argue the case for Lacan's importance other than by assertion or by an appeal to the authority of
Althusser. In a series of articles and editorials a certain schematism is,
perhaps, to be expected in that they are not a fully appropriate setting
for a full archaeology of Lacan. After all, not all studies in theology have
to begin by proving the existence of God. Missionaries, on the other
hand, do normally use more convincing arguments than 'as such',
'necessarily' and 'a necessary component'.

A similar use of rhetorical switch-words and of connotation pervades
Coward and Ellis's *Language and Materialism*, which contains one of
the coherent expressions of the *Screen* version of Lacan. Lacan

> provides the foundation of a materialist theory of the subject in the social
> processes, a subject constructed as always already included in those social
> processes, but never simply reducible to being a support. Lacan's subject is
> *therefore* this new subject of dialectical materialism: a subject in process.[79]

At a lexical level, this claim involves a conceptual condensation: the
terms 'support' and 'always already' are Althusser's rather than Lacan's.
Like *Screen*'s 'as such', 'therefore' allows an assertion to pass for a
demonstration. It is also argued in exactly the same terms that 'Lacanian
theory is rooted in materialism *because* the constitution of the language-
using subject is a continuation of the same process as that by which the
ego is constructed.'[80] Lacan's supposed materialism is then invoked in
attacks on what is dubbed 'bourgeois linguistics', an expression redolent
of the most dismal period in the history of Marxism and of the disastrous

opposition between bourgeois and proletarian science. And, as will be argued later, it is difficult in the extreme to reconcile the proposition that Lacan supplies a materialist theory of language with his own repeated appeals to the quintessentially idealist and theological theses that 'In the beginning was the Word'.

Many of the arguments and assumption informing *Screen*'s presentation of Lacan are transposed virtually intact into the hypothesis that his work can be exploited to produce a theory of the construction of a gendered subject and that it is therefore of direct relevance to feminism. The problems posed by and for a feminist appropriation of Lacan are examined in chapter 6 below but, without wishing to anticipate too much upon the arguments put forward there, it seems opportune to make at least some general comments and to introduce some initial political markers.

  Juliet Mitchell's *Psychoanalysis and Feminism* marks the beginning in Britain of a specifically feminist appropriation of psychoanalysis, or at least of a reassessment of its potential value to feminism. In a wide-ranging discussion of psychoanalytic writing on women and femininity Mitchell argues strongly for a return to Freud, stressing that many feminist rejections of his work have been predicated upon popular (mis)-representations rather than upon any detailed reading of the theories they convey. More specifically, it is argued that those theories are descriptive rather than prescriptive. In short, Freud's analysis of the psychology of women

> takes place within an analysis of patriarchy. His theories give us the beginnings of an explanation of the inferiorized and 'alternative' (second sex) psychol-ogy of women. Their concern is with how the human animal with a bisexual psychological disposition becomes the sexed social creature – the man or the woman.[81]

Lacan is frequently evoked in *Psychoanalysis and Feminism*, usually in relation to the mirror stage and the role of the symbolic father, the implication being that his work can further Freud's tentative explan-ation. He thus becomes an ally in the critical analysis of patriarchy. Lacan remains, however, a somewhat shadowy presence whose import-ance is asserted rather than demonstrated; as Jane Gallop notes, Mitch-ell's precise views on Lacan remain unclear. He is a ghost in the text rather than a real interlocutor.[82]

  Lacan is not the only ghost haunting the text. *Screen* hovers in the middle distance when Mitchell argues that the analysis of patriarchy requires the articulation of historical materialism and psychoanalysis,[83] but another shadowy figure emerges with the reference to the existence in France of 'the large and important women's liberation group calling itself *Psychanalyse et politique*', whose manifesto is quoted with qualified approval in the introduction. *Psychanalyse et politique* is described as 'a Marxist part of the *Mouvement de libération des Femmes*' which 'explicitly opposes what it sees as bourgeois and idealist tendencies within, largely, American radical feminism.'[84] The actual membership of *psych et po*, as the group was normally known, has never been quantified, but it was certainly extremely important and influential, not least because of its ownership of a number of bookshops and control over the successful des femmes publishing house. The group emerged from the May events, but its relationship with feminism has never been as straightforward as Mitchell implies. An undated leaflet circulated by the group (probably in 1973) does speak of the need to articulate psychoanalysis and Marxism, but its criticisms of other tendencies are by no means restricted to radical feminism. On the contrary, it goes on to call for a struggle against all 'sectarian feminist ideology' and against any feminism which puts forward sociopolitical demands [*idéologie féministe revendicatrice*].[85] In an interview quoted in *Le Nouvel Observateur* in 1973, Antoinette Fouque, the leading figure in the group and herself a psychoanalyst, denounces feminists as 'a bourgeois avant-garde that maintains, in an inverted form, the dominant values' and as women who are 'becoming men'.[86]

If the seven demands put forward by the Women's Movement in Britain in the 1970s are taken as a minimalist feminist platform (and many groups in France would support them), it is hard to see how that platform could be extended to take in *psych et po*. In subsequent years, the *psych et po* position leads to a rejection of any participation in politics and to a call for women to abstain from voting in the 1979 elections on the grounds that 'We are not representable'.[87] This is an eminently Lacanian argument, but it is not one likely to achieve say, equal pay for equal work or equal job opportunities. *Psych et po* actually refuse to be mentioned in the history of French feminism published by des femmes, and refer to feminist history as a liability [*ce passif*]. The group then writes itself out of the history of feminism by dismissing it as 'the obverse of an old humanism'.[88] It also seems improbable that the group's practice of organizing mixed study groups at Vincennes to further the struggle against 'feminist sectarianism' would have been acceptable to many English or American feminists in the mid 1970s.[89]

The later history of the group is, if anything, even more dubious. In 1979 it registered with the police as an association formed under the term of the 1901 law, and took MLF (*Mouvement de Libération des Femmes*) as its legal name. Lawsuits against other groups using that

acronym promptly followed.[90] *Psych et po*'s overt hostility to many
forms of feminism has often been reciprocated; the feminist guide to
France published by the 'Carabosses' collective, for example, lists no
addresses for it or for the des femmes bookshops on the grounds that
their role has long been to combat feminism.[91] In retrospect, Mitchell's
favourable references to *psych et po* prove to have been singularly unfortunate. The group's political practices do not invalidate the theoretical
standpoint of *Psychoanalysis and Feminism,* but they do illustrate the
dangers in the assumption – which was only too current in 1974 – that
'Made in Paris' is a guarantee of theoretical-political rectitude.

Many of Mitchell's theses as to the possibility and desirability of using
psychoanalysis and Lacan to analyse patriarchy and to understand the
production of gender have been widely adopted and have become a
recognizable, though by no means universally accepted, strand within
feminism. In their polemical reply to Richard Wollheim's rather patronizing review of *Psychoanalysis and Feminism,*[92] the Lacan Study Group,
for example, argue that 'It is only an elaboration of Marxism in relation
to the Freudian unconscious that will make possible the conceptualization of a feminist practice which has as its aims the challenging of
unconscious sexual formations.'[93] In a paper read to the 1976 Conference on Patriarchy, Ros[alind] Coward, Sue Lipschitz and Elizabeth
Cowie state: 'As feminists, the development of psychoanalysis has made
it possible for us to see how women are constructed in a sexuality
dominated by relations of reproduction.'[94]

As so often with attempts to articulate Marxism and psychoanalysis in
an analysis of patriarchy, a semantic slip appears to occur here between
(sexual) relations of reproduction and (ideological) reproduction of the
relations of production, but a more important criticism relates to the use
made of Lacan's concept of a mirror stage. The authors argue that, for
Lacan, the ego is not pre-given but is constructed, initially during the
mirror stage: 'The mirror phase is the moment when the ego is constituted in the child, precisely as a misrecognition of itself as a whole, in the
face of an experience of his own lack of co-ordination and power.' They
then add in a footnote: 'This is a crucially important part of Lacan's
theory ... the "I" is constructed and not pre-given. This, we believe, is
of crucial importance for feminism since the whole theoretical premise
of feminism is that "femininity" is constructed culturally and socially, and
not something "essential".'[95]

That femininity is a cultural and social construct is not in dispute, but to
map its construction on to the mirror phase is surely a misrecognition of
that phase's theorization by Lacan. The subject or ego constructed by
the encounter with the mirror or its equivalent is a universal without any
class or gender determination. 'Le Stade du miroir' is no more

concerned with the construction of femininity than it is concerned with Miller's 'modern ego': it deals with an ungendered universal. (And given that 'universal' inevitably 'means' male, Lacan's subject will be referred to here as 'he'.) When Lacan does finally turn to the discussion of femininity in 'La Signification du phallus' (1958) and 'Propos directifs pour un Congrès sur la sexualité féminine' (1960), he does so in terms of a long-standing debate within psychoanalysis and makes no specific reference to the mirror stage. The joint authors of 'Psychoanalysis and Patriarchal Structures' effectively 'gender' the mirror stage and the subject by fiat. A similar authorial fiat can be observed in Laura Mulvey's 'Visual Pleasure and Narrative Cinema', the first explicitly feminist contribution to *Screen*: 'Psychoanalytic theory is ... appropriated here as a political weapon, demonstrating the way the unconscious of patriarchal society has structured film form.'[96]

Screen's project began with the deployment of psychoanalysis in a search for what is repressed in film; psychoanalysis is now being deployed to explore the effects of the unconscious of a patriarchal society. A number of assumptions remain unchanged. On the one hand, psychoanalysis (which tends to be synonymous with Lacan) can be unproblematically appropriated or deployed within contextualization because it is a body of theory entire unto itself. On the other, the subject can be gendered, or society made patriarchal, without there being any need to alter or question categories which were originally constructed as universals. Juxtapositions and extrapolations are transformed by fiat into 'articulations'.

To sum up. For the above presentations or appropriations of Lacan, there exists an unsituated and unchallengeable authority or master. If need be, his authority can be reinforced by an appeal to that of Althusser or of certain French feminists whose work is rarely, if ever, described in any concrete detail. In the case of *Screen*, the importation of Lacan goes hand in hand with a virulent intellectual terrorism and with a haughty presumption of knowledge on the part of the reader. All the arguments are predicated upon the existence of a final state which requires no contextualization and upon the reproduction of the induced amnesia which has characterized psychoanalysis itself ever since Freud destroyed his past.[97] They result in the creation of a monolith which is rendered unnecessarily difficult of access, and they present the reader with a stark choice between total acceptance and total rejection of Lacan. It has been convincingly suggested by one psychoanalyst that this choice is at least in part the outcome of a transference effect whereby Lacan is so cathected that he must be followed without hesitation or rejected as a charlatan.[98] The phantasy that the analyst is omnipotent and omniscient has certainly been often observed in transference

situations, and it is not conducive to fruitful dialogue or to the formulations of objective judgements as to the value of the analyst in question.
Perhaps one way to dissolve that phantasy and its aura of timelessness is
to begin to place the master in a variety of contexts, to look at some
earlier states rather than remaining fixated on the final state, and to
resist the blandishments of amnesia and amnesiacs.

2

Retrospective

The early history of psychoanalysis in France is not a happy one.[1] In June 1907 Freud writes to Jung of their 'difficulties with the French', observing that they are probably 'due chiefly to the national character; it has always been hard to import things into France.'[2] In 1914 he is forced to conclude that 'Among European countries France has hitherto shown itself the least disposed to welcome psychoanalysis.' True, some indications of sympathy have come from Régis and Hesnard in Bordeaux, but their 'exhaustive presentation' is 'not always understanding and takes special exception to symbolism', whilst

> In Paris itself, a conviction still seems to reign (to which Janet himself gave eloquent expression at the Congress in London in 1913) that everything good in psychoanalysis is a repetition of Janet's views with insignificant modifications and that everything else in it is bad.[3]

Janet's report on psychoanalysis to the 1913 International Conference on Medicine does give voice to many of the criticisms that will foster French resistance to Freud. The origins of psychoanalysis are, he claims, to be found in the work of Charcot, and Freud's research merely provides confirmation of Janet's own findings. The interpretation of dreams is an arbitrary process, and free association depends for its effects on the power of suggestion; the term 'libido' is used so extensively as to be almost meaningless; sexual disturbances are more likely to be the result than the cause of neurosis. 'Psychoanalysis' itself is simply another term for Janet's 'psychological analysis'.[4]

Freud returns to the topic of resistance to psychoanalysis in France in his *Autobiographical Study*, where he speaks of 'objections of incredible simplicity, such as that French sensitiveness is offended by the pedantry and crudity of psychoanalytic terminology'. More seriously, a Professor of Psychology at the Sorbonne has declared that the whole mode of thought of psychoanalysis 'is inconsistent with the *génie latin*'. In the same study he speaks of receiving 'a number of papers and newspapers from France, which give evidence of a violent objection to the acceptance of psychoanalysis'.[5] Unfortunately, Freud does not state just which newspapers from France he received in 1924, and the Professor at the Sorbonne remains anonymous, but his remarks are by no means unjustified. Anti-German feeling is a factor in French hostility to psychoanalysis, and the press makes no distinction between Berlin and Austria. Psychoanalysis, like phenomenology, is a Teutonic invention to be kept at bay at all costs. In September 1923 *La Presse* describes Freudianism as 'the theory of a *Boche* scientist', whilst a writer on *La Patrie* refers to psychoanalysis 'infiltrating' France and spreading 'obscenity and demoralization'.[6] At the same time, the hope is sometimes expressed that the destructive effects of Freud's theories will be introverted and will further corrupt the enemy defeated in 1918. In 1928, the conservative *Le Temps* cites the Minister for Education as saying: 'I am assured that German youth is being poisoned by Freud. Freudianism is a northern phenomenon. It cannot succeed in France. Beyond the Rhine, Freudianism will complete the work of dissolution begun by the war.'[7]

Whilst Freud's allusions to 'national character' and to '*le génie latin*' may seem naive they are in fact an accurate reflection of the terms of the debate, and anti-German feelings and the desire to defend the national genius of France are by no means confined to those who are overtly hostile or at best indifferent to psychoanalysis. On the contrary, they are shared by the few sympathizers he finds within the citadel of French psychiatry. In the preface to the second edition of the 'exhaustive presentation' he wrote together with Régis (who died in 1918), Hesnard states quite baldly that without 'scientific nationalism', science can be neither living nor fertile:

> And the doctrine of Freud, which springs, not as it has sometimes been said from the French genius of Charcot, but rather from Germanic philosophy, could not meet a more useful ally in its search for the truth than the sense of moderation which is the inspiration behind the French genius.[8]

Hesnard again refers to France as the home of moderation in an article published in 1924 and then goes on to remark that, whatever its merits, psychoanalysis is too marked by Germanic philosophy and its passion for system-building; if it is to become acceptable in France, it must renounce the outrageous notions of 'pansexualism' and 'libido'.[9] In their initial presentation of Freud, Hesnard and Régis use the same military metaphors as *La Patrie*: psychoanalysis has gradually *invaded* the domain of nervous and mental pathology, and it is now attempting to *occupy* that of the psychoses.[10] It is as though the Battle of Verdun is about to be re-enacted on the psychiatric front.

In the circumstances, Freud's comment that their study of his work is 'not always understanding' seems mild in the extreme, and Lacan's laconic description of Hesnard as 'astonishing' a masterpiece of under-statement.[11] The position of Freud's allies is made very clear by the statement of principle published in the first (April 1925) issue of *Evolution psychiatrique*. On the one hand, it seeks to centralize information on all research carried out in France with the help of Freudian methods. On the other, it seeks to translate and explain psychoanalytic theory and technique by 'adapting them as well as possible to the spirit of our race'. In order to do so it will be necessary to abandon the dogmatic and doctrinaire terrain on to which German psychoanalysis has strayed, and to subject Freud's discoveries to 'strictly scientific controls'.[12] The contributors to the first issue include Raymond de Saussure, René Laforgue, Angelo Hesnard and Edouard Pichon; all four will be founder members of the Société Psychanalytique de Paris.

Objections to psychoanalysis are not always based upon crude chauvinism, though an anti-German current (which may, one suspects, mask a considerable element of anti-Semitism) is never far from the surface. In his survey of the French literature on psychoanalysis up to 1920, Saussure rightly detects two main criticisms: French authors criticize Freud for foregrounding the importance of sexuality and for overextending the meaning of 'sexual' so far as to make it a source of confusion, and they attack him for the facile generalization of his theories.[13] The defence of Freud therefore often takes the form of an attempt to 'translate' his theories into more acceptable terms. Hesnard, for example, admits that the theories may sound shocking, but insists that if they are shorn of their external features, it will become immediately apparent that Freud is saying no more than what the poets have always said.[14]

In a later polemic with Politzer, who accuses the SPP of being sterile and dogmatic in its use of Freud, Hesnard accepts that it has indulged in dogmatism and has flirted with a Germanic devotion to method, but contends that the theoretical tools which French psychoanalysis has borrowed will soon be discarded and that future developments will be guided by 'French clarity'.[15] René Allendy, another founder member of the SPP, propounds the far from uncommon view that Freud's 'libido' is little more than a variant on Bergson's *élan vital*, and defends him against the charge of 'pansexualism' by maintaining that the theory of sexuality is not an essential part of psychoanalysis, his evidence being that other analysts have established rational systems without it. His chosen example is Adler and his 'desire for power'.[16] At such moments, it becomes difficult to determine precisely where the defence ends and when the prosecution takes over.

Other objections to Freud take rather different forms. Charles Blondel, who teaches at the University of Strasbourg and who achieves a certain notoriety by describing psychoanalysis as a 'scientific obscenity', views Freud's theories as the dogma of a church. Combining the 'dogma' theme with that of 'pansexualism', he then elaborates a curious seduction theory of his own: the psychoanalytic neophyte is persuaded by his analyst that he is an Oedipus and, regardless of the facts, the natural love he once felt for his mother becomes retroactively sexualized.[17] Dalbiez adopts the 'generalization' charge, and claims that Freud combines a method and a doctrine. The former is acceptable on pragmatic grounds, but the dogma or metapsychology is dismissed as a confused and nebulous philosophy.[18]

A policy of assimilationism is commonly used to equate Freud with Janet or Bergson or to reduce the theory of the unconscious to the Proustian theme of involuntary memory.[19] According to the philosopher Léon Brunschvicg, lecturing at the Sorbonne in 1929–30, there is no clinical theory in Freud which cannot be found in the work of Bernheim and the *Ecole de Nancy*; as a philosopher, Freud is comparable with Darwin and Hobbes in that all three promote theories in which human activity is reducible to the satisfaction of instincts and in which the difference between the human and the bestial vanishes.[20] Claude, the eminent psychiatrist whose 'benevolent neutrality'[21] allowed certain psychoanalysts to practice on a limited basis at the Sainte-Anne hospital in Paris, takes the view that Freud provides a 'psychological medication' (the phrase is Janet's) which can help only a small number of patients; for the vast majority of 'Latin patients', a classic Janetian psychological analysis will suffice.[22] Taking a rather more Olympian view, Daniel Parodi, sometime *inspecteur général de l'instruction publique,* opines that Dumas is quite right not to discuss psychoanalysis in his *Traité de psychologie,* as it has had little or no impact on any serious scientist in France.[23]

In a footnote added to 'On the History of the Psycho-Analytic Movement' in 1923, Freud notes that his writings are now arousing keen interest, 'even in France', but adds, no doubt somewhat ruefully, that the interest is 'more active in literary circles than in scientific ones'.[24] Literary interest in France is real, although its extent has sometimes been exaggerated and its real focus misrecognized, and it will be examined in more detail in the next chapter. It was in part stimulated by the presence of Paris of Eugenia Sokolnicka (her forename duly Gallicized as 'Eugénie'), who was dispatched by Freud from Vienna to act as his representative and as a training analyst. The favourable welcome given

to Sokolnicka by Gide and the *Nouvelle Revue Française* circle must
have been some consolation for her rejection at the hands of the medical
establishment. Reputedly an excellent clinician, she had worked briefly
at Sainte-Anne, where she specialized in child analysis, but was dismissed by Claude for two reasons: she possessed no medical qualifications,
and she was a woman. Sokolnicka subsequently worked in private
practice and contributed greatly to the future history of French psychoanalysis by becoming the analyst of both Pichon and Laforgue. Her
uncomfortable position in the early 1920s, rejected by the clinical world
and courted by the literary salon, seems to sum up the uneasy atmosphere in which the SPP was founded in the winter of 1926, seven years
after the foundation of the British Society, fifteen years after that of the
New York Association, and eighteen years after that of the Berlin
Association.[25]

The SPP is initially a small body, with only twelve members at the end
of 1926 and with René Laforgue as its first president.[26] In 1938 it had
twenty-five full members (*titulaires*). In its first incarnation it is of
necessity short-lived, its members dispersed and its activities suspended
by the outbreak of war. Perhaps inevitably, its activities are fairly
restricted and it may be a reflection of its relative lack of international
standing that Jones refers to it so rarely in his *Life* of Freud. The 1938
Paris Conference of the IPA, for example, is remembered for controversies over lay analysis and organizational issues rather than for any
contribution from the host Society. No major theorist or clinician
emerges from the ranks of the founder members, and the SPP produces
no one of the stature of Anna Freud or Melanie Klein in its early years.
Loewenstein's claim to fame must rest on his post-war work in the
United States rather than on anything accomplished during his brief
years in Paris, and even the names of the original members of the SPP
are now almost unknown except to specialist historians.

Relations with Freud himself are rather distant. Initially, his main
correspondent in Paris is Laforgue but, after theoretical disagreements,
Laforgue is replaced in that role by Marie Bonaparte. The death of
Sokolnicka in 1934 means that Bonaparte is the one member of the SPP
to have been analysed by Freud himself, and the prestige this confers
upon her, together with her financial power and the role she plays in
establishing the Institut de Psychanalyse, means that she rapidly
becomes the dominant figure.[27] Her personal importance in the history
of French psychoanalysis is not, however, reflected by any theoretical
pre-eminence, and her published work is characterized by a curious
combination of biologism and literalism. The biologism, in part no doubt
a reflection of her tenacious support for a medicalized psychoanalysis
despite the fact that she has no medical qualifications, emerges particu-

larly clearly in her writings on female sexuality and in the insistence that
frigidity, to take only one example, has an organic basis.[28] Her literalism
leads her to undertake an extraordinary search for the real participants
in the primal-scene memories that emerge in her analysis with Freud and
in her autobiographical writings. A detailed interrogation of a former
servant results in a confession which confirms the accuracy of Freud's
constructions; he and a wet nurse did indeed indulge in the practice of
fellatio in the presence of the infant Marie.[29]

A similar reductionism informs her study of Poe which, although it is
subtitled '*étude analytique*', is very close to the classic genre of patho-
biography. Thus 'The Purloined Letter' is read in terms of Poe's supposed
identification with the Minister, who represents a hated but admired
father. The tale itself is seen as illustrating a regret for the maternal
phallus and a reproach to Poe's mother for having lost it.[30] In both her
autobiographical writings and her *Poe*, Bonaparte displays a reductionist
literalism which parallels the consistent reduction of psyche to soma in
her writings on sexuality. Even so, Bonaparte is regarded for a long time
as the guardian of Freudian orthodoxy in Paris and as its defender
against the chauvinist tendencies of Pichon, Laforgue and others. Paradoxically, it is the second group who prove to be most relevant to Lacan.

In 1927, the *Revue Française de Psychanalyse* begins publication,
under the patronage of Freud but without the hoped-for contribution
from him in its first issue. Freud declines to contribute even a 'non-
scientific' paper on the tasks facing psychoanalysis in France on the
grounds that he might offend French sensibilities and thus weaken the
position of the young SPP.[31] Freud's refusal to contribute testifies to the
fragility of the new journal, but it also seems to shadow the uneasy
nature of its subsequent publishing programme. The programme begins
with an absence, and then proceeds in a most haphazard manner.
Volume 8 (1933), for example, carries Anne Berman's translation of
'The Taboo of Virginity', the third part of the 'Contributions to the
Psychology of Love'; Parts One and Two ('A Special Type of Object
Choice Made by Men' and 'On the Universal Tendency to Debasement
in the Sphere of Love', both translated by Berman in collaboration with
Bonaparte) do not appear until the following year, despite the fact that
they were, respectively, written six and eight years earlier. The quality of
the translations is, moreover, distinctly uneven.

The publication of Freud in book form does not proceed any more
smoothly. The SPP does not establish any permanent arrangement with
any one publishing house, and there is certainly no French equivalent to
the fruitful alliance forged between the Hogarth Press and the Institute
of Psycho-Analysis in London. No translation of *Jokes and their
Relation to the Unconscious* is available until 1930 and the *Papers on*

Metapsychology do not appear in French until 1940, scarcely the most auspicious of publication dates. Whilst the unsystematic and almost random order in which Freud's works are published in Paris is not the responsibility of the SPP alone and must reflect a general unease on the part of the publishing industry, it does foster an atmosphere in which it is almost impossible to read Freud seriously, and in which discussion has to be based largely on secondary sources.[32] Lacan's almost religious devotion to the letter of the Freudian text becomes more than under-standable in the light of the intellectual climate that prevails when he enters the analytic community. This early period had also left a sad legacy in that there is still no French equivalent to the Standard Edition or the *Gesammelte Werke*; the English edition of Laplanche and Ponta-lis's *Language of Psychoanalysis* does not deign to refer to the French translations of Freud. Rights to various works by Freud are held by three different publishing houses (Payot, Gallimard and Presses Univer-sitaires de France) and although they reached provisional agreement on a projected 'Complete Works' in 1965, the project has come to nothing.[33]

The precise extent of Lacan's participation in the life of the SPP is not easy to assess, nor is the way in which he is viewed by its members. When he is accepted for membership and goes into analysis with Loewenstein, he has an established reputation as a psychiatrist but has had little impact in psychoanalytic circles. The doctoral thesis of 1932 is hailed by the surrealists, noted by Janet and referred to favourably by Dalbiez, but it is not even reviewed in the RFP.[34] Lacan certainly becomes an active and vocal participant in the discussion of papers presented to the SPP from 1933 onwards, but few of his interventions add up to anything substantial.[35] He publishes a translation of Freud's 'Some Neurotic Mechanisms in Jealousy, Paranoia and Homosexuality' in the RFP in 1932, but no original papers.[36] The papers on '*schizogra-phie*' and on the problem of style appear in journals published outside the psychoanalytic milieu,[37] whilst 'Au-delà du "Principe de réalité"' appears in the special 'Freudian Studies' issue of *Evolution psychia-trique*, which has now forsworn its overt chauvinism and describes itself as 'liberal and eclectic'.[38] The paper entitled 'De L'Impulsion au complexe', which was read to the SPP in October 1938 – and criticized by Odier for its 'excessive length' – survives only in the form of a *ré-sumé*, and is basically a condensation of the much longer study of the family published in the *Encyclopédie Française.*[39] Despite its subsequent fame, the 1936 paper on the mirror stage does not appear to have occasioned any discussion within the SPP, and it is 'La Famille' which fully establishes Lacan's reputation. In other words, Lacan finally achieves recognition on the very eve of the temporary eclipse of psycho-analysis in France.

The thesis of 1932 aside, this is by far Lacan's most ambitious production to date and, in the absence of the *Ur*-version of the mirror-stage paper, it is the major primary source for the period. Displaying what is already a fearsome erudition, Lacan draws heavily on both anthropology (Malinowski, Frazer and Mauss) and psychoanalysis to outline a cultural theory of the family institution in a two-part study dealing in turn with the complex as concrete factor in mental pathology, and 'family complexes' in pathology. Many recognizable themes are already in evidence: the need to supplement the theory of the ego with a theory of the imaginary functions which provide its structural underpin-nings; the characteristic interweaving of Freudian and Hegelian strands; the insistence that the individual's history is to be seen as crystallizing around a sequence of stages and moments of separation and division. 'La Famille' is also important in that it provides a concise summary of Lacan's early views on psychosis. In terms of its overall scope and ambition, it looks forward to totalizing texts such as 'Fonction et champ de la parole et du langage en psychanalyse', but there is one significant absence in that no reference is made to linguistics; the importance of that discipline is to be a post-war discovery. It is relatively easy to read the text prospectively, in other words to find in it the seeds of future developments. Reading it retrospectively is rather more difficult, par-ticularly given Lacan's silence as to his sources and his loyalties at this time.

Lacan has remarkably little to say about the early days of the SPP or even about his entry into the psychoanalytic world. If he does feel any nostalgia for the psychoanalytic past, it is for the golden age of the phallic-stage debate of 1928–32 and for the attendant passion for doctrine,[40] not for the days of Sokolnicka's lonely mission to Paris. The cultural and literary references which punctuate his writings are predom-inantly to the avant-gardes of the interwar period, and they promote the impression that surrealism and the early phenomenological movement are more germane to his concerns than any debate in the pages of the *RFP*. That impression is not entirely unfounded, but there are soft echoes in his work of a period which he appears to consign to the silence of prehistory.

These echoes are particularly insistent in 'La Famille', and one founder member of the SPP helps to amplify them considerably. Signifi-cantly, he is the only founder member of whom Lacan speaks with any real respect or affection in *Ecrits*: Edouard Pichon, 'who, both in the indications he gave for the development of our discipline and in those that guided him in people's dark places, showed a divination that I can attribute only to his practice of semantics.'[41] Pichon is a somewhat curious figure who, presumably not without difficulty, combines membership of the SPP with membership of the monarchist Action Française, which is not noted for its enthusiasm for 'German-Jewish' phenomena such as psychoanalysis. He is also a linguist and philologist and, together with his uncle Jacques Damourette, the author of a multi-volume French grammar. That study provides the raw material for what is in effect the first attempt in the SPP to outline a study of relations between the unconscious and language, albeit on a distinctly traditional basis predicated upon a direct correspondence between 'words' and 'ideas' and upon a vehement rejection of the Saussurean thesis that the linguistic sign is arbitrary.[42] Pichon is also the author of the first article to be devoted to Lacan, and he reads him with remarkable attention and acuity.[43] Before going on to look at his article – and to listen to the echoes it summons up – it is necessary to situate him within the main tendencies discernible in the SPP.

There is a general consensus among historians that Pichon is a leading figure in one of the two main tendencies in the SPP, the other being centred on Bonaparte. Laforgue is generally agreed to occupy something of an intermediate position. For Roudinesco, the Pichon group represents a 'French medical chauvinism' in that it rejects lay analysis and inherits many of the anti-German sentiments of the 1920s. The Bonaparte tendency, which includes Loewenstein, represents an unthinking loyalty to the IPA and an 'adaptational current' which foreshadows ego psychology.[44] Paul Bercherie describes the Bonaparte tendency as 'capitulationist' (perhaps a somewhat unfortunate term, given its connotations in the history of Franco–German relations) in that it relies almost entirely upon imported theories and produces little original work. He accepts that the Pichon tendency is basically xenophobic, but argues that with the help of Laforgue's theoretical work it establishes the basis for a distinctive platform which will do much to inform Lacan's later work. Unlike Roudinesco, he takes the project of creating a psychoanalysis *à la française* very seriously. For Bercherie, that project leads to the elaboration of a theory in which the history of the subject is organized around a sequence of pathogenic traumas and conflicts.[45]

In 1938 Pichon describes the edifice built by the French school of psychoanalysis as having its foundations in the concepts of scotomiz-ation, captativity, oblativity, schizonoia and that of the 'vital resultant' [*résultante vitale*]. The relevance of scotomization will soon become apparent, but the other terms are now so unfamiliar as to require some definition. Captativity and oblativity refer respectively to the young child's tendency to appropriate the outside world and to his willingness to turn to the outside world and to give of himself. The vital resultant is the balance that is struck between these tendencies, and refers to the sum total of affect available to the child in his relations with the outside world and with other people.[46] Schizonoia describes what Laforgue terms a 'dual organization' in which transcurrent mental activities develop: an ideal upon which the subject's entire phantasy-activity is concentrated, and the id, which is anchored to the anal-sadistic level and whose activities are manifested outside the realm of conscious activity.[47] All these concepts relate to Laforgue's work on schizophrenia, the subject of his doctoral thesis, and they lead to the one instance of an open dispute between Freud and a member of the SPP.

In both a paper published in German in 1926[48] and in his *IJPA* paper of the following year, Laforgue describes the young child's affective processes as egocentric:

> His mother is to him equivalent to nutrition – she is a thing. She belongs to the child, and he is the point around which she revolves. But in time the centre of gravity is displaced from the child to the father. The father, in whose favour the child resigns the mother, then becomes the head, the pivot on which everything turns.[49]

This is equivalent to a 'far-reaching process of weaning' and, should the child fail to undergo it in satisfactory manner, the consequences may be equally far-reaching. If, on the other hand, the process is accomplished satisfactorily, the child will achieve oblativity: 'that competence to which the psyche attains through the satisfactorily accomplished weaning of the child's libido from the mother or mother-substitute.'[50] Freud, however, will have none of Laforgue's thesis of a 'trauma of weaning' and dismisses it as a concealed form of 'the denial of the castration complex'.[51]

The issue of scotomization leads to further controversy. Freud and Laforgue discuss the question in their correspondence, but the exchange results in a dialogue of the deaf. Laforgue proposes a distinction between repression and scotomization (from 'scotoma': an obscuration of part of the visual field due to a lesion on the retina) and defines the latter as 'a process of psychic depreciation, by means of which the individual attempts to deny everything which conflicts with his ego'. Scotomization indicates a failure of the mechanism of repression: 'contrary to what happens in normal repression, the mind in spite of outward appearances is really simply trying to evade a situation in which it has to endure frustration and which it apprehends as a castration.'[52] The schizonoiac learns to deal with stimuli which conflict with ego interests by scotomizing them, or acting as though they did not exist; he

excludes them from his psychic field of perception. Freud's immediate
response is to say that he simply does not understand the reason for the
proposed distinction between scotomization and repression and that he
sees no need for Laforgue's innovation.[53] He returns to the issue in the
addendum to *Inhibitions, Symptoms and Anxiety*, where he describes
Laforgue's scotomization as a kind of anticathexis, 'a special kind of
vigilance which, by means of restrictions of the ego, causes situations to
be avoided that would entail dangerous perceptions.'[54]

Freud also effects a displacement here, by relating scotomization to
hysteria rather than to Laforgue's schizophrenia. In 'Fetishism' Freud
refers to the dangerous perception that a woman does not possess a
penis, and remarks that 'Laforgue would say in this case that the boy
"scotomizes" his perception of the woman's lack of a penis.' He again
insists that there is no need for a new technical term, as no new fact has
been discovered; the concept of repression can already account for this
mechanism. If it is thought necessary to make a distinction between the
vicissitude of the idea and that of the affect, the terms 'repression'
[*Verdrängung*] and 'disavowal' [*Verleugnung*] are already available.
Finally, '"Scotomization" seems to me particularly unsuitable, for it
suggests that the perception is entirely wiped out, so that the result is the
same as when a visual impression falls on the blind spot in the retina.'[55]
The debate is closed. In his subsequent paper on the mechanisms of
schizophrenia and neurosis, Laforgue makes no use of his 'scotomization' and refers simply to the '"walling-up" of the patient's mind'.[56]

Pichon detects traces of all these concepts in Lacan's 'La Famille'. His
article is in many ways eulogistic of Lacan, whom he praises as 'one of
the most brilliant minds of the younger generation'.[57] The theory of the
mirror stage is singled out as 'a solid and coherent psychological
doctrine supported by the facts. It seems to me that, henceforth, all
psychologists will have to take it into account.'[58] The praise is not,
however, unmixed. Pichon criticizes Lacan for his 'sectarian jargon' and
'preciosity', for his use of 'dialectics' in its Hegelian-Marxist rather than
its Greek sense, and for referring to 'culture' (an individual phenomenon in Pichon's view) in preference to 'civilization' (a collective
phenomenon).[59]

This last criticism may result from a simple misunderstanding, as
French does use 'culture' to refer to an individual's accumulated capital
of knowledge; Lacan, however, is clearly using it in a wider anthropological sense. However, it has more serious implications too. On the one
hand, it reflects the difficulty of finding an adequate equivalent to
Freud's *Kultur*; both the English and the French versions of *Das
Unbehagen in der Kultur* fall back on 'civilization', defined in the collective sense in which Pichon understands that term. On the other, it brings

to Pichon's text echoes of earlier controversies, and even of the First World War, when a philosopher and Academician like Emile Boutroux could assert that 'German culture' was *une barbarie savante*,[60] and when the word *Kultur* was used with bitter irony in France. Beneath the culture/civilization opposition, lies a German/French opposition, and even a Republican/Monarchist opposition: the 'sturdy and living' French civilization which Lacan has betrayed by flirting with Germanic jargon and philosophy is the civilization which survived the Reformation, the 'bloody masquerade' of 1789–99 and the democracy that was the child of 4 September 1870, the date of the Parisian insurrection which heralded the fall of the Second Empire.[61] In other words, Pichon's 'French civilization' is the expression of Hesnard's *génie français*. Not all Pichon's anti-German jibes are so serious; the reference to one 'Charles Marx' and the decision to render 'Wien' (Vienna) as 'Vienne-en-Autriche' (as distinct, presumably, from the French town of Vienne in the Isère) surely indicate little more than a heavy-handed attempt at humour.

The underlying implication is, however, serious indeed: Lacan has a specifically French heritage, and he is in danger of betraying it. And that heritage includes 'French psychoanalysis'. Pichon indicates the existence of that part of Lacan's heritage by making several suggestions and emendations. Lacan speaks of 'narcissistic identification' in connection with the mirror stage; Pichon suggests that it might be more appropriate to speak of *captation*, the term he and Codet introduced into the analytic vocabulary.[62] Lacan concedes the point, and begins in 1948 to refer to 'a first captation by the image in which the first stage of the dialectic of identification can be discerned'.[63] Pichon also detects in Lacan's reference to weaning as trauma a veiled allusion to the work of Laforgue, noting that a more generous author might have thought fit to make this clear.[64] A similar reproach could be directed to Lacan in 1946, when he speaks of the physiological prematuration of the human infant resulting in a traumatism of birth and then a traumatism of weaning,[65] or in 1948, when he refers to 'the great phases that the libidinal transformations determine in human life: weaning, the Oedipus stage, puberty ...', and to 'conceptions that stressed the value of the liberated libido, one of the first of which can be attributed to French psychoanalysts under the register of *oblativity*.'[66]

Pichon also finds in 'La Famille' allusions to the theory of scotomization. Thus, Lacan describes a defence used by the subject when a symptom might lead to the fragmentation of his personality: he wards off the danger by forbidding himself access to the reality in question.'[65] For Pichon, this reveals the 'extensive role M. Lacan grants to scotomization, even though he does not mention the struggles M. Laforgue waged as early as 1926 to make M. Freud recognize the interest of this process, which the master from Vienna had yet to grasp fully.'[68] Pichon also cites and emends a sentence from Lacan: if the subject remains in a narcissistic identification, he will 'cling to the refusal of the real and to the destruction [i.e. scotomization] of the other'.[69]

The term 'scotomization' does not figure in Lacan's other texts of this period, but it suddenly reappears in 1955 in the Seminar on the psychoses. In the course of a discussion of 'Neurosis and Psychosis' and 'The Loss of Reality in Neurosis and Psychosis', the papers in which Freud begins to outline the mechanism of disavowal or denial [*Verleugnung*], Lacan unexpectedly remarks that when the subject triggers his neurosis, he 'elides or scotomizes, to use a later term, part of his psychic reality, of his id. That part is forgotten, but it continues to make itself heard.'[70] The expression is used only once more in an allusion to 'Fetishism' where, according to Lacan, Freud revises the distinction between neurosis and psychosis by saying that 'in the psychoses, reality is reworked, ... a part of reality is suppressed ... and reality is never really scotomized.'[71] This is a fairly free version of Freud's text, and Lacan appears to be citing from memory; Freud in fact speaks of the ego allowing itself to be 'induced by the id to detach itself from a piece of reality'.[72] Scotomization is not, however, a major issue in the Seminar; Lacan is looking for a translation of Freud's *Verwerfung* (repudiation). At the very end of the year's seminar, he finds it: *forclusion*.[73]

Before the discovery of this translation, Lacan has defined *Verwerfung* as 'the rejection of a primordial signifier which, henceforth, will be lacking at this level. That is the fundamental mechanism which I assume to lie at the basis of psychosis.'[74] That definition is further refined and is given its canonical form in the related paper on the possible treatment of psychosis: it refers to an accident in the register of the signifier, to 'the foreclosure of the Name of the Father in the place of the Other ... the failure of the paternal metaphor'. This is 'the defect that gives psychosis its essential condition, and the structure that separates it from neurosis.'[75] In a footnote to his response to Hyppolite's paper on *Verneinung*, Lacan observes that this mechanism is best described as *forclusion*, a term which has prevailed 'by my offices'.[76] Previous translations such as *retranchement* ('cutting off' or 'detachment') are now discarded. Foreclosure differs from negation in that no 'judgement of attribution' is involved; it is as though the foreclosed element had never existed, not as though its existence had been registered and then denied. The Freudian support for the concept is derived from a celebrated passage in the discussion of the Wolf Man case, to which Lacan returns again and again:

He rejected castration. ... When I speak of his having rejected it, the first meaning of the phrase is that he would have nothing to do with it, in the sense of having repressed it. This really involved no judgement upon the question of its existence, but it was the same as if it did not exist.[77]

In his attempt to establish a 'forclusive' mechanism distinct from repression, Lacan is in effect following a path originally traced by Laforgue's tentative theorization of the notion of scotomization. His choice of the term *forclusion* is also an echo of an earlier debate. The term is originally Pichon's. Pichon uses it in both a grammatical and a psychological sense. In its grammatical sense it refers to 'the second part of negation in French, which is constituted by words like *rien, jamais, aucun, personne, plus, guère*, etc....' (nothing, never, no, no one, no longer, scarcely). This form of negation, as opposed to the absolute negation of *ne ... pas*, applies to facts which the speaker regards as not being part of reality: 'Those facts are, in a sense, foreclosed, and we therefore term this second part of the negation the "*forclusive*".'[78] The term itself is used neologistically; the legal meaning of *forclore* is 'to deprive of a right which has not been exercised within a specified period', and Damourette and Pichon play on its etymological components *for* (outside) and *clore* (to close). The use of neologisms is one of the distinctive features of *Des Mots à la pensée*, and its terminology is so arcane as to require a special index; there is something very ironic, therefore, about Pichon's complaint that Lacan indulges in jargon and preciosity. The category of the 'forclusive' has not become part of standard grammatical terminology and is not discussed by modern grammarians such as Grevisse,[79] whereas Damourette and Pichon's work on the 'enclitic' or 'pleonastic' *ne*, which they describe as an 'attenuated negation', is widely recognized as being innovatory.[80] For Pichon, words reflect ideas, and language is a mirror of the depths of the unconscious. The use of the 'forclusive' can therefore be related to the affective register of 'regret' [*le repentir*] and to the wish that 'something in the past ... had never existed'. The French language uses the 'forclusive' to 'express a wish for scotomization' and to 'translate a normal phenomenon' which is found in exaggerated form in mental pathology.[81] In short, a fact which really existed in the past is affectively excluded from the conscious mind, which forms 'mental "blind spots"', as Laforgue puts it.[82]

Whilst Pichon is certainly the first psychoanalyst in France to suggest that the study of language can be a means to explore the unconscious, it would be hazardous to suggest that the Lacanian thesis that the unconscious is structured like a language derives directly from his work. Pichon's version of linguistics is distinctly – even defiantly – pre-Saussurean, and his use of *le repentir* indicates a reliance upon a very traditional theory of the passions. It is probable that he would endorse

Boileau's observation that 'Each passion speaks a different language',[83] but very unlikely that he would subscribe to Lacan's views on the signifier. It is, however, clear that Lacan's foreclosure does originate in debates which Pichon at least saw as contributing to a distinctively French psychoanalysis. To trace its archaeology is to follow a path which leads back to Laforgue and Pichon as well as to Freud, a path which was first followed by Roudinesco in one of the most valuable sections of her *Histoire*.[84] There appears to be a danger of its being obscured anew. In a recent article on Freud's approach to psychotic hallucinations and on his use of *Verwerfung*, Sauvagnat merely notes in passing that Lacan 'borrows' the term foreclosure from Pichon, and then moves into a detailed – and in many respects valuable – discussion of the psychiatry and psychoanalysis of hallucination. Laforgue's debates with Freud and the issues raised by psychoanalysis *à la française* are not discussed.[85]

In their *Language of Psychoanalysis*, Laplanche and Pontalis define foreclosure as follows:

> Term introduced by Jacques Lacan denoting a specific mechanism held to lie at the origin of the psychotic phenomenon and to consist in a primordial expulsion of a fundamental 'signifier' (e.g. the phallus as signifier of the castration complex) from the subject's symbolic universe.[86]

As a definition of foreclosure in its final state this is admirably concise, and the subsequent discussion of Freud's *Verwerfung* and related terms is both erudite and instructive in the extreme. But at no point are the names of Pichon and Laforgue mentioned. The authors' silence reproduces Lacan's own silence, whilst their initial reference to a 'term introduced by Lacan' echoes his own claim that the concept was promoted by his offices. The reasons for Lacan's silence have yet to be explained in a satisfactory manner. Roudinesco takes the rather charitable view that, for Lacan, the use of a term is in itself a sufficient index of its origins and that he sees no need to provide references to authors, adding only that he has been criticized for this and reserving her criticisms for Laplanche and Pontalis.[87] In other words, he makes a classic appeal to a 'reader presumed to know'. But her attempt to defend Lacan against the potential charge of simply having replaced scotomization by foreclosure by pointing out that the Laforgue–Freud correspondence had not been published when he adopted the latter term is surely disingenuous;[88] back issues of the *IJPA* were most certainly available, and Freud's allusions to his discussions with Laforgue in 'Fetishism' are there for all to read. Whatever the reasons for Lacan's silence, its effects are only too evident. It promotes, by omission, a theoretical variant on the myth of the lonely psychoanalytic hero, of a sort of theoretical parthenogenesis. The history of the concept's vicissitudes as it is displaced from schizophrenia to fetishism and then to psychosis, and from traditional grammar to the theory of the signifier, has simply been suppressed. Its suppression does not result in the appearance of an absence or a gap in the theoretical text; on the contrary, it promotes the illusion of its plenitude and self-sufficiency.

Psychoanalysis *à la française* is not Lacan's only inheritance. He originally trained as a psychiatrist, and his work contains trace elements of the instruction he received while working under Claude and then Clérambault, his 'only master in psychiatry'.[89] As has already been noted, he retains the traditional ritual of the *présentation des malades* and even describes it as providing an *in vivo* demonstration of his theories.[90] In his writings on female sexuality he makes significant use of the concept of erotomania, thus promoting the revival of a diagnostic category which was of little interest to Freud but was central to the work of Clérambault in the 1920s.[91] But it is a translation problem which provides the clearest indication of the nature of Lacan's psychiatric inheritance. He occasionally uses the term *automatisme de répétition* to translate Freud's *Wiederholungszwang* ['compulsion to repeat' or 'repetition compulsion'].[92] In so doing he departs from standard French usage. The translation proposed by Pichon and adopted by the SPP in 1928 is *compulsion de répétition*; this is also the term given by Laplanche and Pontalis. The alternative *tendance à répétition* is sometimes used, as in Jankélévitch's version of *Jenseits des Lustprinzips*.[93] Lacan's use of automatism in this context is, then, quite distinctive and in 1954 he admits that it is not really appropriate in that it has neurological overtones, and suggests *insistance* as a more acceptable alternative.[94] His own reservations notwithstanding, he does in fact continue to use 'automatism', as in the Poe seminar.[95] The connotations of automatism are not only neurological; the term is inevitably associated with Janet, whose thesis on *Automatisme psychologique* appeared in 1889. It is also a key term in Breton's programmatic definition of surrealism. A more significant association is made in the Seminar on the psychoses when mental automatism is linked with the name of Clérambault, whose work is said to be 'absolutely indispensable' in the domain of the psychoses.[96]

Clérambault appears to have had little knowledge of or interest in Freud, and his work is based upon a traditional and intellectualist theory of the faculties of the mind.[97] He is also a convinced organicist, looking for somatic causes for the syndromes he describes with such precision in his diagnostic notes on the patients he examines in the Special Clinic attached to the Préfecture de Police in Paris. Automatism itself is held to be the delayed result of intoxication or from physical infection. The syndrome of mental automatism, as found in psychosis and dementia praecox, is characterized by hallucinations, verbal or otherwise, by dissociation of the personality, and by the repeated or 'automatic' use of phrases and neologisms for which there is no rational explanation. These form the core or kernel of the syndrome; the associated delusions of persecution or of interpretation are secondary, intellectual formations which the subject elaborates in an attempt to explain the automatism. That Lacan does not fully endorse Clérambault's theories is evident from his doctoral thesis, where he suggests that delusions of interpretation indicate a 'primitive' distortion of perception and are in effect pseudo-hallucinations; they are not the product of a local or elective influence on a neuronal system.[98] He further suggests that automatism and delusions are contemporaneous and not sequential phenomena, thereby anticipating a curious exchange with Salvador Dali, but moving further away from Clérambault.

Despite these early disagreements, and despite the fact that Lacan does not appear to refer to him in the intervening period, in 1956 Clérambault is given the credit for having attempted to analyse the elementary phenomena of psychosis in such a way as to initiate a search for the link between an affection and its expression in language. For Clérambault, the source of the affection would be found at a somatic level, in a neuronal structure. Lacan endorses the notion of a structure, but insists that it must be conceptualized in terms of a structure internal to language:

> The weakness of his aetiological or pathogenic deduction is of little relevance to us compared to what he highlights, namely the fact that the kernel of psychosis must be linked to the subject's relations with the signifier in its most formal sense, in its aspect as a pure signifier, and that anything else that is constructed is merely an affective reaction to the primary phenomenon, to the relationship with the signifier.[99]

Despite their organic framework, Clérambault's insights help to reveal the externality of the psychotic subject's relations with the signifier, and that in turn raises the question of whether or not the psychotic has really entered into language. It is in this sense that Clérambault is indispensable. In 1966 Lacan asserts that, despite its mechanistic ideology, the notion of mental automatism comes closer to providing elements of a structural analysis than anything else in French psychiatry.[100] It would probably be an error to make too much of Lacan's debts to his old master, but it is clear that the combination of automatism and Freud's repetition is the major element in the emergence of the idea of the insistence of a repressed signifier in the Other, and of a scotomized signifier making itself heard.

Lacan's debts to psychoanalysis *à la française* and to psychiatry have a single focus in that they all relate in some way to a theory of psychosis and paranoia. They concern, that is, the subject of his original research (Aimée, the psychotic woman whose case is discussed below) and the area in which he is usually regarded as having been most innovatory. Whereas Freud comes to psychoanalysis via hysteria, Lacan comes to it via paranoia. It is therefore to be expected that his debts to the twin traditions he inherits should be most conspicuous in this area, but it was not to be expected that they would be so stubbornly forgotten.

3

Baltimore in the Early Morning

In October 1966 Lacan reads a paper entitled 'Of Structure as an Inmixing of an Otherness Prerequisite to Any Subject Whatever' to the Johns Hopkins symposium on the Languages of Criticism and the Sciences of Man.[1] As he speaks, he alternates between English (a language he does not speak well) and French, at times lapsing into a composite of the two; the published text is an edited transcript and paraphrase. It has become something of a commonplace to compare Lacan's weekly seminars in Paris with the equally memorable public performances of Jean-Martin Charcot, but this excursion into a pseudo-bilingualism carries with it an echo of something slightly more recent: the simultaneist recitals of Zurich Dada[2] and the performance art of surrealism. The echo is not an auditory hallucination, a link with surrealism being made perfectly explicit in the discussion that follows the paper. In response to a point raised by Jan Kott, Lacan comments: 'At least I feel a great personal connection with surrealist painting.'[3] He does not elaborate any further. Describing, in the body of the paper, his preparations for his 'little talk', he recounts how he sat at a window overlooking Baltimore. It is not quite daylight; the traffic is heavy; a neon sign flashes. Everything he can see, except for the trees, is

> the result of thoughts, actively thinking thoughts, where the function played by the subject was not obvious. In any case the so-called *Dasein*, as a definition of the subject, was there in this intermittent or fading spectator. The best image to sum up the unconscious is Baltimore in the early morning.[4]

The conceit is extravagant, preposterous even for Lacan, yet taken in conjunction with his reference to his affinity with surrealist painting it becomes an indication of his debt to surrealism, which he describes in 1956 as 'a movement of people who manipulated signs and symbols in

44

curious fashion'.[5] The deserted townscape is of course a recurrent theme in surrealist painting, providing it with certain of its more disturbing icons. One thinks, for instance, of the haunting neo-classicism of de Chirico's proto-surrealist *Gare Montparnasse (Melancholy of Departure)*,[6] of the imaginary cities and railway stations of Paul Delvaux, and of Dali's *Suburb of the Paranoiac-Critical Town; Afternoon on the Outskirts of European History.*[7] The same image reappears in a number of key surrealist texts. In *Le Paysan de Paris* (1928), Aragon and Soupault wander through the park at the Buttes Chaumont, looking out over a sleeping city; in both *Nadja* (1928) and *L'Amour fou* (1937) André Breton walks by night through a deserted Paris, a city haunted by desire and populated mainly by statues.[8] The similarity between the image of Paris in *Nadja* and Lacan's vision of Baltimore in fact borders on the uncanny; one of the features Breton describes is an illuminated sign advertising Mazda light bulbs, a direct ancestor of Lacan's neon sign. The image of Baltimore in the early morning might have been culled directly from the iconography of surrealism.

Overt references to surrealism are not infrequent in *Ecrits.* Of the forty or so French literary authors included in the name index, more than half belonged to the surrealist group at one time or another, or were claimed by the surrealists as their forebears. Surrealism is the only identifiable 'school' to which Lacan refers so consistently; most of his other literary references and allusions indicate the possession of a very broad cultural knowledge, but no overriding interest in any one movement. The passing allusion made to *En Attendant Godot* in 1956, for example, may signal a familiarity with the early theatre of the absurd, but it does not indicate any lasting interest in Beckett himself.[9]

It could be argued that surrealism is not a particularly arcane reference, that it is in the public domain and that no special significance should be attached to it. But whilst certain surrealist texts are now common cultural coinage, anyone who can suggest that a novice psychoanalyst would have found Breton's *Introduction au discours sur le peu de réalité* (1927) a useful adjuvant to the work of interpretation certainly has more than a superficial knowledge of the subject and rather more than a passing interest therein.[10]

The frequency with which Lacan alludes to surrealism is all the more striking in that it is not a major reference for the post-war avant-garde to which received opinion would have him belong. Neither Barthes, Sollers nor Kristeva has anything very positive to say about it. For Lacan, it provides a constant stock of allusions and illustrations, as when Magritte's 'window paintings' are used in the 1962 Seminar to illustrate the structure of phantasy. As Leclaire remarks in that connection, 'A phantasy is like a picture fitted into the opening of a window', a description which is particularly appropriate to one of the Wolf Man's oneiric experiences.[11] And the names of René Crevel and Salvador Dali still have a positive value for Lacan in 1966.[12]

Not all Lacan's nods towards surrealism are as obvious as this, but the more indirect references are equally significant. The cover of S XI is illustrated with a reproduction of Hans Holbein's *The Ambassadors* (National Gallery, London), which depicts two splendidly dressed men surrounded by classic icons of *vanitas*.[13] The foreground of the painting is occupied by a strange, vaguely phallic object which is described by Lacan in the *Ethique* Seminar as

> an enigmatic, elongated form which has roughly the shape of a fried egg. If you stand at a certain angle to it, an angle at which the relief of the picture disappears because of the vanishing lines, you will see a death's head appear; an insignia of the classic theme of *Vanitas*.[14]

The Ambassadors is of course a perfect example of the use of anamorphosis in painting. In 1964, Lacan says of it: 'Holbein makes visible for us something that is simply the subject nihilated – nihilated in a form that is, strictly speaking, the imaged embodiment of the *minus-phi* $[(-\phi)]$ of castration.'[15] In almost the same breath he suggests that Dali belongs to the same tradition as Holbein, and it is true that anamorphosis is an important feature of the paintings of Dali's paranoiac-critical period. A second, and perhaps more significant, connection between the two artists remains unspoken: *The Ambassadors* was always one of the surrealists' favourite classical paintings.[16] Baltimore in the early morning as an image of the unconscious; a deserted townscape embodying *Dasein*; the surrealists wandering through deserted cities; Holbein and Dali as iconographers of the subject nihilated. It is perhaps time to look seriously at surrealism, which Lacan once described as 'a tornado on the edge of an atmospheric depression where the norms of humanist individualism founder'.[17]

Surrealism is pertinent to a contextualization of Lacan in a number of ways. The young Lacan is known to have associated with the group surrounding Breton, and to have been on very close terms with Dali. His publishing career begins on two fronts: while he is publishing clinical articles of neurology in medical journals, he is also making more typically 'Lacanian' contributions to surrealist reviews, and even publishes a sonnet which is stylistically reminiscent of the work of Pierre Jean Jouve.[18] It is in surrealist circles that his doctoral thesis on paranoia receives its most enthusiastic welcome. According to his own account, his room at Sainte-Anne was once adorned with the legend '*Ne devient pas fou qui veut*' ('Not everyone has the good luck to go mad'), a motto which rivals Buñuel's 'Thank God I am still an atheist' in its paradoxical logic.[19] A reference to psychoanalysis is an integral part of surrealism. The surrealists are the first group in France to welcome psychoanalysis with open arms, and their enthusiasm does not a little to popularize the Freudian cause. Indeed, Henri Ey is reliably reported to have said that he first discovered psychoanalysis via surrealism rather than through medical textbooks.[20] Finally, the iconography of sexuality – and especially of female sexuality – elaborated by the surrealists in the 1920s and 1930s (and in part derived from a medico-psychiatric discourse) does much to inform Lacan's later explorations of the 'dark continent'. The point is not to argue that Lacan 'is' a surrealist, a reincarnation of Crevel or Breton's alter ego, but to demonstrate that the inflections of his discourse are profoundly marked by his encounter with the tornado of surrealism.

It is not possible to provide a comprehensive account of surrealism here or even to begin to chronicle the multiple schisms and personal-political conflicts which make up its history.[21] It is probably equally impossible to recapture its original aura of revolt and excitement. Aragon once called surrealism 'a new vice' and 'the child of frenzy and darkness', and in 1929 Walter Benjamin could not unreasonably claim that: 'Since Bakunin, Europe has lacked a radical concept of freedom. The surrealists have one.'[22] Current usage tends to equate 'surreal' or 'surrealistic' with 'bizarre', 'incongruous', or simply 'whimsical'. Magritte's paintings, without doubt the most intellectualized products of the movement, have been recuperated, trivialized and transformed into advertisements for whisky and cigarettes. As so often, a revolt has been turned into style. Our perceptions of surrealism have, perhaps inevitably, become distorted. Thus, received opinion would have it that Dali is the archetypal surrealist painter, yet he was associated with the movement for a relatively short time and his relations with Breton in particular were rarely less than stormy. His contribution to surrealist art is of course both immense and lasting, but that should not be allowed to obscure his differences with the other surrealists: an indifference to politics, a taste for classicism and the academic rather than the gothic, an unfortunate enthusiasm for Catholicism and Franco, and a talent for self-promotion and commercialization that led Breton, never the most tolerant of men, to dub him 'Avida Dollars'.[23]

In retrospect, it is the intellectual breadth and verve of the movement that are so striking. In a philosophical landscape dominated by the dreary ideologues of the Third Republic's educational apparatus, the surrealists at least begin to read Hegel, commenting on French ignorance of his work in *Le Surréalisme au Service de la Révolution*

(SASDLR) even before Kojève began his pioneering series of lectures on
The Phenomenology of Mind in 1933. Their work and enthusiasms
anticipate – and to a degree overlap with – those of the Collège de
Sociologie, the curious intellectual society founded by Bataille in 1937,
whose relevance to Lacan is discussed in the next chapter. A medicalized psychiatry shored up by the spiritualism of Bergson and still capable
of deploying the notion of mental degeneracy is challenged in the name
of an enthusiasm for Freud, and even by an embryonic anti-psychiatry.
Sexuality is foregrounded in a manner impossible to imagine only a few
years earlier, even if the debate is vitiated by a pervasive sexism and
heterosexism.[24] Surrealism is also a highly politicized movement, though
Breton's account of his unhappy experience as a member of the Parti
Communiste Français is a sadly eloquent testimony to the naivety of its
voluntarism.[25] Above all it is an inflammatory movement, deliberately
courting scandal. In short, nothing is left untouched and nothing is left
innocent.

In terms of poetry, surrealism brings about a far-reaching revolution
whose effects are still being felt. Surrealist poetry does not rely upon any
identifiable linguistic theory as such, but it is highly self-conscious and
its theorists do in some ways prefigure the structuralism of later decades.
Language, that is, is not seen as a nomenclature or as a transparent
medium without any materiality of its own. Meaning is seen as being
produced through the juxtaposition of images and the clash of associations rather than as deriving from some ideal correspondence between
sign and referent. Lacan may not entirely accept the poetic theories of,
say, Breton, but they are more than able to contribute to his discussions
of the nature of metaphor. Nor are these intuitions restricted to the field
of written language; an important part of Magritte's *œuvre* can be read
as an exploration of the arbitrary nature of the sign.

Much surrealist poetry – and notably that of Breton himself – is
hermetic, yet the movement probably did more to promote a public and
popular poetry than any of the self-conscious attempts to foster a
populist or proletarian literature. The poetry of the Resistance is
perhaps the last great renaissance of a popular-political poetry in
Western Europe – the only parallel that springs to mind is the work of
Pablo Neruda – and three of its best-known exponents (Aragon, Desnos
and Eluard) are all veterans of the surrealist campaigns, as is Jacques
Prévert, probably the only modern poet, other than the ubiquitous
Rimbaud, that virtually everyone in France can quote from memory.[26]
There are certainly major differences between their resistance poems
and the work of the surrealist period – Aragon, for instance, returns to
rhyme and regular metrical schemes in a deliberate imitation of the
lyrical traditions of the medieval troubadours – but it is quite clear that

they do not renounce the lessons of their earlier experiments or the heritage of the surrealist revolution.[27] To that extent, the more democratic aspirations of the original surrealist group were finally fulfilled, albeit it in a somewhat unexpected context.

Surrealist prose writings are, if anything, even more hermetically enigmatic than the poetry. Traditional genre distinctions break down, giving way to hybrid and almost unclassifiable texts like *Nadja*: part novel, part prose poem, part theoretical-aesthetic essay. Descriptive passages are excised and replaced by photographs. A text like this might be said to signal the birth of the modern, were it not that in the France of the late 1920s 'the modern' tends still to refer to debates over naturalism and Impressionism rather than to what Anglo-American criticism understands by modernism. And a surrealist who speaks of his admiration for *le style moderne* is more likely to be thinking of the wrought-iron Métro entrances built for the Exposition Universelle rather than of a poem by Eliot or a Bauhaus building.

Surrealism's most productive period is the late 1920s and early 1930s. The movement goes into eclipse during the war, is overshadowed by 'committed literature' and never regains its former strength, except perhaps in the films of Buñuel, a true surrealist iconoclast to the last (and one admired by Lacan[28]). Yet these manipulators of signs and symbols irrevocably altered the intellectual landscape of France. It was in effect they who first mapped out the literary canon of the 1960s and 1970s. Sade and Lautréamont would probably have remained in limbo without the surrealist intervention and would certainly not have enjoyed the prestige accorded them by Barthes and the *Tel Quel* group. Names like Artaud, Michaux and Ponge supply further evidence of the hidden continuity between the two avant-gardes. But the structuralists forget or simply repress their historic debt, excluding surrealist poetry from their pantheon just as Marcelin Pleynet excludes surrealist painting from his avant-garde canon.[29] And in so doing they forget a lot about Lacan, a central point of reference in all their work.

The process of forgetting becomes particularly apparent with the Summer 1971 issue of *Tel Quel*, which carries four highly critical articles on surrealism.[30] Not one of the contributors thinks fit to admit or recall that he would have been unable to read Lautréamont, a key reference for the journal at this time, had not Breton transcribed the one surviving manuscript of the *Poésies* held by the Bibliothèque Nationale, and had not his colleague Soupault prepared a complete edition in the 1920s. The belligerent tone of the criticisms addressed to Breton is that of high Althusserian Maoism (which, within a few years, is to give way to High Atlanticism as *Tel Quel*'s politics fall into line with a new orthodoxy).

Guy Scarpetta, for instance, complains that Breton never once used

the words *pratique* or *processus*,[31] key terms in the avant-garde
discourse of 1971 but not in that of 1921 or 1931. This is akin to
complaining that Louis Armstrong never quite perfected the later style
of Miles Davis. Breton is further reproached for having 'misrecognized'
(a classic Lacanian-Althusserian term, often used with distinctly intimid-
atory intent) the true import of psychoanalysis. He is in fact being criticized for failing to anticipate the final state of *Ecrits*. The Freudian
corpus available to Breton is not specified, and no mention is made of
his association with the young Lacan.

One brief detail is symptomatic of what is at stake. Houdebine approvingly cites Paul Nizan's review of Lacan's thesis, omitting to add that a
much longer and more interesting discussion of it appeared in the pages
of *SASDLR*.[32] The appeal of Nizan is obvious: he is writing in the PCF's
daily newspaper, and he finds that Lacan's work is influenced by dialectical materialism. He appears, that is, to be anticipating *Tel Quel*'s
enthusiasm for articulating Marxism and psychoanalysis. Appearances
are deceptive: this is only one of two references to Lacan to be found in
Nizan and one of the few, if any, allusions to him to be found in PCF
literature prior to Althusser's 'Freud and Lacan'.[33] Some aspects of
Nizan's novels do suggest a certain sympathetic interest in psychoanalysis, but on the whole he is quite content to endorse the PCF's official
views on the matter, to denounce attempts to produce a 'Freudo-
Marxism' as idealistic and to write off Bataille and the surrealists as 'men
singularly obsessed with sexual questions'.[34] Nizan is simply not a
precursor of *Tel Quel*. If there is a precedent for the Freud-Marx articulation, it is to be found in Crevel's attempts to elaborate a 'psychodialec-
tic', on the fringes of the surrealist movement and, in a rather different
sense, in the work of Politzer, but not in the mainstream PCF. *Tel Quel*'s
intellectual and political arrogance has rarely been equalled; its
amnesiac talents are rivalled only by those of the international psychoanalytic movement.

Many of *Tel Quel*'s criticisms of Breton derive from Jean Starobinski's
rather more measured essay on 'Freud, Breton, Myers'. Starobinski
rightly notes that Breton owes at least as much to classical psychiatry as to Freud, and that key notions such as that of automatism
derive from nineteenth-century debates around artificial somnambulism
and hysteria rather than from psychoanalysis as such. It is also probably
true that Myer's parapsychological notion of a subliminal self is as
relevant to Breton as the Freudian concept of the unconscious.[35] Starobinski fails, however, even to begin to reconstruct the theoretical and
epistemological conditions in which it was possible for Breton to read –
or misread – Freud. When Breton began to study psychoanalysis
towards the end of the First World War, Freud's work was in a state of

flux and he was very much an unknown quantity in France. The discrete corpus now known as 'Freud' did not exist. If it is relevant to point out that Binet and Janet used automatic writing as a therapeutic method long before Breton transformed it into an *ars poetica*, it is also relevant to point out that related notions of automatism feed into French psycho-analysis itself. Breton's theoretical references may well seem confused by the standards of 1970, but they are also those of the first French psychoanalysts. It is impossible to imagine Starobinski lapsing into such ahistoricism in his studies of Rousseau and the eighteenth century, but when he turns to the history of psychoanalysis he exhibits all the classic symptoms of amnesia.

As Breton acknowledges in his first 'Surrealist Manifesto' of 1924, the noun 'surrealism' derives from *surréal*, the neologism coined by Apolli-naire in 1917 to describe his play *Les Mamelles de Tirésias*. In the Manifesto, Breton defines surrealism 'once and for all' as:

> Pure psychic automatism, by which we propose to express the real functioning of thought, verbally, in writing, or by any other means. The dictation of thought, in the absence of any control exercised by reason and regardless of any aesthetic or moral preoccupations.

It is further specified in more philosophical terms as 'a belief in the higher reality of certain forms of associations which have hitherto been neglected, in the omnipotence of dreams and in the disinterested play of thought'.[36]

Surrealism is not intended to be merely an artistic style; on the contrary, it inherits from Dada a healthy disrespect for most conven-tional definitions of art. In the eyes of its principal theorist it is closer to being a total and transcendental world-view, the transcendental element being indicated by the prefix *sur* (*super*, or *higher*). Surrealism, that is, is intended to go beyond and above all forms of realism and to attain the realm of pure, unmediated thought and perception. This interest in the transcendental lies at the heart of the surrealists' subsequent enthusiasm for Hegel, who is seen as a potential ally in transcending the antinomies of positive and negative. It also no doubt explains their fascination with the 'marvellous', their cult of *l'amour fou*, and their interest in mysticism and the occult, which becomes rather more marked after the Second World War. In the present context, however, it is more important to note that it is inseparable from their interest in Freud, whose discovery of the unconscious will help them to go beyond the limitations of conventional thought and its outmoded poetic expression, beyond the banal opposition between dream and reality.

Breton's initial definition of surrealism is indelibly marked by a psychiatric discourse; terms such as 'higher reality', 'automatism' and 'dictation of thought' all derive from the clinical debates of the nineteenth century. To that extent, surrealism and psychoanalysis are distant relatives and it might be possible to explain Breton's interest in the subject in terms of a certain perception of their kinship. It can also be explained simply in biographical terms. During the First World War Breton served as a medical assistant in Nantes, then at the Second Army's psychiatric centre in Saint-Dizier and at the Val-de-Grâce, the great military hospital in Paris, before working under the neurologist Babinski at the Hôpital de la Pitié.[37] It was at this time that he began to read Charcot and Kraepelin and was lent copies of Régis's *Précis de psychiatrie* (1884) and Régis and Hesnard's *Psychanalyse des névroses et des psychoses* by his superior officer Dr Leroy, who once suggested that he should write a thesis on 'Delusions of Interpretation in Freud'. Although Breton never qualified as a doctor, his knowledge of psychiatry was considerable and was based upon what were at the time standard texts. His knowledge of psychoanalysis is based upon the texts which first introduced many members of the SPP to Freud. The future surrealist had discovered 'dementia praecox and paranoia, twilight states, the German poetry of Freud and Kraepelin'.[38]

According to his own account, Breton soon began to experiment with Freudian therapeutic techniques in Saint-Dizier and at the Val-de-Grâce, carefully recording and attempting to analyse the dreams and nightmares of traumatized troops. He also began to experiment on himself, and his analyses of his dreams contributed much to the imagery of his poetry. In a letter to his friend Théodore Fraenkel, Breton cites Régis's account of the techniques of dream interpretation: 'The subject must take notes with the absolute neutrality of an outside observer ... or that of a mere recording apparatus.'[39] The expression 'a recording apparatus' reappears in the first *Manifeste du surréalisme* and is a major reference in its discussion of automatic writing, an activity which was of vital importance to the early surrealists and which can be described as: 'a monologue which is as rapid as possible, on which the critical mind of the subject passes no judgement ... and which is as accurate a representation as possible of *spoken thought*.'[40] Automatic writing is basically an attempt to produce a stenographic record of dreams, and of the images and phrases that come to one on the verge of sleep; the 'writer' is a recording apparatus, and has the sensation of taking down dictation from an unknown source.[41] Attempts were also made to reproduce the process experimentally by inducing hypnotic trances, Robert Desnos being an excellent subject for hypnosis. The numerous accounts of dreams that figure in reviews such as *La Révolution surréaliste* represent variations on the same experimental theme.

Automatic writing had long been used by Janet in his experimental demonstrations of the hypothesis that hysteria results from personality dissociation and not from a functional lesion,[42] but a similarity can also be seen between Breton's description of the process and Freud's prescriptions for dream interpretation. The fundamental rule of non-omission, for example, applies in both. For Breton the dream is the royal road to poetry rather than to the unconscious, but his remarks about 'the absence of any control exercised by reason' correspond quite closely to what Freud terms 'the required attitude of mind' and 'the abandonment of the critical function'. Freud also notes that, if Schiller is to be believed, 'poetic creation must demand an exactly similar attitude' to that required for dream interpretation.[43]

Lacan, at least, is convinced that automatic writing is at least partly Freudian in its inspiration, and that the pioneers would not have attempted the experiment if they had not been 'reassured by the Freudian discovery'.[44] He disputes the theory of the doctrine, but not its quasi-analytic origins. As a method for poetic production automatic writing does not in fact prove to be entirely satisfactory, and most published examples show clear signs of reworking. Dream images and fragments of phrases which appear to emerge of their own free will do, however, provide a vital starting point. Breton's own attitude to automatic writing varies considerably over the years, but in 1960 he is still prepared to claim that the phrases it produced 'set the emotional tone' and that it therefore remains a central part of the poetic process.[45]

Surrealism is, among other things, an exploration of and a meditation upon the production of signification. The central concept of its poetics, as defined by the *Manifeste*, is that of the image produced by the almost random juxtaposition of two or more terms. The clash between the juxtaposed terms produces a 'spark', and the value of the resultant image is determined by the beauty of that spark. Whilst the concept of the image itself clearly owes a lot to the practice of automatic writing, the attempted theorization derives, as Breton notes, from the work of Pierre Reverdy, the most important of the surrealists' immediate predecessors. Following Reverdy, Breton argues that the juxtaposition of images and objects far removed from one another is the highest task that poetry can set itself; it gives them a poetic power or value which they cannot possess in isolation. Rimbaud's alchemy of the verb makes way for something new: a poetics in which 'words make love'.[46] Words, that is, react upon and against one another. Meaning is produced, and not pre-given.

This implies a definite break with a purely instrumental or representational view of language, and Breton goes so far as to argue that it represents a problematization of language and even of man's *raison d'être*.[47] Automatic writing and the related theories are the site of a contradiction which Breton never resolves. On the one hand surrealist poetics does imply a questioning of the assumption that language is by definition representational, and to that extent it prefigures certain of the tenets of more recent linguistic theory. On the other, the surrealists cling to the notion that automatism can provide immediate access to an unmediated subjectivity, and readily lapse into a romantic theory of expressivity. That the contradiction remains unresolved is scarcely surprising, given that they are working without reference to any specific linguistic theory and with intuitions inherited from Mallarmé, Lautréamont and Reverdy rather than with any formal philosophy or theory of meaning.

It is in the visual arts that we find the most sophisticated and sustained challenge to the notion that signification is a mere nomenclature, and that the unity of the sign is questioned most rigorously. Lévi-Strauss, for example, can easily read Duchamp's ready-mades through a Saussurean grid:

> The bottle-drainer in the cellar is a signifier of a certain signified: in other words, it is a device used for draining bottles. If you put it on a drawing-room mantlepiece, you obviously break and explode the relationship between signifier and signified.[48]

Exhibiting a urinal in a gallery has a similar, if more provocative, effect. In the late 1920s René Magritte begins to explore signification in a series of canvases which Schneede aptly describes as 'language paintings'. The series includes the well-known *Use of Speech*, a large painting depicting a smoking pipe and inscribed with the legend '*Ceci n'est pas une pipe*' ('This is not a pipe').[49] Although an element of humour is present, as so often in Magritte, this is more than a visual joke. The painting can be read as a comment on the radical non-correspondence between the visual image and the object it represents, the underlying thesis being that an image of a pipe is not a pipe. To use a more formalized terminology, the relationship between signifier, signified and referent is shown to be arbitrary.

Related images occur again and again in Magritte, and a pictorial essay published in *La Révolution surréaliste* reveals the extent to which he is quite consciously exploring a theory of meaning that comes surprisingly close to Saussure. The essay consists of a series of small sketches, each with a caption and each helping to illustrate the thesis that: 'Everything points to the fact that hardly any relationship exists between an object and that which represents it'.[50] Much of Magritte's *œuvre* can be seen as an investigation of the classically modernist problem of the relationship between the process of depiction and the object depicted, and in this essay he comes close enough to the insights of theoretical linguistics for one critic to discuss him in connection with both Pierre Fontanier's classic treatise on rhetoric and Wittgenstein's philosophy of language.[51] Saussure was not a reference point for the surrealists; an extremely systematic and sophisticated investigation into language and signification was part of the very air they breathed.

Lacan's rare discussions of surrealism (as opposed to allusions to it) should be read in this light. In the discussion that followed the presentation of 'Fonction et champ' to the 1953 Rome Congress of the SFP, Didier Anzieu remarked that Lacan's position might perhaps be elucidated by reference to surrealism, to the illuminism of poets like Nerval and Rimbaud and to their fascination with the power of the word. Lacan did not dissent from this view, and went on to describe surrealism as 'a stage in the unveiling of man's relationship with the symbolic'.[52] In his subsequent work Lacan attempts to theorize that relationship with the aid of linguistics, structural anthropology and finally mathematics; the implication of his remarks in Rome is that surrealism is an anticipation of these later developments. As was noted earlier, he also describes surrealism as contributing to the destruction of the norms of humanist individualism, a view that is curiously similar to Sartre's perception of it as a revelation that the individual subject is no more than an inconsistent decoy.[53] What is at stake in surrealism, then, is language itself, the symbolic, and therefore the status of the individual subject. Lacan's 'personal connection' with surrealist painting is very real.

In his discussion of poetry in 'Les Mots sans rides', Breton refers to several of surrealism's ancestors or precursors. That he should cite Reverdy, Lautréamont, Mallarmé and Rimbaud is quite predictable, but it is perhaps surprising to see the puns published by Marcel Duchamp in *Littérature* being praised as one of the most remarkable things in poetry to have been published for a long time.[54] The puns are in fact the work of Duchamp's female persona Rrose Sélavy,[55] and they include such masterpieces as: '*Rrose Sélavy trouve qu'un insecticide doit coucher avec sa mère avant de la tuer; les punaises sont de rigueur*' ('Rrose Sélavy thinks that an insecticide should sleep with his mother before killing her; bugs are *de rigueur*'). The cover of the seventh issue of the review is illustrated with a drawing based on another: '*Lits et ratures*', a play on 'literature' and 'beds and erasures' which anticipates 'Lituraterre', the title of Lacan's 1971 contribution to a very different journal entitled *Littérature*. Rrose Sélavy's wordplay is of course intended to amuse and infuriate in equal proportions, but it is also just as serious as Duchamp's experiments with his ready-mades. The ready-mades challenge conventional assumptions as to the nature of the art object, and can be read in quasi-Saussurean terms; the wordplay is a much more overt challenge to the notion that language is transparent, and an assertion that it is both material and malleable. Sélavy is, in short, an expert at the glossological games to which Lacan refers when he describes language as a knot of signification and not as a sign.[56]

The master referred to by Lacan on that occasion is Michel Leiris, whose 'Glossaire' began to appear in *La Révolution surréaliste* in April 1925.[57] The *glossaire*, or 'Glossaire, j'y serre mes gloses' to give it its full title (which might be rendered as 'Glossary, where I air my glosses'), consists of definitions of words arrived at by using a complex process of substitution, often involving the exploitation of assonance. Two of the more translatable examples are: 'PSYCHOANALYSIS: lapsus channelled by means of a couch' and 'PSYCHOSIS: hypostasis in question'. As in the example created by Sélavy, the ludic content is self-evident, but glossology is also a serious application of the principles behind a subsequent description of language: 'The arachnid tissue of my relations with others transcends me, spreading its mysterious antennae in every direction.'[58] Lacan's style owes much to a similar process of word-play, but it has to be admitted that examples such as *Je père sévère* ('I persevere/ I, strict father') seem positively mundane compared to the grandiose productions of his predecessors.[59] It was argued in 'The Final State' that Lacan's style reflects a widespread taste for puns and word games; it can now be seen to be equally indebted to a highly self-conscious intellectual tradition which rests upon a specific and sophisticated view of language, but refers to no identifiable school of linguistics. His style cannot, then, be dismissed as an idiolect or as a mere aberration. Curiously enough, a sustained attack on Lacan illustrates the point very clearly.

François George's *L'Effet 'yau de poêle* is basically an attempt to prove that the psychoanalytic emperor has no clothes and that he is simply hiding behind a screen of linguistic mystification.[60] George describes the Lacanians as a secret society known as the *Confrérie des 'Yau de poêle*, and their mission in life as the destruction of all reason and meaning. Their password is, he claims, the greeting '*Comment vas-tu, 'yau de poêle*', a phrase which requires some elucidation. '*Yau de poêle* is an abbreviated form of *tuyau de poêle*, meaning 'stovepipe' and, by extension, 'stovepipe hat'. In slang, however, *une famille tuyau de poêle* is an 'amoral' family or, more specifically, one in which incest has been or is being committed: as the author of a classic slang dictionary laconically observes, 'Stovepipes fit into one another'.[61] Given the propensity of Lacan's followers to imitate his style as closely as possible, textual incest might not be an inappropriate description of certain of their practices, but that does not exhaust the signification of the alleged password of the *Confrérie des 'Yau de poêle*. The expression '*Comment vas-tu, 'yau de poêle*' comes from a sexually equivocal scene in *La Fête au village*, the third and final part of Raymond Queneau's verse autobiography *Chêne et chien*, which first appeared in 1937.[62] George, then, directs the reader of Lacan back to Queneau.

Raymond Queneau, who died in 1976, is one of the more intriguing figures in twentieth-century French literature and thought. He is probably best remembered for novels like *Zazie dans le métro* (1959) and *On est toujours trop bon avec les femmes* (1947), which Lacan once described as 'A pornographic little book ... one of the most delightful one could hope to read.'[63] Much of the appeal of Queneau's fiction – and *Zazie* in particular has achieved lasting popularity – stems from his use of populist settings and from his creation of a *néo-français*, a semi-phonetic transcription of spoken French that surpasses even Céline in its inventiveness. His *néo-français* relies for its effect on a 'reform' of spelling, and Lacan too has been known to call for a 'sane orthographic reform' which could capture something of the force of Freud's 'Famillionaire' joke; the examples he proposes are *fauphilosophie* (false philosophy, but also a philosophy which worms its way into things; from *se faufiler*) and *flousophie* (a combination of *flou* – vague – and *sophie*, a variant on *sophia*).[64] Other instances of orthographic reform reveal an even closer connection between the two men. In *Zazie*, Queneau transcribes the phrase '*apprends-nous ce que c'est*' ('tell us what it is') as *apprends-nous cexé*; in *Encore* Lacan adopts an almost identical transcription, transforming '*c'est ce que c'est*' ('it is what it is') into *sekecé*.[65] The similarity between the puns Lacan and Godard construct on the basis of *femme, diffâmer* and *infâme* illustrates the extent to which Lacan's style can overlap with a popular ludism; the parallel with Queneau exemplifies how almost populist concerns can intersect with much more intellectualist discourses.

Queneau's career and even personality are a good example of that intersection. His activities are by no means confined to fiction. He is a mathematician, an influential figure in publishing and the editorial director of the highly prestigious *Encyclopédie de la Pléiade*. As a young man he was on the fringes of the surrealist movement and made minor contributions to *La Révolution surréaliste*, but later broke with Breton (for personal rather than ideological reasons). Like Prévert and the Resistance poets, Queneau is proof that surrealism was not, as it is sometimes claimed, destined to become hermetically sterile and did contribute, however indirectly, to the emergence of works that are both highly sophisticated and genuinely popular. At a very different level, Queneau is the editor of Kojève's *Introduction à la lecture de Hegel*, the text which informs a whole generation's perception and understanding of *The Phenomenology of Mind*, and whose importance to Lacan is almost incalculable.[66]

Like Leiris, Duchamp and Lacan himself, Queneau is a past master at glossological games, his talents in that direction being one of the hallmarks of his style. They also emerge in his contributions to the work of the *Ouvroir de Littérature Pontentielle* (OULIPO), the group of experimental writers established in 1960. OULIPO's activities include glossology, and they have a considerable ludic content. But they are also extremely serious and are based on the thesis that 'We are language from head to toe', and that 'Language is a concrete object'.[67] It follows that language can be treated like any other concrete object and can become the subject of scientific experimentation. Such experimentation includes the use of mathematical theories and models to generate poems and narratives, the most awesomely successful experiment in that field being Georges Perec's monumental novel *La Vie, mode d'emploi*.[68] Lacan is not the only person to have made the somewhat curious transition from surrealism to mathematical theory via the perception that language is a material object. Indeed, there is evidence that two individuals who were to become leading figures in OULIPO helped him to make that transition: the first indication that a form of mathematics is to be integrated into his discourse comes from two papers written immediately after the war. The puzzle discussed in one of them was brought to his attention by Raymond Queneau, and invented by Queneau's longtime associate François le Lionnais.[69]

Whilst the OULIPO authors have at their disposal theoretical tools that were not available to the surrealists (linguistics, mathematics), they share many of the premises and perceptions of their precursors. Rrose Sélavy's 'insecticide' is never far away. Their glossological games also relate to the widespread use of a sophisticated wordplay in less intellectualized artefacts such as the immensely popular spook thrillers of San Antonio, which are a kind of grotesque cross between Queneau and Mickey Spillane. They also relate to one positively banal pastime: crossword puzzles. Perec, for instance, saw no contradiction whatsoever between his membership of OULIPO and the compilation of crosswords for newspapers. This point might be borne in mind when reading Lacan's pithy advice to young psychoanalysts: 'Do crossword puzzles.'[70]

Psychoanalysis met with considerable and lasting resistance in French medical circles, and it was in the literary milieu that it found its first favourable reception. But when Lacan remarks that it was in the circle of Jacques Rivière and the *Nouvelle Revue Française* that the Freudian message really caught on, he is endorsing received wisdom to an alarming degree.[71] The influence of the NRF should not be exaggerated, as it does relatively little to promote the psychoanalytic cause and tends, rather, to absorb it into an established literary discourse. In a discussion of Freud (based largely upon Jankélévitch's translation of the *Vorlesungen*) published in the NRF, Jules Romains suggests that psychoanalysis is unlikely to be anything more than a passing fashion and claims that is an art rather than a science; the insights it provides are comparable to the psychological analyses of Racine and Stendhal.[72] This is a literary equivalent to the psychiatric assimilationism practised by Hesnard and others. Gide's comments on first reading Freud are equally complacent: he suddenly realizes, he says, that he had been practising psychoanalysis (by which he presumably means self-analysis) for fifteen years without knowing it.[73] That is, there is nothing in Freud which he has not discovered from introspection. Even so, he does condescend to lie on Sokolnicka's couch for a few hours, and paints a thinly disguised picture of her in his novel *Les Faux-monnayeurs*.

The most sustained expression of the NRF position is contained in the three lectures given by Jacques Rivière at the Vieux-Colombier theatre in January 1924. For Rivière, there are three major themes in psychoanalysis: the theory of the unconscious, the concept of censorship, and the libido theory. The theory of dreams and slips of the tongue is seen as a late, and minor, addition. Rivière finds parallels between Freud and Proust's theory of associations and argues that the theory of the unconscious itself has already been promoted by Racine, and given a new impetus by Rousseau and the Romantics.[74] Psychoanalysis can, that is, be inscribed within a tradition of literary introspection; its texts are an extension of what Lacan terms 'the psychopathological monographs which make up a genre of our literature'.[75] If the NRF group welcomes Freud, it is not because of his radical originality but precisely because he can be reinscribed within a tradition it holds dear. It does not, however, do a great deal to promote a detailed knowledge of psychoanalysis. In the interwar period, the NRF itself publishes only one article on the subject (in addition to Romain's 'aperçu'), some undistinguished notes on a case-history by Reverchon-Jouve and Jouve, and two reviews.[76] In 1934, Pichon remarked that the literary vogue for psychoanalysis in the early 1920s was superficial and had no lasting impact.[77] In terms of literary history, he was perfectly right; the mood of introspection soon gives way to a literary cult of action associated with Malraux and Saint-Exupéry and their belief that man [sic] is what he does, not what he thinks, consciously or unconsciously.

The reception given to psychoanalysis may not have been over-enthusiastic, but it was at least cordial. Even the geography of Paris seems at times to hint at a peaceful coexistence of literature and psychoanalysis; for some time the members of the *Evolution psychiatrique* group met in the apartment of Henri and Odile Codet at 10 rue de l'Odéon, almost next door to Adrienne Monnier's legendary bookshop and Sylvia Beach's Shakespeare & Co., the birthplace of *Ulysses*; and according to one account, it was in Monnier's shop that the young Lacan was first introduced to the high priest of surrealism.[78]

For the surrealists, psychoanalysis is not a continuation of an existing tradition. On the contrary, it is an explosion which they hope to harness to further their self-proclaimed revolution. Freud is an ally in their attack on the bourgeoisie and all its works. Part of that attack is a denunciation of prevailing conceptions of mental health and of the repressive use of psychiatry. In the notorious 'Lettre aux médicins chefs des asiles de fous' of 1925, mental hospitals are denounced as 'frightful jails' and their inmates are described as 'the individual victims of a social dictatorship'.[79] With the publication of *Nadja* in 1928, matters become more serious. The eponymous heroine is finally revealed to be an inmate in a psychiatric hospital and towards the end of the text Breton states that if he were ever to be interned in such an institution, he would take advantage of any remission to kill any doctor within his reach.[80] This clearly touched a raw nerve, as the conservative *Annales Médico-Psychologiques* seriously suggested that Breton's remarks were tantamount to incitement to murder and even considered the possibility of bringing a prosecution. Breton duly – and no doubt with a certain grim satisfaction – published the whole discussion at the beginning of the Second Manifesto of 1930 and pressed his own charges in a related article, claiming that the primary function of psychiatry is one of social repression and that its definitions makes 'pathological' synonymous with 'socially deviant'.[81]

Such statements can of course be read as an extension of a late Romantic celebration of madness and of the cult of the *poète maudit*, a phrase that might have been coined with Artaud in mind, but it would be no great exaggeration to describe their authors as the precursors of the anti-psychiatry of the 1960s. Freud is recruited (or co-opted) into the struggle against establishment psychiatry, not least because he, like the surrealists, regards the distinction between the normal and the abnormal as rather less than self-evident. René Crevel, for instance, argues that Freud has finally put paid to the very notion of 'normality' and invokes both his name and that of Lacan – whose thesis he regards as a major contribution to the nascent science of personality – in his diatribes against the 'ladies and gentlemen of psychiatro-psycho-philosophy' and in his contention that psychoanalysis is already being distorted and used to shore up the very institutions it ought to be destroying.[82]

It is, however, true to say that French surrealism has little or no real interest in the therapeutic potential of psychoanalysis. It is a source of polemic and an addition to their poetic arsenal rather than a clinical practice or even an aetiology. British surrealism tends to adopt a rather different stance, with Hugh Sykes Davies arguing that so long as the world of dreams and phantasy remains 'hidden, unseen, not understood', it is potentially dangerous. In his view, the aim of surrealism is to make that private world public. Pailthorpe, for his part, is of the opinion that the object of surrealism is 'to know the self' and that, like psychoanalysis, it strives 'to free the psychology of the individual from internal conflict so that he or she may function freely'.[83]

The surrealists' enthusiasm for Freud is not reciprocated. Breton did in fact meet Freud in October 1921, but nothing came of the encounter. In 1932, he corresponds with Freud over the omission of Volkelt from the bibliography appended to the French edition of the *Traumdeutung*; it transpires that the name had been unintentionally omitted from the German text from which the French translator worked. Freud's replies to Breton are brief and unfailingly courteous, but he comes to the conclusion that he has no understanding of what surrealism is and no idea of what it wants.[84] Given his personal and moral conformism and his conservative tastes in literature and art, it comes as no surprise to learn that he has little interest in Aragon's child of darkness and frenzy. Indeed, his general view is that Breton and his acolytes are 'complete fools (let us say 95%, as with alcohol)'.[85]

But as his comments on Schiller and poetic creation begin to suggest, Freud may have had more in common with the surrealists than he knew or cared to admit. According to one pilgrim to Vienna, a reproduction of Fuseli's *Nightmare* hung alongside Rembrandt's *Anatomy Lesson* in the apartment at Berggasse 19;[86] a curious juxtaposition of an old surrealist favourite, which Freud never mentions in his writings, and a classic, even hackneyed, icon beloved of so many medical men, and perhaps a reminder of the distant kinship between surrealism and psychoanalysis. Breton and Freud share a taste for Jensen's *Gradiva*, and the subject of Freud's essay of 1907[87] – known to the surrealists in Marie Bonaparte's 1931 translation – provides both the name for the art gallery opened by Breton in 1937 and the inspiration behind a major painting by Masson. It also supplies Dali with a highly productive obsession.

In July 1938, Dali is introduced to Freud by Stefan Zweig. Surprisingly, the two make a favourable impression on one another. According to Dali, Freud tells him that, on seeing a classical painting, one immediately looks for an unconscious element; on looking at a surrealist painting, one looks for the conscious element.[88] As a result of the encounter,

Dali produces three drawings of Freud – including what must be one of his finest works in pen and ink[89] – and Freud modifies his previous views on surrealism by remarking that 'It would indeed be interesting to investigate analytically how he came to create that picture.'[90] Sadly, Freud did not live to write what would indeed have been an interesting analysis; 'that picture' was the *Illuminated Pleasures* of 1929.[91]

Dali's enthusiasm for Freud and psychoanalysis is unsurpassed, even in surrealist circles. Breton observes in later years that 'No one was more passionately interested in psychoanalysis', but adds, somewhat censoriously, that Dali uses it primarily to cling jealously to his complexes and to make them ever more extravagant.[92] Dali appears to have read *The Interpretation of Dreams* while he was still a student in Madrid, and claims that it inspired in him 'a real vice of self-interpretation';[93] many of his paintings of the early surrealist period do indeed centre on lovingly cultivated obsessions, with sexual themes figuring prominently. Automatism has its part to play, but it is soon replaced by the critical-paranoiac method, Dali's most distinctive contribution to surrealism. In his first contribution to SASDLR, Dali claims that by using 'a process of thought which is both active and paranoiac in character' it will soon be possible to 'systematize confusion and to contribute to the total discrediting of the world of reality'. Paranoia is then described as 'using the outside world to promote an obsessional idea' and as having the disturbing property of 'making the reality of that idea valid for others'.[94] In terms of artistic practice the method promotes the use of the double image, as in the Tate Gallery's *Beach with Telephone* (1938),[95] in which a certain similarity can be seen with Holbein's anamorphic *Ambassadors*.

In the paintings of this period images multiply and shift as the eye moves across the canvas, bringing different elements into and out of focus. It is at this point that Dali's practice intersects with Lacan's theory and with his comments on the productions of subjects like Aimée. In such productions, Lacan finds what he terms 'an iterative identification of the object':

> The delusion proves in fact to be very fertile in phantasies of cyclical repetition, of the ubiquitous multiplication and endless periodic return of the same characters, sometimes in the form of hallucinations of a splitting and reduplication [*dédoublement*] of the person of the subject.[96]

In such statements, and in Lacan's 'admirable' thesis, Dali finds a confirmation of his own intuitive views.[97] And when the two meet, at Dali's suggestion, the painter is extremely flattered to learn that 'one of the most brilliant young psychiatrists' should find something of scientific interest in his ideas.[98]

Lacan's 'La Conception du style' and Dali's paranoiac-critical interpretation of Millet's *Angelus* appear together in the first issue of *Minotaure*, the glossy review published by Albert Skira and Tériade. There are definite parallels between their thinking at this time, and certain of Dali's double or multiple images might be illustrations of Lacan's remarks about *dédoublement* in paranoia, *The Metamorphosis of Narcissus* (1937) being a particularly clear example.[99] To the extent that the images are simultaneous and that the depiction of the obsessional idea and of its visual interpretation are inseparable, they are also a reminder of the issue over which Lacan departs from the orthodoxy of Clérambault by contending that automatism and delusions of interpretation (or pseudo-hallucinations) are contemporaneous and not sequential phenomena. The question of possible mutual influences is less important than a parallelism which testifies to the fertility of the borderlands between psychiatry, psychoanalysis and surrealism. A similar notion of *déboublement* and of simultaneous perceptions is apparent in some of Lacan's references to the mirror stage and to the narcissistic construction and function of the ego. Lacan describes the perception of the mirror image as involving pre-formed images and *Gestalten*, and occasionally refers to as 'paranoiac knowledge' (*connaissance paranoiaque*). The individual thus has a pre-formed and illusory knowledge which is simultaneous with his very existence, and Lacan describes it by exploiting Claudel's pun on *co-naissance* ('knowledge' and 'co-birth').[100] An element of paranoia is, that is, implicit in the narcissism of the ego.

Whilst the surrealists have no official mandate from Vienna, they do contribute to the popularization of Freud in their own way, not least by freeing discussion of his work from purely literary or purely clinical considerations. Extracts from Bonaparte's translation of *The Question of Lay Analysis* first appear in *La Révolution surréaliste* in October 1927 illustrated with reproductions of paintings by Tanguy and de Chirico. At the time, fewer than a dozen works by Freud are available in French, and this is by no means an insignificant addition to the literature. Other works by Freud are either reviewed or discussed in the journal, often by Jean-Frois-Wittmann, who enjoys the reputation of being a 'surrealist psychoanalyst'.[101] In purely quantitative terms the surrealist contribution to the dissemination of psychoanalytic knowledge may not be great, but it cannot be ignored, if only because of its relevance to Lacan. The surrealist interest in psychoanalysis is not purely theoretical, and Freud is not simply a source of poetic raw material.

A number of individuals associated with the movement do go into analysis, but little is known of their reactions. Both Bataille and Leiris spend periods in analysis with Adrien Borel; Bataille comments that, whilst analysis did help him to overcome his day-to-day difficulties, it did nothing to allay his 'inner intellectual violence'.[102] Leiris never speaks directly of his experience, but it is clear that psychoanalysis is a major influence on the series of autobiographical writings that begins with *L'Age d'homme*, which Pontalis reads as an exploration of the thesis that the ego is an imaginary construct, and which Lévi-Strauss regards as initiating a study of the unconscious structuring of vocabulary.[103] Queneau too goes through what he calls *psychanasouillis* ('psychoanasullying'), and gives an entertainingly irreverent account of his period on the couch in *Chêne et chien* ('I lay down on a couch/and began to talk about my life/what I thought of as my life. ... Then one day I had to pay/things began to get serious/there were fees to be paid'[104]). The analyst in question cannot be identified with any certainty, but Queneau later remarks that his *psychanasouillis* was no more pleasant than the childhood which presumably made it necessary.[105] Rather more seriously, Artaud had some unfortunate dealings with René Allendy (who also analysed Anaïs Nin) and spent some time as a patient in Sainte-Anne, where an anonymous doctor commented in his fortnightly report that his 'literary pretensions' might be justified 'in so far as delusions can provide a source of inspirations'.[106] His remarks unwittingly pinpoint an important moment in the history and discourse of surrealism: the inevitable convergence of the concern for language and the interest in psychoanalysis and psychiatry.

In 1928, Aragon and Breton celebrate hysteria as 'the greatest poetic discovery of the late nineteenth century'.[107] Two years later, Breton and Eluard begin to explore twilight states and German poetry in greater depth in *L'Immaculée Conception*, one of the most important texts of the heroic period of psychoanalysis. This is a collection of short texts which are at times reminiscent of the colliding images and aphorisms of *Les Champs magnétiques* (1920), Breton and Soupault's first joint venture into the uncharted waters of automatic writing. The central section, entitled 'Les Possessions', represents something new. The authors deliberately simulate five pathological states corresponding to major nosographic categories in classical psychiatry: mental debility, acute mania, general paralysis, delusions of interpretation and dementia praecox. The simulation takes the form of the production or reproduction of the discursive 'style' of each state, but Breton and Eluard are at pains to stress that they are interested in producing a mere pastiche or imitation of the appropriate symptoms. Their stated ambition is to demonstrate that the 'poetically trained mind' can, without ill effect, explore and exploit the 'hitherto unsuspected resources' offered by languages 'which, rightly or wrongly, are regarded as being most inadequate to their objects, and it is fully in line with *Nadja*'s contention that there is no definite boundary between madness and non-madness.[108]

Although the simulation project implies considerable knowledge of psychiatric literature, the authors are not concerned with therapy, diagnosis, or even with the aetiology of the pathological. They are simply using an existing discourse on the pathological in an attempt to find something that can profitably replace outmoded genres such as the ballad, the sonnet and the epic. The implications of *L'Immaculée Conception* are, however, far-reaching. The classically surrealist thesis that the pathological is not meaningless but a mode of expression which has its own validity is taken further than ever before; the states simulated here are specifically referred to as languages. The whole enterprise depends upon the premiss that an equivalence between psychic states and discursive modes can be constructed. It implies, that is, that the unconscious and its formations can be linguistically simulated and studied.

It has been suggested that Lacan's famous dictum that the unconscious is structured like a language may owe much to 'the surrealists' attention to the linguistic expression of psychic phenomena',[109] even though the nosography used in *L'Immaculée Conception* is clearly pre-Freudian. Whether or not Lacan's formula derives ultimately from Breton and Eluard is probably impossible to prove or disprove, and Pichon's thesis that language 'reflects' the unconscious must also be taken into account. Lacan did know the text, and refers to it in his 'Ecrits "inspirés": Schizographie', a paper read to the Société Médico-Psychologique in November 1931. Here, he speaks with admiration of 'the experiments carried out by certain writers on a mode of writing they call sur-realist [which] ... show the remarkable degree of autonomy which graphic automatism can reach without any hypnosis', and adds that similar mechanisms can be observed in pathological cases.[110]

Twenty-five years later, he refers to this paper in the Seminar on the psychoses: 'A case of schizophasia in which one can in fact find the structure of what is known as schizophrenic disintegration at every level of discourse, in both the semantemes and the taxemes.'[111] A description of 'psychotic speech' in the same seminar reminds one even more strongly of Breton and Eluard's early explorations of the unexpected resources of the pathological; when listening to a psychotic patient, Lacan tells us: 'You have the feeling ... that here is someone who has penetrated more deeply into the very mechanism of the system of the unconscious than most mortals are privileged to.'[112] He further contends: 'It is the register of speech which creates all the richness of the phenomenology of psychosis; it is there that we see all its aspects, decompositions and refractions.'[113]

But it is Luce Irigaray who, perhaps unwittingly, comes closest to reproducing the underlying assumptions of *L'Immaculée Conception*. In an influential essay on linguistic and specular communication she characterizes psychosis, neurosis and hysteria in terms of the subject's handling of pronoun functions, and argues that his discourse is determined by the modalities of the experience of the mirror stage. In short, 'Distortions of language can ... be related to a distortion of the specular experience.'[114] Irigaray's linguistics is, it goes without saying, infinitely more sophisticated than the intuitions of Eluard and Breton, but she shares their view that a formal correlation can be established between psychic phenomena and linguistic-discursive formations. To that extent, a text like *L'Immaculée Conception* does prefigure aspects of Lacanian and Lacanian-derived theory, so much so that at least one historian of psychoanalysis can argue that the surrealists were the first to realize that psychoanalysis is essentially a question of language.[115]

The hysteria celebrated by Aragon and Breton as the greatest poetic discovery of the late nineteenth century clearly owes more to Charcot than to Freud, and their text is illustrated with a spread of six plates from the second volume of the *Iconographie photographique de la Salpêtriére*.[116] They show a patient known as 'Augustine' in the throes of a hysterical attack, and are captioned 'Les Attitudes passionnelles en 1875'. Technically, that term applies to the third phase of the attack: a hallucinatory phase in which the subject relives scenes with a high emotional charge and acts them out in theatrical gestures.[117] Breton and Aragon tend, however, to apply it to the whole phenomenon of hysteria. For them, hysteria is 'a mental state based upon a need for mutual seduction. Hysteria is not a pathological phenomenon and can, in all respects, be considered a supreme means of expression.'[118] Years later, Breton in fact admits that the object of their interest is not hysteria itself, but the iconography of *les attitudes passionnelles*.[119] Hysteria becomes an iconography of femininity.

The brief text published in 1928 becomes central to what can only be described as a cult of hysteria and gives rise to an extensive series of icons. Man Ray's photograph of Meret Oppenheim and the fetishistic shots of Lya Lys in Buñuel's *L'Age d'or*, provide minor examples of the genre,[120] but it is Dali who supplies the ultimate icons of hysteria in his *Phénomène de l'ecstase*, which appears in the December 1933 issue of *Minotaure*.[121] This is a collage of photographs of women in a variety of rhapsodic poses and of the heads of statues of women by the Catalan sculptor Gaudi; the similarity with the Salpêtrière photographs used by Aragon and Breton is unmistakable and by no means coincidental. In the accompanying text, Dali makes the connection quite explicit:

Psychopathological parallel – Invention of 'hysterical sculpture' – continuous erotic ecstasy – contractions and attitudes without precedent in the history of statuary (it concerns women discovered and known after Charcot and the school of the Salpêtrière). ... Direct connections with dreams, reveries, waking phantasies.

Just whose dreams and phantasies are depicted in the *Phénomène* is a matter for some speculation, but a male figure bearing a distinct resemblance to the artist appears voyeuristically at the top and bottom of the collage. There is also a related pen-and-ink drawing by Dali entitled *L'Arc hystérique*; this depicts a woman in the classic *arc* position, bent backwards until her arms touch the ground, her face contorted into an ecstatic grimace.[122] The strained pose seems to anticipate the tortured forms of the better-known *Soft Construction with Boiled Beans: Premonition of Civil War* and *Autumn Cannibalism* (both 1936), which suggests that the iconography of hysteria became an integral part of his visual lexicon. But it is not specific to Dali alone; Maurice Heine produced a 'lesbian' variant on the *Phénomène*.[123] One of the installations at the 1938 Surrealist Exhibition in Paris was a 'bedroom for a hysteric' surrounded by a swamp and aquatic vegetation and designed 'to set emancipated young women from the provinces dreaming'.[124]

This iconography immediately evokes the last words of Breton's *Nadja*: 'Beauty will be CONVULSIVE, or it shall not be.' But it is in *L'Amour fou* that Breton comes closest to providing a comprehensive description of convulsive beauty: the beauty of natural phenomena or works of art which 'give me the feeling of wind brushing against my temples, and which produce a real *frisson*'.[125] He adds that there is only a difference of degree between this sensation and erotic pleasure. The original manifesto of convulsive beauty is to be found in Lautréamont's *Chants de Maldoror* and, more specifically, in the famous passages which begin 'As beautiful as ...' (these are supposedly random associations, but the passage most appreciated by the surrealists – 'As beautiful as the chance encounter of an umbrella and a sewing machine on a dissecting table' – is a somewhat transparent metaphor for sexual intercourse). In *L'Amour fou*, Breton provides his own exemplary similes: as beautiful as 'the eyes of Isis, the eyes of the omen thrown to the lions, the eyes of Justine and Juliette, those of Lewis's Matilda, and those of certain portraits by Gustave Moreau'.[126] In the summer of 1933, convulsive beauty is made flesh by three killers: Violette Nozières and the Papin sisters. As Xavière Gauthier demonstrates at length in her *Surréalisme et sexualité*, 'woman-as-victim' is a common theme in surrealist art ('women thrown to the lions', Justine, the collages in Max Ernst's *Les*

Femmes cent têtes . . .). This time, it is the Juliette side of the family that comes into its own.

On 28 August 1933 eighteen-year-old Violette Nozières was arrested and charged with the murder of her father, a railwayman whose sole claim to fame was that he had once driven the President's train, and with the attempted murder of her mother, who gave evidence against her only child. Violette's unsucessful defence rested upon the claim that she had been the victim of incest since the age of twelve, and that she had acted out of desperation. The court, however, took the view that she had poisoned her father in order to lay hands on his savings of 165,000 francs, which she intended to give to her lover, and she was condemned to death.[127] In 1937, she finally retracted the incest story. The surrealists accepted her original version of the events leading up to the murder and produced a celebratory volume of poems and drawings, publishing it in Brussels to reduce the risk of prosecution.[128]

For Breton, Violette no longer resembles anyone living or dead and is 'mythological to her fingertips'; according to Eluard, she 'dreamed of undoing and then undid the dreadful serpents' knot of blood ties.'[129] Her act is seen as one of exemplary revolt, of absolute rebellion against the hypocrisy of the bourgeois family; as one of those offences against public morality and against the person which violently reveal 'the monstrosity of the laws and constraints which create monsters'.[130] Violette's extreme youth, the suspicion of incest and her reputed promiscuity no doubt add to the *frisson* produced by her convulsive beauty which, in 1977, was to have precisely the same appeal for the film-maker Claude Chabrol. Breton's own attitude towards her reveals a certain ambiguity. On the one hand she is the victim of a father who, in her words, 'sometimes forgets that I am his daughter' and whose ultim- ate intentions were always inscribed in the first two syllables of the name he gave her: Breton stresses that '*viol*' means 'rape'. To the extent, she is a sister to Sade's Justine. On the other hand she is an avenging angel, a destructive force which reveals the hypocrisy of petty-bourgeois morality in all its obscenity, a parricide, and a sister to Juliette.

That he definitely associates her with Sade is shown by the similarity between the imagery of his contribution to *Violette Nozières* and that of a poem dealing with the Divine Marquis, written only a year later. In the former, the young schoolgirl from the Lycée Fénelon returns to a home where 'A moral window is opening on to the night'; in the latter Sade has the eyes of a young girl, and the mysterious orders he gives 'open up a breach in the moral night'.[131] The breach opened up by Sade is a form of liberation, a transgression of norms which will allow Breton to love the women to whom the poem is addressed 'as the first man loved the first woman, in complete freedom'. The moral window which opens up in the Nozières home is more ambiguous. Breton's sympathies clearly lie with the supposed victim of incest, and he celebrates her revolt and the vengeance she takes on her father. In that sense, the moral window sheds light on what can happen behind the shutters of respectable homes. On the other hand, the notion of incest does seem to appeal to his more prurient instincts; and, in Sade's terms, incest is by no means reprehensible. Ultimately the ambiguity centres upon the figure of Violette herself: a composite figure of Justine and Juliette.

No such ambiguity attaches to the Papin sisters, who are closer still to the ideal of convulsive beauty; Eluard and Péret describe them as springing 'fully armed' from the writings of Lautréamont, which is high praise indeed.[132] Christine and Léa Papin were servants employed in the home of Monsieur Lancelin, a lawyer in Le Mans: two convent-educated girls who were devoted to one another, two docile and retiring maids. A summer thunderstorm causes a power failure, and when the lawyer's wife and his daughter Geneviève come home to a darkened house, they berate the sisters for something that is obviously beyond their control. The servants' reaction is as unexpected as it is horrific:

> They each grab an adversary, and tear out her eyes from the socket while she is still alive – something which is, they say, unheard of in all the annals of murder. Then, using whatever comes to hand – a hammer, a pewter jug, a knife – they fling themselves on the bodies of their victims, smashing in their faces, exposing their genitals, lacerating their thighs and buttocks, and daubing them with each other's blood. Then they wash up the instruments they used for their atrocious rites, clean themselves up and go to sleep in the same bed. 'What a mess.' That is the very formula they use. It seems to capture the tone of the emotional sobering up that comes after their orgy of blood.

The description is Lacan's.[133]

Like Violette Nozières, the Papin sisters are immediately elevated to the status of surrealist heroines. Eluard and Péret argue that their crime is fully justified because they are the victims of social oppression; it was inevitable that an anger fed by humiliation and fear would eventually explode into violence. All three women have committed crimes which are in some way equivalent to what Breton called the most basic surrealist act: going out into the street and opening fire at random.[134] They become figures in a pantheon of female killers.

Their immediate forebear is Germain Berton, the anarchist who assassinated Maurice Plateau, an Action Française leader, in 1923, and whose photograph appears in *La Révolution surréaliste* in December 1924 surrounded by portraits of the surrealists. She is described by

Aragon as 'an admirable woman in every respect'.[135] Presumably anyone who assassinated a man like Plateau would have found favour with the surrealists, but Berton's sex is without doubt a determining factor. Whilst the surrealists delight in the crimes of Gilles de Rais, the somewhat inflated criminal reputation of Sade and the anarchist outrages of Ravachol, they pay little attention to living criminals. It is, for instance, left to Jean Genet to celebrate the murderous exploits of Weidmann in *Notre Dame des Fleurs*.[136] It is the female killer who excites the surrealists, who procures the eroticized *frisson* of terror and admiration. We can now add new icons to the list of compulsive beauties given in *L'Amour fou*: as beautiful as the eyes of Germaine Berton, the eyes of Christine and Léa Papin ... and the eyes of a woman known simply as 'Aimée'.

Aimée was a thirty-eight-year-old railway clerk who inexplicably attacked one of the best-known actresses in Paris, wounding her with a knife as she entered the theatre one evening. No charges were brought against her in connection with the attack, but she was admitted to Sainte-Anne for psychiatric reports. The initial diagnosis made by Dr Truelle indicated paranoia characterized by delusions of grandeur, megalomania and erotomania. Aimée consistently maintained that the actress, Mme Z., and a novelist and Academician referred to as 'P.B.' had been spreading slander about her and that the life of her son had been threatened. She had never met either of her alleged persecutors. Aimée had literary ambitions, but her novels and poems had been repeatedly rejected by one publisher after another. She insisted that her work had been plagiarized by well-known writers. It was the burning significance of her writings which first led Lacan to take an interest in her case,[137] and they later ensured her a minor place in the surrealist pantheon when Bousquet published extracts from them in the first issue of *14 rue du Dragon*, and when Eluard reprinted them in his anthology *Poésie involontaire et poésie intentionnelle*.[138] Sadly, the only remnants of Aimée's poem and of her novel *Le Détracteur* are these fragments, originally published by Lacan in his doctoral thesis. When asked what had become of the manuscripts, Lacan said he could only assume that Aimée threw them away or destroyed them when she left hospital.[139] Aimée, on the other hand, claimed that Lacan refused to return them and that she had every intention of publishing them.[140]

Lacan discusses the Aimée case at length in his thesis, and incorporates certain of his conclusions into later and more general elaborations – a résumé is given in 'Propos sur la causalité psychique' (1946) and references to it can be found in the Seminar on the psychoses. Although it is not always apparent from his later accounts – and it is certainly not apparent from references to Aimée in the work of his followers – Lacan did not analyse Aimée; he had yet to qualify as a psychoanalyst.[141] The text of the thesis, which Lacan was apparently reluctant to republish,[142] bears all the hallmarks of its academic origins: a survey of existing theories of paranoia, a cumbersome array of notes and references, and a bibliography which prompted Georges Heuyer, the holder of France's first chair in child neurology, to write to its author to say that he felt sorry for anyone who had read so many background books.[143] It is probably best regarded as a transitional text midway between classical psychiatry and psychoanalysis; in 1955, Lacan will say that Aimée took him to the 'threshold of psychoanalysis'.[144]

Lacan's observations lead him to the conclusion that Aimée is suffering from 'self-punishment paranoia'; that her assault on Mme Z. was in fact a means of punishing herself by attacking her ideal. The diagnosis is not in itself original in that 'self-punishment' mechanisms were very much on the French psychoanalytic agenda in the early 1930s;[145] Lacan's originality lies in his attempt to outline a structure of personality as alienation and in his ability to incorporate Aimée into an iconography of femininity.

Aimée attacks an ideal image of a woman who enjoys social freedom and power, the very type of woman she hopes to become by pursuing a literary career.[146] She lives in a dual world, dreaming in her writings of a world of universal fraternity and peace, and at the same time suffering persecution at the hands of the domineering figures she admires. 'The dominating woman she envies',[147] and who comes to be her persecutor, is initially embodied by her sister and then by a close woman friend to whom Aimée once admitted: 'I feel that I am masculine'.[148] Aimée's condition, then, is rooted in a problem of identification, in a confusion of self and other. She wishes to be a rich, influential novelist, and attacks the incarnation of her ambition: an actress who effectively represents her ego ideal. She feels herself to be masculine, and suffers from frigidity.[149] Her uncertainty as to her sexual identity recalls the curious statement made by Christine Papin in prison, where she was separated from her sister for the first time in her life: 'I really do think that in a different life I should have been my sister's husband.'[150] Lacan's comments on both the Papin case and that of Aimée rely heavily on Freud's argument that paranoia is in part a defence against homosexuality, a process of disavowal which gives rise to the delusion of persecution and to the identification of the loved one with the persecutor.[151] In both the cases he discusses, self and other merge all too easily and gender becomes uncertain, which may explain why Genet found the Papin case so attractive and used it as the basis for his play *Les Bonnes*. It is also very apparent that Lacan is as fascinated by the Papin sisters as Breton is by Violette Nozières; the very tone of his loving description of their atrocious rites certainly indicates rather more than an objective clinical interest.

In one sense, Lacan's interest in these convulsively beautiful criminals is not surprising. His recent career has included a year working under Clérambault in a clinic attached to the Préfecture de Police; its main task is to prepare psychiatric reports on criminals and vagrants. In 1931 he is awarded his Diplôme de médecin légiste, which qualifies him as a forensic psychiatrist. His interest in the psychiatric study of female criminality is, that is, professionally determined, and the bibliography appended to the thesis provides amply evidence of his wide knowledge of the clinical literature on criminology. His article on the Papin sisters is, however, published in *Minotaure*, alongside work by Dali, Leiris, Masson and Breton. The decision to go into print in such company surely indicates a high degree of overdetermination by the cults of hysteria and convulsive beauty then prevailing in surrealist circles. In 1977, Lacan plaintively asks: 'What has become of the hysterics of the past, of those marvellous women like Anna O. and Emmy von M?'[152] It is not difficult to imagine him musing over the fate of Léa, Christine and Aimée in the same nostalgic tone. Psychoanalysis owes a great deal to its marvellous hysterics. Lacan's debts to his convulsive beauties are considerable; they are his first guides to the dark continent of femininity.

The last icons of convulsive beauty to be found in Lacan are not culled from case-histories or from crime reports but from mysticism, from the histories of Hadewijch of Antwerp and Teresa of Avila.[153] The transcript of the 1972–73 Seminar, is supposedly 'Lacan's most direct attempt to take up the question of feminine sexuality',[154] yet it contains references at the iconographic level which take us back to Dali rather than beyond Freud. The cover illustration is a reproduction of a detail of Bernini's *Ecstasy of St Teresa*, which depicts the saint at the moment of her transverberation. In her vision, she sees an angel carrying a golden spear which is tipped with fire:

> This he plunged into my heart several times so that it penetrated to my entrails. ... The pain was so severe that it made me utter several moans. The sweetness caused by this intense pain is so extreme that one cannot possibly wish it to cease, nor is one's soul content with anything but God.[155]

Lacan's version is rather less poetic: 'She's coming, there is no doubt about it.'[156]

The title given to this volume of the Seminar is *Encore* (again, more, still), and it refers partly to Lacan's surprise – or feigned surprise – at once more [*encore*] giving a seminar and at still [*encore*] having an audience.[157] The layout of the cover artwork introduces a rather different dimension. The word *Encore* appears immediately above the head of the saint, and seems to have issued from her parted lips. Given St Teresa's own description of her transverberation, the layout is not inappropriate: 'The soul is conscious that it is fainting away almost completely into a kind of swoon ... once the ... faculties have begun to grow drunk on the taste of this wine, they are very ready to give themselves up again in order to enjoy some more.'[158] To imitate Lacan's more robust phraseology, she is saying, '*Baise-moi encore*' or '*Fais-moi jouir encore*' ('Fuck me again', 'Make me come again'). Whatever else Lacan may have to say about femininity in *Encore*, one thing is abundantly clear: the iconography he selects to illustrate his text belongs to the realm of Dali's continuous erotic ecstasy and participates in the celebration of convulsive beauty. In the painter's *Phénomène de l'ecstase*, a male figure watches ecstatic women. The text and artwork of *Encore* implicitly reproduce that configuration. Once again [*encore*] a man watches a woman coming again [*encore*].

In an important passage in 'Fonction et champ', Lacan refers to the unconscious as a chapter in the history of the subject that has been censored and which is now marked by a blank or occupied by a false-hood. The truth about that chapter has not, however, been destroyed and it can be found elsewhere in monuments, in archival documents and in the subject's semantic evolution.[159] Application of these archaeologi-cal, palaeographic and philological metaphors to the corpus of Lacan's own *œuvre* reveals a great deal about a chapter which, if not censored, has all too often been overlooked in readings centred solely upon a final state and informed primarily by the assumptions of the avant-gardes of the 1960s and 1970s. His textual body bears scars from the past, the stigmata of past encounters. Its monuments and archival documents make up an image stock (and this is a possible translation of *imagi-naire*), a storehouse of allusions, references and asides, many of them to surrealism. The documents are illustrated, and the plates are drawn from an iconography which includes the terrible beauty of the Papin sisters and the ecstasies of St Teresa. They are stations on a journey that takes us from a legendary encounter in Adrienne Monnier's bookshop to a room overlooking Baltimore in the early morning.

Lacan defines 'semantic evolution' as 'the stock of words and accept-ations of my own particular vocabulary'. If his words and acceptations are glossed in terms of their context, it becomes apparent that they are part of what Leiris terms an arachnid tissue, a web of discourses which encompasses surrealism, the glossological games of Rrose Sélavy, the experiments of Queneau and Perec, and even the humble art of the crossword puzzle. To regard this web as an 'influence' would be myopic in the extreme. Lacan is not influenced by surrealism, as though it were some external factor impinging upon his subjectivity; his writing is part of the same web. He spins it together with his manipulators of signs and symbols. In 1973 Lacan opens a televised conversation with the words: 'I always tell the truth; not the whole truth, because you cannot succeed in telling the whole truth.'[160] No truth is absolute or final, not even that provided by documents and monuments. The neon light that flashes over Baltimore does not and cannot provide a full illumination, but it does throw certain things into relief.

4

Philosophy and Post-Philosophy

Psychoanalysis has in the course of its history generated a considerable body of philosophical writing, but the bulk of this has been produced outside the psychoanalytic community itself, which usually remains untouched by the more theoretical debates around Freud and his work. The *International Journal of Psycho-Analysis*, for example, is not noted as a forum for philosophical or epistemological debate, and gives pride of place to clinical and technical literature. Lacan's foregrounding of philosophy and his willingness to enter into theoretical-epistemological controversy are very much the exception to the rule. One cannot imagine, say, Anna Freud, Ernest Jones or Melanie Klein discussing Descartes or Heidegger with anything like his sophistication. Nor is Lacan's evident relish for theoretical *alpinisme* a national or generational characteristic. There is some truth in the clichéd opposition between Anglo-American empiricism and French high theory, but by no means all French analysts display Lacan's talent for abstraction; Bonaparte, Nacht and Lagache being obvious examples. Yet the ease with which a French author can speak so readily of 'important French philosophers, like Lacan and Althusser', and with which a book entitled simply *Lacan et la philosophie* can be published masks some important problems and contradictions.[1]

Freud himself shows relatively little concern for philosophy; literary and historical references abound in his writings, but allusions to identifiable systems or discourses are comparatively rare. His sole comment on an author who will be of major importance to Lacan is a passing reference to 'the obscure Hegelian philosophy in whose school Marx graduated'.[2] Although he at times displays a certain nostalgia for *Naturphilosophie* and occasionally detects a certain kinship between his own work and that of Kierkegaard or Nietzsche, in general Freud tends to view philosophy and its 'artifices' with profound distrust and suspicion.[3] In his *Autobiographical Study* he even claims to have deliberately avoided any contact with 'philosophy proper', explaining that 'this avoidance has been greatly facilitated by constitutional incapacity.'[4]

Such claims are, as one might reasonably suspect from Freud's own comments on the mechanisms of denial, rather more ambivalent than they might seem. The writings on anthropology and on the theory of culture certainly do not suggest that their author was constitutionally incapable of speculation, and there is some evidence that Freud regards them as being equivalent to a philosophy. In a revealing letter to Wilhelm Fliess, Freud confesses: 'As a young man, I knew no longing other than for philosophical knowledge, and now I am about to fulfil it as I move from medicine to psychology.'[5] Freud's longing is never fulfilled within the arena of 'philosophy proper', perhaps because it is inhibited by methodological and epistemological considerations, but it does find expression in contiguous areas of speculation.

Freud's epistemologically and metapsychologically based suspicions of philosophy are voiced on a number of occasions, but rarely more clearly than in the *New Introductory Lectures* of 1932–33. Here, he explicitly argues that psychoanalysis is antithetical to the elaboration of a specific *Weltanschauung*. In so far as it does generate a world-view, it is simply expressing the *Weltanschauung* of science, which Freud defines in terms of its empiricism, in terms of its assertion that: 'there are no sources of knowledge of the universe other than the intellectual working-over of carefully scrutinized observations – in other words, what we call research'.[6] It is the weight given to the primacy of observation in scientific research that provides Freud with grounds to distrust philosophy, which he habitually equates with speculation.

A dichotomy is thus introduced between the slow, empirical progress of science and the hasty speculations of the philosophers. Although both philosophy and science are 'higher mental activities',[7] the former departs from the latter by 'clinging to the illusion of being able to present a picture of the universe which is without gaps and is coherent'.[8] Science, in contrast, is content with more modest ambitions and with approximations which are susceptible to modification as science progresses:

> The transformations of scientific opinion are developments, advances, not revolutions. A law which was held at first to be universally valid proves to be a special case of a more comprehensive uniformity, or is limited by another law, not discovered till later; a rough approximation to the truth is replaced by a more carefully adapted one, which in turn awaits further perfecting.[9]

A holistic or totalizing *Weltanschauung* provides a feeling of security, and satisfies basic emotional needs by supplying an intellectual construction which solves all the problems of existence uniformly on the basis of one overriding hypothesis, which, accordingly, leaves no question unanswered and in which everything that interests us finds its fixed place.[10]

The prototypes for this illusory satisfaction are the great religions and philosophical systems; in clinical terms the model for philosophy is provided by paranoia, in which 'the construction of systems ... dominates the symptomatic picture.'[11] Freud's epistemological distrust of philosophy thus merges with his metapsychological and clinical categories. Both totalizing *Weltanschauungen* and paranoia are characterized by 'an overevaluation of the magic of words',[12] to that extent, they are reminiscent of animism. The criticisms of the artifices and speculations of philosophy can therefore be integrated into a broad evolutionary vision which recalls Comte's theses on the theological-metaphysical-positive sequence that characterizes human history: 'The human race ... have in the course of the ages developed three ... systems of thought – three great pictures of the universe: animistic (or mythological), religious and scientific.'[13] The same vision inspires the hope that the 'scientific spirit' will eventually establish a 'dictatorship in the mental life of man'.[14] In other words, Freud's objections to philosophy are in part based upon a cultural evolutionism which he fails to recognize as 'one overriding hypothesis'.

It is, then, on the basis of an empiricist-positivist epistemology and of metapsychological considerations pertaining to the clinical symptomatology of paranoia that Freud voices his distaste for 'clear and sharply defined basic concepts' and advances the view that 'the advance of knowledge ... does not tolerate any rigidity even in definitions'.[15] His admission that he is 'not at all partial to the fabrication of *Weltanschauungen*'[16] and his dislike of the speculations of philosophy do not, of course, prevent Freud from advancing his own speculative hypotheses. They are, however, subject to subsequent modification and to further revision, as 'Only believers, who demand that science shall be a substitute for the catechism they have given up, will blame an investigator for developing or even transforming his views.'[17] Thus the concept of the unconscious is a hypothesis or assumption which has to be justified by an appeal to experimental or experiential data (post-hypnotic suggestion, or psychoanalytic practice itself).[18] Similarly, the pleasure principle is a speculative assumption arrived at 'in an attempt to describe and to account for the facts of daily observation in our field of study'.[19]

The need for observation combines with the exploitation of speculative insights to produce a constant interrogation and reshaping of basic, but provisional notions. 'Metapsychological speculation and theorizing' are necessary if knowledge is to advance, but they can easily take the form of phantasy, and are not to be trusted; metapsychology itself is a 'witch' whose services may be necessary, but whose charms and spells are to be resisted.[20] Lacan cites the opening paragraph of 'Instincts and their Vicissitudes' as evidence that Freud's empiricism implies a high degree of conceptualization.[21] Advances in knowledge, that is, are impossible without the constant renewal and enrichment of the work of conceptualization. Freud's empiricism is by no means naive or non-reflexive, but it remains an empiricism.

The critique of philosophy is also a defence of psychoanalysis. Following Freud, Ferenczi warns against the danger of adapting it to 'a specific philosophical attitude' on the grounds that premature system-building is an obstacle to new discoveries. It follows that psychoanalysis must be allowed to develop without interference from the philosophers: 'Surely an off-season, like that in which game may not be shot, should be granted to a young science such as psychoanalysis, and a substantial delay should elapse before it is approached with the armament of metaphysics.'[22] Psychoanalysis does not hold itself accountable to philosophy. It does, on the other hand, claim that philosophy must take it into account: 'the setting up of the hypothesis of unconscious mental activities must compel philosophy to decide one way or the other and, if it accepts the idea, to modify its own views on the relation of mind to body so that they may conform to the new knowledge.' Moreover, philosophy can 'derive a stimulus from psychoanalysis' by 'becoming a subject of psychoanalytic research'.[23] Freud thus both excludes psycho-analysis from the field of philosophy and reserves it the right to pronounce upon philosophy. Objections from philosophers can be parried by arguments elaborated on the basis of the hypothesis they have most difficulty in accepting (that of the existence of the unconscious), and their systems can be challenged on clinical grounds. A distinctly unequal relationship has been established.

Whilst Freud does on the whole steer clear of 'philosophy proper', his broader speculations are by no means confined to working hypotheses applicable to clinical psychoanalysis and its applications. He also makes spectacular – and at time spectacularly unfortunate – forays into anthropology and into the theory of religion, notably in *Totem and Taboo*, a text to which he was singularly attached but which it is now almost impossible to read without embarrassment, so tightly are its references to 'the most backward and miserable of savages, the aborigines of Australia ... these poor naked cannibals' enmeshed within the Eurocentric prejudices of late-nineteenth-century and early-twentieth-century anthropology.[24] Here – and in related texts such as *Moses and Monotheism* and *Civilization and its Discontents* – Freud moves away from hypotheses grounded in or justified by clinical practice to speculations based upon theses as to 'the analogy between neurotic processes and religious events'[25] and as to 'Some points of agreement between the mental lives of savages and neurotics', to quote the subtitle of *Totem and Taboo.*

It is on this analogical basis that the history of the Jewish people can be written in terms of a latency period and a return of the repressed. The basis for Freud's analogical reasoning derives ultimately from Haeckel's basic biogenetic law (ontogeny as 'the short and rapid recapitulation of phylogeny'[26]) and it can be integrated without difficulty into his quasi-Comtean vision of the evolutionary march of history. But in positing such analogies, Freud unwittingly prepares the ground for one of the more dubious tendencies to be observed in psychoanalysis: the marked propensity to regard sociopolitical phenomena as strictly analogous or even reducible to the symptoms it finds in clinical work. Paradoxically, this propensity can be explained in terms of the well-known mechanism of projection. By projecting clinical findings on to areas in which their validity may be less than self-evident, psychoanalysis can discover truths which can then be introjected as proof of its original hypotheses or findings. Thus, if it is the case that 'the mental life of savages' is a picture of an 'early stage of our own development', it follows that a comparison between the psychology of primitive peoples and that of neurotics 'will be bound to show numerous points of agreement and will throw new light upon familiar facts in both sciences.'[27] That 'light' will inevitably be a reflection of the original hypothesis. Projection is, of course, a defence, and the projection of analogies enables Freud to defend a system he denies having, as projected findings replace demonstrations.[28]

The reductionism implicit in this tendency to project – which is remarkably innocent of any theory of the social, not to mention the economic – must surely pose serious problems for any Marxism–psycho-analysis 'articulation', yet it has rarely been rigorously examined in recent work on that subject. The work of Janine Chasseguet-Smirgel, a distinguished training analyst and a vice-president of the IPA, provides a by no means atypical example. In her major study of the ego ideal she illustrates the phenomenon of the fusion of individual egos into a collectivity by referring to 'the sports meetings of young people in totalitarian countries where, with the help of streamers or coloured placards, a group of individuals create immense slogans or gigantic portraits.'[29] The phenomenon she describes is readily recognizable and might be construed as exemplifying Freud's theories of group dynamics, but the slide into a quasi-political discourse is illegitimate, unless it can be argued that the Los Angeles Olympics also took place in a totalitarian country. In short, Chasseguet-Smirgel has nothing concrete to say about totalitarianism, young people or sports meetings. Her assertion has all

the cogency of the legendary statement: 'Paul Valéry is a petty-
bourgeois intellectual', to which Sartre rightly retorts that not every
petty-bourgeois intellectual is a Paul Valéry.[30] It is founded upon
Freud's analogical reasoning, and it permits – or requires – the elision of
any reference to a theory of the political.

Just as psychoanalysis can call philosophy to account without being
accountable to philosophy, so it can pronounce upon the political whilst
refusing to be politically judged. Chasseguet-Smirgel also cites a *Le
Monde* article on the occupation of the Sorbonne in May 1968; it is
entitled 'Le Bateau ivre' (after Rimbaud's poem), and she comments
that the metaphor 'demonstrates ... the intrauterine (the boat) and
elated (drunk) nature of the group regression.'[31] Freud's speculations
thus pave the way for a reductive, or projective, identification of the
political with the pathological. It is statements of this order which
authorize and lend credence to the psychoanalytically inspired cultural
sociology of, say, Christopher Lasch, in whose writings the clinically
observable phenomenon of narcissism becomes a cultural category of
almost infinite elasticity.[32] It should be noted in passing that, on the
whole, Lacan and his followers eschew such sweeping political judgements and reserve their speculative energies for other projects. The one
area in which they do lapse into the type of argument deployed by
Chasseguet-Smirgel and Lasch lies on the borders of the dark continent
of femininity; here, as will be seen in a later chapter, the 'the political is
pathological' argument applies in all its force.

The analogical reasoning which underpins Freud's more speculative
ventures into anthropology and related areas is itself symptomatic of an
unresolved tension that lies at the very heart of psychoanalysis. In his
survey of the main current in post-Freudian psychoanalysis, Bercherie
notes a certain confusion between the view that analysis is a science of
the entire psychic field and the more modest view that it is a specific
technique and practice.[33] It would appear that the origins of the confusion can be traced back to Freud himself. On the other hand, Freud
advances arguments and hypotheses based upon empirical clinical
observations in order to elaborate a theory of the unconscious as it is
revealed in psychoanalytic practice. Within this domain he considers his
work to be characterized by the modesty of science, as opposed to the
vaulting ambitions of speculative philosophy. On the one hand, he also
makes speculative extrapolations with a universal application on the
basis of analogies grounded in a supposedly fundamental biogenetic law.
There is considerable evidence to suggest that he views the results of his
speculations as an equivalent to the philosophical knowledge for which
he once longed: 'My interest, after making a lifelong detour through the
natural sciences, medicine and psychotherapy, returned to the cultural

problems which fascinated me long before, when I was a youth scarcely old enough for thinking.'[34]

His manifest aversion to holistic theories notwithstanding, Freud does effectively admit to a desire for a quasi-philosophical knowledge, whilst his use of analogical projection affords the feeling of security proffered by universalist theories. His work is thus the site of a tension between a desire for modesty and the theory of a specific practice, and a desire for a speculative universal theory. As the example of Chasseguet-Smirgel indicates, the ambiguities surrounding the theoretical object of psycho-analysis can therefore be exploited, consciously or otherwise, to justify political and cultural arguments which appear to be supported by the authority of empirical clinical practice, but which in fact rest upon purely analogical foundations. Despite his theoretical sophistication, Lacan will consistently reproduce these ambiguities at a number of levels.

Lacan clearly does not subscribe to Freud's tacit positivism but he does display the same overt distrust of philosophy, arguing that the very term 'world-view' is antithetical to psychoanalytic discourse[35] and even that all 'philosophical -*ologies* (onto, theo, cosmo and psycho alike)' contradict the basic tenet of the existence of the unconscious.[36] Like Freud before him, Lacan objects strongly to the totalizing ambitions of philosophy and to its pretensions to being able to tell the whole truth. But whereas Freud chooses to identify his work with the slow, halting march of science, and therefore refuses the comforts of speculation (at least at the manifest level), Lacan opposes philosophical totalization on the grounds that it is simply not possible to tell the whole truth. As he tersely puts it at the beginning of *Télévision*, the words that might allow one to do so are simply not there.[37]

His objections to the project of totalization crystallize in the critique of the 'discourse of the Master', one of the four discourses identified in *L'Envers de la psychanalyse*, the unpublished Seminar of 1970, the others being the discourse of the University, that of the hysteric, and psychoanalytic discourse.[38] Very schematically, the discourse of the Master originates in the attempt to attain the moment of Absolute Knowledge described by Hegel in *The Phenomenology of Mind*: 'This last embodiment of spirit – spirit which at once gives its complete and true content the form of self, and thereby realizes its notion, and in doing so remains within its own notion – this is Absolute Knowledge.'[39] For Lacan, such knowledge can only be illusory in that it implies an unattainable unity; as Hegel has it, it implies 'Knowledge which unites the objective form of truth and the knowing self in an immediate unity.'[40] In Lacanian terms, unity – or the illusion thereof – belongs within the realm of the imaginary and of the narcissistic functions of the ego.

The link between the discourse of the Master and the agency of the ego is best illustrated by a punning sentence in *Encore*: '*Je suis m'être, je progresse dans la m'êtrise, je suis m'être de moi comme de l'univers.*'[41] The sentence depends for its coherence on the play on *m'être* (a neologistic reflexive verb meaning roughly 'to be myself' and generating the noun *m'êtrise*, or 'my-being') and for its wit on the allusion to *Cinna*, Corneille's heroic drama of 1640, which ends with the Emperor Auguste proclaiming that he has achieved both a truly Cartesian mastery of the passions of his own soul and political mastery of Rome. It is not a particularly erudite allusion; '*Je suis maître de moi comme de l'univers*' is one of the most familiar quotations from any classical French drama. Lacan's sentence, which might be rendered as 'I am my-being; I progress in my-being/mastery; I am master/my-being of myself and of the universe', posits a link between the illusion of mastery and absolute knowledge or power, and the illusory identity of the ego. Not even 'his Majesty the Ego'[42] is an absolute monarch. The allusion to *Cinna* is apposite in that Auguste's triumph depends upon the voluntary submission of Cinna, the erstwhile rebel; even apparent absolutism or autarky is based upon a dialectic between self and other. Elsewhere, the illusory nature of absolutism and mastery leads Lacan to remark that Hegel's Master is 'the great dupe, the magnificent cuckold of historical evolution'.[43]

The discourse of the Master is a concept relatively late in Lacan's career, but its implied critique of all attempts at totalization is anticipated in the 1938 essay on the family. Here the metaphysical mirage of universal harmony, the mystical abyss of affective fusion and social uptopianism are all seen as expressions of a desire to return to a lost prenatal paradise or of an aspiration towards death, as a 'nostalgia for the whole' or, more abstractly, as a desire 'for the perfect assimilation of the totality into being'.[44] In this early paper, then, Lacan is very close to Freud's theses on the illusory satisfaction afforded by holistic systems; a trace of the analogical reductionism of Freud's anthropology can also be observed in the assimilation of the social (utopianism) to the pathological.

Lacan endorses Freud's suspicions of philosophy. He also endorses the totalization/psychosis (paranoia) parallel by playfully remarking in 1975: 'Psychosis is an attempt at rigour. In that sense, I would say that I am psychotic. I am psychotic for the simple reason that I have always tried to be rigorous.'[45] It will also become apparent that, like Freud, he holds philosophy accountable to psychoanalysis, but contends that psychoanalysis has no accounts to render. In view of this manifest distrust of philosophy and its ambitions, the conspicuous references to philosophy that punctuate his work may seem somewhat anomalous or even contradictory. As though aware that their status is not always self-evident, he frequently asserts that they are primarily pedagogic devices and illustrations, whilst denying that they imply the adoption of any specific philosophical position.

In many cases, such assertions can be taken at face value. Thus, a quotation from St Augustine's *Confessions* is consistently used from 1938 to 1973 to illustrate the structures of jealousy that are bound up with the transivitism and the mirror stage, but its use does not necessarily betoken any serious interest in patristics.[46] Other allusions have a less obvious pedagogic function, but again they do not connote any especial interest in the authors concerned. The passing references to Malebranche in *Ecrits*, for instance, surely indicate little more than the possession of a broad intellectual culture and can, depending upon one's level of tolerance, be interpreted as either an entertaining discursive playfulness or a terroristic pedantry.[47] But it is clear that there is no pressing need to engage at any length with Malebranche in order to read Lacan. In other cases – notable those of Hegel and phenomenology – Lacan's claim to be exploiting the philosophical field to purely pedagogic ends must be open to question, but before going on to examine that issue it is to be noted that despite his reputation for subversive iconoclasm, Lacan takes a surprisingly conventional view of philosophy.

Lacan normally assumes the philosophical field to be an ahistorical arena in which Augustine and Descartes can speak to one another across the ages, and in which existential phenomenology can be viewed as a minor variation on the theme of Cartesianism. No fundamental distinction is drawn between materialism and idealism, and the former tends to be invoked in its eighteenth-century sensualist guise rather than in its later – and rather different – Marxist incarnation. The field is approached, or traversed, in totally apolitical terms. The ethical implications of, say, *L'Etre et le néant* are ignored in favour of its theory of perception. When, in 'Le Temps logique', Lacan does invoke the Sartrean notion of freedom, he misconstrues it. The blunt statement: 'I am not one of these recent philosophers for whom the constraints of four walls simply do more to promote the goal of human freedom' indicates a certain failure to come to terms with Sartre's apparently paradoxical claim that the French had never been so free as they were under the Occupation; the whole issue of freedom as necessary choice and commitment is simply elided.[48]

There is, moreover, no real attempt on Lacan's part to theorize or problematize the production of philosophy. Whereas Althusser would discuss philosophy in terms of its relationship with the sciences and would view it as 'class struggle in theory', and whereas Derrida would

deconstruct the various discourses invoked by Lacan as so many
variations on the narratives and metaphors of 'Western metaphysics',
Lacan himself tends to take the philosophical field as a given, as something natural: philosophy is philosophy is philosophy. The resounding
assertion that 'the formation of the *I* as we experience it in psychoanalysis ... leads us to oppose any philosophy issuing directly from the
Cogito'[49] cannot alter the fact that in so far as it constitutes a field of
reference, the field of philosophy remains largely intact and conventional.

Its conventionality is exemplified by the reluctance to address philosophical systems as such, and by the marked tendency to reduce them to
certain of their constituent moments. The entire Hegelian system is
reduced to the master–slave dialectic and to its resolution through
symbolic recognition, although discussion can extend to take in the
theme of the beautiful soul. Descartes is discussed solely in terms of the
cogito; the issue of how the cogito articulates with the physics, or with
the physio-psychology of *Les Passions de l'âme*, is never raised. For
Descartes, the *Discours de la méthode* is but a prolegomenon to an
exposition of the sciences that will make men masters and possessors of
nature; for Lacan it is simply the eternal moment of the cogito. There is
of course no a priori reason why a psychoanalyst should rewrite or
deconstruct the history of philosophy, but recognition of Lacan's oddly
conventional vision of its field does provide a healthy corrective against
the exorbitant philosophical claims that are sometimes put forward on
his behalf.[50]

The conventional nature of the philosophical field exploited by Lacan
can be illustrated by an examination of the opposition he establishes
between Descartes and the 'perverse genius' of La Rochefoucauld.[51] La
Rochefoucauld is the great theorist of *amour-propre*, which is usually
translated as 'self-love', though in a psychoanalytic context it might not
be inappropriate to regard it as approximating to 'narcissism'. For
Lacan, the notion of *amour-propre* represents a glimpse into the nature
of the ego.[52] According to the *moraliste, amour-propre* is the secret
motivation behind even the most apparently altruistic action; it is the
mainspring behind all human behaviour, but it never manifests itself as
such, being a protean force or even instinct which conceals itself behind
countless masks and disguises. Hence Lacan's comment:

> What is scandalous about La Rochefoucauld is not that, for him, *amour-
> propre* is the foundation of all human behaviour, but that it is deceitful, inau-
> thentic. There is a hedonism specific to the ego, and it is precisely that which
> deceives us.[53]

In other words, the author of the *Maximes* pinpoints the irreducibly narcissistic structure of the ego.[54] He can therefore become an ally in the denunciation of the certainties as to the identity of the subject that can be derived from the cogito. Like Lacan, he proclaims that the truth is always elsewhere; like Rimbaud, he proclaims that '*Je est un autre.*'[55] He may also be an ally in other senses; it is difficult not to imagine this perverse genius whispering to Lacan as he aphoristically remarks that Reich's error was to mistake armorial bearings (those of the ego) for 'character armour', a *bon mot* which has all the cutting edge of the seventeenth-century master.[56]

One of the characteristic features of maxims is their susceptibility to a form of reversal into the opposite. Pascal's 'The heart has reasons of which reason knows nothing' can, for example, easily be perverted into 'Reason has emotions of which the heart knows nothing.' Lautréamont exploits this potential to great effect in his *Poésies*, where he parodies the maxims of the *Pensées* with merciless accuracy. Nor are his reversals totally alien to the tradition from which both Pascal and La Rochefoucauld emerge; the coining of maxims is in part a social game, and a high value is accorded to incisive witticisms. It is perhaps not totally unreasonable to suggest that Lacan is playing a similar game when he perverts the cogito into 'I think where I am not, therefore I am where I do not think', or 'I am not where I am the plaything of my thought; I think of what I am where I do not think to think.'[57] Lacan is not simply a reincarnation of La Rochefoucauld or Lautréamont, but he has learned their lessons well.

Lacan usually invokes La Rochefoucauld in order to supply a corrective to the certainties of self-identity and to the associated notion of a transparent subjectivity. A similar shaft is directed against self-identity and self-assurance by the allusion to *Cinna* in *Encore*, and although the perverse genius of the *Maximes* is not mentioned there, there is a remarkable consistency to Lacan's exploitation of seventeenth-century literature and philosophy. The psychology which inspires Auguste's triumphant '*Je suis maître de moi ...*' derives directly from Descartes's *Les Passions de l'âme.* In so far as the Cartesian subject can be identified with the ego, Lacan can therefore appeal to the Descartes/Corneille/La Rochefoucauld opposition to demonstrate his thesis that 'in so far as the subject is placed within the register of the ego, everything is in fact dominated by a narcissistic relationship.'[58] Illuminating as a reference to La Rochefoucauld may be in this context, and useful as he may be for Lacan's assaults on ego psychology, the opposition which lies behind it is scarcely original. Lacan is appealing to arguments very similar to those advanced by Paul Bénichou in a classic study of the seventeenth century which demonstrates that the target of the *Maximes* is precisely the

heroic psychology of Descartes and Corneille.[59] Lacan never refers to
Bénichou, but his work is sufficiently well known to be regarded as fall-
ing within the public domain. Lacan's illustrative use of La Rochefoucauld may have been something of a novelty to the psychoanalytic
community of the early 1950s; it would not have been innovatory for
anyone from the world of literary or cultural studies. There is, however,
one fundamental difference between Lacan and Bénichou. For the
latter, the Descartes/La Rochefoucauld opposition is deeply political
and reflects the decline of a feudal nobility in the face of the rise of
absolutism. Lacan, as always, excludes the political from his account and
produces a vision of the philosophical field in which notions of subjectivity can compete unsullied by politics.

Lacan's pronouncements as to the historical status of La Rochefoucauld are so ambivalent as to border on the contradictory. In 'La Chose
freudienne' (1955) he argues that Freud's discovery is not reducible to
the *moraliste* tradition of humanist analysis that includes Balthazar
Gracian, La Rochefoucauld and Nietzsche.[60] Ten days later he appears
to argue the opposite case, claiming that La Rochefoucauld and the
Nietzsche of *The Genealogy of Morals* do represent a proto-Freudian
tradition: 'It is into this hollow, this bowl, that the Freudian truth is
poured. Of course you are deceived, but the truth is elsewhere. And
Freud tells us where it is.'[61] At such points Lacan appears to be hesitat-
ing between an insistence on the specificity and radical originality of
psychoanalysis, and a rather banal search for precursors. And La
Rochefoucauld is no stranger to the 'precursors' debate; on the contrary,
it is almost a cliché to regard him as one of Freud's intellectual ancestors, even though Freud himself, perhaps surprisingly, gives no indication of having read him. Sartre, for instance, writes in 1936 that the
theory of *amour-propre* is in effect the first reference to the existence of
the unconscious.[62]

The hesitations displayed here by Lacan indicate something of the
ambiguity of his relationship with philosophy. Philosophy, defined in
very conventional terms, provides him with an arsenal of references and
allusions which can be used to make illustrative or pedagogic points. It is
a field in which tactical alliances can be formed and exploited to
promote the Freudian cause, but the formation of those alliances
presupposes the existence of an unproblematic and a political vision of
the history of philosophy. In both these senses, the philosophical field
must remain intact if it is to fulfil its supportive role. Finally, the
ambiguities surrounding the reference to La Rochefoucauld imply both
that psychoanalysis is 'other than' philosophy (or even a post-philosophy) and that it can be inscribed within a philosophical continuum; both
that its history is inaugurated by a break and that it represents a continu-

ation of philosophy by other means.

If Lacan's claims to be exploiting the philosophical field to purely pedagogic ends raise – and mask – some important theoretical issues, they are certainly consistent with his stated views as to the need for a broad curriculum in the psychoanalytic institute and with his refusal to allow psychoanalysis to be or become a purely medical speciality. He is a staunch defender of the position outlined by Freud in *The Question of Lay Analysis*, the 1926 paper which argues that a 'college of psychoanalysis' should study 'branches of knowledge which are remote from medicine' and that its curriculum should include such topics as 'the history of civilization, mythology, the psychology of religion and the science of literature'.[63] At one level, the argument in favour of a broad curriculum is largely pragmatic; unless the would-be practitioner is at home in these subjects, he or she will probably make little of much of the material brought up by the analysand. It is, however, also part of the more general claim that, desirable as they may be, medical qualifications are not an essential prerequisite for practising psychoanalysis, and that the presence of 'lay' persons within the analytic community is to be positively welcomed.

Freud's stance is not prompted by pedagogic concerns alone. It is a response to the unsuccessful prosecution brought against Theodore Reik in Vienna for quackery – that is, for practising medicine without the appropriate and recognized qualifications. The defence of lay analysis is therefore part of the defence of the specificity of psychoanalysis, and a reflection of Freud's reluctance to seeing doctors of medicine gaining a monopoly on its practice. A letter written in 1938 further suggests that it may indicate a lingering anti-Americanism; medicalization is simply one aspect of 'the obvious American tendency to turn psychoanalysis into a mere housemaid of psychiatry'.[64]

The issue of lay analysis is contentious and provokes controversy in virtually all the national Societies at some point. It resurfaces in France in the late 1940s and is directly relevant to the schism within the SPP that leads to Lacan's departure and to the foundation of the SFP. *Mutatis mutandis*, Lacan also invokes basically pragmatic reasons for the need for a broad curriculum, contending that given the primacy of language in psychoanalysis, illiteracy is not a quality to be desired in its practitioners.[65] He therefore takes Freud's proposed curriculum more seriously than some. Anna Freud, for example, regards the ideal college as a 'utopia', as a 'piece of "fantastic" wishful thinking'.[66] Not so Lacan. His proposed statutes for the Institut de Psychanalyse, drawn up in 1953, are prefaced by Freud's remarks on the ideal college. The earlier (1949) proposals are informed by the same position, and in them Lacan refers to 'the fertile kernel of knowledge' supplied by the humanities.

Elsewhere, he argues that it is because the humanities 'designate man's relations with the signifier' that they are such an essential element in psychoanalysis.[67] Similar points are made, if anything more forcefully, towards the end of 'La Chose freudienne', and in the 1954–55 Seminar Lacan even contends that psychoanalysis is the human science *par excellence*.[68] In retrospect, there is a pleasing irony about these statements; Lacan, reputedly one of the prophets of the 'death of man' and the theorist of a theoretical anti-humanism, deliberately places his project under the aegis of the traditional humanities, and in 1949 even takes comfort from the fact that their organization is underpinned by 'traditional teaching'.[69]

Like Freud's *Lay Analysis*, the documents of 1949 and 1953 are part of a complex controversy involving pedagogic, legal and political issues. The 1953 proposals were drafted in response to those put forward by Sacha Nacht, who prefaces his statutes with a quotation from Monakow and Mourque implying that psychoanalysis is little more than a sub-speciality within human neurobiology; Lacan duly reproduces the quotation with heavy irony at the beginning of 'Fonction et champ'.[70] The Institut envisaged by Nacht would award a diploma to medically qualified analysts and would endeavour to obtain state recognition of the said diploma, thus establishing a *de facto* medical monopoly on psychoanalysis. In other words, the conflict between Nacht and Lacan is a re-enactment of the earlier debate over lay analysis. The pedagogic issues are the same, and so are the legal issues. A prosecution had recently been brought against Mme Clarke-Williams, an American-trained therapist working at the Centre Psychopédagogique Claude Bernard, on grounds identical to those used against Reik.[71] When Lacan writes to Loewenstein in an attempt to rally support for his position, one of the points he makes is that Nacht's proposals imply a refusal to defend lay analysts against the possible threat of prosecution.[72]

The most serious issue of all, however, is the defence again of the specificity of psychoanalysis, the refusal to allow it to become a handmaid to either psychiatry or neurobiology. Lest it be thought that Lacan's position indicates an excess of liberalism, it should be recalled that his proposed rules exclude from membership of the Institut and the profession anyone suffering from epilepsy, and anyone unfortunate enough to display 'an ugliness likely to vitiate the basis of the imaginary support which the person of the analyst gives to transferential identifications through the generic homeomorphism of the imago of the body: shocking deformities, visible mutilations or manifest dysfunctions'.[73] No mention is made of 'deviations' such as homosexuality, but it can safely be assumed that it too is a disqualification.

Lacan's didactic references to philosophy are, then, to be understood in terms of a general view of psychoanalysis which stresses the need for interdisciplinarity and for the incorporation of the humanities into the training programme. That view is inscribed in both the draft statutes of 1949 and the founding documents of the SFP. It is put into practice in no uncertain terms by the programme of activities for 1953–54: this included a series of *séminaires extraordinaires* by speakers ranging from Koyré to Lévi-Strauss, from Merleau-Ponty to Benveniste.[74] According to Lacan, the *séminaires extraordinaires* have a twofold importance. On the one hand, they allow analysts in training to crystallize questions pertaining to issues raised by his own *séminaire de textes*; at a more general level, the need for interdisciplinarity reflects the fact that a young science frequently needs to borrow from other sciences in order to further its own elaboration.[75]

The SFP's openness to the human sciences is one of its hallmarks, and most contemporary observers comment upon it in very favourable terms. In a review of the first issue of *La Psychanalyse*, Valabrega remarks that its openness is reminiscent of Freud's 'heroic period', whilst Blanchot describes the SFP's early publications as instituting a return to Freud that will enrich psychoanalysis by instituting a dialogue with 'certain forms of contemporary philosophy and thought'.[76] The insistence on a broad curriculum goes some way towards explaining the heady intellectual climate in the SFP, and that climate may in itself contribute to the accusations of 'intellectualism' that are levelled against Lacan during the schism, though they undoubtedly refer primarily to his failure to analyse, or even to take seriously, the role of affects.[77] It also explains his bitterness towards psychoanalytic institutes which dispense a purely 'vocational' training whose intellectual content is worthy of that of a school of dentistry.[78] The SFP's programme for 1953–54 contrasts starkly with the syllabus for the first semester of 1981 at the Department of Psychoanalysis at Vincennes; there are no speakers from outside a small Lacanian circle, and no topics which cannot be discussed solely on the basis of an exegesis of Lacan's own texts. Openness gives way to closure, excitement to introspection.[79]

It is not uncommon for non-French observers, and especially those reared on a diet of what passes for empiricism in Britain, to explain the foregrounding of philosophy within Lacan's vision of the humanities in terms of the general intellectual climate of France, or to argue that the inclusion of philosophy in the school curriculum in itself produces a greater and more intellectualized sophistication than is normally to be observed in the English-speaking countries. In her discussion of French feminism and the impact Lacanian psychoanalysis has had upon it, Claire Duchen, for example, explains the 'relative importance of intel-

lectual life in France compared to British anti-intellectualism' in terms of
the French child's familiarity with 'certain philosophical ideas' and of his
or her participation in a compulsory class in philosophy.[80] There is a
grain of truth in this, but the importance and influence of the *classe de
philo* should not be over-estimated. By no means every *prof de philo* is a
budding Jean-Paul Sartre, and all too often the apprentice philosopher
subsists on a meagre diet of predigested knowledge culled from stereo-
typed textbooks and a very restricted range of set texts. In itself, the
classe de philo is no more designed to produce theoretical sophisticates
than the 'religious instruction' provisions of the 1944 Education Act are
intended to produce theologians. And Lacan is distinctly less than
sanguine about the intellectual qualities of its *alumni*, complaining that
their formation has provided them with no more than 'a mishmash of
formulae, a shambles of a catechism which anaesthetizes them against
the possibility of ever being surprised by the truth'.[81]

   In terms of his own career, Lacan's philosophical propensities can
scarcely be explained in terms of any experiences he may have had in
the state ideological apparatuses of the Third Republic. He belongs to
the same generation as Sartre, Lévi-Strauss and Nizan, a generation
which rose in open revolt against the academic philosophy of the 1920s
and 1930s. Indeed, it was largely a reaction against the philosophical
climate typified by Léon Brunschwicg's neo-Kantianism that drove
Sartre to Berlin and phenomenology, Lévi-Strauss to Brazil and anthropology, and Nizan to Aden and Marxism. In the mid 1930s Lacan
himself writes bitterly of the 'intellectual stagnation' that is affecting
psychology and psychiatry, and explains their poverty in terms of their
traditional philosophical inheritance.[82] The incorporation of philosophy
into the school curriculum was the achievement of the state ideologues
of the Republic, and the encouragement of original or innovatory theoretical work was the very least of their concerns. On the contrary, they
saw their curriculum as a means of incorporating republican ideology
and of resisting change.[83] The expression 'state ideological apparatus' is
Althusser's, but it was not for nothing that in 1932 Nizan described
philosophy as a 'state apparatus' and philosophers as the watchdogs of
the bourgeoisie.[84]

   The philosophical reference which comes to dominate Lacan's
discourse from the mid 1930s onwards, namely Hegel, is quite alien to
the hegemonic philosophies of the Third Republic. When, in 1930,
Koyré reported on the 'state of Hegelian studies in France' to a congress
in The Hague, he had to admit to having nothing to say, so great was the
influence of the return to Kant and of the Cartesian tradition.[85] Neo-
Kantianism is strongly associated with Brunschwicg, 'the philosopher of
the regime', as Sartre dubs him,[86] and one does not have to resort to *ad*

hominem arguments to conclude that French ignorance of Hegel has a
lot to do with his position as chairman of the jury awarding the *agréga-
tion de philosophie*. When he dismisses Hegel, along with Wolff, as a
'conceptual schoolman' and claims that Hegel's philosophy of history is
as weak as his philosophy of nature because it provides no appropriate
method for understanding the real, Brunschwicg is speaking not as an
individual but as an ideological state apparatus personified.[87]

Ultimately, it is reason of state which explains Hegel's virtual exclusion from the official philosophical field; since the defeat of 1870, he has
been seen as the apostle of pan-Germanism.[88] Freud is not the only
'German' thinker to have been declared anathema by the defenders of *le
génie français*. Lacan's philosophical interests, as opposed to his exploitation of a conventional field whose existence is to some extent
supported and reproduced by the *classe de philo*, cannot be explained in
terms of the discourse of educational apparatus of the Third Republic.
As will be demonstrated, they relate, rather, to the concerns of the
marginal or dissident avant-gardes which provide his natural habitat in
the interwar period.

There is, however, one sense in which the very existence of the *classe
de philo* may shed some light on Lacan. It institutionalizes and reproduces a definition of the philosophical field as being contiguous with
psychology. Traditionally, the philosophy syllabus is subdivided into
four sections: logic, ethics, 'general philosophy', and psychology. The
lycée clearly does not institute this definition, but it does legitimate it and
symbolizes a recognition of the existence of a borderline area where
speculative philosophy and academic psychology can mingle and merge
to a remarkable degree.

Indeed, it has long been a criticism of French psychology and psychoanalysis that philosophers are overrepresented in these disciplines. In
1945, Georges Devereux attacks American psychoanalysis for its indifference to philosophy ... and French psychoanalysis for its continued
failure to emancipate itself from the Faculty of Philosophy.[89] A generation or more later, the Department of Psychoanalysis at Vincennes is
attached to the Faculty of Humanities [*sciences humaines*], not to the
Science Faculty. It was in fact only in 1947 that a nationally recognized
degree in psychology was established, even though Lagache had instituted a degree course at Strasbourg before the war. Inevitably, teaching
posts in psychology (as opposed to the medicalized discipline of psychiatry) tended to be filled by philosophers. When Piaget left the Sorbonne
for Geneva in 1953 his chair in child psychology was filled by Merleau-
Ponty, who, as Anzieu remarks, had never examined a child in his life.
Anzieu does, on the other hand, give him credit for being one of the first
academics in France to discuss Klein and Anna Freud in any detail.[90]

Historically, this curious borderline area has proved remarkably fertile, Bachelard and Bergson being only two of its inhabitants. Sartre is no clinician, but he does study psychology at the Ecole Normale Supérieure and writes extensively on the subject in the early stages of his career. His contribution to the anti-psychiatry of Laing and Cooper is in part the fruit of that period. Rather more recently, the collaborative work of Deleuze and Guattari further testifies to the intellectual fecundity of the alliance between the philosopher and the psychologist and psychoanalyst. Seen against this tradition, Lacan's intellectualism becomes part of a tradition instituted and reproduced by the educational apparatus, although he would rightly object to even the suggestion that he might be deemed a psychologist. For the historian, the curriculum of the *classe de philo* contains one final irony: since 1968, the young philosopher has had the possible option of studying Freud.[91] The recent publication of a collection of essays on Lacan intended for use by final-year *lycée* pupils and undergraduates suggests that Lacan may be about to join him on the syllabus. Indeed, Bordas advertised it in *Le Monde* by announcing that Lacan was now one of the classics and by asking, no doubt rhetorically, whether he might not soon be on the *bac* syllabus.[92] Despite their stated hostility to philosophy, both Freud and Lacan seem likely to become defined as philosophers by the educational apparatus and by related sections of the publishing industry.

The existence of a fluid psychology–philosophy borderline, together with the fact that Lacan locates psychoanalysis in such close proximity to the humanities, is certainly conducive to a constant cross-fertilization between psychoanalysis and philosophy, but its effects can be more problematic than might be supposed. As will become obvious later, the category or concept of desire is especially aporetic in this respect, but problems also arise on the border between the ego – defined in psychoanalytic terms as an agency of the psyche – and the subject, as defined in much broader philosophical terms. Lacan often uses the two synonymously, and appears to be almost deliberately exploiting one of the most ambiguous areas in French psychoanalytic terminology.

The standard French translation of Freud's *Ich* is *moi*. It was originally adopted, after considerable debate within the SPP, in preference to *je* or even *ego* precisely because it is broad enough to refer both to Freud's agency and to a traditional philo-psychological notion of selfhood.[93] As a recent and well-informed observer notes, by adopting this convention 'the French translators took the risk of assimilating the psychoanalytic concept to a very traditional philosophical one.'[94] The term *moi* has a much wider semantic field than *ego*; it can, for instance, be made virtually synonymous with Descartes's 'soul' or with Pascal's 'hateful self', and it can refer to Kant's 'transcendental ego'. That it is also the emphatic form of the first person pronoun introduces a further register, again equating it with subjectivity.

One of the constants running through Lacan's Seminar on the ego is the argument that the *moi* is a philosophical construct which emerges at a specific moment in history; that the importance accorded to the *moi* is a historical contingency relating to the prestige granted to consciousness in so far as the latter is an irreducibly unique and individual experience.[95] The *moi* is also made synonymous with the 'subject', which term has the further ambiguity of referring both to a grammatical and a legal category. It can then be argued that the 'inaugural moment of the emergence of the subject' occurs at the beginning of the seventeenth century.[96] The claim that a shift within the definition of the subject, and even within the experience of subjectivity, occurs in the seventeenth century would be accepted by many of the writers associated with Lacan in the 1960s, and it coincides fairly closely with the periodization introduced by Foucault.[97]

Whether or not the same claim can be applied to the agency described by Freud is another matter. Lacan asserts the historicity of the *moi*, points to its philosophical origins, and insists that ego psychology implies a return to an uncritical and pre-Freudian notion of the *moi*. He does not address a central problem inherent in his assertions. It would surely, that is, be difficult to argue in strictly Freudian terms that any agency of the psyche emerges at a given historical moment. The term 'human nature' may have embarrassing connotations for Marxists, Lacanians and post-structuralists alike, but Freud has no inhibitions about using it. Disconcerting though it may be to his more modernist followers, Freud does implicitly operate with the notion of an unchanging human nature. And if psychoanalysis deals with a human nature, the various agencies of that nature can scarcely be historicized. Lacan's assertion of the historicity of the *moi* also conflicts with one of his favourite illustrations of its functions. That is, it is difficult to sustain the claim that the *moi* appears at the beginning of the modern era and, at the same time, to insist that St Augustine's account of jealousy epitomizes one of its essential structures. Lacan's use of *moi* both generates and reproduces a contradictory vision of the philosophical field as being at once historical and capable of expressing eternal and ahistorical truths. This is not the only instance of his reliance upon a very curious concept of intellectual history and historiography; as will be seen in the next chapter, Saussurean linguistics is said to represent both a break with all previous theories and a continuation of the discourse of Augustine. The contradictions already noted in relation to Lacan's appeal to La Rochefoucauld are, that is, reproduced in his theory of the *moi* and in his discussion of linguistics.

* * *

The academic constitution of philosophy as a discursive field bordering
on psychology, and by extension psychoanalysis, does influence Lacan's
ability to appropriate or exploit philosophical references and therefore
helps to compound the aporetic nature of certain of his formulations,
but it does not supply him with the major philosophical themes or
philosophemes that run through his work from the 1930s onwards. They
derive, rather, from the concerns of the marginal or dissident avant-
gardes of the Third Republic, and many of those avant-gardes emerge in
the wake of surrealism. ('Dissident' is to be understood here in the sense
of dissidence with respect to the dominant philosophical-cultural
discourse, not in any narrowly political sense. The political sympathies
of the dissidents do, generally speaking, lie with the left but, with a few
honourable exceptions, organized left groups such as the PCF are almost
as philistine as the Sorbonne.)

It was not the academic philosophers who imported Hegel and
Heidegger into France but more marginal figures, many of them
immigrants like Kojève, whose lectures on Hegel were to have an
immense impact. *La Revue de Métaphysique et de Morale*, the prestigious journal that occupied the centre of the official philosophical stage,
did little to promote novelties such as phenomenology; that was to be
the task of organs such as *Recherches philosophiques*, the annual journal
edited by Koyré, Peuch and Spaier (and modelled on Husserl's *Jahr-
buch*), which published Sartre's first major essay on phenomenology.

Of all the marginal groups of the period, it is probably the Collège de
Sociologie which is most relevant here. The Collège was founded in
1937 by Bataille and his associates, and its activities focused upon the
sociology of the sacred and of ritual. Its work is inadequately chronicled,
not least because it functioned in semi-secrecy, but its importance
should not be underestimated.[98] Lacan appears not to have been an
active participant, but was clearly aware of its existence and interest; the
original discussion that led to its foundation involved Leiris, Bataille and
Caillois, and took place in Lacan's apartment.[99] Active members and
speakers at its meetings included Klossowski, Kojève and several of
Lacan's old *Minotaure* associates, as well as individuals involved with
Recherches philosophiques. In many respects, the Collège can be
regarded as a transitional group bringing together veterans of the
surrealist period and the initiators of the phenomenological movement
of the future; Lévi-Strauss remembers it as a meeting place for sociolo-
gists and surrealist painters and poets, adding that the experiment was a
success.[100]

Although the Collège's primary interest is sociology, defined in somewhat idiosyncratic terms, one of its proposed offshoots was a 'Société de
psychologie collective'. The initiative for this new venture, which

appears to have come to nothing, came from Bataille himself with the support of Leiris, Allendy and Borel. The programme drawn up for 1938 centred on 'Attitudes Towards Death' and was to have included papers from Leiris on Dogon funeral rites and from Lagache on the work of mourning; it is not known whether the discussions actually took place.[101] The Collège thus begins at least to outline an intellectual space in which psychoanalysis, sociology and anthropology can merge and cross-fertilize one another. The 'fertile kernel' of the humanities to which Lacan refers in 1949 is, with hindsight, quite recognizable as the matrix that was to give rise to structuralism. It is all too easily forgotten that small groups like the Collège de Sociologie were already operating in an equally heady 'interdisciplinary' atmosphere in the late 1930s. The missing element is, of course, linguistics, but 'Baltimore in the Early Morning' has already demonstrated that an extremely sophisticated perception of language was also an ingredient in this atmosphere.

It has already been argued that Lacan's work contains many monuments to his early association with the surrealist movement. His publishing history also provides evidence of the importance to him of the avant-garde represented by the Collège de Sociologie. The majority of the papers included in *Ecrits* first appeared in professional psychoanalytic journals, but there are some interesting exceptions. Two of the *écrits* first appeared in *Critique* ('Jeunesse de Gide' and 'Kant avec Sade), whilst 'Le Temps logique' (and its companion piece, 'Le Numéro treize') was published in *Cahiers d'art.* Both journals originate in the work of the avant-gardes of the 1930s. *Critique* was founded by Bataille and former members of the Collège de Sociologie, whilst *Cahiers d'art* is a direct descendant of *Minotaure.*[102] A decision to publish in these journals is surely a form of testimony to the ties of intellectual kinship formed by Lacan in the interwar years. The presence of Marcel Griaule at the Seminar in 1955, when he spoke on symbols and symbolization in the Western Sudan, serves as a further reminder of the importance of this period.[103] Griaule may now seem an almost forgotten figure, but he was the leader of the 1932 Dakar–Djibouti expedition which meant so much to Leiris and to those who worked on *Minotaure.*

It is sometimes assumed that the series of lectures given at the Ecole des Hautes Etudes by Alexandre Kojève between 1933 and 1939 represent the starting point of Hegelian studies in France, and they have taken on a legendary importance.[104] There is a degree of hyperbole in this assumption, and indeed in Koyré's comments at the 1930 Hague conference. Charles Andler did, for example, lecture on the *Phenomenology* at the Sorbonne in 1928–30, and Jean Wahl's *Le Malheur de la conscience*

dans la philosophie de Hegel appeared in 1929. An earlier precedent had been set by the shadowy figure of Lucien Herr, librarian at
ENS and *éminence grise* behind many a conversion to socialism, who
contributed a substantial general article on Hegel to the *Grande Encyclopédie* in the early 1890s but whose cherished project of writing a full-
scale study sadly never came to fruition.[105] There must, then, have been
at least a certain familiarity with some Hegelian themes prior to Kojève's
lectures, even though non-Germanists can have had only a second-hand
knowledge of the subject; it is only in 1939 and 1941 respectively that
the two volumes of Jean Hyppolite's translation of the *Phenomenology*
appear.

Kojève's lectures were, however, of almost incalculable importance,
and many elements in the 'left Hegelianism' and Marxist humanism of
the post-war decades can be traced back to them. Regular attenders
included Aron, Bataille, Koyré, Klossowski, Queneau and Lacan, and
the company was occasionally joined by Breton. These names represent
a cross-section of the avant-gardes of the period, and if one wished to
develop a Balzacian cultural geography of the dissident Paris of the mid
to late 1930s, Kojève's lecture room would lie at its heart.

In some ways, it is difficult not to see the lectures as a precursor of
Lacan's Seminar. In both cases, the reputation of the master was initially
spread by word of mouth and was confined to a relatively small circle. In
both cases, the resultant text is the work of a disciple. Even in institutional terms, there is a parallel. Kojève's lectures were given at the EHE,
always the most marginal of the Parisian institutes and one originally
founded as a research centre designed to circumvent the perceived
sterility of both the Sorbonne and the *grandes écoles*. In the 1930s it
offers a congenial home for the German and Russian expatriates who
did so much to introduce France to phenomenology; in later years it
provides Barthes with a strategic base, and Lacan with a temporary
home.

The published text of the lectures is fragmentary in the extreme.
Kojève rarely wrote up his lecture notes, and the text is based on the
notes taken on the spot by Queneau; it was not revised by its original
author. Kojève's actual reading of Hegel is often regarded by subsequent
Hegelian scholars as eccentric or at best idiosyncratic, not least in that
he insists that Hegel elaborated a 'philosophical anthropology' rather
than an account of the self-realization of reason.[106] Kojève describes an
extremely violent world-view focussed upon moments of rupture and
struggle rather than of synthesis, and it has often been suggested that a
certain Nietzschean influence is at work. His vision of Hegel is also
marked by contemporary as well as historical considerations; Kojève is
reported as contending that the true world-historical individual who

ushers in the end of history is not Napoleon but Stalin, a claim which accords well with his description of himself as a 'right-wing Marxist', but tells us little about Hegel.[107]

For Kojève, as for Wahl before him, it is the *Phenomenology* rather than the *Logic* or the *Encyclopaedia* which is the key text and, within that text, it is the master–slave dialectic which is foregrounded to the exclusion of almost everything else.[108] For Hegel, the struggle between these figures is the 'trial by death' from which an independent self-consciousness arises on the basis of the recognition accorded by the other: 'Self-consciousness exists in and for itself, in that, and by the fact that it exists for another self-consciousness; that is to say, it *is* only by being acknowledged or "recognized".'[109] The price of recognition is the willingness to risk death in the struggle with the other; self-consciousness and recognition are predicated upon a life-and-death struggle. Kojève habitually refers to this as a struggle for 'pure prestige', a term which frequently figures in Lacan's various accounts of the constituton of individual subjectivity, but which is not used by Hegel himself.

In Kojève's reading, the master–slave dialectic is the central moment in the emergence of consciousness and individuality and, by breaking the immediate unity of the ego, it further introduces a mediation which differentiates 'human' from 'animal'. The human community, that is, is founded upon a conscious encounter with death and with a concomitant 'recognition' of the individual. 'There is no mediation in the purely natural, vital world, because there is no Society in which individuals "recognize" themselves in their reality and dignity.'[110] The emergence of individuality also revolves around desire (defined as 'going beyond' the biological) in so far as it implies a dialectic between self and other. Desire is human only to the extent to which it is oriented towards 'other *Desire* and an *other* Desire'.[111] As Kojève writes in his panoptic introduction:

> It is ... in and through 'his' Desire – or, more accurately, to the extent that he is his Desire – that Man is confronted, constituted and revealed – both to himself and to others – as an Ego, as an Ego which is essentially different to and radically opposed to, the non-Ego. The (human) ego is the Ego of a Desire, or of Desire.[112]

The themes outlined here, and even the vocabulary in which they are couched, are recognizably 'Lacanian', as is obvious from the most casual reading of 'Subversion du sujet' or of Lacan's remarks on Hyppolite's paper on *Verneinung*: 'The dialectic which supports our experience ... obliges us to understand the ego as being constituted from top to bottom within the movement of progressive alienation in which self-consciousness is constituted in Hegel's phenomenology.'[113] A certain parallel between Kojève's description of the constitution of the ego and Lacan's mirror stage is also evident in that both stress that it is a conflict with the other that is constitutive of the self, whilst Kojève's references to recognition and pure prestige as defusing or sublimating a potentially murderous aggression anticipate Lacan's later description of language and the symbolic as being founded upon a pact or act of mutual recognition.

To return to Kojève after reading Lacan is to experience the shock of recognition, a truly uncanny sensation of *déjà vu*. A return to Hegel induces the feeling that there is a kinship between the philosopher and the psychoanalyst, but not the same overwhelming shock. This is perhaps less surprising if one recalls that there are relatively few indications of Lacan having any extensive knowledge of Hegel himself; virtually everything is filtered through the words of Kojève, the 'master' who initiated him into matters Hegelian,[114] so much so that it might be more accurate to say that Lacan is a Kojèvean rather than to suggest that he is a Hegelian.

It is difficult to determine precisely when Kojève-Hegel becomes a reference point for Lacan, but it may be surmised that it is during the mid 1930s. The doctoral thesis is devoid of any reference to Hegel, and the *Ur*-version of the mirror-stage paper is not extant. 'Au-delà du "Principe de réalité"' contains no explicit allusions to Hegel, but the discussion of the animal world's 'relations of connaturality' with the environment has distinctly Kojèvean overtones.[115] By 1938, the Kojève–Hegel reference has become a central element in 'La Famille', where Lacan ascribes to Hegel the formula: 'the individual who does not struggle for recognition will never become a personality before he dies.'[116] Ten years later Hegel is credited with having produced the 'ultimate theory' of the function of aggressivity in human ontology, and he is finally claimed to have elaborated a 'general formula' for the phenomenology of madness.[117] The chronology of the absorption of Hegel into Lacan's discourse may remain regrettably unclear, but one thing is increasingly obvious. Although Lacan claims in 'Subversion du sujet' and elsewhere that Hegel is merely a propaedeutic reference designed to facilitate his critique of ego psychology,[118] these are more than purely illustrative allusions. There is, moreover, an anachronistic or retroactive note in the reduction of Hegel to an adjuvant in the struggle against ego psychology; the seeds of Lacan's critique of that current are indeed contained within the theorization of the mirror stage, but the controversy over the ego dates from the post-war period, not from 1936 or 1938.

The theory of the mirror stage does not derive solely from Lacan's reading of Hegel and Kojève. As the 1949 paper makes clear, the empirical evidence for its existence is drawn from the work on child development undertaken by Charlotte Bühler. Her work also informs Lacan's second empirical source: the lectures on psychology given by Henri Wallon in 1930–33.[119] The more abstract theoretical references, like the illustrative allusion to St Augustine, are, that is, grafted on to an empirical account of developmental psychology. In other accounts of the mirror stage, Lacan draws heavily on ethology to exemplify the different functions of recognition in animals and human beings by means of some curious reflections on the behaviour of pigeons and migratory locusts.[120] In the 1953–54 Seminar sticklebacks are pressed into service to make a general point about *Gestalten*, and in 'Fonction et champ', the wagging dance of bees is invoked to demonstrate *a contrario* the function of human language.[121]

Given Lacan's reputation for militant anti-biologism, there is something improbable, even uncomfortable, about this repeated appeal to developmental psychology, ethology and biology. At one level, it reflects a Kojèvean-Hegelian concern to make an ontological distinction between the human and animal kingdoms, but Hegel's community of animals is a moment within the development of consciousness rather than one pole in a binary opposition. The assertion, made in 1948, that Harrison's work on pigeons and Chauvin's observations of locusts reveal facts that prove the validity of Lacan's own insights into the importance of the mirror stage implies that a very different discourse is impinging upon Lacan's theories.[122] Lacan places 'facts' within inverted commas, a mark, perhaps, of a certain epistemological embarrassment at having to fall back upon an empirical argument. The same illustration appears in 'Some Reflections on the Ego', where the facts are shorn of their inverted commas and where Lacan adds that 'psychoanalytic experience substantiates in the most striking way the speculations of philosophy.' The facts, that is, provide an a posteriori verification of a hypothesis. In a sense one is reminded of Freud's views on the need for a combination of speculation and slow, halting observation. Less charitable observers might note that Lacan comes perilously close here to the received wisdom of the *classe de philo* itself, which traditionally defines the philosopher as a specialist in generalities and the scientist as the specialist who deals with a specific, concrete object.[123]

Alain Juranville expresses a widely held view of the nature of Lacan's debt to philosophy when he argues, at considerable length, that his use of that discipline represents a constant attempt to introduce a new theoretical rigour into psychoanalysis, and a stage in an uninterrupted movement towards the quasi-mathematical abstraction of his late manner.[124] According to his view, Freud's basic empiricism prevents him from elaborating any truly satisfactory concept of the unconscious;

Lacan, in contrast, is able to work at a much more abstract level, thanks, in part, to his ability to exploit the resources of the philosophical field. Yet the curious manner in which Lacan combines his Hegelian-Kojèvean borrowings with an appeal to the 'verifications' supplied by ethology and biology must cast some doubtful shadows across this image of a writer who moves constantly and relentlessly towards the abstraction of the 'matheme'.

Juranville's reading is, moreover, predicated upon a teleological final state in that it subordinates everything to a development which is late in terms of both chronology and its implications. In similar fashion, the final-state readings of the late 1960s and the 1970s stress Lacan's apparent kinship with the rationalist epistemologies of Bachelard, Koyré and Canguilhem, and – no doubt stimulated by certain of Althusser's interventions – emphasize the role of epistemological breaks and obstacles in the history of psychoanalysis. All these readings can be grounded in Lacan's texts, but only if they are read in purely synchronic terms. Among other things, they must ignore or repress the fact that for a surprisingly long time Lacan effectively inscribes his work beneath the slogan 'Towards the Concrete', to use the title of Jean Wahl's essay of 1932,[125] even though that slogan appears to be completely at odds with his more Hegelian leanings.

The phrase 'towards the concrete' encapsulates many of the concerns of a generation in revolt against a 'world of philosophical politeness',[126] but in terms of Lacan's theoretical evolution it is Politzer's 'concrete psychology' which is the essential landmark.[127] Politzer's influence on Sartre and his posthumous contribution to existential psychoanalysis have attracted a certain interest but his relationship with Lacan is less familiar, not least because Lacan himself tends to dismiss him in rather summary terms in later years.[128] The 'correctness' or otherwise of Politzer's reading of Freud is less important than the parallel between his notion of a concrete psychology and the stated ambitions of the young Lacan. Nor is there any imperative need to enter here into a discussion of Politzer's later adoption of a classically Stalinist position which rejects psychoanalysis as an idealism.

The object of Politzer's critical attentions is 'classical psychology' from Wundt to Bergson,[129] the main reproach addressed to it being that it consistently eliminates any individual meaning from the phenomena it examines and forces them into a straitjacket of a priori categories and abstractions which are not far removed from the old 'faculties of the soul'. A neurosis, for example, is a wonderful nosographic entity embodied in the individual neurotic in the same way that the soul is incarnated in the body. Politzer is drawn to psychoanalysis in that, by uncovering the meaning of dreams, it reveals a concrete meaning specific to the individual dreamer. Its disadvantage is that it constantly lapses back into the world of classical psychology by constructing a collection of unconscious entities which exist in and for themselves. The *Traumdeutung* exemplifies the antagonism that exists within psychoanalysis between abstract and concrete tendencies; Freud at once analyses dreams in terms of what might be termed a signifying intentionality, but then integrates his findings into an abstract metapsychology.[130]

Here, it will be noted, Politzer's criticisms intersect with the more academic doubts about Freud's metapsychology voiced by Dalbiez and others. In order to remedy what he sees as a failing, Politzer proposes the marriage of elements of Freudian psychoanalysis with a more general and 'concrete' psychology which will take as its object the specific life of a specific individual, or life 'in the dramatic sense of the word': life defined as a concrete drama written by concrete individuals.[131] This concrete psychology will approach the subject 'in the first person', abandoning the abstractions of classical psychology and Freud's metapsychology alike in favour of the analysis of the specific acts and dramas that make up an individual life. A text like *Group Psychology and the Analysis of the Ego* can then be appropriated to outline a theory of identification which Politzer defines as a segment of the life of a particular individual, as a section through the human drama enacted in the first person. The subject's identifications thus become an effective part of his life; identification provides the key to understanding a whole series of attitudes and behavioural patterns. Finally, the Oedipus complex becomes 'not a process, and still less a state', but a 'dramatic schema'.[132]

Whilst much of Politzer's project may now seem naive (particularly the crudely Manichaean opposition between abstract and concrete), and whilst his reading of Freud may appear aberrant, there is a link between his proposed concrete psychology and Lacan's early work. Lacan concludes his doctoral thesis by arguing that:

> The key to the nosographic, prognostic and therapeutic problem of paranoid psychosis must be sought in a *concrete* psychological analysis which applies to the whole development of the subject's personality, in other words to events in his *history*, to the development of his consciousness and to his reactions within the social environment.[133]

In the 1938 paper on the family he comes closer to adopting Politzer's terminology by describing the *fort-da* game, the mirror stage and the 'drama of jealousy' in which both ego and other are constituted as so many stages within the 'existential drama of the individual'.[134] At an interindividual level, the twin notions of complex and imago, defined in

terms reminiscent of Politzer's 'identifications', are said to be categories
which allow the family to become the object of a concrete analysis rather
than of purely moralizing pronouncements. The paper is clearly not
simply a reprise of Politzer's arguments, as Lacan does not endorse the
criticisms of Freud and definitely does not display Politzer's leanings
towards a Watsonian behaviourism. Nor does he share Politzer's
Marxism, though there may be a trace element of it in the frequent use
of 'dialectical' in 'La Famille'. But whilst the references to developmental 'stages' recall Laforgue and psychoanalysis *à la française*, the
vocabulary of 'dramas' and 'concrete analysis' is quite definitely Politzerean.

The reference to a Politzerean notion of the concrete, in particular, is
surprisingly slow to disappear. In 1949 Lacan defines psychoanalysis as
the 'cornerstone of any concrete psychology', and in 'Propos sur la
causalité psychique' he both refers to Politzer as 'a great mind' and
endorses the call for a science of concrete psychology to be constituted.[135] In 1950, the incestuous and parricidal wishes accompanying the
Oedipus are a 'situation' generating 'a dramatic crisis which resolves
itself into a structure'.[136] For a considerable length of time, Lacan
operates with notions – or even slogans – which derive from the generational revolt of the 1920s and 1930s. His critical remarks on
Minkowski, whom he accuses of attempting to reduce phenomenology
to a revised version of Bergsonian intuitionism, represent a minor, but
telling, contribution to that revolt.[137] More specifically, the criticisms of
associationism put forward in the first half of 'Au-delà du "Principe de
réalité"' are distinctly reminiscent of Politzer, as is the call to arms in a
struggle against a 'scholastic' psychology which operates with categories
inherited from centuries of philosophical discourse.[138]

The almost simultaneous presence of Politzer and Hegel-Kojève as
reference points for Lacan must inevitably frustrate attempts to present
his work as a unified whole or – to use a phrase in distinctly bad odour
with the proponents of the final states of the 1960s and 1970s – as an
expressive totality. They reveal the extent to which his work is, at least
until the mid 1950s, torn in two conflicting directions: towards a
concrete individual psychoanalysis which might have resulted in something akin to the Sartrean notion of situation (the Politzer pole) and
towards a much more abstract and philosophical theory of the subject
(the Hegel-Kojève pole). The latter tendency finally comes to prevail,
and results in a certain area of weakness in the critique of ego psychology, but it does not imply a linear movement towards mathematical
abstraction in that it is often bound up with a curious appeal to the
'facts' of ethology or of analytic practice to 'guarantee' or verify its more
speculative features.

Rather than trying to reconcile the irreconcilable, it is surely important to recognize the existence of contradictions and conflicts within the
Lacanian corpus. To a large extent, the contradictions exemplify Lacan's
inevitable engagement with the preoccupations of his contemporaries
and mirror the changing intellectual climate; they also suggest that his
true genius is a talent for syncretism rather than a gift for innovation.
Finally they suggest, in more general terms, that his relationship with,
and use of, philosophy cannot be satisfactorily interpreted in any unila-
teral fashion.

Similar points can be made with respect to Lacan's rather tortured
relations with Sartre. Although Lacanian psychoanalysis and Sartrean
existentialism might appear to be polar opposites in that Lacan would
probably regard the project of authenticity as simply a variation on the
discourse of the Master and in that Sartre for a long time effectively
denies the very existence of the unconscious, their discourses intersect
on a number of occasions. The kinship is, perhaps, most apparent in the
links that can be found between Lacan's mirror stage and Sartre's early
essay, *La Transcendance de l'ego*.[139] Originally written during a stay in
Berlin in 1934, the essay attempts to lay the foundations for a rigorous
phenomenology and outlines certain of the themes of the later *L'Etre et
le néant*. In striving to establish a pure phenomenological field purified
of all egological structures, Sartre posits a distinction between the *je* (the
positive aspect of the personality) and the *moi* (the concrete psycho-
physical totality of the personality), and defines the *ego* as emerging
from the convergence of the two, as a 'virtual focus of unity'.[140] He then
argues that it is as though 'consciousness constituted the Ego as a false
representation of itself, as though it became hypnotized by the Ego it
had constituted, and became absorbed into it, as though it made it its
safeguard and its law.'[141] The ego is not, that is, the agency which founds
consciousness, but a focus (in the optical sense) of alienation and
inauthenticity. It is therefore to be apprehended as existing in the world,
as 'other than' consciousness; the true reflexive attitude is encapsulated
by Rimbaud's *Je est un autre*.[142]

The parallel with the ego of the mirror stage is startling; in both cases
the ego is viewed as an illusory representation, as a source and focus of
alienation. Both authors make use of optical metaphors, and both relate
their theorizations to Rimbaud's formula.[143] Both recruit La Rochefoucauld as an ally. Lacan and Sartre are of course working from different
starting points and to different ends. In philosophical terms Lacan's
mirror stage takes its inspiration from Kojève-Hegel, whereas Sartre's
pure phenomenology owes its primary inspiration to Husserl. But the
structural descriptions they give of the ego function are broadly similar,
and both Lacan's psychoanalysis and Sartre's phenomenology are

designed to transcend and overcome egology or ego-ology.[144] Whether or not they were aware of one another's work at this time is not known, but Vauday finds the similarity between their positions so great that he suggests it is possible to speak of a creative reprise of phenomenological research on Lacan's part.[145] In more general terms, Sartre and Lacan are both writing against the unproblematic primacy accorded to consciousness by the hegemonic neo-Kantianism of the period. The slogan 'towards the concrete' could be applied to and by a wide variety of individuals and projects, but they inevitably had the same enemies.

A second intersection between the trajectories of Sartre and Lacan can be seen in the latter's Seminar of 1953–54, where *L'Etre et le néant* is described as essential reading for psychoanalysts because of the acuity of its presentation of the phenomenology of the perception of the other and of the gaze. Sartre's phenomenology of 'being in love' is simply pronounced 'irrefutable'.[146] As with the claim that Hegel provides the ultimate theory of aggressivity or a general formula for madness, the absolute tone of these pronouncements makes it almost impossible to read them as purely, or even primarily, illustrative references. Sartre's phenomenology is recommended as essential reading because it provides a corrective against the alleged tendency within psychoanalysis to overlook the vital question of intersubjectivity. Lacan's subsequent criticisms of phenomenology notwithstanding, Sartre is thus credited with the ability to contribute to psychoanalysis. The philosophical field is therefore a source of conceptual inputs, and not merely a referential or illustrative field.

It has already been suggested that both Sartre and Lacan owe something to Politzer, but it is undoubtedly because of the shared reference to Heidegger that Lacan can read Sartre with such marked sympathy in the 1950s. Lacan's reading of Heidegger has a considerable impact on his thinking on language, and will be discussed in that context, but there is one other area in which the paths of Lacan, Sartre and Heidegger cross: that of the temporality of the subject. The structure of the mirror stage implies a temporal as well as a visual dimension, and the 'jubilant assumption' of the specular image is a *prefiguration* of 'the symbolic matrix in which the I is precipitated in a primordial form'. Thus, 'The mirror stage is a drama whose internal thrust is precipitated from insufficiency to anticipation.'[147] The identification it generates implies, then, a relation to the future, and it might be articulated as a future perfect: 'What I will have been'. The illusory or alienating nature of the ego's identifications (or of the ideal ego) is not simply a matter of untruth; it involves an anticipatory, futural dimension. Identity is not stable and is constructed around a dialectic of projection; in his paper on transference, Lacan writes: 'there is no progress for the subject other than through the integration which he arrives at from his position in the universal: technically through the projection of his past into a discourse in the process of becoming.'[148] But it is, perhaps, in 'Fonction et champ' that Lacan comes closest to spelling out his views on the temporality of the subject: 'What is realized in my history is not the past definite of what was, since it is no more, or even the present perfect of what has been in what I am, but the future anterior of what I shall have been in the process of becoming.'[149]

Elsewhere in the 'Rome Discourse', Lacan makes it clear that such formulations derive from Heidegger's *Being and Time* by stating that both hysterical and waking recollections of dream material 'constitute the subject as *gewesend* – that is to say, as being the one who has been.'[150] In a contemporary paper read to the Collège philosophique, the temporal aspect of subjectivity and the Heideggerean strand in its theorization are further emphasized by the link established between the 'thrownness' [*Geworfenheit*] of the subject and the rift instituted in him by the anticipatory dimension of his history.[151] The temporality invoked here is that of Heidegger's 'being towards' [*Sein zu*], by definition an anticipatory mode of being. Being towards is, for Heidegger, futural in so far as it implies 'the coming in which *Dasein* ... comes towards itself', a formula in which one recognizes something of Lacan's 'what I will have been'. In terms of the past history of the subject, the corollary of being towards is '*Dasein* as an I-am-having-been' [*bin-gewesen*]:

As authentically futural, *Dasein* is authentically as 'having been'. Anticipation of one's uttermost and ownmost possibility is coming back understandingly to one's ownmost 'been'. Only in so far as it is futural can *Dasein be* authentically as having been. The character of 'having been' arises, in a certain way, from the future.[152]

A similar, if less opaque, description of the temporality of the *pour-soi* may be found in *L'Etre et le néant*: 'It is a flight away from co-present being and from the being that once was towards the being it will be.'[153]

Broadly speaking, Lacan, Heidegger and Sartre are all mapping out a similar temporality, despite a slight variation in their use of tenses. The similarity between Sartre and Lacan can be particularly striking; Sartre writes: 'I *am* not my past. I *am* not my past because I *was* my past'; and Lacan: 'History is not the past. History is not the past in so far as it is historicized in the present – historicized in the present because it was lived in the past.'[154] The opacity of the terminology masks the relative ease with which this temporality can be applied to the identificatory structures implicit in the ideal ego to which the subject strives to conform, or to the self-images of wish-fulfilment. When, for example,

Freud writes to Fliess and expresses the hope or phantasy that 'someday' a marble tablet will be mounted on the wall of the house where he discovered the secret of dreams,[155] he identifies with the great man he will have been. The history of his recollection of that hope or desire is neither the history of what he has been nor that of what he is, but the history of what he will have been when his discovery will have been publicly acknowledged.

Lacan will of course shrug off his phenomenological borrowings, claiming, for instance, that no more than a 'propaedeutic' reference was at stake in the distinctly Heideggerean tone of certain of his reflections on language.[156] Yet again, the evidence of the text, and even the text of the supposed manifesto of Lacanian psychoanalysis, indicates that such disclaimers, which are habitually made after the event, cannot be taken at face value. The ease with which Lacan imitates Sartre's vocabulary and syntax reveals a remarkable gift for discursive mimicry, but the text also indicates more than an ability to exploit the resources of philosophy; there is a definite tendency to import certain of its products into the allegedly antithetical discourse of psychoanalysis. And in the case of Heidegger and Sartre, Lacan is not seeking confirmation for speculations. The theory of the temporality of the subject elaborated in the early 1950s is philosophically founded and it is imported directly into the Freudian field.

There is never any final settling of accounts between Lacan and Sartre, and the intersections between their trajectories culminate in a dialogue of the deaf rather than in a fertile exchange. Sartre tends in later years to associate Lacan with the structuralist horde and overlooks the phenomenological strand in his work. He claims to have no difficulty in accepting the thesis that the unconscious is the discourse of the other, but immediately reinterprets it on the basis of his own distinctive philosophy. Thus he will argue that during any speech act, verbal sets are structured as pratico-inert sets and that they 'express or constitute intentions which determine me without being mine'.[157] Lacan, for his part, does not discuss Sartre's later work, and confines his criticisms to *L'Etre et le néant*. Whilst he praises its analysis of the self–other dialectic, he holds that Sartre is unable to go beyond a dual situation in that each of the subjects involved in that dialectic remains his own centre of reference, and that phenomenology therefore cannot come to terms with the oedipal triad.[158] Similar, if not harsher, criticisms are addressed to Merleau-Ponty, even though he displays more sympathy towards psychoanalysis than Sartre himself. Merleau-Ponty is accused of clinging to notions of totality and unity and of claiming that they are, ultimately, amenable to an instantaneous *prise de conscience*.[159] Finally, it is claimed that he is propounding a phenonemology of perception predicated upon the abstract eye 'presupposed by the Cartesian concept of extension, with, as its corollary, a subject, a divine module of universal perception'.[160]

Such criticisms are, to say the least, reductive. Whilst it may be true that Sartre and Merleau-Ponty do assert the primacy of consciousness and do cling to a central notion of the subject, the phenomenological subject is by no means as unproblematical as Lacan suggests here, or as received post-structuralist wisdom would have it. In so far as the subject does remain a central category for Sartre, it is a subject which is constantly being constituted and reconstituted by a play between *en-soi* and *pour-soi*. The final moment of union between the two (the asymptotic moment of *en-soi-pour-soi*) is at least as elusive as Lacan's moment of *m'êtrise/maîtrise*, and a subject who claims to have attained it is living in bad faith. The debt to Sartre which Lacan contracts in his description of the temporality of the subject remains, meanwhile, unacknowledged in these criticisms, and is therefore left outstanding. And Lacan's failure to settle accounts with Sartre is all the more striking in that certain phenomenologically derived themes feed directly into his critique of ego psychology.

Ego psychology is so often the object of Lacan's philosophical-theoretical scorn that it is essential to outline its central tenets before going on to look at Lacan's critique and the perspectives it opens up for what might be termed a 'post-philosophy'. Ego psychology is a major current within post-Freudian psychoanalysis; it derives its metapsychological premises from the second topography of id, ego and superego, as transmitted by Anna Freud in her 1937 study of the ego and its defences.[161] In many respects, however, the true founding father is Heinz Hartmann, whose *Ego Psychology and the Problem of Adaptation* provides the current with its initial manifesto.[162] Subsequent elaborations are due largely to Hartmann's collaborative work with Kris and Loewenstein, who together make up the unholy trinity that figures so conspicuously in Lacan's demonology, whilst the annual *Psychoanalytic Study of the Child* (Founded in 1945 by Kris, Hartmann and Anna Freud) provides a major institutional platform. Although Lacan and his followers display a marked tendency to see ego psychology as a quintessentially American phenomenon[163] – and even to use their objections to it as a pretext for dismissing 'American psychoanalysis' *in toto* – it is in fact quite clear that its origins are distinctly European. Hartmann was a member of the Vienna Society until his departure from Europe, and Loewenstein a much-travelled graduate of the Zurich school and a sometime member of the SPP. It would be a foolhardy historian who described Anna Freud as the daughter of any American revolution.

Many of the adepts of egopsychology did migrate to the USA as a result of the wartime psychoanalytic diaspora, and it did find a fertile environment there, but its influence is not confined to North America. It is a component element in the work of the Hampstead Child Therapy Clinic, which owes so much to Anna Freud's psychoanalytic pedagogy and informs the concept of the self used by many British analysts working in the tradition of Winnicott, even though they may not endorse all Hartmann's theses.[164] Nor, it might be added, is its appeal restricted to the Anglo-American sphere of influence; it proves, for example, to be of some considerable relevance to the concerns of Sacha Nacht. Even within the USA not all ego psychology takes the form of a crude social engineering, as the Lacanian critique would suggest; it can also merge with a general – and generous – humanism, and the work of Bettelheim suggests that 'ego strength' may also provide a basis for resistance to totalitarianism and oppression in the extreme situation of the concentration camp.[165]

For Hartmann and his associates, the three agencies which coexist within the psyche are to be defined in terms of the functions ascribed to them, and, as is the case with most forms of functionalism, their theory is not without its teleological and even tautological implications. Id functions are, that is, centred upon basic needs and upon a striving for instinctual gratification (which is often defined in purely biological terms); ego functions centre upon adaptation to external reality; super-ego functions focus upon moral or social demands.[166] All three functions are defined somewhat prosaically; the external reality to which the ego must adapt is discussed in totally unproblematic terms and has none of the complexity of, say, Lacan's concept of the real. In developmental terms, the ego is seen as emerging from a primary and undifferentiated id–ego matrix via a process of maturation (a process of growth which is relatively independent of environmental factors) and development (in which environmental factors and maturation interact). The ego also contains within it innate elements which mature and develop into a 'conflict-free ego sphere' which transcends instinctual ambivalences and conflicts, and which is therefore regarded as autonomous and as a prerequisite for the establishment of reality-relations.[167] In clinical terms, interest centres upon the way in which the ego neutralizes instinctual drives and the strength of the id, harnesses them and uses them to further the work of adaptation. Ego strength tends to be equated with both biological maturation and successful socialization. Psychopathological states are, accordingly, viewed in terms of the survival of archaic elements. Although this view readily merges into social psychology, it can also be interpreted as a rather pale reflection of Freud's underlying cultural evolutionism.

At a general theoretical level, psychoanalysis is redefined as moving towards a 'general development psychology',[168] and the ego is identified with the traditional object of clinical and experimental psychology. It is this 'redefinition' which promotes the emergence of a 'sphere in which a meeting of analytic with physiological, especially brain-physiological, concepts may one day become possible'.[169] It is probably the prospect of a meeting with neuropsychology that appeals so much to Nacht, who suggests that the innate 'rudiments' of the ego can be identified without further ado, though he also argues in more banal terms that 'normality' indicates the existence of an ego which can at once satisfy the id, respect the reality principle and resist the superego; the objective of the analysis is therefore to strengthen the ego.[170] Further meetings are contrived with Erikson's culturalism,[171] with Piaget and even with Sullivan's behaviourism. There is, then, a constant attempt to expand psychoanalysis's field of reference – and its field of clinical indications – through the formation of alliance with a wide variety of disciplines ranging from social psychology to the behavioural sciences.

Ego psychology further implies that psychoanalysis itself must adapt, just like the ego, and that it must be amenable to integration with other disciplines. Lacan not unreasonably regards this as a search for respectability, commenting on one occasion that the IJPA's decision to print an article by Masserman on 'Language, Behaviour and Dynamic Psychiatry' betrays the editorial board's adoption of the criteria of an employment agency and alleging that, in their search for respectability, they 'never neglect anything that might provide our discipline with "good references".'[172] The plague bacillus which Freud and Jung believed they were smuggling into the USA (according to Lacan[173]) has become anodyne and respectable, a mere addition to the national formulary.

Hartmann notes, perhaps with a degree of false modesty, that his ego psychology is based upon 'some of Freud's later and not yet fully integrated findings' and that it is therefore a 'mixture of synchronizations and reformulations'.[174] In other words, its elaboration necessitates the establishment of a final state; only the second topography is taken into account, and the many other connotations acquired by the term 'ego' in the course of the trajectory that takes Freud from the *Project* of 1895 to the *Outline* of 1938 are silently ignored. As André Green observes, Freudian and post-Freudian theories of the ego constantly oscillate between seeing it as a 'part-agency' within the psychic apparatus and erecting it into a unitary entity, a totalization of the personality.[175] Neither the ego psychologists nor Lacan are immune to the effects of that oscillation. In a very general historical sense, ego psychology is a product of the ambiguities surrounding Freud's own writings on the ego, but that in itself implies that its origins can be traced back to certain of his formulations, such as those of *The Ego and the Id* or 'Analysis Terminable and Interminable', where Freud argues that 'The business of the analysis is to secure the best possible psychological conditions for the functions of the ego.'[176] If, as Lacan will insist, ego psychology is a revisionism, it must also be admitted that Freud himself could be a revisionist.

Hartmann's 'reformulations' are far-reaching, particularly in terms of the theory of sexuality. Instinctual maturation and the development of ego strength are often described in terms of sexualization, a process combining sublimation and aim-inhibition. For Nacht, desexualization and the concomitant emergence of an autonomous ego open up the utopian prospect of an escape from ambivalence, the most 'pernicious poison' that infects the psyche.[177] Lacan, in stark contrast, consistently gives precedence to a theory of the ego which is grounded in Freud's writings on narcissism and thus places sexuality at the very core of the ego, even at the very heart of being. Ego psychology even desexualizes the analytic situation itself by introducing the notion of a therapeutic alliance between analyst and analysand on the grounds that analysis is a process whereby the analysand gradually comes to identify with the strong ego of the analyst.[178] The notion of a 'therapeutic alliance' comes in for severe criticism from Lacan, but one does not need to be a devout Lacanian to object that the idea of a desexualized therapeutic situation implies a somewhat naive view of transference and countertransference.[179] It might also be added that the identification model is an encouragement to ignore the explicit advice of Freud, who warns against the 'temptation of the analyst to play the part of prophet, saviour and redeemer'.[180]

Ego psychology is, in intellectual and theoretical terms, the least distinguished of all the currents within post-Freudian psychoanalysis. Its theorists lack both the emotional power of Klein and the intellectual excitement of Lacan, and lapse all too easily into a banal social psychology in which development is a linear process involving an unproblematic subject and an equally unproblematic reality. Despite these limitations ego psychology can provide a relatively coherent description of specific developmental stages, and thus helps to pinpoint one of the major weaknesses of Lacanian psychoanalysis: its apparent inability to furnish an account of the emergence of individuality which is couched in terms more specific than the ritual references to the subject's insertion into the symbolic. Sartre often bemoans Marxism's penchant for describing social existence solely in terms of entry or insertion into relations of production and for ignoring the world of childhood in favour of an adult world of labour. Lacan often commits a symmetrical error in that his descriptions of insertion into the symbolic are couched in such totally abstract terms that they become an obstacle to formulating any account of how an individual reaches, say, adolescence or puberty, just as his concentration on the symbolic or mythic aspects of the *fort-da* game mask the absence of any theory of how natural languages are acquired by specific social speakers.

A critique of ego-psychology runs through all Lacan's post-war work. It has been argued above that the original co-option of Hegel-Kojève was not designed to facilitate any attack on Hartmann and his associates but to construct a distinct theory of the origins, structure and functions of the ego. Lacan's claims to the contrary and his suggestions that the philosophical references are purely illustrative are either a screen-memory or a back-projection. The philosophemes are, that is, constituent elements of his theorization and not pedagogic or critical adjuvants.

The critique is frequently violent, and can take the form of *ad hominem* arguments (and *ad feminam* arguments, in the case of Anna Freud) though it is to be noted that Lacan usually spares Loewenstein his venom, perhaps out of a lingering respect or affection for his old analyst. The splenetic and exasperated rhetoric which denounces ego psychology as, among other things, 'the reduction of a distinguished practice to a label suitable to the "American way of life"' or a 'theology of free enterprise',[181] and the savagery of the 1966 *Cahiers pour l'analyse* interview are notorious, but Lacan's criticisms can be more subtle than this. When he does not lapse into polemic, he deploys arguments which, if open to dispute, are based upon Freud's metapsychology. But these arguments constantly bring in their wake concepts culled from the philosophical field, and therefore undermine his claim not to be fighting on a philosophical front.[182] Lacan often exploits the ambiguities of the French *moi*, the term designating both the Freudian ego and the traditional subject of psychology and philosophy alike. In a sense, he becomes a prisoner of the discursive borderline area he exploits so well in other respects.

Lacan's views on the ego derive primarily from Freud's 'On Narcissism: An Introduction'. Thus, he argues in a 1956 lecture on 'Freud dans le siècle' that the theory of the ego does not begin with the second topography, but with the transitional paper of 1914: 'In Freud, the theory of the ego is ... designed to show us that what we call our ego [*moi*] is a certain image of ourselves ... which gives us a mirage, a mirage of totality.'[183] This reading of 'Narcissism' accords well with Lacan's long-standing interest in identification, an interest evinced by the discussion of the Aimée case in his thesis, and combines with the theory of the mirror stage to produce the thesis that: 'The core of our being does not coincide with the ego.'[184] It follows that, for Lacan, the ego cannot be regarded as centred upon the perception-consciousness system, or as organized by the reality principle, precisely because all its structures are characterized by the effect of misrecognition [*méconnaiss-ance*].[185] Needless to say, this implies a rejection of Freud's second topography and therefore a challenge to the ego psychology which is one of its clinical expressions.

It is on this basis that Lacan sardonically described Anna Freud's *The Ego and the Mechanisms of Defence* as marking the triumphal return of 'the good old ego', in other words as signalling a regression to a pre-psychoanalytic and primarily philosophical notion of the ego.[186] The current it inaugurates is a disavowal of the essence of Freud's discovery: the decentring of the subject from the ego; under Anna Freud's influence, the entire history of psychoanalysis becomes a return to 'not a traditional, but an academic conception of the ego as a psychological function of synthesis'.[187] Lacan's strictures against the ego psychologists imply rather more than a controversy internal to psychoanalysis; because of the overlap between the agency and the subject implicit in his use of *moi*, they imply nothing less than a philosophical revolution.

The subtitle of 'The Agency of the Letter' is therefore to be taken quite literally; Lacan's concern is with 'Reason since Freud'.[188] The psychoanalyst who hoped he would be remembered for having discovered the secret of dreams is credited with having launched a philosophical revolution. Given the manifest distrust of philosophy exhibited by both Freud and Lacan, this can only mean a revolution against philosophy. Psychoanalysis, that is, opens up the vista of a post-philosophy inaugurated 'since Freud': '*Ça parle*: a subject in the subject, transcending the subject, has, since the *Interpretation of Dreams*, been asking the philosopher its question.'[189] Whilst this proclamation sounds innovatory, it also recalls the defensive stance adopted by Freud and Ferenczi: psychoanalysis can interrogate philosohy, or call it to account, but it has no accounts to render.

In 1955 Lacan refers to this revolution as 'worthy of the name of Copernicus', and later alludes to the 'so-called Copernican revolution to which Freud himself compared his discovery' and to 'what Freud in his doctrine articulates as constituting a "Copernican" step'.[190] Lacan often appeals to a concept of scientificity which owes a great deal to the French rationalist school of epistemology associated with Bachelard, Canguilhem and Koyré (his overt references are usually to the latter), and the Copernican revolution is a classic paradigm for its history of the sciences. Freud does on a number of occasions compare himself to Copernicus, but the key terms in this description of the Freudian discovery – 'revolution in knowledge' and 'Copernican step' – are Lacan's, and do not figure in Freud.

The effect, if not necessarily the intention, of Lacan's formulations is to lend Freud the discourse and accents of an epistemology which is quite alien to him and, at the same time to induce a certain misrecognition of the role played by the name 'Copernicus' in Freud's imaginary. Freud's first allusion to Copernicus appears in his reply to a 'Questionnaire on Reading', where he describes the astronomer's works as being amongst the ten most significant books in the history of science. In *Leonardo*, the importance of Copernicus is compared to that of Bacon and Leonardo himself, but it is only in the *Introductory Lectures* of 1915–17 that Freud actually identifies with Copernicus and claims that the discovery that the ego is not even master in its own house is a 'third major blow to the naive self-love of men', the first and second blows having been struck by Copernicus and Darwin respectively.'[191] The same point is made in almost identical terms in 'A Difficulty in the Path of Psycho-Analysis' and in 'The Resistances to Psycho-Analysis', whilst a final allusion comes in the *New Introductory Lectures*, where psychoanalysis is situated within a schematic history of the sciences punctuated by the names 'Kepler, Newton, Lavoisier, Curie, Copernicus. . . .'[192] For the rationalist epistemologists, certain of these names are associated with epistemological breaks, but it is almost improbable that they have the same resonances for Freud, who specifically rejects the view that the history of science is dependent upon revolutions or breaks. On the contrary, he believes it to be dependent, at a methodological level, on a decidedly hesitant mode of progress and upon slow, halting advances.

The evidence of the *New Introductory Lectures* implies something of a contradiction here in that it appeals to a classic 'Great Men' vision of history, with all the heroic imagery that implies.[193] The latter vision is, however, quite in keeping with Freud's tendency to identify with the great men of the past: Hannibal, Cromwell, Napoleon, the conquistadores. According to his own account, such identifications date back to his childhood,[194] and they are later exemplified by the letter to Fliess and by the wish to be commemorated by a marble tablet. In short, the Copernicus allusions and identifications have at least as much to do with Freud's imaginary ideal ego as with any explicit epistemology or history of the sciences. In so far as a self-conscious history of the sciences is present here, it is of a very different nature to that evoked by Lacan. In a detailed reading of the Copernicus references, Paul-Laurent Assoun notes that the name is always coupled with that of Darwin and that, whilst Copernicus had been viewed as a precursor of modern science since at least the Enlightenment, the combined Copernicus-Darwin figure is defined and codified by Haeckel.[195] Haeckel views Copernicus and Darwin as the heroes who destroyed geocentrism and anthropocentrism respectively, and Freud is in effect quoting his words in the *Lectures*. Freud himself thus describes his own discovery within the

history of a continuum, and takes as his authority for doing so a figure
who is unlikely ever to be associated with any Bachelardian epistemological break.

Given Freud's heroic identifications and views on the history of
science, there is something unfortunate about Lacan's reference to the
Freud-Copernicus figure. The reference is introduced to support the
contention that Freud inaugurates a revolution heralding the era of post-
philosophy, a contention predicated largely upon a reading of 'On
Narcissism'. Yet Freud's most explicit references to Copernicus postdate
the problematic of that paper and are contemporary with the elaboration
of the second topography which, according to Lacan, signals a counter-
revolutionary return to philosophy. In the *Introductory Lectures*, in
particular, Freud refers explicitly to the synthetic functions of the ego,
and to the fact that the decisive factor for that agency is 'the relation to
the external world'; and in the *New Introductory Lectures* it is because
of the pressure exerted by the id that the ego 'has scanty information
about what is going on unconsciously in its own mind' and that it is not
master in its own house,[196] not because it is constituted on an irredeem-
ably narcissistic basis and therefore functions according to a mode of
méconnaissance. Lacan therefore selects a rather unhappy support for
his revolutionary claims.

In terms of the epistemology to which Lacan alludes in his presentation of the Copernican Freud, the claim that a revolution has begun
would have to be supported by a much more exhaustive reading of the
history of the relevant sciences or protosciences than anything provided
by either *Ecrits* or the Seminar. Koyré, for instance, is not merely a
theorist of epistemological breaks, but primarily a historian. His studies
in the scientific thought of the sixteenth and seventeenth centuries rely
for their coherence upon a detailed and sympathetic reconstruction of
the very theories that are abandoned as a result of breaks, which are by
definition perceptible only with hindsight.[197] Lacan does not provide any
comparable history of pre-Freudian psychiatry and psychology, yet that
would be the only history that might justify his claims on the basis of the
epistemology he invokes.

Lacan's wild analysis of Freud's Copernican identifications and the
attendant notions of an epistemological break are not the only harbing-
ers of the supposed dawning of the age of post-philosophy. Its advent is
also signalled by the foregrounding of desire, which is held to subvert
the notion of the unified subject that is central to both traditional philosophy and ego psychology.[198] In the article on 'Wish (Desire)' in their
Language of Psychoanalysis, Laplanche and Pontalis note in rather
neutral terms that Lacan has 'attempted to reorientate Freud's doctrines
around the notion of desire, and to replace this notion in the forefront of

analytic theory'.[199] Desire is of course merely one term in the need-demand-desire triad, but it is noteworthy that the other two persons of the trinity receive distinctly less attention. Need can be defined in basically biological terms, and demand in terms of the linguistic expression of need in an appeal to the other as a potential source of satisfaction, the obvious example being the demand for love that accompanies the need for nutrition. Desire is that which goes beyond demand and conveys the subject's wish for totality, or, in the case of the pre-oedipal child, a wish for immediate unity with the mother. To cite one of Lacan's classic descriptions of the imbrications of the trinity: desire is 'what is evoked by any demand beyond the need that is articulated in it, and it is certainly that of which the subject remains all the more deprived to the extent that the need articulated in the demand is satisfied.'[200] Rather more succinctly, 'Desire begins to take shape in the margin in which demand becomes separated from need.'[201] The re-orientation proposed by Lacan is so profound that '*Desidero* is the Freudian cogito'.[202]

Like *le moi*, *désir* offers an extensive semantic field which is amenable to exploitation in a number of ways. It too is a borderline signifier which readily facilitates movement between the contiguous fields of philosophy and psychoanalysis, particularly when the latter is placed in such close proximity to the humanities. *Désir* also reflects certain translation problems and some of the weakness of French renditions of Freud. These in turn reflect a serious semantic difficulty in that the obvious alternative translation of Freud's *Wunsch* – *vœu* – is not appropriate in all contexts. As a result, *désir* is used rather indiscriminately to refer to both *Wunsch* (wish, as in wish-fulfilment: *Wunscherfüllung*; *accomplissement du désir*) and the less frequent *Begierde* and *Lust*, which have rather broader connotations and which are perhaps closer to the English sense of 'desire'. This usage can result in some startling differences between the English and French texts of Freud; it can also lead to some major problems when Lacan's English translators render his terminology without referring to the English or German texts he cites in French. The problem becomes rather more difficult where the 'phallus' is concerned, but two minor examples will illustrate some of the difficulties pertaining to *désir*.

In a brief discussion of *Hamlet* and *Oedipus Rex* in *The Interpretation of Dreams*, Freud speaks of 'the child's wishful phantasy' [*Wunschphantasie*]; the French version cited by Lacan in his Seminar on *Hamlet* has '*les désirs de l'enfant*'.[203] If the latter phrase is translated simply as 'the child's desires' its meaning changes considerably, not least in that the *Phantasie* element vanishes. And such translations are adopted. Freud tells the story of the butcher's wife and her 'wish for a caviar sandwich';

in the French this becomes '*un désir de caviare*', in Sheridan's version, it is a 'desire for caviar'.[204] These are by no means minor issues related to an arcane theory of translation. On the contrary, they indicate that the ambiguities of the French text produced by Freud's translators, together with Lacan's foregrounding of a general theory of *désir*, lead not to a return to Freud but to a departure from the letter of his text. And in this instance at least, the English version departs further still from it by lending Freud Lacan's terminology.

The ambiguities of *désir* are at their greatest when the term is used in the singular, as it is inevitably overdetermined by centuries of philosophical usage. It can encompass Hegel's *Begierde* and Spinoza's *cupiditas*, and *désir* is also a key term in traditional theories of the passions of the soul, as in Descartes's 'desire to acquire something one does not yet have, or to avoid an evil one thinks may happen'.[205] But the classic dictum that 'man's desire is the desire of the Other' has a more modern ancestry, and seems designed to conjure up echoes of Kojève's definition of desire as being human only to the extent that it is oriented towards 'other *Desire* and an *other* Desire'.[206] The 'reorientation' of Freud's doctrine thus involves a further appeal to philosophy. The genealogy of Lacan's *désir* is not to be found in Freud, but in a corner of the philosophical field occupied by Kojève-Hegel and phenomenology. 'Desire of the Other' has a definite Kojèvean ring to it, as does the notion of desire going beyond the biological, but it is Sartre who speaks of man being torn between a 'desire to be' and a 'desire to have', and who defines desire itself in terms of a 'lack of being' [*manque d'être*].[207]

It is surely impossible, therefore, to ignore the link between Sartre's ontological-phenomenological categories and Lacan's dialectic of having and being the phallus. Indeed, Lacan himself points to the connection when he defines *objet-a* as supporting the subject's relationship with what he does not have, and adds that his formulation take us slightly further than 'what traditional and existential philosophy formulates as the negativity or nihilation [*néantisation*] of the existing subject'.[208] And the Sartrean note is unmistakable in the sentence: 'The experience of desire ... is that of the lack of being which means that any being [*étant*] might or might not be the other, in other words is created as an existant.'[209] A phenomenology of temporality is not the only thing Lacan has in common with Sartre; they come close to sharing a concept of desire which it would be difficult to find in Freud.

The most obvious effect of Lacan's incorporation of a philosophically derived concept of desire into psychoanalytic discourses is the displacement of libido. In the Seminar of 1964–65, libido is described as 'the effective presence, as such, of desire', which effectively demotes it to epiphenomenal status.[210] The very term 'libido' is quite simply absent from 'Subversion du sujet', the text in which the most far-reaching claims for desire are advanced. Lacan always uses 'libido' surprisingly sparingly, and it is effectively displaced or even ousted by 'desire'. The displacement often takes the form of a substitution, as in 'La Direction de la cure', where Lacan speaks of 'the frustrations in which Freud's desire is fixed (Freud's *Fixierung*)'.[211] Yet Freud uses *Fixierung* to refer to the binding of libido to persons or imagos, or to fixation at a stage of libidinal development; the term is not applied to *Wunsch* or *Begierde*, which are the closest equivalents to *désir*. Desire also extends to cover other distinct concepts in Freud, as in the discussion of *The Interpretation of Dreams* in 'La Chose freudienne', where Lacan describes the motives of the unconscious as being 'limited to sexual desire', and then refers to 'the other great generic desire, that of hunger'; Freud is referring here to love and hunger as 'the major vital needs'.[212] For Freud, hunger is a need, an expression of a 'nutritive instinct' which is analogous to 'libido', the name used to describe the force of the 'sexual instinct.'[213] Neither hunger nor libido is collapsed into a generic category of desire.

By expanding the semantic and conceptual range of desire' in this way, Lacan overlooks Freud's rationale for using the term he borrows from Moll; the first sentence of the *Three Essays on the Theory of Sexuality* makes it clear that 'libido' is used to make a distinction between the sexual and the nutritional instincts; a footnote added in 1910 points out that *Lust* is unsuitable because it is so ambiguous.[214] The very distinction which Freud wished to preserve becomes lost in Lacan's use of desire. Once more, it is not merely terminology which is at stake here; Freud's libido knows stages and gives rise to character types, but there is no indication that the same can be said of Lacan's *désir*, which often appears to operate according to the modalities of an eternal essence.

For Althusser at least, the shift from libido to desire has considerable appeal in that the designation of desire as 'the basic category of the unconscious' is part of the work of dispelling the 'temporary opacity' cast over Freudian theory by its reliance upon the hydraulic and energetic metaphors it uses to describe libido.[215] Lacan himself can refer to libido as a 'fluidic myth', whilst the striking absence of 'libido' from the index to *Ecrits* and the concomitant over-representation of 'desire' strongly suggests that that view is shared by Miller, who argues elsewhere that anyone who believes that libido is a 'real energy' is not a true psychoanalyst and, in a classic flourish of *reductio ad absurdum*, that belief in libido leads inevitably to the construction of Reichian orgone accumulators.[216] If it is true that 'libido' is merely an embarrassing metaphorical survival from the past, it will require more than the

substitution of one term for another and sarcasm to rid psychoanalysis
of its effects.

Lacan holds that the theory of desire subverts the subject and therefore, it might be assumed, inaugurates the dawn of post-philosophy, or
at least of the revolution against philosophy. Yet it can be shown that
'desire' trails with it clouds of philosophemes, that its theorization
requires a number of appeals to Kojève-Hegel and to Sartre. It also
implies a move away from distinctions established by Freud. In 'Position
de l'inconscient', Lacan describes his appeal to Hegel as 'an *Aufhebung*
which allows the avatars of a lack' to replace the 'leaps of an ideal
progress'.[217] For once, he appears to have forgotten the lessons he
learned from his master Kojève. The moment of the *Aufhebung* is not a
moment of abolition; it preserves that which it transcends. The constant
appeal to philosophers in an attempt to escape the philosophical field
merely reproduces what post-philosophy or 'reason since Freud' seeks
to abolish. The death of philosophy has often been proclaimed, but the
rumours of its demise inevitably prove to be both premature and greatly
exaggerated. The obituary notice posted by Lacan is no exception to the
rule.

Lacan's career spans fifty years of French intellectual life, and it is
only to be expected that it should reflect many of the cultural shifts that
occur over that period. The successive references to Politzer, to the
Hegelianism of Kojève, to Sartrean and Heideggerean phenomenology,
and finally to a linguistically based structuralism are so many pointers to
both Lacan's own evolution and to changes in the more general intellectual climate. It takes a great deal of charity to see them as consistently
and 'purely' propaedeutic references designed to promote the understanding of any final state. Perhaps André Green is closer to the truth
when he remarks with some sadness that all too often Lacan's
undoubted talent for speculation was used to satisfy the demands of the
changing climate rather than to help psychoanalysts solve their own
problems.[218] François Perrier makes a not dissimilar point, if rather
more cynically, when he remarks that it was at one stage *de rigueur* in
Lacanian circles to refer to what later became known as '*objet-a*' as '*Das
Ding*' ... 'because Lacan was reading Heidegger at the time.'[219]

The traffic between Lacan's psychoanalytic field and that of philosophy and its environs is not a one-way flow. A number of his theorizations have fed into philosophy and its derivatives, a process which
provides further evidence of the fertility of the borderline area. Perhaps
the most obvious case in point is the mirror stage, which Simone de
Beauvoir integrates so easily into her phenomenology of childhood in
Le Deuxième Sexe, and which Fanon appropriates for an analysis of
racism grounded in both clinical psychiatry and phenomenology.[220]

Decades later, the Lacanian concept of desire, which owes at least as much to generations of philosophers as it does to Freud, will meet with a similar absorption into philosophy. In Lacan's own discourse, desire tends to be eclipsed gradually by *jouissance* – itself a mixed psychoanalytic-philosophical concept[221] – but his *désir* will feed into the various philosophies of desire that flourish in the 1970s, just as the figure of the Master (but not the critique of his discourse) will readily be absorbed into the demonic cosmologies of the so-called 'New Philosophers'.[222] To the extent that Lacan – no doubt inadvertently, but ineluctably – promotes their speculative enterprises, his career has not been that of a Copernicus but that of a latter-day philosophical sorcerer's apprentice.

It is, however, with the late theory of the four discourses that Lacan comes closest to surrendering to the attractions of speculation and, in so far as it represents an attempt at rigour, to paranoia. At this point, his teachings as to the nature of analytic treatment are so displaced as to apply to culture in its entirety.[223] The discourse of the Master has already been seen to relate to the illusory moment of Absolute Knowledge, but Lacan now effectively makes it synonymous with the discourse of philosophy as such.[224] The philosopher, like the Master, seeks a totality of illusory knowledge. Matters of style and reference aside, it is not difficult to reconcile this view of philosophy with Freud's remarks about totalizing or holistic *Weltanschauungen.*

At the opposite discursive extreme, the hysteric constantly poses questions and re-enacts the Socratic role of putting the Master 'up against the wall' by demanding knowledge.[225] It is at the insistent urging of the hysteric that science takes wing;[226] after all, it was the female hysterics who finally stimulated or goaded Freud into discovering psychoanalysis itself. Master and hysteric thus coexist in a state of symbiosis, with the hysteric demanding knowledge and the Master striving to attain absolute knowledge in response. The discourse of the University, in the meantime, is that of the Master reinforced by obscurantism.[227] It too is concerned with mastery in the sense that one might speak of mastering a discipline or corpus of knowledge, but at every stage it is forced to confess to the inadequacy of its acquired knowledge, thereby reproducing the non-mastery of its students or would-be initiates.

Finally, psychoanalytic discourse subverts the discourses of both the Master and the University by insisting that the whole truth can never be spoken, that totality is an imaginary, illusory notion. At the same time it allows the hysteric to speak, thus stimulating the drive towards knowledge, but also undercutting the hysteric's illusion that the Master knows all. Lacan insists that his discourses exist within a system of permutations; only 'a quarter of a turn' separates the discourse of the Master

from that of the University; the discourse of science – and by extension
of psychoanalysis – and that of hysteria have 'almost' the same structure.[228] By the same criterion, it can be argued that they require one
another's existence. The University requires a Master to justify its teachings and to sanction its students' non-mastery of their disciplines; the
Master requires recognition, just as Auguste requires the submission of
Cinna to endorse his *m'êtrise/maîtrise*. Hysteric and analyst also need
one another; Dora needs someone to answer her questions, but Freud
needs hysterics to lead him to psychoanalysis.

Lacan's theory of the four discourses clearly goes beyond the practice
of psychoanalysis and has pretensions to a universal application. Whilst
some of its features are readily recognizable as applicable to an analytic
context, and whilst one (the discourse of the University) is instantly
recognizable to anyone who has ever been trapped in its signifiers, the
overall thrust of the theory is towards a universal system of discursive
classification, in other words towards the rigour and clarity of definition
which both Freud and Lacan see as characteristic of philosophy and
paranoia. Freud thought that he had found the satisfactions of the
philosophical knowledge he once sought in his theory of culture. Lacan
appears to find the philosophical totalization he denies seeking in a total
theory of discourse, just as he constantly finds verifications, justifications
and conceptual inputs in a philosophical field whose very existence he
tries to contest by elaborating the notion of the discourse of the Master.
By ceaselessly raising the one question he claims it cannot answer (that
of the unconscious), he in fact sanctions its existence, just as the hysteric
sanctions the existence of the analyst, and the University that of the
Master.

Lacan insists that identification is one of the key discoveries of
psychoanalysis, and it is true that Freud's youthful identifications prove
to reveal a great deal about the ambitions that inspire his work. Lacan's
identifications are equally revealing. The history of psychoanalysis
records the careers of many excommunicants, but in the lonely hour of
his own 'excommunication' from the IPA Lacan identifies, not with
them, but with Spinoza.[229] In so doing he in effect admits to his ambivalent views on philosophy: it is both other than psychoanalysis and an
object to be absorbed by psychoanalysis, an object of identification.
In the moment of his identification with Spinoza, the vision of post-
philosophy fades into one of psychoanalysis as philosophy.

5

Linguistics or *Linguisterie*?

in many

·ch

ᵤₜ

... communic-

_..ₗₜ of view. For Lacan,

...c strongest and most absolute of

...cₙ are its sole field and its sole medium.

...ₑ other hand, does not become part of the theoretical

..ᵥc until the 1950s, and it is incorporated into an existing structure of philosophemes and anthropological references without undermining its foundations. When, in 1949, Lacan refers to the fertile kernel of knowledge supplied by the humanities, linguistics is not privileged in any way; when, in 1953, he speaks of the need to restore the primacy of speech in psychoanalysis, 'speech' is not defined with reference to any specific theory of linguistics.[1] Even after this date, the linguistics invoked by Lacan represents a curiously truncated or incomplete version of the discipline.

At the level of authorities, the canon is effectively restricted to the Saussure–Jakobson axis; there is, for example, no substantive discussion of Hjelmslev, Martinet, Harris or Chomsky, to take only a random selection of names familiar to any student of linguistics.[2] At the level of areas and categories of linguistics theory and analysis, the debate is equally restricted. Saussure's theory of the sign (with important 'modifications') and Jakobson's work on phonemic analysis and on aphasia provide the main parameters, but references to grammar are more likely to be Damourette and Pichon's *Des Mots à la pensée*, an enormous multi-volume survey of French grammar based upon historical–philological principles and an unlikely claimant to the title of 'modern linguistics', than to any transformational or generative theory. There is little or no

121

discussion of sociolinguistics, and the allusion to 'semantic evolution' in 'Fonction et champ' reads like a description of an idiolect rather than a theory of semantics.[3] Victor Hugo's romantic etymologies are pressed into service on a number of occasions, and whilst Hugo's importance as a poet is not in dispute, a question mark must surely hang over his competence in theoretical linguistics. Lacan's only reference to language acquisition is to the *fort-da* game described by Freud in *Beyond the Pleasure Principle*, but, whilst the game may provide a mythical illustration of a theory of symbolization, it cannot supply a convincing model for the acquisition of natural language, that being a process of adapting the infinite possibilities offered by the human vocal apparatus to the conventions of a given language, and not a process which begins in silence and then leads to the manipulation of a pair of phonemes.

It is also significant that Lacan's reflections on language have not entered the discourse of mainstream linguistics, however great their appeal for literary theorists or for the adepts of a generalized structuralism or post-structuralism. A standard and highly competent survey of linguistics such as that provided by John Lyons is innocent of any reference to Lacan; in their encyclopaedic study of the sciences of language, Ducrot and Todorov relegate discussion of Lacan to an appendix.[4] In short, even a cursory glance at the linguistic authorities referred to by Lacan and at the mainstream discipline itself begins to suggest that his relationship with 'modern linguistics' is at best one of marginality.

It is also striking that Lacan should devote so little time and space to discussing the extensive psychoanalytic literature on language and linguistic phenomena.[5] The major exception is of course the critique of Jones's theory of symbolism in *Ecrits*, but that is a contribution to Lacan's own theory of metaphor and of the phallus rather than a detailed reading of Jones in his own right.[6] And despite the repeated assertions that Freud's writings are alive with references to philology and language, no real attempt is made to reconstruct his discourse on language as it moves from the early papers on aphasia to the discussion of thing-presentations and word-presentations in the papers on metapsychology. Unlike Todorov, Lacan never writes any substantial study of – nor delivers any seminar on – 'Freud's Rhetoric' or 'Freud on Enunciation'.[7] His discussion of language tends to be highly intellectualist and to be articulated with broad anthropological or philosophical concerns; the question of the body–language relationship is not posed, and the issue of the affective content and nature of language is not raised.

It is in fact difficult to take Lacan at all seriously as a linguist as opposed to a psychoanalyst who is fascinated by language, who explores it in a variety of ways and to a variety of ends, who exploits elements of linguistic theory for some two decades before effectively abandoning them in the 1970s, and whose own use of language intersects with a variety of identifiable registers ranging from popular slang to poetics. But just as Lacan is fascinated by language, so it is easy to become fascinated by his fascination. The ease with which one becomes fascinated by his reflections is no doubt in part the effect of his successful use of rhetoric and style, but it is also an index of the very real intellectual excitement to be had from reading an author who engages, however marginally, with such a vast array of theories and theorists. Whole passages of his *Ecrits* and of the Seminar generate the impression that Lacan's thought is a thought in search of itself, a thought which is constantly open to revision and to innovation rather than a codified body of dogma. But when his references to the theories he co-opts are examined in more detail or are traced back to their origins, difficulties begin to arise; inconsistencies, divergences and contradictions become increasingly apparent, and the sense of excitement may become dulled by an impression of confusion. It is dangerous to mistake a fascination with language for linguistics, exploration for cartography.

Yet the linguistic model does tend to dominate many of the classic presentations of Lacan. For Althusser, it is the 'emergence of the new science of linguistics' which permits Lacan's theorization,[8] whilst Lemaire's influential study discusses Lacan in almost solely linguistic terms, and in fact extends the debate far beyond Lacan's own frame of linguistic reference. The *Screen* and *Tel Quel* presentations tend to take a broadly similar view, and inform the not uncommon belief that Lacan has a major contribution to make to some materialist theory of language, even though it is almost impossible to describe Lacan as operating with or within any one theory of language as opposed to a kaleidoscope of theories and philosophemes, a shifting set of prisms through which the phenomenon of language can be viewed in a variety of ways. At its most basic, the 'linguistic' presentation of Lacan may be summarized by reference to the dictum that the unconscious is structured like a language, and Lacan himself is often prone to collude in a final-statism by claiming that he has 'always' said that this is so.[9]

The record of his published work does not bear him out. No such formula appears anywhere in the pre-war writings, and even in the 1950s it appears in a bewildering and confusing variety of guises. In the Seminar on the psychoses, the unconscious is said to be a language that has to be translated; in 'Fonction et champ' it is the symptom that is structured like a language whereas the dream has the structure of a sentence, but it is also stated that the symptom is the signifier of a repressed signified; in 1956, however, the symptom is a signifier which connotes the subject's relation to the signifier.[10] Such variants on and around the consecrated formula may seem minor, but they are an indication of the manner in which his references to language can slip and slide, an index of the worrying imprecision of his linguistic terminology, and a reminder of the dangers of final-state readings.

The primary constant in all Lacan's reflections on language, regardless of whether they take a philosophical or a more strictly linguistic form, is a high degree of ambiguity and a conflation of levels and terms of analysis. Signifier, sign and symbol are sometimes used almost interchangeably, whilst at other times they refer to distinct and even oppositional entities. Arguments based upon the primacy accorded to the synchronic dimension by post-Saussurean linguistics intertwine with references to a pre-structuralist tradition of philology; the discussion of Saussure and Jakobson coexists alongside a Heideggerean exploitation of the poetics of phenomenology and of the resources of wild etymologies. A similar degree of ambiguity is present at the referential level, as Lacan constantly shifts from a description of the role of speech and language in the psychoanalytic encounter to a universalist description of language *qua* language; from a discussion of the nature of a therapeutic dialogue to a theory of human intersubjectivity as such. Indeed, the shift from one register or level to another can occur within the space of a single sentence, and the ambiguity is present throughout 'Fonction et champ'. Lacan thus reproduces in a very specific area the tension between universals and specifics in the analogical reasoning deployed by Freud in his anthropological writings; theses propounded with respect to language within psychoanalysis are projected on to language as such.

Lacan also tends to distance himself from conventional linguistics at crucial moments, even if it means contradicting his earlier pronouncements. The issue of metalanguage and of the 'necessarily' discursive construction of reality is a case in point. In an early Seminar, Lacan puts forward the unremarkable view that 'any language implies a metalanguage. ... It is because every language is potentially to be translated that it implies metaphrase and metalanguage, language speaking about language.'[11] Few linguists would disagree. Jakobson, in Lacan's opinion one of the rare individuals to have succeeded in speaking about language without being stupid, takes the view that the language/metalanguage distinction is one of symbolic logic's major contributions to linguistics, speaks very favourably of Carnap, and argues forcefully that the metalingual operation of interpreting one sign by means of another is an integral part of language acquisition.[12] In his early essay on semiology, Barthes takes it as self-evident that linguistics is a metalanguage.[13] When Lacan asserts that there can be no metalanguage because there can be no meaning of meaning,[14] he is not merely contradicting his own previous statements; he is going against the authority of his linguistic mentors and against the discourse of a discipline to which he claims to owe so much. Assertions to the effect that there is no pre-discursive reality and that the shape of Cleopatra's nose changed the course of history only because it was already inscribed in discourse take him further away from Jakobson. And they do not represent a gesture towards some materialist theory of discourse; Lacan's claim that 'In the beginning was the Word' is overdetermined by a theology of creation, and it is a challenge to the quotation from *Faust* which closes *Totem and Taboo*: 'In the beginning was the Deed.'[15]

Lacan's contradictory views as to the possibility and impossibility of metalanguage cannot be reconciled by referring to some occult unifying principle, but they can be seen as an effect of the manner in which language is viewed through shifting prisms. For a linguist or a semiologist the existence of a metalanguage is a methodological *sine qua non*, but for a philosopher such as Heidegger, it is axiomatic that there is no Archimedean point of leverage 'outside' language and that it is impossible to step outside the house of being. It is, according to Heidegger, by abandoning the traditional procedures of linguistics or language studies that we take the way to language itself: 'Instead of explaining language in terms of one thing or another, and thus running away from it, the way to language intends to let language be experienced as language.'[16] If we take this road the experience of language is inescapable, and what purports to be a metalanguage proves merely another room in the house of being. From this perspective, the fact that we are in some sense obliged to use language in order to talk about language proves that we cannot escape it in order to arrive at some metalinguistic level.[17]

In its own terms, and at its own level, the argument is far from unconvincing, but it is precisely the issue of terms and levels that is constantly blurred by Lacan. If, as he remarks at one point, linguistics is 'the study of existing languages in their structure and in the laws revealed therein',[18] it is by definition a positive and descriptive discipline which is not concerned with the 'experience of language' in any phenomenological sense. The question of 'the locus in which language questions us as to its very nature'[19] may be of burning interest to a hermeneutic philosopher, but not, surely, to the professional phonologist or sociolinguist. Nor, one can safely say, is a linguist likely to be greatly impressed by the claim that we can aphoristically paraphrase the statement that 'no metalanguage can be spoken' as 'there is no Other of the Other'.[20]

Contradictory statements as to the possibility or otherwise of constructing a metalanguage also plague Lacan's attempts to introduce a mathematical component into his reflections on language. In 1956 mathematicians are said to use a language of pure signifiers, a metalanguage *par excellence*; in 1960, the use of algorithms and analogous schemata is held not to imply the existence of a metalanguage because they are 'indices of an absolute signification'.[21] Finally, it need scarcely be pointed out that a critical and exegetical discourse of a seminar centred on a reading of Freud necessarily proceeds at a *meta* level, nor that the identification of a given figure of speech as an example of metaphor or metonymy is in itself a metalingual operation.[22] The blanket rejection of the *meta* dimension obscures the fact that linguistic, philosophical and psychoanalytic references to language are not necessarily references to the same object; Heidegger is not concerned with the laws of phonemics, and Saussure shows little interest in the architecture of the house of being. More importantly, it obscures the issue of levels of linguistic analysis and of the nature of many linguistic practices.

At the level of 'pure signification' it can be convincingly argued that there is no point at which one emerges from the network of signifiers, and that dictionary definitions never relate to a referent but only to other signifiers. And in terms of analytic practice, Lacan's position presumably precludes interpretations based upon a 'simultaneous translation' of symbols which move directly from, say, 'house' to 'female genitals'. It may, that is, reflect a valid concept of the use of language in psychoanalysis, but it does not in itself resolve the *meta* issue. For a variety of language practices, the assumption of the existence of a *meta* or referential level is quite essential. A verbal description of a painting may contain the expression *nu au pinceau*. If analysis is restricted to the pure signifiers contained in that syntagm, it can be translated as either 'nude holding a paintbrush' or 'nude drawn with a brush'. The ambiguity can be resolved only by looking at the painting (a referential operation) and then interpreting the grammatical function of the preposition *au* (a metalingual operation). It is of course perfectly true that a painting is not 'the real', but it is also true that it is not merely a verbal signifier caught up in a dictionary of other verbal signifiers. The issue of metalanguage and the contradictory positions to which it gives rise exemplifies the manner in which Lacan slides from one level to another, from one field of theoretical discourse to another. It typifies the co-presence within his discourse of radically different, even mutually contradictory, elements. The variegated colours and textures of that discourse may be exciting and seductive, but they do not merge into any harmonious fabric.

As though aware of these problems, in *Encore* Lacan finally renders unto Jakobson what is Jakobson's and unto himself what is his own, and admits that the dictum 'the unconscious is structured like a language' does not belong within the field of linguistics.[23] It, like his other views on the foundation of the subject and on the nature of the unconscious, belongs to what he terms the realm of *linguisterie*. The neologism is apt. The French suffix *erie* often connotes derivation, and it is therefore possible to see *linguisterie* as belonging to a paradigm which also includes *chinoiserie*, a generic term for Western imitations or evocations of Chinese art, most of them derivative and owing at least as much to the conventions of Western taste as to the supposed originals. *Chinoiserie* has its charms and its beauty, but it would be a major error for an art historian to identify a piece of Chinese Chippendale as a product of the Celestial Empire; it would be fradulent practice for a dealer to do so. With the coinage of *linguisterie* psychoanalysis becomes, not an extension of the field of linguistics, but a 'practice of chatter' which puts speech on the same level as blather or spluttering.[24] And as Lacan abandons linguistics for *linguisterie*, a note of parody is introduced: Saussure's *langue* becomes *lalangue* as the article is condensed with the noun to produce an onomatopoeic effect and as linguistic scientificity gives way to splutters. It will be argued below that this noisy departure from linguistics in fact represents a return to Lacan's earliest concerns and to a fascination with the stuff of pathological language rather than with the theoretical object of Saussure's *Cours de linguistique générale*.

To turn, however, to the period that precedes the encounter with any recognizable linguistics, structural or otherwise. The second section of *Ecrits* brings together five papers dating from the years 1936 to 1950[25] and is prefaced by 'De Nos Antécédents', the short, dense text in which Lacan retraces his entry into psychoanalysis. Here, he remarks that the five *Ecrits* outline his 'reference to language', but warns against retrospective readings which project the future into the past.[26] The degree to which these papers refer to language varies considerably, but they are all characterized by the absence of any mobilization of linguistic theory and of any reference to the 'linguistic' Freud of *The Interpretation of Dreams, Jokes and their Relation to the Unconscious* and *The Psychopathology of Everyday Life*.[27] Lacan is still reading Freud in order to explore the themes of identification and of the imaginary construction of the ego, and has yet to turn his attention to the classic formations of the unconscious or to its rhetoric. His references to language are couched in terms deriving from the Kojève-Hegel philosopheme and from the practices of the literary avant-gardes of the 1930s. Thus, the allusion to language being a 'knot of signification' in 'Propos sur la causalité psychique' proves to be a gesture of homage to Leiris's glossological prowess, and not a comment on Saussure or even a reference to the 'nodal points' of *The Interpretation of Dreams*.[28] The typology of pathological discourse proposed here and the suggestion that tracing knots of signification will make it possible to study the 'significations of madness' are reminiscent of *L'Immaculée Conception* and of Lacan's earliest writings, but they do not extend to a discussion of what will come to be termed 'man's relation to the signifier'. In other words, the 'phenomen-

ology of madness' is still of greater interest than the linguistic or rhetorical structures of the unconscious.

The mirror-stage paper itself has little to say about language, and
concentrates upon the visual perception and construction of the image
or imago of the 'I'. The paper on the functions of psychoanalysis in
criminology, a reminder of Lacan's early work at the special clinic
attached to the Préfecture de Police, is concerned with language only in
so far as both the criminal's confession and the analytic encounter
involve elements of a dialogue which reveals a universal function implicit in the institution of language.[29] The remaining écrits in this section
discuss language slightly more specifically, but the dialogic element is
still described in terms deriving from the Kojève–Hegel philosopheme:
language is seen as a medium which permits mutual recognition and thus
defuses the aggressivity generated by any encounter with the other.

Within the analytic encounter itself, the essential property of
language is the implication of an interlocutor; before it comes to signify
something, language signifies for someone, even though that interlocutor
may be imaginary.[30] It implies, then, a signifying intention on the part of
the subject: 'It can be said that psychoanalytic action is developed in and
through verbal communication, that is, in a dialectical grasp of meaning.
It presupposes, therefore, a subject who manifests himself as such to the
intention of another.'[31] Intentionality can be expressed in one of two
different modes. Either it is expressed but not understood by the subject
– in which case it takes a symbolic form amenable to interpretation – or
it is masked by the mechanisms of negation and disavowal. In the latter
case, the analyst-interlocutor's role is to frustrate the analysand's
demand for recognition by his silence and eventually to provoke the
emergence of images expressing the disavowed intentionality. Lacan's
phenomenological description of the psychoanalytic encounter is recognizable as a variant on the implications of Freud's 'Negation' paper. It is
also possible to detect in it elements of later descriptions of the analyst's
silence and of the view that his non-intervention is in itself a response to
a demand, but it takes a phenomenological and not a linguistic form. In
'Aggressivité', a Sartrean note is struck by the reference to the 'facticity
of the I', but the assertion that Hegel supplies the 'ultimate theory' of the
ontology of aggressivity indicates that the original philosopheme is still
firmly in place.[32]

Although these écrits outline a reference to language, they do not
indicate any debt to linguistics. The poetic practices of Lacan's old
associates are a major point of reference; Saussure is not. In short, this is
a period of language without linguistics in which communication is
viewed in philosophical terms as 'a relationship of mutual knowledge
between two subjects caught up within a space of representation'.[33]

Between 1936 and 1950 Lacan also begins to make reference to an anthropology of language and to suggest, following Mauss, that the universals of language imply the existence of unconscious symbolic structures.[34] The implications of the extension of the debate into the anthropological field and the question of the precise weight to be given to 'unconscious' in this context are best reserved for an exploration of Lacan's relations with Lévi-Strauss, who will soon replace Mauss and Malinowski as his primary source. For the moment, it is sufficient to note the absence of any reference to Saussurean linguistics.

It is in fact only in retrospect that the absence of Saussure from these early *écrits* is surprising. As Mounin remarks, ignorance of Saussure in this period is no great epistemological crime.[35] The linguist had yet to enter the intellectual public domain, and even within more specialist circles his reputation rests on his work on philology rather than on the theory of sign, signifier and signified which is so central to the structuralism of the post-war years. For the dean of the Faculté de Lettres de Paris, writing in 1936, Saussure's contribution to the understanding of sound laws is invaluable, but he is not, as he will become, the founder of modern linguistics.[36] Eleven years later, the linguist R.L. Wagner argues that Saussure's great innovation is the synchrony–diachrony distinction, not the theory of the sign.[37] There is certainly no article in the pre-war RFP which indicates any great knowledge of the *Cours de linguistique générale*, and even in 1950 psychoanalytic discussions of language in France are far more likely to refer to Damourette and Pichon and to Piaget's developmental theories than to Saussure.[38] Pichon, by far the most sophisticated linguist in the early SPP, rejects the thesis that the sign is arbitrary, and Raymond de Saussure, son of Ferdinand, appears to have had no inkling of the importance of his father's work.

According to Roudinesco, Lacan began to read Saussure in about 1946, but whilst this seems probable, there is no direct textual evidence to support the suggestion.[39] The first specific references to Jakobson and structural linguistics – but not to Saussure – appear in 1950, during Lacan's stormy intervention at the International Congress on Psychiatry and Psychoanalysis. In an attack on Raymond de Saussure's attempts to combine Piaget and Freud and on his promotion of the old notion of a 'prelogical mentality', Lacan raises the banner of linguistics – as exemplified by Jakobson's work on phonemes – and of anthropology – as personified by Lévi-Strauss. He argues that the significations contained in language mobilize images which determine both the conduct and the organic functions of the subject, that language does more to explain psychology than psychology can do to explain language, and that slips of the tongue and puns are specifically linguistic phenomena. The intervention is relatively brief, but it begins to introduce characteristic themes, not least in that it rapidly becomes an attack on the account of ego psychology given by Franz Alexander, at the time the President of the American Psychiatric Association. It does not, however, ascribe any particular importance to Saussure.[40]

The terms 'signifier' and 'signified' occur sporadically in the earliest recorded sessions of the Seminar and punctuate 'Fonction et champ' at fairly regular intervals, but it is only in 'La Chose freudienne' (1955) that Saussure becomes the 'founder of modern linguistics' and emerges as a major figure.[41] Before this Saussure tends to be subsumed into a much broader and more general discussion of language, and the supposed radical specificity of his theories is far from apparent. In the 1954 Seminar, for example, the mention of Saussure provokes a lengthy discussion of St Augustine, and in 'Fonction et champ' itself, *parole* is used in a sense which owes much more to a theological tradition than to Saussure's *langue/parole* distinction. And if, as it has often been suggested, 'Fonction et champ' is the manifesto of Lacanian psychoanalysis, it is to be noted that Heidegger has as great a hand in writing it as Saussure, although that may be more obvious if the original circumstances of its publication are taken into account than if only *Ecrits* is considered. When it appeared in the inaugural issue of *La Psychanalyse*, it was flanked by Lacan's translation of Heidegger's 'Logos' and by articles by two seminar members in which a use of Heideggerean etymologies is all too evident. In this context, Benveniste's essay on Freud and language begins to resemble a minority report from an outnumbered and embattled structuralist camp.[42]

The incorporation of Saussure into Lacan's theoretical discourse is, then, surprisingly slow and hesitant. The linguist's importance has already been established for philosophy by Merleau-Ponty, albeit via a somewhat idiosyncratic reading of the *Cours*,[43] and for anthropology by Lévi-Strauss, who begins to apply a linguistic model to the analysis of kinship systems in 1945.[44] To that extent Lacan does not innovate but follows a general shift within the human sciences, bringing psychoanalysis into advances already made elsewhere. At this stage in his career, the psychoanalyst does not authorize himself; he is authorized by other discourses and other agencies.

The invocation of Saussure becomes, moveover, the occasion for a number of significant displacements. In the 1954 Seminar, Lacan links Saussure with the classically structuralist theory of the differential nature of signification and of the oppositional nature of phonemes. His remarks prompt Louis Beirnaert, a Jesuit Father and a teacher of dogmatic theology, to comment that everything he has said can be found in the first section of Augustine's *De Magistrato*: the *Disputatio de locutionis significatione*.[45] Lacan immediately concurs and a discussion of the *Disputa-*

tio ensues, the general conclusion being that it has taken linguists fifteen centuries to rediscover the theses elaborated and expounded by Augustine. The exchange is remarkable not only in that it represents one of the very few instances of the Seminar turning into a dialogue rather than a monologue from Lacan, but because of its implications. The 'rediscovery' theme implies a very different vision of the history of the sciences to that which prevails in 'Instance de la lettre', where Lacan argues that the reclassification of the sciences around linguistics signified a 'revolution in knowledge'; or in 'Radiophonie', where he writes: 'Saussure and the Prague Circle produce a linguistics which has *nothing in common* with what previously went by that name, even if the key to it is to be found in the hands of the Stoics.'[46] Lacan frequently alludes to a history made up of breaks and ruptures, but this is a cyclical history of recurrence and repression analogous to the history which sees La Rochefoucauld as a precursor of Freud. Saussure becomes the heir to a lost tradition rather than the author of the 'algorithm' which founds the science of modern linguistics. The point is not that Beirnaert and Lacan are simply in error – indeed, this is a fairly standard argument and the claims put forward for Augustine here can also be made on behalf of Plato – but that this discussion is at variance with Lacan's usual history of the sciences. It is also significant that his first reaction on encountering Saussure is to allow discussion to veer off into historical and theological considerations. His second, and more decisive, reaction is to emend and correct Saussure.

In November 1955, Lacan tells his audience at the Neuro-Psychiatric Clinic in Vienna to read Saussure ('If you want to know more, read Saussure'), and then expounds his own reading of the *Cours* in a remarkably dense account of the signifier–signified distinction.[47] The need for such an exposition strongly suggests that Saussure is still not a familiar reference for a psychoanalytic public, but if Lacan's audience did follow his advice and did turn to the text of the *Cours*, they must have been startled to find that much of the discussion concerns the diachronic aspect of language, that the central unit of Saussure's general linguistics is the sign and that the *langue/parole* opposition is crucial. None of this is apparent from Lacan's account. He is concerned with a distinction between *langage* and *parole* – a distinction which has no Saussurean ancestry – and he describes language as consisting of two networks which never overlap. The first is that of the signifier, a synchronic structure in which each element is defined purely in terms of the difference between it and every other element; whilst the model is supplied by the binary opposition between phonemes, it is at least implied that a similar opposition pertains at every level of language. The second network is that of the signified, a diachronic set of discourses which reacts historically upon the first network and in which the 'unit of signification' is dominant. Signification is never a matter of reference to the real; each signification refers only to another signification. It is the signifier alone which guarantees the unity of the whole. The unity of Saussure's sign, a compound of signifier and signified, has been decisively broken.

Nor is this the only modification introduced by Lacan. For Saussure, diachrony refers to the historical dimension in which *langue* develops and changes; for Lacan it is a temporal dimension internal to a 'unit of signification' which remains alarmingly ill-defined.[48] At this point, Saussure effectively vanishes from Lacan's paper as it moves into a violent attack on ego psychology and then into an account of the role of speech [*parole*] in psychoanalysis. As in 'Fonction et champ', this *parole* has little to do with Saussure and a great deal to do with the gift relationship analysed by anthropology. The meaning of key concepts such as 'sign', '*langue*', diachrony and '*parole*' have all been modified considerably, and largely without direct reference to the original.

Lacan also emends the interpretation of the schema which Saussure uses to represent the division of *langue* into a plane of 'confused ideas' (A) and a plane of 'sounds' (B):[49]

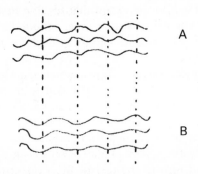

In the Seminar, Lacan reinterprets this as a distinction between 'signification' and 'discourse' or 'what we hear', even though that is a distinctly odd definition of discourse. He insists, moreover, that the schema implies the existence of a diachronic element in which there occurs a sliding of the signifier, adding later that 'the signifier is there as a pure chain of discourse, a succession of words in which nothing can be isolated.'[50] The same schema is discussed in 'Instance de la lettre', where it is said to run counter to all our experience; it must be supplemented by Lacan's own theory of the *point de capiton* (literally an upholstery stud) which represents the mythical point where the sliding of the signifier comes to an end. Whereas Saussure subordinates signifier and signified to a prior division of the sign into 'sound' and 'thought' elements, but insists on their co-presence, Lacan asserts the primacy and independence of the signifier.[51]

Before going on to examine the implications of the theory of the *point de capiton*, it may be appropriate to examine certain of the most effects of the 'primacy of the signifier'. The most obvious effect is to signal, albeit unintentionally, a move away from any concrete linguistic analysis. At a conceptual level, the signifier–signified distinction is of vital importance in that it breaks down the naturalist thesis that there is a spontaneous correspondence between language and other realms of reality, and makes it impossible to maintain that language is a nomenclature. It is, however, quite impossible to analyse even a simple sentence by means of the concept of the signifier alone. In a totally banal sentence such as 'The cat sat on the mat', /the/, /cat/, /sat/, /on/, /the/ and /mat/ are all signifiers; unless their grammatical, syntactic and semantic functions are taken into account, analysis cannot proceed beyond the truism that a sentence consists of signifiers. That this is a problem for Lacanian analysis will emerge from a discussion of the examples Lacan chooses to illustrate his theory of metaphor, where it will become apparent that references to the 'sliding of the signifier' have little more precision or scientificity than references to the 'drift of meaning' would have.

At a rather more general level, Lacan's departure from Saussurean orthodoxy results in what Anderson nicely terms a 'gradual megalomania of the signifier'.[52] 'Signifier' comes to be deployed in so many ways that it eventually becomes void of any conceptual relevance, as in Sollers's observation that 'the religious signifier' is obsessional whilst the 'philosophical signifier' is paranoid.[53] The observation may be valid at the level of religious and philosophical discourse but surely not at that of individual signifiers, assuming of course that a unit such as 'a religious signifier' actually exists. Whilst it is undeniable that Sollers has an almost unrivalled talent for accumulating and generating clichés, and that this is beyond Lacan's control, it is also true that Lacan cannot be totally absolved of responsibility for such pronouncements. The inflationary promotion of 'the signifier' leads inevitably to its conceptual devaluation. It can also lead to palpable absurdity. At an EFP day school held in November 1975, one G. Hadad argued that 'labour is structured like a language' and that all the features of language can be found in it. Assembly-line work is therefore metonymic because it involves the displacement of a signifier and because the workers' activity becomes meaningful only at the end of the line.[54]

Saussure's modest schema is, for Lacan, reminiscent of 'the wavy lines of the upper and lower Waters in miniatures from manuscripts of Genesis'.[55] The association is intriguing, if only in that it introduces a biblical note which never appears in Saussure and in that it is consonant with the theological connotations which are so often present in Lacan's use of *parole*, whilst the reference to Genesis begins to hint at a search for origins which is quite alien to most of modern linguistics. A brief discussion of the same schema in the Seminar on the psychoses leads immediately into an exploration of Racine's *Athalie* (1691), a tragedy dominated, as Lacan notes, by the fear of God.[56] But what begins as an illustration of the role of the signifier rapidly becomes a hunt for privileged key signifiers, all of which relate to the structure of the Oedipus complex on the grounds that the fear of God is very close to the notion of the oedipal father. A discussion of Saussure leads, seemingly ineluctably, to a primal oedipal level. In the course of this displacement of the discussion, 'signifier' comes to acquire a bundle of poetic, theological and metapsychological connotations which remove it further and further away from the orbit of Saussure's discourse and inscribe it in a very different theoretical construct.

Lacan frequently refers to the 'privileged signifier' – the fear of God which permeates *Athalie* being one instance of its workings – as a *point de capiton* (an 'anchoring point' in Sheridan's translation). The best-known definition of its function is that given in 'Subversion du sujet': it is the anchoring point 'by which the signifier stops the otherwise endless movement of signification'.[57] In diachronic terms – and for Lacan diachrony is a dimension internal to the unit of signification – its function can be seen in the organization of a sentence; each term is anticipated in the linear construction of the sentence, and at the same time it seals their meaning by its retroactive effect. Only when the sentence has been completed does its signification emerge. The diachronic function of the *point de capiton* is, then, to put a halt to the otherwise endless process whereby signifier refers to signifier. Its synchronic function is said to be 'more hidden'. Lacan adds that it takes us to the 'source' [*origine*]:

> It is metaphor in so far as the first attribution is constituted in it – the attribution that promulgates 'The dog goes miaow, the cat goes woof-woof', by which the child, by disconnecting the animal from its cry, suddenly raises the sign to the function of signifier, and reality to the sophistics of signification.[58]

Whether or not this is a true metaphor by any standard other than that of Lacan's own definition ('one word for another') must be open to doubt, particularly as the game in question relies upon a systematic and indeed stereotypical distortion which has little to do with the defiance of usage implicit in most effective metaphors.[59] More importantly, the move from the diachronic to the synchronic function of the *point de capiton* involves a somewhat treacherous shift of level. Its diachronic function is observable in an identifiable lexical-grammatical unit (the sentence), but the same cannot be said of its synchronic function. On the contrary, it is not located in any identifiable unit, whilst the reference to 'origins' implies the existence of a primal level and the allusion to metaphor seems to hint at the old theory that all language originates in that figure of speech. Elsewhere, Lacan gives a rather different definition in which the lexical element disappears altogether: here, the *point de capiton* is the element which pins a chain of signifiers to a chain of signifieds, but it is mythical in that no one has ever been able to pin a signification to a signifier without entering into the endless stream of signification itself.[60] Both these definitions, difficult as they may be to reconcile, relate to a universalist concept of language, but in the Seminar on the psychoses, this is not exactly the case. There, the reference is to a minimal number of *points* attaching signifier to signified, 'minimal' being the criterion which will determine whether an individual is or is not psychotic: if the two registers are attached at too few points, psychosis will ensue.[61] Precisely how the universalist and the psychopathological points of view are to be articulated is not explained.

More generally, the *point de capiton* is a point of convergence. Just as an upholstery stud is the centre for the converging lines or creases on the surface of a taut fabric, so the linguistic *point de capiton* provides a vantage point from which everything that happens in a given discourse can be situated both retroactively and prospectively. The example given in the Seminar is the fear of God which dominates *Athalie*, but it might be noted that traditional literary criticism can easily identify this as a theme without any assistance from Lacan. It is, however, rather more important to note that, far from being a supplement to Saussure or a mere solution to the difficulties inherent in Lacan's theory of the sliding of the signifier, the *point de capiton* is a device which allows Lacan to move from positive linguistics to primal levels of language, from signifier to symbol. A similar displacement can be observed in 'Instance de la lettre', the site of the most startling of all Lacan's emendations of Saussure.

In 'Instance', Lacan describes the emergence of the discipline of linguistics as being signalled by the algorithm which founds it:

$$\frac{S}{s}$$

The capital 'S' in this formulation represents the signifier, whilst the italicized lower-case *s* represents the signified.[62] The line between the two does not indicate proportionality. It is a bar [*barre*] which is resis-

tant to signification and which causes the signifier to slide over the signified; aficionados of word games will note that *barre* is an anagram of the
arbre (tree) which figures in Saussure's classic image of the signifier–
signified relation. The reformulation gives primacy to the signifier, and
again indicates a veering away from the original theory of the sign.
Lacan himself noted that the algorithm does not in fact appear in the
Cours, but insists that Saussure should still be given credit for it. The use
of the term 'algorithm' is of course a gesture towards the mathematization which Lacan so often describes as an integral feature of any move
towards a greater scientificity, but it is a singularly unfortunate gesture in
that this is not in fact an algorithm or a rule for solving a problem in a
finite number of stages, but merely a fairly arbitrary, if convenient,
notation.[63]

Having introduced his purported algorithm, Lacan immediately
makes a new and yet more radical innovation. Saussure's 'classic yet
faulty' image

Tree
———

is replaced by Lacan's

Ladies   Gentlemen

According to Lacan, the doubling of the noun through the juxtaposition
of the terms 'Ladies' and 'Gentlemen' results in an

> unexpected precipitation of an unexpected meaning: the image of twin doors
> symbolizing, through the solitary confinement [*l'isoloir*] offered Western man
> for the satisfaction of his natural needs away from home, the imperative that
> he seems to share with the great majority of primitive communities by which
> his public life is subjected to the laws of urinary segregation.[64]

There follows the well-known fable, its humour now somewhat dimmed by repetition, of the two children arriving at a station by train. The boy immediately remarks that they have arrived at 'Ladies', only to be told by his sister that they are at 'Gentlemen'. The railway lines 'materialize' the bar in the algorithm, but that does not exhaust the fable's potential, as 'only someone who didn't have his eyes in front of the holes ... could possibly confuse the place of the signifier and the signifed in this story.'

Lacan's illustrative fable could scarcely be less arbitrary or more motivated. What began as a discussion of the sign, by definition arbitrary for Saussure, becomes a foray into the most motivated area of all: that of symbols of sexual difference. Tellingly, the twin doors do not *signify*; they *symbolize*. Saussure's humble tree is replaced by a binary pair of symbols governed ultimately by the phallus (the role of the phallus as primal symbol is discussed in the next chapter). Indeed, the setting of the fable is rife with psychoanalytic 'symbolism' in the most banal of senses. A train enters a station. In the Dora case, Freud comments on his patient's use of 'station' to represent the female genitals and explains in a footnote that 'A "station" is used for the purpose of *Verkher* ["traffic", "intercourse", "sexual intercourse"].'[65] Nor are trains neutral or arbitrary signifiers in analytic law. Lacan himself criticizes Melanie Klein for her rather heavy-handed interpretation of train and station symbols in the Little Dick case, and her ready identification of 'train' with 'penis'; he does not contest the identification, merely the manner of its introduction.[66] No psychoanalyst can spin tales involving trains and stations with impunity. There is nothing unexpected about the meaning precipitated here.

The claim that 'no signification can be sustained other than by reference to another signification'[67] reads like a classic extrapolation from the Saussurean thesis that language consists of differences, or like an example of Lacan's own views on the play of the signifier, but it immediately gives way to a scenario in which symbols of sexual difference are legislated by a 'law of urinary segregation' which can only be a clumsy euphemism for the prohibition of incest. The fable is a primal myth, a discursive equivalent to the primal scene. It is also clumsy at the most empirical of levels; as many a tourist has found to his or her consternation, the law of urinary segregation is much less strictly enforced in France than in the English-speaking world. More conventional criticisms of the 'Ladies and Gentlemen' schema can be made from within linguistics itself. As Descombes notes, the 'signifiers' in question are in the plural, and that usage is governed by grammatical rules, in other words by laws which apply at a level higher than that of the signifier. Moreover, 'Ladies' does not signify an acoustic concept, but the statement 'This door is exclusively for ladies'. Such a statement is composed of signifiers; it is not itself a signifier in any Saussurean sense.[68]

The celebrated reading of Poe's 'Purloined Letter' involves a similar set of shifts and departures from Saussurean linguistics, though that may be more obvious from the original Seminar version than from the text included in *Ecrits*. For Lacan, the tale illustrates the 'major determination the subject receives from the trajectory of a signifier',[69] the 'signifier' in question being the stolen missive. In technical terms the missive is not a signifier, but a fragment of discourse made up of more complex units (clauses, sentences ...). It is only in metaphoric terms that it can be designated a signifier. Even in the terms deployed by Lacan, it rapidly becomes apparent that it is a symbol of the pact between the king and the queen, of the pact which unites man and woman, which has an essential value for society as a whole and which is the traditional mediator between the natural cosmos and the social order.[70] Elsewhere – and notably in 'Fonction et champ' – this will be the role of the primal or founding *parole*. Here the drift away from the Saussurean signifier is quite obvious, but it is also eminently clear that Lacan's discourse has none of the terminological and conceptual coherence which he himself associates with scientificity. Again and again the level of the debate is displaced from signifier to symbol, from differences to difference. Lacan occasionally notes that Freud's *Enstellung* can be translated as both 'displacement' and 'distortion'. It is apparent that he subjects Saussure's signifier to both these vicissitudes. This is *linguisterie* writ large.

Lacan parts company with Saussure in the matter of the signifier, but nowhere is the radical difference between the linguist and the psychoanlyst more obvious than in the realm of etymology. Saussure's familiarity with and contribution to philology is indelibly stamped on the text of the *Cours*, and so is a knowledge of etymology, but he is careful to make a crucial distinction between diachronic and synchronic linguistics, insisting that whilst diachronic facts have their own *raison d'être*, the specific synchronic consequences to which they give rise are quite alien to them.[71] The diachronic fact that the negative adverb *pas* and the noun *pas* (footstep) derive from the same source has no effect upon their respective positions and functions in the synchronic operation of modern French.[72] To confuse diachrony and synchrony is to go against the whole dynamic of the *Cours*. As Benveniste notes, the revolutionary nature of structuralism lies in its privileging of the synchronic set: elements of a given language are studied in relation to that set, and not in relation to earlier states which are assumed to be 'causes'.[73] Whilst Lacan does endorse this orthodoxy he also departs from it at a number of significant points, abandoning structural linguistics in favour of what he calls 'etymological soundings' and claiming that the promotion of etymology conforms to Freud's belief that the in-depth study of language is the best way to rediscover the accumulated experience of tradition.[74]

Lacan puts etymology to a variety of uses. It can introduce a judicious note of emphasis, as in the use of *in-fans* ('without speech') to stress that the human infant has yet to accede to speech and language. It can be exploited as a rhetorical device, as when Lacan prefaces 'Fonction et champ' with an allusion to Aulus Gellus's rather dubious derivation of Mons Vaticanus from *vagire* to further his claim that even if his speech proves to have been no more than a *vagitus*, it was at least delivered in the right place and at an auspicious moment.[75] This, surely, is no more than an instance of *captatio benevolentiae* – the deployment of a conceit or flourish designed to capture and hold the attention of the audience – but it is also a reminder that classical rhetoric often exploits etymology in a distinctly wild manner. Not all Lacan's etymological flourishes are so innocent. In *Encore*, he suggests that female *jouissance* relates to the fact that there is something which simultaneously shakes [*secouer*] and succours [*secourir*], explaining that a glance at Bloch and Von Wartburg's etymological dictionary will explain the connection.[76] His self-confessed delight in that work is most certainly legitimate, and when he remarks that most of his audience probably do not have a copy he is probably right, but by postulating a causal and semantic connection at a synchronic level and then explaining it in diachronic terms, Lacan is using etymology in precisely the sense denounced by Saussure when he takes the example of *pas*. His memory of the text is also, as it happens, faulty: Bloch and Von Wartburg derive *secourir* from the Latin *succurrere* and *secouer* from *succutere*, and add that the rare forms in which a connection is established between them are based upon false analogies. Lacan's 'something' appears to enter into that category.

A more spectacular example of the same strategy occurs in 'Instance de la lettre', often considered the *locus classicus* of Lacanian linguistics. As he introduces the metaphor/metonymy duality, Lacan remarks that it is from *trope* that the verb *trouver* [to find] comes to us.[77] There is, he suggests, a causal connection between the two. Later in the same paper, he describes Freud's condensation [*Verdichtung*] as 'the structure of the superimposition of the signifiers, which metaphor takes as its field, and whose name, condensing in itself the word *Dichtung*, shows how the mechanism is connatural to poetry.'[78] Condensation and metaphor are poetic, that is, because of the etymological connection between *Verdichtung* and *Dichtung* [poetry]. In terms of the *trope/trouver* doublet, Lacan appears to be correct: *trouver* can be dervied from the Vulgar Latin **tropare* (the asterix indicates a reconstructed form for which there is no supporting textual evidence), which can in its turn be traced back to the Classical Latin *tropus* and the Greek *tropos*. But, as both

Saussure and Benveniste would doubtless observe, that tells us nothing
about the respective meanings or roles of the two signifiers in modern
French.

With *Dichtung/Verdichtung*, Lacan is on shaky ground. Lyotard
points out that there is no etymological link between the two words:
Verdichtung can be traced back to *dihan* [to prosper], but *Dichtung*
derives from the Latin *dictare* [to say often; to cause to be written
down]. Lyotard prefaces his remarks with an apologetic reference to
their pedantry, but his manners are, perhaps, over-polite.[79] Lacan
demands that we read literally [*à la lettre*], and here it is the letter of the
text which betrays him: a pun is being passed off as a philological
argument because of its proximity to a conceit based upon true etymologies.

Other examples of reliance upon spurious etymologies are not difficult to find. In the Seminar on *Hamlet*, Lacan gently mocks those who
transform 'Ophelia' into '*O phallos*' in order to establish a link with
Fenichel's equation between 'girl' and 'phallus'; a phonetic similarity is
mistaken for a proven etymology.[80] Yet his own description of the
process of *séparation* in 'Position de l'inconscient' involves extensive use
of similar devices and conceits. The identification of Freud's *Ichspaltung*
or splitting of the ego is in fact problematic at a metapsychological
level,[81] but for the moment Lacan's exploitation of supposed etymologies is of greater relevance. *Séparer*, like the English 'separate', derives
from the Latin *separare*, but by segmenting it Lacan relates that verb to
se parere, meaning 'to engender oneself' or 'to give birth to oneself'; an
initial syllable becomes a reflexive pronoun by fiat, and the shift from
/a/ to /e/ appears arbitrary. *Parere* can also mean 'to procure' and so,
in order to procure himself an *état civil*, the subject must sacrifice or
separate himself from part of his interests or his being. By becoming part
[*pars*] of the symbolic, the subject loses part of himself by being
castrated, but he also procures himself a new status. *Separare* can then
be transformed into *se parere*, meaning 'to deck oneself out', indicating
that the subject acquires a signifier. In this passage Lacan ostentatiously
rejects the services of Latin etymologists, but at the end same time he
notes that all the verbs he is discussing are interrelated in that they
pertain to the function of the *pars*. He describes his exploration of the
etymologies involved as 'sliding from verb to verb', a term normally
reserved for the synchronic dimension.[82] Once again, supposed etymologies mask a proliferation of puns.

There is something compulsive or obsessional about Lacan's use of
etymology. The effect, as in the *separare* example, is to introduce a
plethora of overdetermined 'meanings' and to negate the thesis that
signifiers are determined synchronically and differentially. The alleged

functions of *trope* and *Verdichtung* bear within them their entire history and the signifiers are forced to recount their supposed origins. Proofs are piled up and accumulated as though to forestall any possible objection to the theses being advanced. Witness the explanation as to why the phallus is chosen as the signifier of desire in 'La Signification du phallus': because it is the most tangible element in the real or sexual copulation, and also 'the most symbolic in the literal (typographical) sense of the term, since it is equivalent there to the (logical) copula.'[83] Proofs real, symbolic, literal, logical and even typographical are accumulated, and are implicitly supported or authorized by the etymology of 'copulation'.

As Forrester remarks, at such points one cannot but be reminded of Bopp's attempts to demonstrate that all verbs in the Indo–European family of languages derive from the 'original' copula '-*s*'. He adds that Lacan's argument would have appealed to Freud's 'etymologizing tendency'.[84] It would, that is, have appealed to the Freud who surrendered to the dubious charms of Abel's *Uber den Gegensinn der Urworte*, a treatise on philology published in Leipzig in 1884 which would surely have been long forgotten were it not for Freud, who reviewed it favourably in 1910.[85] Philology is one of Freud's abiding interests, and he frequently refers to it in his writings on symbolism.[86] Abel provides him with new material for speculation and he is clearly impressed by the essay. A note added to the third (1911) edition of *The Interpretation of Dreams* explains its fascination – Abel's findings reveal that dreams and the most ancient languages behave in precisely the same way as those languages 'have only a single word to describe the two contraries at the extreme end of a series of qualities or activities (e.g. 'strong–weak', 'old–young', far–near', 'bind–sever').'[87] The same evidence is produced in the *Introductory Lectures* to show that the 'archaic' features of the dream-work (reversal of meaning, replacement of something by its opposite, absence of negation) 'are equally characteristic of ancient systems of expressions by speech and writing.'[88]

Unfortunately for Freud, the data supplied by Abel are quite extraordinarily inaccurate, and his speculations are not acceptable to any serious linguist. They are demolished with both elegance and eloquence by Benveniste, who demonstrates that Abel's claims are based upon random associations between individual words and not upon the bedrock of philology: the study of languages on the basis of regular correspondences attested to by recorded usage. They are also based upon faulty derivations: the Old English *bat* [good, better] is simply not related to *badde* [bad]; 'to cleave' derives from the German *klieben* [to sever] and not from *kleben* [to bind], and so on. The discovery of an antithetical meaning in 'without' requires the prior and arbitrary segmentation of the word into the elements 'with' and 'out' in defiance of the elementary procedures of historical linguistics.[89]

Freud's attempt to recruit Abel into his service is as unhappy as his own attempt to relate the German noun *Mutter* to Mut, the vulture-headed goddess of Ancient Egypt.[90] As the *Dichtung/Verdichtung* example indicates, Lacan too can rely upon random associations to make connections which purport to be etymological inferences. He also expresses doubts as to the cogency of Benveniste's critique of Abel, suggesting in darkly enigmatic terms that it leaves intact the question of antithetical meanings and hinting that those meanings relate to the agency or instance of the signifier.[91] Lacan's extravagant claim, in 'Radiophonie', that he was the first to pick up Freud's interest in words with antithetical meanings suggests more than a passing interest in the philological equivalent to *linguisterie*.[92]

Freud and the ghost of Abel are not the only characters in the play of etymologies staged and directed by Lacan. He introduces a third when, during a discussion of repression and the return of the repressed, he insists that Heideggerean arguments have to be introduced and adds: 'Whenever a being enters the dwelling house of words, there is a margin of forgetfulness, a *lethe* which complements any *aletheia*.'[93] This suggestion depends for its coherence on the supposed etymological link between Lethe (the river which washes away memory) and *aletheia* (Heidegger's truth-as-uncovering). Whether or not there is any such connection is less important than the clear indication that there is a common core to the etymological or para-etymological arguments deployed by Lacan and Heidegger. The philosopher frequently fractures or segments words into supposedly significant elements, thereby anticipating and authorizing one of the more irritating mannerisms of Derrida and the deconstructionists, and there is a definite parallel there with Lacan's 'separation' conceit. At a much more abstract level, Heidegger regards etymology as a path leading to a point where language and ontology merge into one, and he frequently takes that path during his explorations of the being of language and the language of being; Lacan also takes it when he uses the neologism *le parlêtre*,[94] which condenses *parler* (to speak) and *être* (to be, or being) and plays on *par lettre* (by letter). This view pervades all Heidegger's work and the etymologies involved can be distinctly dubious, as in *Being and Time*, where a classical fable is pressed into service to further the claim that *homo* [man] derives from *humus* [earth] *because* man is made from earth.[95]

Heidegger explains his special predilection for Greek etymologies in *What is Philosophy?* The Greek language is the *logos* itself: 'In the Greek language what is said in it *is* at the same time in an excellent way what it is called. ... Through the audible Greek word we are directly in the presence of the thing itself, not first in the presence of a mere sign.'[96] The excavation of Greek roots reveals and uncovers a level of truth of being and language that is concealed by mere signs. The claim that prior or more archaic states reveal something that has been lost in current discourse is of course inherent in any etymological argument. Heidegger's claim goes far beyond that, insisting that there is a primordial or ontological level at which what Lacan would term resistance to signification ceases and the etymological archaeologist finds himself in the full presence of the thing itself. For Lacan, it is an indication of the importance Heidegger ascribes to the signifier.[97]

By no means all of Lacan's forays into etymology take place at this level, but his investigations into the origins and etymology of 'symbol' do involve the mobilization of a similar logic. In his introduction to Hyppolite's paper on the concept of *Verneinung*, Lacan speaks of a 'primal field of language' whose 'primordial image is the material of the tessera (in which we find the etymology of symbol)'.[98] That field is intersected by the dimension in which both non-being and reality arise; language and being coincide. The same argument pervades the whole of 'Fonction et champ', subtends the anthropological arguments deployed there, and inevitably comes into conflict with the orthodoxies of structural linguistics, if only because the stress placed on primal fields and origins is at variance with its foregrounding of the relational and the synchronic. It is also present in the early displacement of Saussure by Augustine. Lacan proposes that the Latin *nomen* should be translated as 'symbol': 'The *nomen* is the signifier–signified totality, especially in so far as it serves the purpose of recognition, since it is on that basis that the pact and the accord are established. It is a symbol, in the sense of a pact.'[99]

The drift away from Saussure is obvious: for Saussure this 'totality' would be a sign, not a symbol. And the drift takes Lacan back towards the Kojève-Hegel philosopheme according to which language provides a medium for recognition and thus defuses aggression. Lacan then insists that *nomen* is cognate with *numen* because the two words are related by virtue of their primal form; the symbol can thus be linked to the existence and experience of the sacred. The authority for this claim comes from Victor Hugo's '*Nomen, Numen, Lumen*', a short poem from *Les Contemplations* which describes how Jehovah inscribed the letters that make up his name in the stars of Ursa Major.[100] As in the theory of the *point de capiton*, the logic of Lacan's argument moves away from any linguistic definition of language to a primal and ontological vision of language, but here it is supported by a quasi-Heideggerean exploitation of the supposed etymologies of individual words, and subtended by a theologico–poetic mythology.

'Fonction et champ' provides a further occasion for an excursion to this primal level. In one of its denser passages, Lacan proclaims that *Nul n'est censé ignorer la loi* (the first words of the French penal code, which announce that ignorance of the law is no defence) and immediately identifies the law of man with the law of language. The two have been synonymous ever 'since the first words of recognition presided over the first gifts', the gifts in question being those exchanged by the 'Pacific Argonauts' when they united their island communities into a symbolic network of exchange. Lacan is, however, rather less interested in the anthropology of Melanesia than in the origins of symbolism and law. He continues: 'These gifts are already symbols in the sense that symbol means pact and that they are first and foremost signifiers of the pact that they constitute as signified.'[101] For a linguist, the slide from symbol to signifier and the unspecified use of 'means' must be a cause for some terminological alarm. But Lacan's argument does not brook terminological or conceptual queries: symbol means pact or recognition in the sense that it dervies from *sumbolon*, the Greek term for the tessera, the broken piece of pottery used as a token in mystery religions; initiates recognized one another by piecing together the fragments.[102] Lacan is using 'derivation from' as a criterion to determine meaning and to ident-ify a primal field in which the sliding of the signifier comes to a halt: his *sumbolon* is both signifier and signified, both the pact it institutes and the mode of its institution. And that primal field, it is implied, continues to exist and to inform any symbolic exchange.

The language-as-pact theme appears at its most basic in the repeated references to such statements as 'You are my husband' or 'You are my wife', which begin to appear in the early sessions of the Seminar and gradually become more elaborate.[103] For Lacan, the 'meaning' of these statements is 'I am your wife' or 'I am your husband'; in other words the subject is implicated in an inverted mode of communication. In a more elaborate discussion of this structure, he writes:

Speech [*parole*] manifests itself as a communication in which the subject not only proffers his message in an inverted form in the expectation that the other will render it true; the message transforms him, as can be seen in any declar-ation of faith, where the declarations 'You are my wife' or 'You are my master' signify 'I am your husband', 'I am your disciple'.[104]

This form of communication necessarily opens up the possibility of deceit: speech [*parole*] is a gift of faith [*fides*], but its obverse is a feint [*feinte*].[105] The subject's statement therefore implies the possibility of a feint, but that in itself implies the possibility of discovering the truth in an inverted form; the initial pact can then be mapped on to the famous

joke recounted by Freud: 'If you say you're going to Cracow, you want
me to believe you're going to Lemburg. But I know you're going to
Cracow. So why are you lying to me?'[106] Ultimately, this variation on the
pact theme provides the structure in which: 'The Other is ... the locus in
which is constituted the I who speaks to him who hears, that which is
said by the one being already the reply, the other deciding to hear it
whether the one has or has not spoken.'[107] In philosophical terms the
structure maps on to the recognition theme in Kojève's reading of
Hegel, but certain of its implications are perhaps indicative of something
else. If pronounced in the appropriate ritual context, Lacan's 'You are
my wife' is close to being what Austin terms a performative, and marriage vows are in fact one of the examples he gives: 'When I say "I do"
(sc. take this woman to be my lawful wedded wife), I am not reporting
on a marriage, I am indulging in it.'[108] Ignoring the issue of context,
Lacan at least implies that a performative pact is an essential aspect of
all communication and that it has a foundational import in that it
provides the basis for symbolism and law. Given that *parole* often
acquires theological connotations in Lacan, it is tempting to read the
underlying argument as a veiled reference to a performative uttered by
the divine *logos* itself.

As the full title of the 'Rome Discourse' of 1953 indicates, *parole* is one
pole of an opposition, the other being *langage*, but Lacan's *parole* is not
an equivalent to the Swiss linguist's 'individual act of will and understanding'.[109] Nor is *langage* as transparent a term as one might wish.
Parole in particular poses considerable translation problems because of its
semantic extension. The two translators of the *écrit* have opted for
different solutions to the problem, and it is a measure of the difficulty of
translating Lacan – and, *a fortiori*, of reading him in English without
reference to the original – that both their versions have received his *imprimatur*. On the whole, Wilden prefers 'Word' and normally capitalizes
it, whereas Sheridan usually renders *parole* as 'speech', except when
conditions of readability dictate otherwise. Both solutions have their
advantages and disadvantages, as the precise connotations of *parole* at
any given moment are a matter of contextuality rather than of conceptual or definitional logic. It is probably impossible to determine which
English version is preferable in the abstract, or without a sentence-by-
sentence exegesis of the text in its entirety, but certain general considerations can be advanced. In standard French, *parole* has a number of
senses and connotations that distinguish it from *mot*, which refers
primarily to the lexical unit but also to a particularly concise or witty
expression of thought, as in *bon mot* or *mot d'esprit*. *Parole* covers a
much broader field. It is commonly used in such syntagms as *donner sa*

parole (to give one's word) and *parole d'honneur* (on my word of honour), and thus lends itself well to Lacan's reflections on *fides*. In contexts such as *demander la parole* or *donner la parole*, it signifies requesting or conferring the right to speak in a debate or an assembly. Perhaps more important still, *la parole de Dieu* is the Word of God, and in that acceptation it is cognate with *verbe*.

Le verbe designates the grammatical category, but it also has all force of the Latin *verbum* (and for once etymological considerations are relevant in that they are overdetermined by theological tradition) and, behind it, of the Greek *logos*. In French, the Fourth Gospel begins *Au commencement était le verbe*, and it is *le verbe* that is made flesh and dwells among men. Finally, *le verbe* is also the poetic word *par excellence*, as in Rimbaud's *alchimie du verbe*. A further semantic charge is added by the Heideggerean strand in 'Fonction et champ' when a distinction is made between *parole pleine* and *parole vide* (full and empty speech); the terms correspond to Heidegger's *Rede* (talking, discourse) and *Gerede* (idle talk) respectively. Throughout 'Fonction et champ', Lacan's *parole* plays on all these registers and semantic fields; the implicit reference to Saussure is only one of the elements in play, and it is by no means the most important.

Langage, the other pole of the opposition of the title, has something in common with Saussure's concept of *langage* as total linguistic phenomenon,[110] but in so far as it is described as the system within which 'signs take on their value from their relations to one another in the lexical distribution of semantemes as in the flexional use of morphemes',[111] a parallel must be drawn with *langue*. The degree to which Lacan's cavalier use of linguistic terminology can be both confused and confusing may be gauged from the discrepancy between this description and that proposed in 'La Chose freudienne', where it is the signifier and not the sign which acquires value in this way.[112] Even within 'Fonction et champ' itself, *langage* and *langue* can be surrounded by a high degree of conceptual ambiguity, as when attention is drawn to the fact that 'what defines any element whatever of a language [*langue*] as belonging to language [*langage*] is that, for all the users of of this language [*langue*], this element is distinguished as such in the ensemble supposedly constituted of homologous elements.'[113] It is precisely these features which will later be ascribed to *langage*. If, as Lacan claims in 1950, the demand for internal coherence is the very motor force behind knowledge,[114] there must be serious doubts as to the direction in which he is moving as he enters the field of language and begins to discuss its function.

The final words of the title of the *écrit* introduce a further degree of ambiguity: 'in psychoanalysis'. The ambiguity is at its greatest on the *parole* axis. The explanations with which Freud gratifies the Rat Man are a 'symbolic gift of speech [*parole*] pregnant with a secret pact'.[115] *Parole* thus appears to be defined in terms specific to the analytic encounter, but it also has a much broader phenomenological function in that it is the medium within which man's desire can be satisfied by being recognized 'through the agreement of speech [*l'accord de la parole*] or through the struggle for prestige'.[116] *Parole* thus operates both at the level of the analytic dialogue, where it finds its manifestation in interpretation, and at the universal level of the struggle for pure prestige. It is overdetermined in both these usages by the primal or theological considerations outlined above, and they will facilitate the transition to and from a unversalist anthropology. It functions as a switch-word which allows a variety of theoretical fields to be articulated almost at will.

Within the analytic encounter, *langage* is not the vehicle for individual expression and its relations with *parole* are inimical. *Langage* is often described as a wall, as an obstacle to the emergence of *parole*. The subject becomes lost in its machinations, trapped in the labyrinthine system of a structure in which signifier refers to signifier – Lacan refers to it as a 'deafening buzzing', as noise.[117] It is therefore related to the category of empty speech [*parole vide*], in which 'the subject seems to be talking in vain about someone who, even if he were his spitting image, can never become one with the assumption of his desire.'[118] Here, the subject does not speak; he is spoken by language, trapped in the stereotypical pathological discourse whose stylistics have so long been of burning interest to Lacan. Within empty speech the subject is dispossessed, alienated and inauthentic. Empty speech belongs to the register of the imaginary, and it is an obstacle to positive transference in that it blocks the possibility of full speech [*parole pleine*].[119] The point is perhaps made more clearly in the Seminar than in 'Fonction et champ' itself. The advent of *parole pleine* is 'the advent of a word [*parole*] which aims at or forms the truth as it is established in mutual recognition' and which is enunciated 'at the level of recognition in so far as the Word established between subjects the pact that transforms men and establishes them as communicating subjects.'[120] If language and speech are the medium of psychoanalysis, the liberation of full speech is its objective: the symptom is the language from which this Word or speech must be delivered.[121] In rather more prosaic terms: 'The subject ... begins the analysis by talking about himself without talking to you, or by talking to you without talking about himself. When he can talk to you about himself, the analysis is over.'[122]

The *parole vide/parole pleine* opposition owes something to Heidegger's *Gerede/Rede* distinction. Heidegger insists that the latter category has no 'disparaging signification' in that 'terminologically, it signifies a positive phenomenon which constitutes the kind of Being of *Dasein*'s understanding and interpreting', but it is a mode of speaking which does not allow any real interpretation of Being and which cuts the subject off 'from its primary and primordially genuine relationships-of-being-towards the world, towards *Dasein* with, and towards its very Being-in'.[123] Discourse [*Rede*] alone can truly appropriate Being, and it necessarily implies a relationship with the other: 'Discoursing or talking is the way in which we articulate "significantly" the intelligibility of Being-in-the-World, which in every case maintains itself in some definite way with concernful Being-with-one-another.'[124] Lacan's Word-as-pact can thus be translated into phenomenological terms as a discursive mode which permits recognition of the other and Being-with by re-enacting the establishment of a primordial pact. The dialogic structure of both the pact and the analytic encounter presupposes and establishes an intersubjectivity, even if its presence is signalled by the silence of one of the parties involved. As Heidegger notes, keeping silent is 'an essential possibility of discourse' and reticence can make things manifest and do away with 'idle talk'.[125] Or as Lacan remarks: 'Even if it communicates nothing ... discourse represents the existence of communication; even if it denies the evidence, it affirms that speech constitute truth; even if it is intended to deceive ... discourse speculates on faith in testimony.'[126]

A very similar formulation occurs in the 1951 paper on transference, where 'what happens in analysis' is described as the constitution of a subject 'through a discourse to which the presence of the psychoanalyst brings, before any intervention, the dimension of dialogue'.[127] The subsequent discussion of transference and countertransference, and the reference to the 'Hegelian analysis of the protests of the "beautiful soul"',[128] make it abundantly clear that the structures involved do not depend for their coherence on any incorporation of linguistics as such into Lacan's discourse. Nor do they owe any fundamental debt to Heidegger. Their genealogy can be traced back to the period in which Lacan outlined a reference to language but not to linguistics, to the period dominated by the Kojève-Hegel philosopheme. That the *Rede/Gerede* distinction invoked in 'Fonction et champ' is not a structural element can be seen from its gradual disappearance from later *écrits*; speech [parole] remains a constant, and there are frequent references to a *parole vraie* or true speech which is adequate to its object,[129] but it is no longer part of a bipolar opposition. No use is made of that opposition is either the discussion of Schreber or in 'Subversion du sujet'; in 'La Direction de la cure', only the *parole pleine* dimension is discussed.[130] Perrier suggests that the phenomenological tone of certain of the *écrits* may be no more than a reminder of the period when 'Lacan was reading

Heidegger'.[131] It may, that is, be little more than a monument to a philosophical flirtation which was never consummated, but it did have its practical implications: at least one young psychotherapist who read Lacan in the 1950s saw the work of the SFP as an attempt to promote the analysand's understanding of his existential situation and to facilitate his search for his Being-in-the-World.[132]

Parole is, it was suggested above, the switch-word which facilitates the transition between various theoretical domains or fields. Together with the related notions of 'pact' and 'symbol', it paves the way for the sudden and dramatic incorporation of Lévi-Strauss into the *dramatis personae* of 'Fonction et champ', where an allusion to the Sironga proverb which is epigraph to *The Elementary Structures of Kinship* leads immediately into a restatement of the anthropologist's basic theses: marriage is governed by a preferential order of kinship which, like language, is imperative for the group, but unconscious in its structures: 'The primordial law is therefore that which in regulating alliance superimposes the kingdom of culture on that of a Nature abandoned to the law of mating.'[133] In this perspective the rules governing alliance regulate the exchange of women, thereby instituting the prohibition of incest and institutionalizing the subjective pivot of the Culture–Nature divide, the element which wards off the biblical threat: the abomination of the confusion of generations. The Law which governs this whole structure is identical with the law of language. It is of course on this basis that Lacan elaborates his theory of the symbolic, the dimension of culture into which the child must be introduced through the acquisition of language and through the renunciation of incestuous desires for union with its mother. But the very rapidity with which Lévi-Strauss is introduced and the ease with which *The Interpretation of Dreams* is recast in Lévi-Straussean terms implies that the relationship between the anthropologist and the founder of psychoanalysis is quite unproblematic. A brief examination of Lévi-Strauss suggests that this is not the case and, by implication, that Lacan's own notion of the unconscious may not be pristinely Freudian.

In the autobiographical *Tristes Tropiques*, in many ways the most attractive of his works, Lévi-Strauss describes Marxism, psychoanalysis and geology as having been the 'mistresses' of his youth, the discreet charm of all three being that, in their various ways, they taught him that understanding always means reducing one level of reality to another and that reality is never manifest.[134] All three provided him with a means to criticize existentialism and phenomenology for their assumption that there is a continuity between the real and the lived. Existentialism in particular is savaged because it is a 'sort of shop-girl metaphysics' which elevates personal preoccupations to the dignity of philosophical

problems, a judgement which it is quite impossible to contemplate
without a bitter smile in an era of feminism and of the insistence that
'the personal is political'. As in most autobiographical writing, there is
obviously a retrospective element at work here; whilst phenomenology
did begin to seep through France's theoretical defences in the 1930s,
existentialism itself is very much a post-1940 discourse. It is also
probable that a retrospective vision colours the reference to psychoanalysis and the claim that it was 'during the decade from 1920 to 1930'[135]
must be tested against other historical accounts and against certain of
the material discussed elsewhere in this study.

It is in fact improbable that the young Lévi-Strauss acquired anything
more than a very schematic knowledge of Freud in the 1920s. Indeed,
there is always something schematic about his very references to Freud
and, with the partial exception of *Totem and Taboo*, it is rare for him to
discuss specific texts. His reading of Freud is, moreover, highly personal
and, as he confirms in an interview, both intellectualist and rationalist.[136]
Like Marxism, and presumably geology, psychoanalysis is of interest in
that it reveals meaning behind a semblance of arbitrary irrationality;
Lévi-Strauss shows little or no interest in libido or 'desire', and admits to
being unconvinced by the wish-fulfilment theory of dreams. Nor does
the theory of sexuality itself concern him to any great extent; the only
moment of psychosexual development to be taken into account is that of
the Oedipus. The one register of sexuality to be discussed is the prohibition of incest, which is seen as the moment 'where nature transcends
itself', the moment of the transition 'from the natural fact of consanguin-
ity to the cultural fact of alliance'.[137]

All Lévi-Strauss's discussions of the unconscious are characterized by
a high degree of intellectualism. In his introduction to the work of
Mauss, for example, he refers to the unconscious as a 'category of
collective thought'.[138] The use of the noun form – 'the unconscious' – is
relatively rare; normally it is the adjectival form which predominates, as
in 'Language and the Analysis of Social Laws', where the author
remarks that 'much of linguistic behaviour lies on the level of unconscious thought. When we speak, we are not conscious of the syntactic
and morphological laws of our language', and as in *The Elementary
Structures of Kinship*, where the structures of exchange are said to be
'always present to the human mind, at least in an unconscious form'.[139]
The authority for these references to unconscious thought and unconscious laws is not derived from Freud. The contention that 'an internal
logic directs the unconscious workings of the human mind' is prompted
by a discussion of Radcliffe-Brown, and it is Boas who is given credit for
'defining the unconscious nature of cultural phenomena'.[140]

For Lévi-Strauss, unconscious structures and activities are motivated by laws which are not immediately amenable to conscious reflection but are ultimately accessible to intellectual analysis. In the famous discussion of the parallel between shamanism and psychoanalysis, the unconscious is described as being reducible to a symbolic function and as being 'as alien to mental images as is the stomach to the foods which pass through it'.[141] It imposes structural laws upon non-articulated elements which originate elsewhere and, as such, it can be assumed to be universal. The preconscious, in contrast, is an individual lexicon, but its vocabulary becomes significant only when the unconscious structures it in accordance with its laws, and transforms it into language. It is difficult to reconcile this account with Freud's picture of a realm of 'instinctual representatives seeking to discharge their cathexes', of a realm characterized by 'exemption from mutual contradiction, timelessness and the replacement of external by psychical reality'.[142] In Lévi-Strauss's account it is the anthropological and sociological tradition of Radcliffe-Brown, Boas and Mauss which functions as a vanishing point rather than Freud. That vanishing point, together with the prevalence of the adjectival mode, suggest that Lévi-Strauss is working with a philosophical notion of 'unconscious' as denoting simply that which is not immediately amenable to the observations of the conscious intellect.

The notion of 'an unconscious level' is by no means rare in the history of either linguistics or philosophy. It might be said that Chomsky's deep structures are unconscious in that no individual speaker is aware of them at the moment of their operation, but they are more akin to Descartes's innate ideas than to Freud's drives. Even Kant's a priori knowledge might be termed un-conscious or non-conscious to the extent that it is quite independent of experience and even of sense-impressions. And in the 'Overture' to *The Raw and the Cooked*, Lévi-Strauss agrees that Ricoeur is quite right to observe that his reference to the unconscious involves a 'Kantism without a transcendental subject', and a 'Kantian rather than a Freudian unconscious, a combinative, categorizing unconscious'.[143] In short, Lévi-Strauss's rationalist vision of the unconscious is very close to what Lacan condemns as 'the rational unconscious ... or the metaphysical unconscious implied by "the act of the mind"'.[144]

There are, of course, obvious disparities between Lévi-Strauss and Lacan. The anthropologist's formulation would, for instance, appear to imply that it is the workings of the preconscious which are analogous to rhetoric, not the mechanisms of the unconscious. For Lacan, monuments, archival documents, semantic evolution and traditions are the key to the unconscious; for Lévi-Strauss, they are no more than a reservoir of 'recollections and traditions amassed in the course of a lifetime', but 'not always available to the individual'.[145] Despite these differences, Lacan insists that Lévi-Strauss provides 'objective foundations' for the theory of the unconscious and, ignoring the anthropologist's distaste for phenomenology, incorporates him without further ado into the variegated tissue of 'Fonction et champ', in which the Heideggerean strand is so obvious. If, however, Lacan's own references to unconscious structures are traced back through the corpus of his work, the differences may prove more apparent than real.

Lacan's earliest references to symbolic structures being unconsciously conveyed by or inscribed in language predate his discovery of Saussure and, like Lévi-Strauss, he derives them from an anthropological tradition. In the 1938 paper on the family, Freud's description of the Oedipus is said to be confirmed by the sociological data supplied by Frazer; in the 1950 paper on psychoanalysis and criminology, it is Mauss who provides an outline theory of unconscious symbolism.[146] In the latter écrit, Lacan makes it quite clear that psychoanalysis is to be situated in a continuum which includes anthropology and even Pauline eschatology; that it is a technical extension of those discourses in that it explores the impact upon the individual if a dialectic between culture and nature which goes back to the childhood of society.[147] Elsewhere, he refers in similar vein to the preconscious inscription of the Ten Commandments.[148] Such comments are reminiscent of Freud's evolutionism and of his use of analogical reasoning in his anthropological writings; they also exemplify Lacan's own tendency to invoke other discourses as an authority which can support his claims, as when ethology is pressed into service to supply an a contrario demonstration of the functions of human language. The effect is to inscribe the Freudian revolution within a continuum, despite the fact that Lacan also insists upon its radical and irreducible originality, but these theses also indicate that Lacan's writings on the unconscious contain a rationalist strand and owe something to the classic sociological tradition. That debt is most apparent in the stress placed on relations of exchange and in the references to the gift as 'total social fact' in 'Fonction et champ' and related texts. It is the existence of that strand which prepares the ground for the incorporation of Lévi-Strauss into the 'Rome Discourse'.

The reliance upon Lévi-Strauss for the theorization of unconscious symbolic structures is apparent throughout 'Fonction et champ' but it is even more patent in 'La Chose freudienne', where it is again stressed that anthropology and psychoanalysis form a continuum:

With his discovery of the unconscious ... Freud was taken at once to the heart of this determination of the symbolic law. For, in establishing, in *The Interpretation of Dreams*, the Oedipus complex as the central motivation of the unconscious, he recognized this unconscious as the agency of the laws on which marriage alliance and kinship are based. This is why I can say to you now that the motives of the unconscious are limited ... to sexual desire. Indeed, it is essentially on sexual relations – by ordering them according to the law of preferential marriage alliances and forbidden relations – that the first combinatory for the exchanges between nominal lineages is based, in order to develop into an exchange of gifts and in an exchange of master-words the fundamental commerce and concrete discourse on which human societies are based.'[149]

The passage is quoted at some length, not only because of the clarity of its exposition but also because it calls for comment at a number of levels.

The first comment is of a historiographical nature: the reading of The *Interpretation of Dreams* evoked here is tendentious in the extreme in that it implies a negation of textual and conceptual history. Lacan suggests that that text contains in its entirety the theory which he himself is in the process of elaborating with the aid of Lévi-Strauss: a theory of the symbolic structure which founds human societies. In the *Interpretation*, oedipal dreams are subsumed within the broader category of 'typical dreams' and Freud's comments are restricted to the observation that our first sexual impulses are directed towards our mother, and our first murderous intentions against our father.[150] No inferences are made in the original edition to the anthropological or foundational implications of the Oedipus myth; they are drawn in a footnote added in 1914 – after, that is, the publication of 'A Special Type of Choice of Object Made by Men', the paper in which the expression 'the Oedipus complex' is used for the first time.[151] It is only in *Totem and Taboo* that the Oedipus is given its foundational import – in terms which can readily be criticized for their reliance upon the archaic illusion so often attacked by Lévi-Strauss. References to oedipal feelings can also be found in the correspondence with Fliess, where Freud observes that being in love with one's mother is 'a universal event in early childhood' which helps us to understand 'the gripping power of *Oedipus Rex*'.[152] In short, *The Interpretation* does not signal the discovery of oedipal motifs, neither does it establish the oedipal basis of the symbolic law. Lacan's reading suppresses the history of a concept, and suggests that concepts have no genealogy and undergo no vicissitudes.

Years later, Miller will sketch the other panel in an astonishingly amnesiac dipytch by insisting that the isomorphism between language and the unconscious can be traced back to Freud's first texts [*sic*]: the trilogy of *The Interpretation, The Psychopathology* and *Jokes*.[153] Lacan thus inaugurates a mode of reading Freud in which history vanishes, in which the atemporality of immaculately conceived concepts abolishes the diachronic dimension of their emergence. A second comment relates to a rather different dimension of history: the history of sexuality. By equating the sexual desires which motivate the unconscious with the laws governing alliance and kinship, Lacan implicitly restricts sexuality to the heterosexual and the genital, if not the procreative. A stage within sexuality is made synonymous with sexuality itself, a point which Laplanche had made at some considerable length.[154] The equation further implies that 'deviations' from the heterosexual and even the genital are simply dysfunctional with respect to relations of exchange, as they tend to be in Lévi-Strauss's account.

The theory of symbolism projected on to Freud here relies heavily upon a theory of exchange and, more specifically, on Lévi-Strauss's account of the exchange of women in a symbolic commerce which subtends the universality of the prohibition of incest. And that account rests upon a *petitio principii* which must seriously undermine any claim to the effect that Lucan can contribute to a non-essentialist or non-naturalistic theory of the gendering of the subject. Despite the stress he places upon the nature–culture divide, Lévi-Strauss's gender categories are profoundly naturalist: women are 'not primarily a sign of social value, but a *natural* stimulant' to a promiscuous male desire which is presumably just as natural.[155] It is the allegedly natural stimulant value of women which, in conditions of scarcity, makes them 'that most precious category of goods' and 'valuables *par excellence*'.[156] The fact that Lacan accepts these theses so readily and makes them such an integral part of his own theory implies that he adheres to a naturalist view of gender which makes his relevance to feminism look distinctly dubious, especially when they are combined with the blatantly sexist formulations he uses in later texts.

It is the symbolic-exchange thesis which provides the basis for the analogy between women and signs (or symbols; Lévi-Strauss is notoriously cavalier in his handling of the distinction[157]), with the notion of value acting as a pivot. Alliance and kinship can, it is argued, be regarded as a form of symbolic language in which women-signs circulate and are exchanged. The fact that women are exchanged is not in dispute, but the analogy does not hold except in the most general and abstract terms. Lévi-Strauss himself modifies his initial analogy by adding that there is a difference between words and women in that, unlike the former, the latter speak and in that 'as producers of signs women can never be reduced to the status of symbols or tokens.'[158] A rather more important difference is passed over in silence: it is scarcity and desire which determine the value of women, but those categories cannot be applied to linguistic units. Natural languages do not display any shortage or scarcity of, say, phonemes; although their numbers are finite, they are by definition commensurate with the needs of the system within which they exist. Phonemes and words can be combined into higher and more complex units, but not even Lévi-Strauss suggests that women-signs are articulated into women-sentences.

Nor, it might be added, are linguistic units normally the object of heterosexual desire. Any attempt to found an analogy between the exchange of women and that of signs stumbles against a further problem in that Saussure's concept of linguistic value is purely differential and does not have any connotations of economic exchange-value or use-value. The acquisition of signifiers does not confer any economic wealth, whereas the institution of polygamy is wealth-based, and political control over the exchange of women in a society based upon a kinship mode of production does confer power. Despite all these problems, Lacan wholeheartedly adopts Lévi-Strauss's analogies and does not even endorse the modest caveat about the difference between women and words:

> Lévi-Strauss demonstrates that, in the structure of alliance, women, who define the cultural order as opposed to the natural order, are the object of exchange, just like speech, which is in effect the object of the primal exchange. No matter what goods, qualities or status are transmitted through the matrilineal line, the symbolic order is, in its initial workings, androcentric. This is a fact.[159]

If it is anthropology which provides the grounds for stating that the unconscious is structured like a language, a number of reservations must be expressed. It would appear that the arguments of Freud's 'The Unconscious' must be supplemented by references to a rationalist and anthropological tradition which has heavy philosophical overtones and which Lacan himself occasionally consigns to a pre-Freudian oblivion. Mauss and Boas must be accorded virtually the same status as Freud, regardless of the insistent claim that psychoanalysis is founded by an epistemological break which radically restructures the human sciences. Lévi-Strauss's analogy between the exchange of words and the social exchange of women must be endorsed, even though it represents something of a departure from Saussure and linguistics and even though it relies for its coherence upon a naturalist view of gender and an implicit restriction of the field of sexuality. Paradoxically, then, the invocation of structural anthropology in an attempt to promote the 'like a language' thesis implies the perpetuation of a number of assumptions which Lacanian psychoanalysis is often held to have discredited. There is, however, a second road that leads to the 'like a language' conclusion. It involves a peregrination through the formal garden in which the flowers of rhetoric bloom, to quote Paulhan.[160]

In 'Fonction et champ', Lacan describes the work of translation inherent in the interpretation of dreams as revealing a 'rhetoric of the unconscious', and catalogues certain of its tropes and figures. Ellipsis, pleonasm, hyperbaton, syllepsis, regression, repetition and apposition are categorized as 'syntactic displacements', and metaphor, catachresis, autonomasis, allegory, metonymy and synecdoche as 'semantic condens-ations'.[161] Four years later, in 'Instance de la lettre', Lacan states that the mechanisms of the unconscious can be classified as, respectively, 'figures of style' (periphrasis, hyperbaton, ellipsis, suspension, anticipation, retraction, negation, digression and irony) and as tropes (catachresis, litotes, autonomasia and hypotoposis). Elsewhere in the same *écrit* Freud's condensation is identified with metaphor, and displacement with metonymy.[162]

Until the late nineteenth century rhetoric had been an integral part of the school and university curriculum in France, and provided the basis for literary studies, but it gradually falls into disrepute during the age of Romanticism and becomes something of a minority interest, albeit one shared by figures of the stature of Valéry and Paulhan. The revival of critical interest in rhetoric in the 1960s is in part stimulated by the appearance of a translation of Jakobson's essay on aphasia,[163] but it is also probable that Lacan himself is a major influence and helps to promote the popularity of rhetoric amongst structuralist critics and theorists. His interest in the topic predates the general vogue, and may have been prompted by Jakobson. Jakobson is not mentioned by name in 'Fonction et champ', but the debt is explicitly acknowledged in 'Instance' and we know from Lacan's earliest comments on linguistics that he was familiar with his work from the 1950s onwards. In 1953, the sonorous roll call of tropes and figures must have had an impressive effect; it has all the splendour of an epic poem, but its music tends to drown out some fairly basic points.

If the unconscious is indeed structured like a language, it follows quite logically that its verbal or para-verbal manifestations of its workings can be classified in rhetorical terms. Paulhan remarks that rhetoric is the most banal of sciences, in that using rhetoric is synony-mous with the act of speaking.[164] Seventeenth-century poets like Boileau and eighteenth-century rhetoricians like Du Marsais, the author of a celebrated treatise on the subject, were well aware of the fact that the devices of rhetoric can be found throughout discourse, and often pointed out that more tropes and figures were used in quarrels in the marketplace than in the formal deliberations of the Académie Française. Had they been informed of the existence of an unconscious structured like a language, they would have taken it as axiomatic that its verbal manifestations would take a rhetorical form. Even so, Lacan's foregrounding of rhetoric does have far-reaching effects, both for psychoanalysis and for a broader literary constituency. It also promotes some unfortunate conflations and misapprehensions, as when Laplanche and Leclaire assume that Lacan has made it possible to identify displacement and condensation with 'scientific linguistic terms'.[165] Rhetoric is not synonymous with linguistics and it is far from being an exact science, as the confusion arising from Lacan's identifications demonstrates beyond any doubt.

Although the metaphor-condensation and metonymy-displacement equations rapidly become an integral part of Lacanian linguistics or *linguisterie*, they rest upon highly unstable definitions. Lacan's own classifications are uncertain: in 'Fonction et champ' both metaphor and metonymy were 'semantic condensations', but in the Seminar of 9 May 1956 condensation, displacement and representation are all said to belong to an order of metonymic articulation which allows metaphor to function. A week earlier, Lacan had been insisting that metonymy is the opposite of metaphor and had established a polarity between the two.[166] The extent of the confusion can be seen from the differences between Lacan and Jakobson, who identifies displacement with metonymy, but condensation with synecdoche. When these conflicting definitions were brought to his notice, Jakobson is reported to have explained them in terms of the conceptual imprecision of Freud's 'condensation' and to have argued that it could encompass both metaphor and synecdoche.[167] Jakobson's comment is not without a certain justification, but it is not only Freud who is lacking in conceptual precision. The history of rhetoric is one of conflicting definitions, and the resurgence of interest in the subject during the structuralist era has done little to clarify certain basic problems.

To take only some examples of the taxonomic confusion that has arisen around Lacan's figure-mechanism parallel. In an early essay on semiology Barthes describes dream symbols as metaphors, and the mechanisms of both condensation and displacement as metonyms; in his seminar of 1964–65 he reclassifies both metaphor and metonymy as 'metaboles' on the grounds that both involve substitution, and contrasts them with figures relying on parataxis. The latter classification will eventually be adopted by Laplanche, regardless of the fact that it destroys what he originally held to be a polar opposition.[168] For his part, Todorov argues in 1970 that there can be no real difference of opinion between Lacan and Jakobson because metaphor is merely a double synecdoche, but in a later and much more substantial study he contends that condensation covers all tropes (including metaphor and metonymy), whereas displacement is not a trope in that it does not substitute one meaning for another, but relates two co-present meanings to one another.[169]

The ongoing controversy merely illustrates the point that the primary difficulty is that rhetoric, despite its fascination, is not a coherent entity or a single taxonomy – still less a precise science – but an extensive field of conflicting and often mutually contradictory definitions. Barthes pinpoints another difficulty when he notes that it is exceedingly difficult to identify a specific poetic feature with a rhetorical category unless one has already mastered the entire system. It may not be difficult to move from definition to example or to find instances of, say, metaphor, but it is difficult to identify the phrase 'Melissa shook her doubtful curls' as an example of hypallage without a working knowledge of the system within which hypallage is defined.[170]

Lacan's chosen examples illustrate the problem perfectly. He identifies the expression 'thirty sail' as a metonymic figure signifying 'thirty ships' (the part for the whole). Pierre Fontanier, author of a standard nineteenth-century treatise on rhetoric, identifies this as a synecdoche, but immediately adds that it could also be seen as an example of catachresis.[141] No doubt both Lacan and Fontanier could find allies to support their respective claims. Lacan habitually takes a line from Hugo – *Sa gerbe n'était point avare, ni haineuse* – as an illustration of the workings of metaphor; the irony, of which Lacan appears to be unaware, being that Hugo naively prided himself on having cleansed poetry of rhetoric. Lyotard, in contrast, argues that a metonymic shift is at work here, and his claim is supported by Genette, perhaps the most serious of all modern students of rhetoric.[172] Rhetoric is not botany, and the precise identity of the two most cultivated flowers of rhetoric known to French psychoanalysis remains sadly ill-defined.

The line from Hugo is initially introduced in somewhat brutal fashion in the Seminar on the psychoses: "*Sa gerbe n'était point avare, ni haineuse*" – Victor Hugo. There's a metaphor.'[173] In 'Instance de la lettre' Lacan uses the same example, adding that it has been chosen at random from Quillet's *Dictionnaire usuel*, 'an appropriate place to find a sample that would not seem to be chosen for my own purposes'.[174] The quotation is from *Booz endormi*, a well-known poem from *La Légende des siècles* which retells the biblical story of Ruth and Boaz;[175] it is difficult to imagine that an audience made up of arts and philosophy students at the Sorbonne would be totally unfamiliar with at least Hugo's version of the tale. Indeed, in June 1964 Lacan contradicts his earlier statement and admits: 'Of all poems, I have taken the one that, in French, may be said to echo in more people's memories than any other. Who did not learn when a child to recite *Booz endormi!*'[176] It is, then, unlikely to have been a random choice in the first place, but Hugo certainly proves to be a useful ally and serves Lacan's purposes admirably.

In the line '*Sa gerbe n'était point avare, ni haineuse*' ('His sheaf was neither miserly nor spiteful'), the metaphoric substitution of *gerbe* for *Booz* produces, according to Lacan, a poetic spark which realizes the signification of paternity. This is in fact the theme of the entire poem; the sleeping Boaz dreams that an oak tree is growing out of his stomach, and exlaims in surprise at the realization that he – an old man – is to be the founder of a race. It would be difficult to arrive at that prophetic intuition on the basis of the single line cited by Lacan; elsewhere, he in fact states that the whole poem revolves around the phallus.[177] His interpretation of the line is therefore overdetermined by his reading of the thematic organization of the entire poem, but knowledge of that reading and even of the poem's organization is withheld from the non-informed reader. A more intriguing piece of information is also withheld by the concentration on only one line: it is in fact Ruth's decision to lie at Booz's feet, 'le sein nu' ('with bare breasts'), which stimulates the dream of paternity. As so often in Lacan, female desire and female sexuality have been elided and eclipsed by phallic imagery. The poem is, moreover, saturated with images of autumnal fertility which appear to have as much to do with pregnancy and birth as with phallic potency.

The elision of the overall context and of the female element promotes a transition similar to that noted in the ladies/gentlemen fable: the transition from metaphor or signifier to paternal metaphor and primal symbol. As in the earlier example, this transition implies a drift away from any linguistic or rhetorical model to the level of highly motivated and non-arbitrary symbols. But the transition is possible only because of the unit chosen for analysis. If a broader context is introduced, the supposed metaphor does not simply generate 'the signification of paternity conveyed by the signifier *gerbe*, but the propositional syntagm: '*une race nâtrait de moi*' ('A race born of me!'; the conditional is used here to express surprise). In an earlier line – '*Ce vieillard possédait des champs de blé et d'orge*' ('This old man owned fields of wheat and barley') – Lacan's analysis is complicated by the obvious metonymic connection between *champs* and *gerbe*, as well as by the anaphoric link between *Booz* and *ce vieillard.* In short, Lacan's metaphor works thanks to the suppression of its context and to a very cavalier use of elements of poetics.

Lacan's signal departure from the norms of linguistics and rhetoric is visible in other areas too. The claim that 'it is in the substitution of signifier for signifier that an effect of signification is produced' is as weak as the earlier definition of metaphor as 'one word for another'[178] (a definition which could apply to many figures of speech, notably euphemism), whilst the ease with which 'word' can be substituted for 'signifier' must cast some doubt on the precision of his linguistic terminology.[179] Lacan's theory of metaphor stems, of course, from Jakobson's metaphor–metonymy polarity, but Jakobson's account makes it clear that the figure necessarily involves an operation of selection and combination. Lacan mentions no such operation, and therefore implies that any substitution will produce a metaphor.

One might have expected at least some indication as to the nature of the paradigmatic set from which *gerbe* is selected and, in terms of poetics, as to the formal constraints governing the choice of the adjectives *avare* and *haineuse*. Lacan's only comment on the formal organization of his chosen example is that a change in the word order would destroy the meaning of the sentence.[180] Quite aside from the fact that this is not a sentence but a clause within a sentence, the word order (and to some extent the choice of lexical units) is in part determined by the formal requirements of rhyme and metre; *haineuse* rhymes with *glaneuse* (gleaner) and a trisyllabic word would be metrically inappropriate. Nor is it enough to argue, as does Lacan in his polemic with Perelman, that 'nothing natural' predestines the substitute signifier *gerbe* to act as a *phora*;[181] nature may not be a pertinent reference here, but a discussion of the highly codified laws of versification would be pertinent in the extreme. A metaphor which may not be a metaphor is given a status which removes the debate from symbol to signifier; female desire is elided by the motivated selection of the unit of analysis; the formal laws of the poetics associated with Jakobson are ignored or flouted. Not surprisingly, Lacan refers approvingly to Humpty Dumpty as the 'master of the signifier'.[182] It will be recalled that Humpty Dumpty's proud boast is: 'When *I* use a word ... it means just what I choose it to mean – neither more nor less.'[183] The degree to which Lacan departs from the norms of linguistics and rhetoric and defies their terminological niceties strongly suggests that he takes a similar view.

Lacan's dispute with Perelman centres on the question of the analogical basis of metaphor. For Perelman, metaphor can be used to construct an expression on the basis of an analogy; the analogy 'A is to B as C is to D' permits the construction of the formula 'C's B' to designate 'D'.[184] Despite Lacan's disparaging reference to 'nature', it is clear that Perelman's 'analogy' is an intellectual construct and that the analogical element in even the most picturesque metaphor does not imply any direct relationship with its extralinguistic referent. By insisting on the analogical element, Perelman is following the traditions of classical rhetoric; he can cite Du Marsais to support his claims, and Fontanier describes metaphor as a trope centred on 'resemblance'.[185] It is, then, Lacan who is out of step with rhetorical tradition. His criticisms of Perelman are presented in 'Instance' and in the much shorter 'La Métaphore du sujet', where he writes:

Metaphor is radically the effect of the substitution of one signifier for another within a chain, without anything natural predestining it to this function as a *phora*, apart from the fact that we are dealing with two signifiers, which are as such reducible to a phonematic opposition.'[186]

The reducibility of signifiers to a phonematic opposition is surely redundant in the context of a discussion of rhetoric, but it is more important to note once more that Lacan's definition suggests that any substitution of signifiers will generate a metaphor. In other words, he fails to specify any conditions of substitutability, just as his discussion of the 'Booz' metaphor fails to indicate the set from which *gerbe* is selected.

It is not difficult to construct a hypothetical example illustrating the importance of conditions of substitutability. Seventeenth-century French poetry and drama normally uses 'flame' [*flamme*] as a metaphor for love or passion; 'My flame burns for you' is acceptable to the point of banality. But the substitution of 'mud' for 'love' and the resultant 'My mud is bubbling for you' are not. Yet it conforms to Lacan's definition of metaphor. Classical references to analogy or resemblance do at least begin to specify a basis for an intuitive theory of conditions of substitutability and acceptability, and to interpret a theory based upon an 'comparison which exists in the mind' – as Du Marsais puts it – as a reference to 'nature' is simply disingenuous.

Lacan uses the same definition of metaphor in 'Instance', but there he also alludes to the surrealist theory that the force of the poetic spark generated by the juxtaposition of two images is proportional to the distance between those images.[187] Logically, this should provide an opportunity to examine the difference between new or unexpected metaphors and tired metaphors. That issue is central to many discussions of poetics, and again raises the question of substitutability and acceptability: at what point does substitution result in an unacceptable metaphor, and how far can the conventions of acceptability be challenged? That Lacan does not take the opportunity is an indirect indication of his reluctance to explore the richness of the field of metaphor, of his seeming lack of interest in just why *gerbe* should be a successful metaphor. He contests the surrealist theory by challenging the ill-defined notion of 'images' and replaces it with the 'substitution of signifiers' argument, again failing to specify the conditions under which it can or cannot occur. If Lacan fails to address the problem that, because of substitutability criteria, not all substitutions produce successful metaphors, he also fails to note that not all poetic sparks are produced by metaphors. Eluard's line *La terre est bleue comme une orange* (The earth is as blue as an orange) is a surrealist classic, but it

centres on the *comme*, not upon a substitution, and on the juxtaposition
of colour signifiers.[188]

Part of the problem with Lacan's theory of metaphor is no doubt an
effect of the insistence that metaphor is part of a binary opposition, the
other pole being metonymy, which receives rather less attention. (Here
at least he does follow the rhetorical tradition which habitually sees
metaphor as the poetic device *par excellence*, and metonymy as a 'poor
figure'). This results in a certain vagueness in the mapping of figures on
to unconscious formations and in a failure to explore the possibilities
opened up by the alleged isomorphism. If, as Freud repeatedly states,
the unconscious ignores the principle of non-contradiction, oxymoron
(Milton's 'darkness visible') would appear to be an appropriate description of at least some of its linguistic expressions. And when Freud writes
that one form of condensation involves 'the total omission of certain
latent elements' from the manifest content, or that displacement can
take the form of shifting the psychical accent 'from an important
element to another which is less important',[189] one thinks surely of ellipsis and litotes rather than of metaphor and metonymy.

Yet Lacan rarely extends the debate beyond those two figures and,
despite his impressive roll calls of tropes and figures, he in fact operates
with a very impoverished rhetoric. The claim that the unconscious uses
the most elaborate forms of style (accismus, metonymy, catechresis,
antiphrase, hypallage, litotes[190]) is simply not pursued. Lacan effectively
reduces rhetoric to a binary opposition displaying oppositional features
which can be found at every level of language:

> The mechanisms described by Freud as those of the 'primary process', where
> the unconscious assumes its rule, correspond exactly to the functions that this
> school [structuralism] believes determine the most radical aspects of the
> effects of language, namely metaphor and metonymy – in other words the
> signifier's effects of substitution and combination on the respectively
> synchronic and diachronic dimensions in which they appear in discourse.[191]

Lacan makes it eminently clear that his references to the 'most radical
aspects' of language derive from Jakobson and, their differences over
synecdoche aside, it seems that they are in agreement as to the need for
and desirability of such a universal taxonomy. Jakobson's research on
aphasia allows him to identify two basic patterns (contiguity and similarity disturbance) which can be mapped on to the metaphor–metonymy
polarity, but the paper in which his findings are presented is remarkable
for the manner in which it moves from 'aspects' to 'axes' of language.
The basic opposition does not, however, derive directly from research
on aphasia but from an earlier and rather less precise distinction

between types of literary forms and genres, in other words from a poetics. Romanticism, symbolism, surrealist painting and the films of Chaplin can be described as metaphoric, whilst historical epics, the cinema of Griffith and realist fiction, as typified by the concentration on Anna Karenina's handbag in the suicide scene, are basically metonymic.[192] In one of his more formalist moods Barthes expands the lists, describing didactic exposés, thematic criticism and aphoristic discourse as metaphoric, and popular novels and press reports as metonymic.[193]

Such broad oppositional classifications are by no means unusual. Wölfflin studies Western art in terms of a 'classical/Baroque' opposition, and a polarity between Classicism and Romanticism is basic to many a banal history of French and other literatures. Originally, the metaphor/metonymy duality is one such broad historical–formal typology. As such it can be applied to an almost infinite number of areas, as when Lévi-Strauss uses it to examine different modes of naming pets in a bravura passage where, as so often, the weight of erudition is quite disproportionate to the topic under discussion.[194] Jakobson, for his part, insists that 'competition between the two processes' can be observed in all symbolic activities, and it is on that basis that the opposition is extended to include dream symbolism.[195]

The metaphor–metonymy opposition functions adequately as a convenient – if schematic – typology of forms, though, as both Jakobson and Barthes's lists indicate, it can easily fall prey to the structuralist enthusiasm for watertight binary systems. If it is applied in more specific areas, difficulties begin to emerge. Lacan inadvertently signals one of the greatest when he refers almost simultaneously to the radical aspects of language and to the appearance of synchrony and diachrony in discourse. Language and discourse are being conflated. In much of contemporary writing 'discourse' is increasingly used in a very loose – but not therefore illegitimate – sense to refer to any process of signification and, in a sense derived largely from Foucault, to the ideological–political constructs described as discursive formations. In most forms of linguistics, the term is used in a much narrower and more tightly defined sense to refer to units of signification of dimensions equal to or greater than a sentence.

To adopt the classic formulation used by Benveniste, discourse can be defined as a manifestation of *langue* in communication, and as having the sentence as its basic unit; *langue*, in contrast, refers to the set of formal signs within which discourse exists.[196] Whereas the sentence is made up of signs and can therefore be segmented into its components, it cannot, unlike those components, be integrated into a higher unit which is differentially opposable to other units. Unlike phonemes, sentences do not form binary pairs. At the level of the sentence, differences pertain to semantics and not to phonematic features; the criterion for analysis is no longer a finite system of signs, but semantic modes of communication. And it is at the level of discourse and communication that rhetoric is traditionally located. It is not, then, perceptible at all levels of language, as Lacan often suggests: a phoneme cannot be a metaphor for another phoneme precisely because the appropriate criterion of semantics does not pertain at its level. If the formations of the unconscious do use all the figures and tropes of rhetoric – which, in view of Lacan's failure to go beyond metaphor and metonymy, must remain non-proven – it would appear that it is structured like discourse, and not like a language.

Lacan's exploitation of rhetoric is, then, somewhat dubious and his invocation of the rhetorical tradition is highly problematic. At the other end of the linguistic scale, his use of and reference to the notion of the phoneme is equally problematic. When the Cheshire Cat asks Alice if she said 'pig' or 'fig', he intuitively identifies /p/ and /f/ as distinctive units in English, in other words as phonemes. Phonemes are identified by a process of segmentation which breaks down language into monemes (minimal units endowed with meaning), and then into phonemes which cannot be segmented into smaller units and which can be defined in terms of distinctive features at the levels of sonority, protensity and tonality.[197] The definition applies only at this level, and the /p/ ≠ /f/ distinction is not in itself pertinent to the semantics of the syntagms 'a pig in a poke' or 'I don't give a fig'. Nor do all phonetic differences indicate the existence of phonemes; the use of the voiced rather than the unvoiced terminal /s/ in the English /us/ may indicate a class or regional sociolect, but not a phonemic difference pertinent to English as a language. The identification of phonemes is not, however, simply a matter of segmentation, as a commutation test is applied to determine the possibility of their being integrated into higher and more complex units; /p/, for example, can be integrated into /pig/, /pug/, and /f/ into /fig/, /fug/, and so on. The criterion of integration centres upon the issue of acceptability within a given language. Thus, the use of the voiced /s/ will not prevent an English-speaker from identifying the word /us/ as distinct from /ut/ or some other hypothetical form, because it does not lead to the production of 'meaningless' or unacceptable forms.

Lacan describes the discovery of the phoneme as a 'form of mathematization' which leads us to 'the subjective sources of the symbolic function in a vocalic connotation of presence and absence', a reference to Freud's *fort-da* game.[198] One characteristic of his *linguisterie* is immediately apparent here: the slide from the phonemic to the symbolic and the conflation of levels of analysis. Phonemes do not symbolize. Precisely what 'connotation' refers to in this context must remain a matter for debate or even speculation, but it appears to have little to do with the denotation/connotation distinction pioneered by Hjelmslev and adopted by Barthes, and its use is a further index of Lacan's lack of conceptual precision and consistency.[199] To describe phonemic analysis as a mathematical operation may be accurate to the extent that it identifies a finite number of units (thirty-four in French, according to Martinet[200]) and to the extent that their possible distribution could be calculated by using a mathematical model, but the integration–commutation operation is not mathematical. Even if we accept the presence of a mathematical element, Lacan appears to be confused as to the unit of analysis. A phoneme is, so to speak, the 'product' of the analysis, but the basic unit of phonemics is the pertinent or distinctive feature or bundle of features which combine to form the phoneme.[201] If Lacan's allusion to phonemic analysis is traced back to the linguistics on which it purports to be based, it becomes apparent that, like so many of his linguistic and rhetorical references, it is surrounded by a serious imprecision and characterized by what he himself will describe as a 'casual' use of linguistics.[202]

The claim that phonemic analysis is a form of mathematization may be dubious in its own terms but it is consistent with Lacan's use of a variety of formal and quasi-mathematical notations, the most obvious being the supposed algorithm which inaugurates modern linguistics and the formulae given for metaphor and metonymy in 'Instance de la lettre'. It is also consistent with the claim that 'mathematical formalization is our goal, our aim'.[203] Lacan's interest in mathematics is long-standing, and can be traced back to the immediate post-war years. Roudinesco dates the beginnings of his fascination with mathematical and logical formulae to the early 1950s when, together with Lévi-Strauss and Benveniste, he worked with Georges Guilbaud, whom he regularly approached for information on mathematical and topological problems.[204] Guilbaud appears to have been something of an *éminence grise* for the early structuralists; it was he who helped Lévi-Strauss to formulate the diagrammatic representation of Aranda social structures and marriage rules that appears in *The Savage Mind.*[205]

The accuracy of Roudinesco's information is not in dispute, but Lacan's interest in a form of mathematics in fact predates the reported association with Guilbaud. In 1945 he contributes the first of two articles to *Cahiers d'art* at the invitation of its editor, Christian Zervos: 'Le Temps logique et l'assertion de certitude anticipée'. A year later, a companion piece appears entitled 'Le Nombre treize et la forme logique de la suspicion'; only the former appears in *Ecrits*. Both deal with logico-mathematical problems, and 'Le Temps logique' is in effect a variant on or precursor of the 'odds and evens' game explored in the

Poe Seminar. A group of prisoners have to identify the combination of black and white discs affixed to their backs in order to gain their freedom; no prisoner can see his own back, and knowledge of his position must therefore be constructed on the basis of his knowledge of the position of the others. In the second paper, Lacan makes it clear that the problem it discusses – a variation on the well-known 'counterfeit coins' puzzle – was invented by François le Lionnais and was brought to his attention by Raymond Queneau.[206] What appears at first sight to be a classically structuralist interest proves to be part of the curious intellectual continuum that stretches from surrealism and glossology to the experiments of OULIPO.

Lacan describes both the *Cahiers d'art* papers as exercises in the formal analysis of a collective logic, and as exemplifying 'the conception of logical forms in which relations between individuals and the collection are to be defined; this definition occurs prior to the specification of the individual as individual, and reveals a logic of the individual.'[207] More specifically, the 'logical birth of the I' in the game described in 'Le Temps logique' is said to parallel the psychological birth of the I, which is defined in terms of the specular transivitism described in 'Aggressivité' and in the 1949 version of the mirror-stage paper.[208] It has already been argued that the theorization of the mirror stage originates in a rather uneasy amalgam of clinical observation, ethology and philosophemes deriving from the Kojève-Hegel matrix. In other words the logic of these sophisms, whatever their technical sophistication, is a restatement or a re-presentation of an existing theorization. Lacan argues in 'Fonction et champ' that they illustrate how a mathematical formalization can provide the science of human action with the structure of intersubjective time.[209] Yet it is difficult to see just how this 'formalization' introduces anything new or moves towards any scientific rigour; it is largely a reworking of something already theorized, a second-degree re-presentation. The same might be said of most of Lacan's models and attempts at formalization, despite the claim that they indicate a gesture towards the mathematicity of the model of science promoted by the rationalist epistemology of Koyré and others.

Before going on to discuss the fate of the models, it seems opportune to look briefly at their origins, which are rather more humble than the later interest in Moebius strips and Borromenean knots might suggest. Both *Ecrits* and the Seminar are punctuated by graphs and formulae which gradually proliferate and become more complex, but the recurrent phrase which accompanies the earliest examples is simply 'in order to fix our ideas'; this strongly suggests that they are no more than mnemonics with a fairly basic pedagogic purpose.[210] For instance, in a discussion of the pleasure principle and the reality principle, Lacan remarks: 'I would like to put this on the board for you', and then matches actions to words in a gesture performed on countless occasions by teachers the world over.[211] The 'inverted vase' experiment in perception which is used to illustrate the structures of the imaginary is said to be 'an apparatus for thinking' and, more significantly, 'a metaphor', whilst the schema introduced in 1955 to represent the construction of the ego is simply a device whose use is necessitated by 'the infirmity of our discursive wit'.[212] As Miller notes in his commentary on the graphs that figure in *Ecrits*, 'All the constructions gathered together here have no more than a didactic role: their relation with the structure is one of analogy.'[213]

Despite Lacan's attacks on Perelman, there would appear to be a role for analogically based metaphors after all. The graphs and schemata are originally no more than convenient images, a sort of visual shorthand which allows a relatively complex structure to be transcribed and, presumably, committed to memory. The degree of formalization they introduce is minimal in the extreme. Even the more complex formulae used to exemplify the workings of metaphor and metonymy represent no more than a minor gesture towards mathematics. Their workings are transcribed as, respectively, $f(\frac{S'}{S})\ S \cong s\ (+)\ s$ and $f(\dots S')\ S \cong S\ (-)\ s$.[214] In the paper on Schreber, a new formula for metaphor is supplied by the notation:[215]

$$\frac{S}{S'} \cdot \frac{S}{x} \to S(\frac{I}{s})$$

Although such formulae have the allure of mathematics, their nature and function remain surprisingly vague. In the first two formulae, for instance, the sign $\cong$ is said to designate 'congruence', but it is not a conventional mathematical notation and its role remains undefined. Although these appear to be equations, no element of calculation is involved; they refer to no quantitative element but merely to the operations of 'the signifier', with all the uncertainty implied in Lacan's use of that term. Nor, as Lacan will later insist, does the 'bar' indicate proportionality; it illustrates the eminently non-mathematical notion of resistance to signification.[216]

Lacan's formulae are habitually accompanied by discursive commentaries. The commentary attached to the first metaphor formula is simply a restatement of Lacan's general position: 'It is in the substitution of signifier for signifier that an effect of signification is produced.'[217] Similarly, the 1955 schema illustrating the imaginary function of the ego and the discourse of the unconscious reappears in simplified form in 'D'Une Question Préliminaire' as

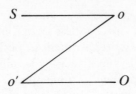

It is said to have the function of 'fixing our ideas', and Lacan proceeds to explain that it

> signifies that the condition of the Subject S (neurosis or psychosis) is dependent upon what is being unfolded in the Other O ... the subject is ... a participator, in that he is stretched over the four corners of the schema: namely S, his ineffable, stupid existence, o his objects, o' his ego, that is, that which is reflected of his form in his objects, and O, the locus from which the question of his existence may be represented to him.[218]

All these points are familiar from other discussions, but the addition of the discursive commentary points to the epistemological weakness of the schema. It may be a convenient pedagogic formula, but it remains referential in that it is supported by a paraphrase and has little or no autonomy. Like the 'prisoners' and 'counterfeit coins' puzzles, it provides no more than a restatement of a point which can be made verbally and introduces no real formalization or abstraction.

A further problem arises with Lacan's system of notation in that its terms are amenable to translation into another natural language. In the above formula, 'o' (other) translates the French 'a' (*autre*); it is a mere coincidence that S (subject; *sujet*, and elsewhere signifier; *signifiant*) does not require translation. Translatability is not a feature of mathematical symbols or formulae: the expression signifying the vector differential $\frac{\partial}{\partial x} + \frac{\partial}{\partial y} + \frac{\partial}{\partial z}$ neither requires nor permits translation from French to English, even though an explanation of its meaning may be required for the non-mathematician, French or English. Lacan's insistence that the expression *objet petit-a* should remain untranslated and that it thus acquires 'as it were, the status of an algebraic sign' hints at the existence of this problem.[219] It does not resolve it; the expression can readily be translated as 'object small o', and no authorial insistence can confer upon it the status of an algebraic sign. Untranslatability may well be a feature of mathematical notations; a refusal to translate the translatable cannot elevate any formula to mathematical status.

Lacan's notations are translatable, but it is perhaps more significant that they are referential in that they are illustrative of a discursive formulation and therefore cannot have the standing of mathematical signs which, according to Lacan himself, can be transmitted integrally but mean nothing in themselves.[220] The development of a metaphor used in 'Instance de la lettre' indicates how a seemingly complex topological structure is in fact little more than an extension or expansion of an illustrative image. The position of the signifier within the order of the signifying chain is compared to that of 'the rings of a necklace that is a ring in another necklace made of rings'. There is, therefore, 'no signifying chain that does not have, as if attached to the punctuation of each of its units, a whole articulation of relevant contexts suspended "vertically", as it were, from that point.'[221] The use of spatial imagery here is obviously purely illustrative, and Lacan does not claim that it is part of some process of formalization or mathematization.

In *Encore*, however, the same image is invoked during a discussion of the properties of Borromenean knots, which, we are told, make it possible to obtain 'a model for mathematical formalization'.[222] Lacan concludes from a demonstration of the knots that they facilitate the representation of the spoken chain. In order to represent the use of language it is necessary to imagine the chain as consisting of a series of links, each attached to other links, with intermediary links floating between them.[223] The repeated use of 'representation' and of 'imagine' is in itself significant in that it indicates that a metaphorical element is still present. The original 'necklace' image has been refined and translated into the more complex imagery of Borromenean knots and topology, but it retains its original illustrative–metaphoric character. No progress has been made towards a purely logical or axiomatic model. Nor is this an isolated instance of what might be termed the secondary elaboration of an existing image or metaphor.

In 'L'Etourdit', Lacan asserts that topology is not a guide to structure: 'It is that structure – as the retroaction of the order of the chain of which language consists.'[224] This is, however, no more than a reworking of the image of the diachronic function of the *point de capiton* in 'Subversion du sujet', where Lacan writes: 'The sentence completes its signification only with its last term, each term being anticipated in the structure of the others, and, inversely, sealing their meaning by its retroactive effect.'[225] The reference to topology in 'L'Etourdit' introduces little that has not already been stated in more concrete and less portentous terms. Nor does the claim that the signifier 'is to be structured in topological terms' and that phonology does effectively topologize it 'in so far as it incarnates the signifier of the phoneme' inspire any great confidence in Lacan's mathematics.[226]

The search for a mathematical formalization leads in the 1970s to the introduction of the controversial 'matheme'. The term is not a standard element in mathematical terminology but a neologism which is presumably created by analogy with mytheme, semanteme and so on. Logically, its probable derivation would appear to indicate something approximating to a minimal or elementary unit of mathematics, but in practice it means little more than 'mathematical sign'.[227] Although the term itself dates from the early 1970s, Lacan had been using the formulae encapsulated by the matheme for some years. The matheme which is discussed most frequently appears in 1962 in 'Kant avec Sade': ($S \diamond a'$). S designates the barred subject, and a objet a, and the symbol $\diamond$ is to be read as 'desire for'.[228] In a variant on this formula, 'D' can be used to designate Demand; it then designates the subject's relation with his verbalized demands. It is immediately obvious that the matheme is open to the translatability criticism; a is translatable as o, and so on. Only the arbitrary $\diamond$ escapes this criticism. The matheme – or mathemes; usage varies between the singular and the plural – is said to be meaningless in itself but amenable to integral transmission. To the extent that it is a convenient notation it is, like the earlier schemata, a pedagogic device, but the notion of 'integral transmission' does seem to introduce a new note. Whilst Lacan often insists that his work does not consist of *ex cathedra* pronouncements and that it is a process of constant exploration, the idea of transmission does imply the existence of a codified body of doctrine to be handed down and passed on.

Although Lacan's stated ideal is not to mathematize the whole of his work or to provide a formal mapping of the entire analytic process, but simply to isolate a 'mathematizable minimum',[229] it is clear that the theory of mathematical formalization derives from the rationalist epistemology associated with Koyré, Bachelard and Canguilhem, or in other words from the tradition which informs his views on the epistemological break which founds both psychoanalysis and Saussurean linguistics. Mathematics, with its purification of discourse through the gradual expulsion of the real and its formalization, is said to be the form 'most propitious' for scientific discourse.'[230] The underlying thesis is that post-Galilean science is typified by the constitution of a form of writing or notation using 'little letters' to encapsulate formulae and to obviate the need for long discursive expositions or digressions. 'Little letters' are not merely a formal shorthand, and represent a move towards a non-verbal level: everything that has been produced as science is non-verbal.[231]

Lacan's exploitation of this version of the history of the sciences is problematic in a number of ways. It tends to be illustrated by constant references to Copernicus and Galileo, and no attempt is made to articulate it with more modern scientific developments. There is, for example, no discussion of particle physics or of any post-Einsteinian discourse. And in a seminar given at Yale, Lacan has obvious difficulty in parrying the objection that geology and biology are also sciences, but make little or no use of the process of mathematization.[232] A rather more obvious problem was not raised at Yale. Mathematization may be a necessary element in the development of certain sciences, but it is by no means a sufficient guarantee of scientificity. The theory of periodicity elaborated by Fliess and Freud in their correspondence is not invalidated by arithmetical errors, but by its purely imaginary nature. Leaving aside the wider issue of the history of science, it is in fact fairly clear that the mathemes and references to mathematization remain illustrative and metaphorical. To say that the continuous single surface of a Moebius strip says something about the nature of ambivalence is to employ a metaphor. And it is difficult to see how that metaphor represents any theoretical advance on the neologistic *hainamouration,* a condensation of *haine* and *enamourer* (hate and enamouration) which encapsulates an important psychoanalytic concept with such economy.[233]

Lacan's use of mathematics has long been controversial. To take only three critical comments from three very different sources. Octave Mannoni maintains that the use of mathematical formulae in the original discussion of metaphor is in itself merely metaphorical and that it does not represent any mathematization of linguistics.[234] When the EFP held a three-day meeting to discuss the matheme in 1975, Leclaire protested that psychoanalysis is above all a matter of speech and that, even if they might have a certain utility, the mathemes are best regarded as graffiti[235] – and anyone who encounters the inscriptions in the margins of *Télévision* for the first time will probably be only too happy to agree. A more recent and more philosophical commentator regards the graphs which support Lacan's claim to have formalized fundamental concepts as 'disastrous', and adds that his diagrams 'are to any authentic formalization what Jarry or Duchamp's "*machines célibataires*" are to ordinary machines'.[236] It might not be inappropriate to suggest, finally, that the mathemes are to mathematics what *linguisterie* is to linguistics. In both cases, elements from a rigorous discipline are appropriated in what Lacan himself admits is a casual manner. If few linguists take the *linguisterie* seriously, there must be even fewer mathematicians or logicians who view the matheme with anything but extreme suspicion or savage amusement. If a summary judgement has to be passed, it could well make use of the coinage *mathématiquerie.*

Not all the controversy surrounding the matheme is epistemological; it also involves a political dimension and may have contributed to the final demise of the EFP. The 1974 Rome Congress of the EFP was noteworthy for the intervention by Miller, later to be one of the main organizers of the matheme day schools. In substance, Miller asserts that if there is a psychoanalytic matheme, non-analysts like himself can contribute to the life and work of the analytic community, and that its existence authorizes their presence within the EFP.[237] Miller had in fact been arguing along similar lines for some years. In the preparatory remarks to a paper read to Lacan's Seminar in 1965, he justifies his presence in the analytic milieu by appealing to topology and by arguing that the Freudian field cannot be represented as a closed surface. It can, however, be represented by a Moebius strip in which 'at a certain point ... inside and outside meet, and the periphery crosses over the circumscription.' It follows that the outsider is an insider, that the non-analyst's presence is authorized by the contributions he can make to the logical formalization of psychoanalysis.[238] During the reorganization of the Département de Psychanalyse at Vincennes in 1974, similar theses were effectively written into the teaching programme:

> If there is a psychoanalytic metheme, something of what the analytic experience is integrally transmissible. . . . The thesis of the matheme therefore implies that only a real commitment to elaborating original work in or on the basis of the Freudian field can in future qualify anyone to hold a post in the department.'[239]

The ascendancy of what will come to be known as the Lacano-Miller tendency implies that acceptance of the matheme thesis is a precondition for continuing to work at Vincennes, and all prospective teachers are required to submit projects proving their commitment to the new line. A number of resignations and departures follow.

Lacan's association with Miller begins in the mid 1960s and leads to his encounter with the *Cahiers pour l'analyse* group at the Ecole Normale Supérieure. It is widely accepted that this encounter gives a new impetus to Lacan's interest in mathematics and formalization and, to that extent, the matheme can be seen as a Baroque variation on older interests, though its promotion is undoubtedly facilitated by the influx of philosophers into the EFP. Its effect, however, are unprecedented. As Miller admits with a certain bravado in his 1965 paper, the thesis that the non-analyst has a role to play within the analytic community goes against the psychoanalytic tradition which, from Freud onwards, has always insisted that: 'No one has the right to join in a discussion of psychoanalysis who has not had particular experiences which can only be obtained by being analysed oneself.'[240]

Taken literally, Freud's remarks would deny the non-analyst, or the non-analysed lay person, the right even to express an opinion about psychoanalysis, but most analysts would probably now interpret them more liberally and would not deny that much valuable work on the history of psychoanalysis – and indeed in applied psychoanalysis – has been undertaken by individuals who have not shared experiences unique to a personal analysis. It is, however, improbable that this tolerance would be extended to cover work within an analytic institution, and membership of most psychoanalytic associations is normally reserved to those who have undergone analysis. The Lacano–Millerian position implies, in contrast, that an academic training in philosophy and logic is a sufficient qualification for theoretical work within the analytic community.

The specificity of psychoanalysis must therefore be in some doubt, as must the basic assumption that its theory is grounded in clinical practice. Throughout the late 1940s and the 1950s Lacan maintained strenuously, and at some cost, that psychoanalysis must not become a sub-branch of neurobiology or a sub-speciality within the Faculty of Medicine. The logic of the matheme – which is the basis for work at Vincennes and, according to Miller, the foundation stone of the EFP itself[241] – strongly suggests that analysis is no more than a sub-topic within a more general programme of mathematical formalization and that its theoretical progress is not primarily dependent upon clinical experience.

To return to less overtly political issues. Miller argues that the concept of the matheme is inseparable from that of *lalangue*:

> Whereas *lalangue* is sustained only by misunderstanding, lives on it and is nourished by it because meanings grow and multiply on the basis of sounds, the matheme, in contrast, can be transmitted integrally ... because it is made up of little letters without any signification.[242]

Their purely logical inseparability may be less than obvious, but they are certainly historically related in that they both emerge as Lacan departs from the field of linguistics and enters that of *linguisterie*. The dichotomy between the rigour of the matheme and the definitional indeterminacy of *lalangue* can be seen as an index of the tension between the discreet charm of linguistic analysis and the fascination exercised by certain experiences of language. Indeed, in *Encore* Lacan states that *lalangue* is the element which allows or obliges him to demarcate his interests from those of structuralism to the extent that the latter 'integrates language into semiology'.[243]

The term *lalangue* itself is an obvious condensation of the definite article *la* and the noun *langue*, and it constitutes an ironic or humoristic reference to Saussure. It also strikes a familiar note; the reduplication of an initial syllable is often used in popular French to produce an affectionate diminutive, as when *Paul* becomes *Popaul* or *fille* becomes *fifille*, a familiar term used to address a little girl. In *Encore*, *lalangue* is described as being used for any purpose other than communication, as the element revealed by the experience of the unconscious, but it is said elsewhere to be the element in which 'each word takes on, according to the context, an enormous and disparate range of meanings, meanings whose heteroclite is often attested to by the dictionary.'[244] The latter definition is reminiscent of the earlier descriptions of the endless flow of the signifier, and when Lacan refers to the 'signifying battery of *lalangue*' he is effectively recycling a description of the signifying chain that dates back to at least 1959.[245]

In that sense the new terminology does not introduce anything novel at a conceptual level and, like the topological illustrations, it signals a secondary elaboration of existing notions, but it may indicate a shift of perspective. As Jean-Claude Milner writes in a study which does much to remedy the nebulous quality of many of Lacan's own definitions of *lalangue*, the term refers to the register which condemns all language to equivocation and ambiguity: '*Lalangue* is a crowd of proliferating tree-structures where the subject hangs up his desire, and any node can be elected by the subject, provided that it makes a sign.'[246] Milner's description here is faithful to Lacan's own comments, but it inevitably recalls the early definition of language as a 'knot of signification'. It is, then a reminder of Lacan's old fascination with the stuff of language and of the productions of writers such as Leiris. As he leaves the field of linguistics, Lacan re-enters familiar territory. He gives few specific instances of the practices he associates with *lalangue*, but when he refers to Joyce as exemplifying the experience of its working, one has the definite feeling that he is returning to old enthusiasms.[247]

In the period following the promulgation of the *lalangue* theses, considerable interest is aroused in Lacanian circles by a curious book originally published in 1970 with a preface by Deleuze. Wolfson's *Le Schizo et les langues* is the autobiography of a 'demented student of languages', a schizophrenic who is forced to reject his English mother tongue because it causes him physical pain and is associated with masochistic sexual phantasies. His defence is to construct an artificial language by isolating elements of language and transposing them directly into other languages. At a very basic level, the word *milk* is replaced by the harmless *milch*, but the process can be much more complex than this. Words are altered by the interpolation of vowels from etymologically related words in, say, the Germanic or Slav languages; *tree*, for instance, is gradually transformed into *derevo* via a complicated – and very sophisticated – series of phonetic and etymological substitutions.[248] The final result is a delirious linguistic construct which is not unreminiscent of Schreber's *Grundsprache*. Significantly, certain commentators also see it as illustrating Lacan's comments on *lalangue* and as displaying a certain kinship with Joyce. For Geneviève Morel, Wolfson's transliteration exercises isolate a letter as a material object which can support signification and thus exemplify the theses of texts like *Télévision*, whilst the search for 'equivalents' in foreign languages recalls both Joyce and the Schreberian tactic of emptying words of their meaning in the *Grundsprache*.[249]

In such pronouncements one cannot but hear distant echoes of Lacan's initial fascination with the beauty of psychotic language and of the burning interest he found in the writings of Aimée. Lacan himself does not appear to have been acquainted with Wolfson's work, but it can reasonably be assumed that he would have recognized certain of his own concerns in the discussions it provokes. Lecercle inscribes *Le Schizo et les langues* within a specific tradition and regards it as a prime example of the literature of desire and *délire*, a term approximating to 'delusion' and 'delirium'; he uses these terms to refer to the linguistic–literary realm where philosophers and poets consort with the March Hare, a sort of linguistic wonderland where communication breaks down and where words proliferate like material objects. Lecercle's tradition includes Schreber and ultra-surrealists like Artaud; it would not be difficult to grant Aimée honorary membership. Many of Lecercle's comments on this tradition overlap with the above descriptions of *lalangue*. With the emergence of the notion of *lalangue*, Lacanian psychoanalysis moves away from any formal analysis of language and begins once more to enjoy the experience of fascination, to experience the fascination of a psychopathological manifestation of language. This may well be more exciting than the mechanics of phonemics or the rather dismal science of philology, but it pertains to *linguisterie*, not linguistics.

No true theory of language emerges from Lacan's prolonged meditations and explorations. Still less do they generate any materialist theory of language. At crucial moments he departs from linguistic orthodoxies, conflating levels of analysis and contradicting the basic premisses of Saussurean and post-Saussurean linguistics by exploiting etymologies and pseudo-etymologies in a manner reminiscent of Heidegger and even Abel, but not of any rigorous historical linguistics. The search for primal signifiers and *points de capiton* leads, not to any recognizable science of language, but to a curious ontolinguistics combining elements of a philosophy of being and of a philosophy of language in which the presence of philosophemes derived from Kojève-Hegel is only too apparent. Later and more abstract mathematical and formalist formulations prove on closer examination to be little more than variations on or secondary elaborations of earlier and rather more concrete metaphors. The excursion into rhetoric unwittingly demonstrates that the formations of the unconscious are structured like a discourse, but not that the unconscious is structured like a language. Despite all the contradictions, there is one constant: the fascination with the stuff of language which takes Lacan from an enthusiasm for schizography in the 1930s to a love for *lalangue* in the 1970s.

6

The Dark Continent

The debate over the 'riddle of the nature of femininity'[1] is probably as old as psychoanalysis itself, but it reaches something of a climax in the period 1923–35. During these years, the controversy centres on the phallic phase and involves many of the leading analysts of the day (Freud, Jones, Rivière, Deutsch, Horney, Klein ...). The various arguments advanced have been widely discussed as a result of recent feminist interest in Freud and psychoanalysis, and need not be reiterated at length here.[2] Very schematically, the ground for the debate is prepared by Freud's contention that there is only one libido, which he describes as masculine, and that the castration complex and the phallic phase are to be observed in children of both sexes. This at least implies that sexual differentiation is not natural, pre-given or founded in biology; if both boy and girl are originally polymorphously perverse and potentially bisexual, share the belief that the mother has a penis, and have to come to terms with anatomical differences in order to identify with masculine and feminine roles respectively, gender itself cannot be pre-given. Freud's account is challenged, primarily by Jones, on the grounds that psychoanalysis concentrates too much upon the development of the boy and that male analysts in particular have taken an 'unduly phallo-centric view of the problems in question'.[3] The challenge to Freud's phallocentrism both derives from and promotes the hypothesis of an innate femininity or disposition towards femininity which is, ultimately, grounded in the little girl's perception of her own sexual organs. The phallic phase then becomes a secondary formation, whereas for Freud it remains the primary instance of psychosexual development. In a sense, then, the entire debate revolves around the question of whether gender is a construct or an innate, 'natural' differentiation founded upon a genital determinism.

The phallic-phase controversy ends – or is adjourned – with the reaffirmation of Freud's phallocentrism as opposed to the naturalism of, say, Jones, but the basic riddle remains unsolved. Throughout his writings on femininity and female sexuality Freud insists that matters remain unclear, that we do not yet know enough to solve the enigma. Frigidity is 'a phenomenon that is still insufficiently understood'; psychoanalytic understanding of the developmental processes that transform a girl–child into a woman is 'still unsatisfactory, incomplete and vague'.[4] Finally, Freud is obliged to ask in exasperation: 'What does a woman want?'[5] The truth of femininity is still in abeyance, still elusive. Given Freud's marked tendency to rely upon paralogisms and near-tautologies, it is scarcely surprising that this should be so. He asserts: 'Psychoanalysis does not try to describe what a woman is – that would be a task it could scarcely perform – but sets about inquiring how she comes into being, how a woman develops out of a child with a bisexual disposition.'[6]

Psychoanalysis sets out to inquire into the coming into being of something it cannot, by its own admission, describe. It discursively constructs femininity as indescribable, as unknowable, and then complains that it cannot describe it. It is probably Hélène Deutsch who comes closest to absolute tautology when she asserts: 'I want to examine the genesis of "femininity", by which I mean the feminine, passive–masochistic disposition in the mental life of women', and: 'A woman who succeeds in establishing this maternal function by giving up the claim of the clitoris to represent the penis has reached the goal of feminine development, *has become a woman*.'[7] Femininity, the object of the investigation, is '. . . the feminine disposition in woman; a woman succeeds in becoming a woman . . . by having become a woman.' As Freud notes, psychoanalysis cannot elucidate the intrinsic nature of 'masculine and feminine'; 'It simply takes over the two concepts and makes them the foundation of its work.'[8] One of the two concepts is defined from the outset as unknowable. By Freud's own admission, the nature of the feminine cannot be elucidated. It is only to be expected that the riddle cannot be solved.

The metaphor of 'the dark continent' is Freud's.[9] In keeping with a rationalist ideology of enlightenment, he frequently applies metaphors of darkness – often drawn from archaeology or exploration – to areas of ignorance, as in his remark that the analysis of early childhood 'leads us into dark regions where there are as yet no signposts'.[10] Such metaphors becomes more pronounced when he turns to female sexuality, 'a field of research which is so difficult of access'.[11] The discovery of a pre-oedipal phase in girls 'comes to us as a surprise, like the discovery, in another field, of the Minoan–Mycenean civilization behind the civilization of Greece.'[12] But the ultimate challenge to the psychoanalytic field-worker lies in the dark continent of the sexual life of adult women. The 'dark continent' is a classic metaphor for Africa, and if we are to accept the admittedly eccentric authority of Eric Partridge it derives from the title of a book by the Victorian explorer Stanley.[13] Freud does associate Africa and femininity in connection with the 'Dissecting my own pelvis dream', when Haggard's *She* is described as 'A *strange* book, but full of hidden meaning ... the eternal feminine ... *She* describes an adventurous road that had scarcely even been trodden before, leading into an undiscovered region ... '[14].

However, he appears to be blissfully ignorant of the political connotations of his metaphor. Within the discourse of late-nineteenth-century colonialism, Africa is dark, moist and unknown. It is, however, amenable to penetration, provided that the appropriate degree of force is used. And penetration is very much on Freud's mind as he approaches the dark continent.[15] Hence such phrases as 'If we penetrate deeply enough into the neurosis of a woman ...' and 'If you want to know more about femininity ... wait until science can give you deeper and more coherent information.'[16] The metaphors of penetration are often accompanied by metaphors of sight and insight derived from a traditional discourse of enlightment for which knowledge is a matter of 'seeing into'.

It is, of course, a psychoanalytical truism that the eyes often stand for the penis and that blinding is, as in Oedipus legend, a metaphor for castration. Penetration and insight are one and the same. Freud wishes to see into femininity, to penetrate it. Yet 'lynx-eyed Freud'[17] remains blind to the fact that his phallic-optical metaphors construct and reproduce femininity as dark, impenetrable and unknowable. Psychoanalysis posits femininity as being in excess of its rationalist discourse, and then complains and exclaims that it cannot explain it. It is as though the obscure object had to remain impenetrable for the desire to penetrate to be sustained. Freud's attempts to explain femininity might be described as an interminable exercise in epistemological foreplay; the final penetrating explanation or insight never comes, precisely because he defines its object as impenetrably obscure.

The feminine is a realm of darkness for Lacan too. He takes the signifying opposition between day and night as an example of symbolization 'because our subject is man and woman'.[18] He refers to the 'obscurity concerning the vaginal organ', but extends Freud's phallic-optical metaphors by referring to the possibility of breaking the seal that keeps it inviolate, thus supplementing the old dream of penetration with a phantasy of defloration.[19] He is also capable of transmuting psychoanalysis's impotent desire to penetrate into woman's desire to 'remain at the blind centre of analytic desire', a notion which is surely a classic instance of projection.[20] Serge Leclaire, for his part, admits to being tempted to

agree with those analysts who are clear-sighted enough to take the view
that women are virtually unanalysable.[21] Such analysts are presumably
clear-sighted enough to see that the object of their scopic-phallic desire
is impenetrable, but not to see that it is their very metaphors which
construct it as such.

The first European travellers to reach the coast of Africa returned
with extravagant tales of strange peoples and even stranger customs;
psychoanalytic field-workers return from the dark continent with their
own wondrous tales and speculations. The extravagance of Deutsch's
tautologies is rivalled only by that of her suggestion that female masochism may lead future generations of women to adopt the practice of infib-
ulation, and of her contention that miscarriages may result if the
aggressive tendencies of the sadistic-anal phase prevail against 'the
tendencies to retain the foetus' during pregnancy, a view which seems
closer to Renaissance theories about the wandering womb than to the
stated scientific ambitions of psychoanalysis.[22]

Marie Bonaparte's contribution to the 'travellers' tales' genre are, if
anything, still more curious. In a pseudonymous article published in
1924 she describes one type of frigidity as resulting from the fact that
there is 'too great a distance' between the clitoris and the vaginal
opening, and recommends surgical intervention as a means of overcom-
ing the problem. Three years later she herself underwent the operation,
but found the results unsatisfactory.[23] She later admits that her 1924
article was 'para-analytic' and erroneous, but compounds the confusion
by remarking that too great a distance between the meatus and the clitoris does not facilitate the normal transfer of sensitivity from clitoris to
vagina. She also comments on a case in which the operation failed and
the incision became infected; this 'temporarily' mobilized the patient's
essential female masochism.[24] It is difficult to decide which is more
shocking: the disastrous and dangerous conflation of psyche and soma,
or the callousness of the comment about masochism. In the late 1940s
Bonaparte is capable of arguing that the fecundation of the female cell is
primordially initiated by a kind of wound, and that the cell is therefore
masochistic.[25] There is no indication that Freud sees such statements as
casting any doubts on Bonaparte's ability as a psychoanalyst.

Freud himself is not averse to telling travellers' tales and his recon-
naissance missions to the dark continent provide the inspiration for one
of his wilder sorties in speculative anthropology. In 'Femininity' he
observes that women have made few contributions to the history of
civilization, but then modifies his generalization and credits them with
the discovery of plaiting and weaving:

Nature herself would seem to have given the model which this achievement imitates by causing the growth at maturity of the pubic hair that conceals the genitals. The step that remained to be taken lay in making the threads adhere to one another, while on the body they stick into the skin and are only matted together.[26]

Bizarre as the speculation may be, it is quite consonant with the iconography Freud applies to the female genitals, an iconography which culminates in the horror image of 'Medusa's Head', a paper which, according to Lacan, deals with 'the primitive object *par excellence*, the abyss of the female organ'.[27] It is not merely the boy-child who is horrified and petrified by the sight; it is psychoanalysis itself. Freud's iconography intersects with the phallic-scopic metaphors. The sight of the impenetrable provokes the horrified petrification of the erection that signifies: 'I am not castrated.' At the same time it both sustains and frustrates the desire to see and to penetrate. Whilst Freud's anthropology is, to say the very least, suspect, his metaphors are remarkably coherent and constant.

Lacanian psychoanalysis has its own contributions to make to this odd literary genre, but they have attracted little attention in recent writing of the feminism–psychoanalysis articulation, perhaps because the wood of sexual politics cannot be seen for the tall trees of theory. Who but a psychoanalyst would be allowed to suggest, without being challenged on the grounds of sexism, that a girl who allows herself to be raped by her father is expressing her desire for the phallus, or even for a penis? The ground for such an eminently political assertion is of course prepared by the disclaimer: 'We are not concerned here with political or philosophical work, but with analytic work.'[28] The same woman analyst appears to believe that women cannot or do not masturbate ('we might say that she masturbated, if the term had any meaning when we are dealing with a woman') and to accept the existence of nymphomania as an objective phenomenon.[29]

An extraordinary sentence in an essay by Piera Aulagnier-Spairani, a respected member of the EFP, holds that pre- and post-pubertal clitoral masturbation is more common in men than in woman; she further argues that one of the essential components in lesbian lovemaking is a theatrical *mise en scène* staged for the benefit of an unseen or imaginary witness who is presumed to know the role played by the phallus.[30] The argument derives from Jones and is endorsed by Lacan,[31] but no one sees fit to mention that this scenario is one of the oldest clichés in pornography, both written and visual. Finally, the extent to which psychoanalytic sophistication can coexist alongside the most banal assumptions about sexuality is revealed by Aulagnier-Spairani's casual remark to the effect that male homosexuals are spontaneously drawn to careers in hair-dressing and dressmaking because they allow them to shape the image of the object of male desire.[32] No sociological or statistical evidence is produced to support this claim which, with the appropriate terminological modifications, might have been culled from the tabloid press. The impenetrability of the dark continent has become a blank screen on which the most fantastic of myths and the most banal of assumptions can be projected at will.

Lacan himself makes no reference whatsoever to the phallic-stage debate in his early writings, even though its later stages are contemporaneous with his own entry into the world of psychoanalysis. Texts like 'Le Stade du miroir' outline a theory of the constitution of the subject but operate with universal categories which are never sexually differentiated. Aimée and the Papin sisters provide him with elements of a theory of psychosis, and with an iconography, but not with a theory of the genesis of the feminine. When the young Lacan does leave the realm of convulsive beauty, his iconography is as banally sociological and normative as anything to be found in Karen Horney's writings on the subject. Thus, in the long 1938 essay on the family, he argues that the act of feeding, holding and contemplating her child satisfies the mother's most primitive desires, and comes very close to Horney's celebration of 'the blissful consciousness of bearing a new life within oneself.... The deep pleasurable satisfaction in suckling it.'[33]

Although there are references to the phallic-stage controversy in the early seminars and in 'D'Une Question préliminaire ...', it is really only in 1958 that Lacan addresses it in any detail in 'La Signification du phallus', 'A la Mémoire d'Ernest Jones' and 'Propos directifs pour un Congrès sur la sexualité féminine'. Lacan now stresses the importance of a debate which represents a true 'passion for doctrine' and takes us back to a golden age that predates the alleged Americanization of psychoanalysis and its degeneration into egopsychology.[34] 'Propos directifs' originally appeared in an issue of *La Psychanalyse* devoted to female sexuality. It was published alongside a number of papers from the original debate; Lacan's 'remarks' are in effect his marginal notes on the controversy and an important moment in the elaboration of his views on femininity. It is therefore essential to note that this *écrit* contains an unexpected reference to a clinical notion which is not really part of the classic Freudian heritage: erotomania, which may, Lacan suggests, be to women what fetishism is to men.[35]

Erotomania is not a major category for Freud, and he does not make any great clinical use of it. It is invoked in the study of the Schreber case, but merely as one example of the possible relations between paranoia and homosexuality, and much more importance is ascribed to delusions of persecution, delusions of jealousy and megalomania.[36] Here Freud discusses erotomania in relation to a male subject, but Lacan clearly associates it primarily, if not exclusively, with women. Perhaps more significantly still, he does not discuss erotomania in 'D'Une Question préliminaire ...', his detailed rereading of Schreber's *Denkwürdigkeiten eines Nervenkranken.*

Erotomania has a long history in French psychiatry, having been first identified as a distinct nosographic entity by Pinel's disciple Esquirol in his *Traité des maladies mentales* of 1837.[37] For Esquirol it is a chronic cerebral condition characterized by an excessive love for a person who may be imaginary or known to the subject, and by the delusion of being loved by that person. In 1975 Lacan describes it rather more succinctly in a seminar given at Yale University: 'Erotomania implies the choice of a person who is, to some extent, famous, and the idea that that person is concerned with no one but you.'[38] Nineteenth-century psychiatric literature abounds in accounts of erotomania, many of them dealing with cases in which a young man develops a passion for an actress or a young woman becomes infatuated with a social superior. Both Kraepelin and Bleuler note the existence of erotomania, but do not foreground it in any way and see it simply as a form of *dementia paranoides* (paraphrenia and schizophrenia in their respective systems) if it is accompanied by hallucinations, and as a form of paranoia if no hallucinations are present. Shortly after the First World War erotomania becomes the subject of renewed interest in French psychiatric circles. The man responsible for the revival of interest is Clérambault, Lacan's 'only master in psychiatry'.

In a series of articles published in the early 1920s,[39] Clérambault defines the syndrome as a *psychose passionnelle* centred upon the delusion of being loved, usually by a prestigious figure, and as being frequently accompanied by extreme jealousy. Classically, erotomania can be divided into three successive phases: a phase of pride in being loved or hope of being loved; a phase of frustration; and a phase of jealousy. In the final phase love turns to hatred, and the love object becomes an object to be persecuted. Real or attempted violence may ensue. Erotomania was part of the diagnosis of Aimée made by Truelle, himself the author of articles on the subject, when she was first admitted to Sainte-Anne after her abortive assault on Madame Z. Many features of the case do seem to be typical of the syndrome: admiration is reversed into hatred; Aimée has a sentimental attachment to the Prince of Wales; she does not suffer from hallucinations. Although Lacan's observations led him to conclude that she was suffering from 'self-punishment paranoia', and he analyses her case in terms of identification with an ideal ego, it is clear that erotomania is also a significant element in his analysis. It is also an element in the aetiology of psychosis elaborated in the Seminar of 1955–56.[40] The Seminar references to the theory of erotomania are not to Freud, but to Clérambault; Lacan's debt to French psychiatry is as apparent here as in the decision to translate *Weiderholungszwang* as *automatisme de répétition*. That he does not theorize erotomania to any great extent is in itself symptomatic. A nosographic category asociated primarily with the French school of psychiatry is appropriated and interpolated into a reading of Freud. He appears to see no contradiction here, just as there is no contradiction between his declared loyalty to the Freudian tradition and his adherence to the ritual of the *présentation des malades*.

Although Lacan himself does not elaborate on erotomania, the concept acquires a certain currency in the EFP in the mid 1960s, with François Perrier devoting a substantial paper to the subject in April 1966. Perrier endorses both Clérambault's characterization of erotomania as a *psychose passionnelle* and Lacan's suggestion that it is gender-specific.[41] He then attempts to integrate it into the Lacanian canon by arguing that the syndrome is found in women who have somehow bypassed the phallic stage. This argument is not followed through completely, but it would appear to imply that erotomania is, like fetishism, an attempt to disavow castration. Perrier, that is, reproduces the thesis briefly put forward by Lacan in 'Propos directifs'. Similar formulations can be found in Aulagnier-Spairani's paper on femininity: whereas the fetishist wishes to sustain his belief in the existence of the maternal phallus, or his belief that his gaze will never fail to find the object he desires, the erotomaniac sustains the belief that she is the object of an omnipresent gaze which confers upon her the status of the desired one.[42] Lemoine-Luccioni, meanwhile, argues that sublimation is the only thing that can save a woman from the Scylla of erotomania and the Charybdis of nymphomania.[43]

All these suggestions are made in texts published in Lacan's 'Champ freudien' collection, and it can be assumed that they therefore have his doctrinal *imprimatur*. Perrier ends his paper on erotomania by speculating that there may be a link between 'the aptitude for erotomania' and 'surrealist inspiration', but does not pursue the argument.[44] Frustrating as his failure to follow through his argument may be, it is an indirect reminder that Lacan returns to Clérambault and erotomania just as he begins to approach the dark continent. The erotomaniac strand in Aimée's symptomatology is in part the inspiration behind the writings which both Lacan and the surrealists admired so much, and the clinical category of erotomania is readily incorporated into the cult of convulsive beauty and of what Dali terms the phenomenon of ecstasy. As will be seen, Lacan's reflections on femininity are never entirely divorced from that cult.

Lacan's contribution to the long-standing debate over femininity is of course the phallus, but its conceptual status may in fact be rather less clear than is sometimes assumed. The centrality of the phallus to his views on femininity means that he does in a sense remain within the mainstream of the Freudian tradition, which has always tended to address the issue in negative, not to say privative, terms. Freud discusses femininity in terms of the absence of the penis; Lacan discusses women in terms of their negative or problematic relation to the signifier 'phallus'. The epistemological aim of introducing the concept of the phallus has often been read in terms of an attempt to rid psychoanalysis of its residual biological and natural references, and to articulate it with the theory of symbolism Lacan derives from structural anthropology and linguistics. Any claim to the effect that Lacan provides a theory capable of accounting for the structuring of a gendered subjectivity that is irreducible to a biological given and that he therefore has something to offer feminism must, so to speak, stand or fall by the phallus. It must also be tested against the process whereby the concept of the phallus is elaborated.

The use of the word itself marks something of a departure from Freud who, Lacanian assertions to the contrary notwithstanding, does not make any systematic distinction between 'phallus' and 'penis'. In, for instance, 'Fetishism' (SE XXI) – the paper from which Lacan derives his notion of the imaginary phallus of the mother – the terms are used interchangeably. The same could be said of 'The Infantile Genital Organization' (SE XIX), where 'phallus' is used only once; in the rest of the paper Freud reverts to 'penis', and it is difficult to sustain the view that the lexical variation signals any major conceptual distinction. As Laplanche and Pontalis note in their *Language of Psychoanalysis*, Freud employs the adjective 'phallic' frequently, but normally reserves the noun 'phallus' for the symbolic phallus of the Ancient World, as in 'The Taboo of Virginity' and in the essay on Leonardo.[45] French psychoanalysts have always tended to use 'phallus' much more frequently, and somewhat indiscriminately. Bonaparte oscillates between *phallus* and *pénis* throughout her *Sexualité de la femme*; in the glossary appended to an anthology of essays by Freud entitled *Essais de psychanalyse*, Hesnard writes: 'Phallus. Ancient name for penis. Male sexual organ, of remarkable significance for its symbolic value'.[46] Lacan's use of 'phallus' must, then, be seen against a rather confused terminological background. The traditional lack of precision leads Melanie Klein to protest about the French translation of her *Psycho-Analysis of Children*, and to complain that the generalized use of *femme* or *mère phallique* obliterated the distinction between Freud's 'phallic mother' and her own concept of the 'mother with a penis'.[47] As will become apparent later, the obliteration of that difference is of direct relevance to Lacan's phallus concept.

Although the concept of the phallus is allegedly an important motif in the final state of the Lacanian system, it is elaborated gradually and with a surprising degree of hesitancy and for a long time the phallus/penis distinction is simply asserted rather than being justified or theorized. In his pre-war work Lacan fails to make any distinction between the two, and in 1951 it is the penis that is defined as being 'dominant in the shaping of the body-image'.[48] Apart from a remarkably opaque reference to a Sanskrit noun which can, according to Wilden, mean both 'signifier' and 'phallus', even 'Fonction et champ' is innocent of any mention of the phallus.[49] If, as Leclaire claims, the phallus is an 'essential psychoanalytic notion',[50] one can only conclude that the original manifesto of Lacanian psychoanalysis is in some way marginal to the final canon. Alternatively, one can argue that 'Fonction et champ' is the true manifesto and that the phallus is a later addition of no great consequence. Whichever option is taken, the theoretical edifice of the final state begins to look rather less stable than many presentations would have us believe.

It is in fact during the Seminars of 1954–55 and 1955–56 that Lacan begins to forge his new concept. Discussing *penisneid* in June 1954, he remarks that there is nothing 'natural' about it; *penisneid* relates to the symbolic, and it is because women are inscribed within an androcentric symbolic order that the penis takes on a symbolic value. He then corrects himself, specifying that it is the phallus, not the penis, that is involved.[51] This sounds more like a classic slip of the tongue – and, in view of later developments, a highly significant one – than the deliberate, feigned hesitation of the rhetor. In 1954 'phallus' is defined simply as something of which a symbolic use can be made. A symbol, that is, is tautologically defined as amenable to symbolization, and the supposed phallus/penis distinction remains remarkably unspecific. Matters are little clearer a year later, when Dora is said to identify with the bearer of the penis and not, as one might expect from later formulations, with the bearer of the phallus. Later in the same seminar Lacan discusses *Booz endormi*, a *locus classicus* for his subsequent comments on sexual differentiation and symbolization, but his remarks apply to the 'royal penis', and not to the phallus.[52]

It is only towards the very end of the 1956 Seminar that 'phallus' is used in its later acceptation and is referred to as the mediating element in the castration complex, as an imaginary object which the child accepts as being in the father's possession.[53] In view of the crucial importance accorded to the phallus in the final state, it should be noted that these early definitions are not merely hesitant; at one point Lacan simply contradicts his own future orthodoxy. In June 1955 he says of the phallus that no symbolic use can be made of something that cannot be seen; in later formulations, precisely the opposite is asserted: the phallus can play its symbolic role only if it is veiled and remains invisible.[54]

The 1955–56 Seminar provides the basis for 'D'Une Question préliminaire à tout traitement possible de la psychose', written in December 1957–January 1958 and first published in 1959. In the process of reworking and writing up, all the hesitations of the Seminar disappear. The phallus now emerges fully armed and entire unto itself; its imaginary function is specified as the 'armature of the Freudian edifice'.[55] The effect, if not the purpose, of the reworking is to erase any mark of difference between Freud and Lacan.

Nor is that the only difference to be silently erased. Lacan refers here and elsewhere to Fenichel's paper on the symbolic equation between girl and phallus,[56] and it is at least implied that the two analysts share a common concept of the phallus. This is not in fact the case. Fenichel does not make any systematic phallus/penis distinction. Whilst the title of his paper refers to the phallus, the first three sentences refer quite indiscriminately to 'a girl with a phallus', 'woman's possession of a penis' and 'a phallic girl'. Lacan's attempts to found a phallus/penis distinction press into service a text in which no such distinction is made. Lacan also makes the suggestion that Fenichel's *Mädchen* might be translated into French as *pucelle*,[57] meaning 'maid' or 'virgin'. 'Virgin' is not the first meaning of *Mädchen* (*Jungfrau* is the normal equivalent to 'virgin'), and the banal *jeune fille* would surely be an adequate translation, especially as Fenichel's paper is not primarily concerned with virginity. There appears to be a perverse logic at work here. Most French-speakers would probably immediately associate *pucelle* with *la pucelle d'Orléans*, in other words with Joan of Arc, the most famous female transvestite in French history. Fenichel's equation originates in an analysis of a phantasy recounted by a male transvestite patient. Transvestism is of course a denial of difference. Lacan uses a text about the denial of difference to deny the existence of a difference between himself, Freud and Fenichel. The phallus is the concept which will be evoked to explain sexual differentiation, but an important moment in its elaboration includes a denial of difference, and a confusion of gender which extends even to the grammatical level; *Mädchen* is a neuter noun, whereas *pucelle* is obviously feminine.[58]

It is of course in 'La Signification du phallus' that Lacan comes closest to stating what he means by 'phallus', but the reasons for his departure from Freud's terminology are perhaps less clear than they might be. In the 1957–58 Seminar on the formations of the unconscious, he does in fact ask: 'Why the phallus and not the penis?' The answer is less than illuminating: 'Because the phallus is not a question of a form or an image, or a phantasy, but rather of a signifier, the signifier of desire.'[59] The word 'penis' is a signifier too, and Lacan is substituting one signifier for another. The description of the structuring effects of the castration complex given in 'La Signification' relies heavily upon Freud's account, and might be taken for a recapitulation were it not that Lacan uses 'phallus' in contexts where Freud normally uses 'penis'.[60] Nor is the only example of substitutionism in this *écrit*. Lacan refers to the phallus as being a part-object, and to its presence within the mother's body as an internal object. This is of course an allusion to Klein, but she speaks of the child's phantasy of the penis inside the mother's body[61] and, as already noted, she strongly objected to the confusion of this idea with Freud's 'phallic mother' in the French translation of her work.

Once more, differences are being elided. 'One signifier (or word) for another' is Lacan's rather dubious definition of metaphor, and if that definition is taken at face value, 'phallus' is little more than a metaphor or euphemism for 'penis'. Although the elaboration of the phallus concept is often said to represent a move away from psychoanalysis's residual biologism, it remains true to say that Lacan does not really depart from Freud's account of the castration complex and merely restates it in symbolic, metaphorical or structural terms.[62] It is difficult to see what has been gained from the substitution of one signifier for another, unless there is some advantage to be had by replacing the notorious 'anatomy is destiny' with 'symbolization is destiny'.

It is far from uncommon for Lacanians to attempt to locate a phallus–penis distinction in Freud himself. As with Lacan's silent substitution of one signifier for another, there is something of a paradox here: on the one hand, it is implied that by introducing the phallus as the key to the symbolic Lacan has gone beyond Freud; on the other, every attempt is made to find that 'beyond' in Freud himself. In an essay on Hélène Deutsch, Nicole Kress-Rosen makes much of Freud's reference to the 'primacy of the phallus' in 'Infantile Genital Organization' and claims to find the phallus–penis distinction in that paper, even though Freud uses the terms interchangeably (and it is to be noted that the Standard Edition is much more faithful to the text of 'Die infantile Genitalorgani-sation' than the translation she quotes).[63] Further evidence in favour of that claim is adduced from 'Femininity', but, once again, the authority of the text to which Kress-Rosen refers simply cannot be taken for granted. The French text has *le désir de posséder un phallus* for the Standard Edition's 'wish for a penis'. Freud's original German is quite unequivo-cal; he speaks of *der Wunsch nach dem Penis*.[64] A phallus–penis distinc-tion has indeed been introduced, but not by Freud. His French translator, Anne Berman, must take responsibility for the innovation. Similarly, the French reference to *le manque de phallus de la femme* is simply a free – not to say libertarian rendition of Freud's *Penislosigkeit des Weibs.*[65]

Berman's translations simply do not have the authority of the Standard Edition (itself open to criticism on rather different grounds[66]), not to mention the German original. It has to be remembered that in France, the 'return to Freud' all too often means a return to the letter of distinctly uneven, and at times simply inaccurate, translations. Yet it is the French translation alone that allows Kress-Rosen to find a phallus–penis distinction in Freud. Until such time as Lacanians deign to provide authority for their claims by referring to Freud rather than to his translators or to Lacan's substitutions, allusions to 'the phallus – which, as Freud makes clear, is not the penis'[67] must be viewed with rather more than a degree of scepticism, particularly when they are not accompanied by any reference to a specific paper by Freud. This also goes for English translations which unquestioningly accept and transmit their unverified and unverifiable claims.

In *Encore*, Lacan notes with malicious glee that all his pupils have got into a muddle over the phallus.[68] Whilst their confusion is no doubt in part a reflection of his own repressed hesitancies and contradictions, 'muddle' is a superb example of litotes. Definitions of the phallus proliferate, become ever more defined, and finally cancel one another out, thus allowing a conceptual regression from phallus to penis. In 1968 Serge Leclaire who was at the time the director of the Département de Psychanalyse at Vincennes and a figure of no small importance in the EFP, refers to the phallus as a word, but adds that it is an unusual word; it designates the penile object, and is at the same time a letter which might be termed the alpha and the omega of the alphabet of desire. It is, moreover, a universal symbol, the differential term which makes the body either male or female.[69] An unusual word indeed. In the course of a seminar at Vincennes, he confidently asserts: 'Nowadays, no one thinks of the phallus simply as a penis', and then goes on to say that the penis is part of the concept of the phallus. That concept has both a biological function (or even two biological functions: excretion and reproduction) and a symbolic function.[70] A concept with one or more biological functions is something of an oddity by any standard, linguistic or epistemological; Leclaire's concepts are every bit as unusual as his words. By 1975 the phallus has become 'the referent of the unconscious order'.[71] Leclaire defines the phallus as, successively, a word, a letter, a symbol, a concept and a referent; no attempt is made to collate or clarify these conflicting, contradictory definitions.

Juan David Nasio's essay 'Métaphore et phallus' is based upon Leclaire's Seminar, and if its content is a faithful reflection of that of the original, it would appear that Leclaire was even more confused than his own text suggests. Nasio describes the phallus as a signifier, a sign, the signifier of an impossible *jouissance*, the sign of castration, the signifier of *jouissance*, and the sign of the impossible object. It is further said to represent the real and the non-representable.[72]

Lemoine-Luccioni has her own contribution to make to the muddle. At the beginning of her *Partage des femmes* the phallus is quite conventionally described as 'the symbol of the penis', but the penis later becomes 'the sign of the phallus', and by the end of the essay the phallus has become 'that which the penis represents'.[73] There is no known system of linguistics or theory of symbolization in which symbol, sign and 'that which represents' are synonymous and interchangeable. The confusion of her definitions notwithstanding, Lemoine-Luccioni is quite happy to use the phallus–penis distinction in a most authoritarian manner. In an account of a dream an analysand mentions the penis, only to be told by her analyst that she really means the phallus.[74] As Jane Gallop notes, there is something deeply shocking about this intervention,[75] not least because it appears to offend against the most fundamental rules of analytic practice. This is not an interpretation, but a violent interpolation on the part of an analyst who takes her role as the subject-presumed-to-know somewhat literally.

Lemoine-Luccioni's interpolation is symptomatic of the way in which all ill-defined and unstable concept can become a source of authority, as in the ritual 'You are confusing the phallus with the penis' that is addressed by Lacanians to everyone from Karen Horney to the unnamed feminists whose criticisms of Lacan's doctrine of the signifier are said to be 'vitiated by their confusion of the penis as an organ of the body with the phallus as signifier'.[76] The degree of definitional and conceptual confusion surrounding the phallus is, however, such that the shrill and oft-repeated cry of 'the phallus, not the penis' begins to sound uncannily close to Freud's classic example of *Verneinung*: '"You ask who this person in the dream can be. It's not my mother." We emend this to "So it *is* his mother." '[77]

Credence is lent to this view by the work of Françoise Dolto and Maude Mannoni. Both make use of the phallus-as-signifier concept in their theoretical expositions, but it is evident from the case-histories they describe that at the level of clinical practice, the phallus–penis distinction becomes blurred. Just as the symbolic Name-of-the-Father tends to regress to being little more than an invocation of the name or imago of the real father, so the symbolic phallus tends to become the biological penis. Accordingly, both these respected child analysts often revert to Freud's original usage and use phallus and penis interchangeably.[78] There is no evidence to suggest that this has ever occasioned any denunciation of their work by Lacan, and Dolto in particular was a close associate of his for many years. Their reversion to Freudian usage and the apparent absence of polemic over the issue might, then, be taken as an indication that, at the level of clinical psychoanalytic practice, the supposed phallus–penis distinction is less pertinent than it seems to be at the purely theoretical level.

Even if the rallying cry of 'the phallus, not the penis' is taken at face value, there is one objection to the phallus-as-signifier theory which remains immune to the repeated *anathemata est*. Lacan's linguistics constantly drifts into *linguisterie* and he often refers to privileged signifiers, thus contradicting the basic tenet that a signifier is defined solely by the differences that mark it out from other signifiers. It is difference alone which allows a signifier to signify; in and of itself, it signifies nothing. Yet the phallus is a 'privileged signifier', or even the 'signifier of signifiers'.[79] It is in itself significant and of itself productive of signification; unlike other signifiers, it becomes the primal signifier of absolute difference. As Derrida points out, this can only mean that it is a transcendental, an element which allows a system to function without being reducible to a part of that system, an element which determines without being determined, and an avatar of the divine *logos*.[80] It is in effect the end-stop which guarantees the stability of a signifying system which would otherwise be in a perpetual state of flux, a first cause which is itself without cause.

Derrida's objection does not rest upon any confusion of the phallus with the penis; on the contrary, it follows through the logic of Lacan's own privileging of the phallus. According to this view, Lacan's supposed attempt to rid psychoanalysis of its residual biologism simply results in phallogocentrism, a disastrous condensation of Freud's undoubted phallocentrism and the logocentrism characteristic of Western metaphysics. A similar, but more explicitly feminist critique of the phallus concept is put forward by Catherine Baliteau, who concludes: 'Ultimately, Lacanian psychoanalysis is the last avatar of Western metaphysics. The symbolic replaces the thing in itself, and the phallus replaces the Prime Mover.'[81] And Lacan does occasionally betray his underlying logocentrism by citing the evangelical 'In the beginning was the Word'.[82]

The attempt to introduce a phallus–penis distinction is open to challenge on a number of grounds. It is not possible to justify it by reference to Freud, unless credence is given to faulty translations and forced interpretations. The supposed concept is so hedged about with contradictory definitions and tautologies that it is highly unstable and, ultimately, little more than a metaphor or euphemism for 'penis'. It is unable to escape Freud's lingering biologism; indeed, the examples of Dolto and Mannoni strongly suggest that the phallus concept is the site of a regression towards the biological organ. If the phallus is integrated into the theory of the symbolic derived from Lévi-Strauss, it has to be articulated with a theory which founds sexual difference in natural gender categories. If it is rigorously theorized as a signifier, a transcendental metaphysics – or even a theology – is silently introduced. Ernest Jones's 'In the beginning ... male and female He created them'[83] – an endless source of amusement to Lacanians – is supplanted by a phallogocentrist 'The transcendental phallus–*logos* created them as male and female signifiers.' If the phallus is the conceptual compass that will allow Lacan to go beyond Freud in the exploration of the dark continent, the expedition sets off under an inauspicious sign.

As noted above, it is in the Seminars of 1954–56 that Lacan tentatively begins to elaborate his concept of the phallus. In March 1956, he also briefly addresses the issue of femininity itself during a discussion of the Dora case. Dora, according to Lacan, asks 'the hysterical question': 'What is a woman?' or 'What does it mean to be a woman?'[84] Dora does not in fact ask any of these questions in so many words. In her dreams, she repeatedly asks: 'Where is the key?' and 'Where is the box?', and Freud immediately and somewhat brusquely interprets these as 'questions relating to the genitals'.[85] Freud speaks on behalf of Dora, and Lacan in turn speaks on behalf of Freud, transforming 'questions relating to the genitals' into the question 'What is a woman?' The question of femininity becomes a question of or pertaining to genitals. It is perhaps significant that the old scopic metaphors re-emerge at precisely this point; for Lacan, the meaning of Dora's two dreams is 'transparently obvious'.[86]

Just as Lacan is attempting to move towards a theory of the symbolic as the source of sexual differentiation and to elaborate a concept of the phallus which is not reducible to the biological, he regresses towards genital determinism as an explanation for the riddle of femininity. This minor instance of genital determinism has to be related to Lacan's subsequent remarks about femininity's 'resistance to symbolization', as it at least implies the equating of 'symbolic' with 'masculine' and of 'natural' or 'biological' with 'feminine'. In 1938 Lacan actually spelled out that equation by observing that, whereas the early phases of the 'maternal function' reveal instinctual features pertaining to the biological family, paternity owes much to 'spiritual postulates'.[87] The masculine–feminine dichotomy is, it is strongly implied, isomorphic with a spiritual–biological dualism. Lacan never disowns or criticizes the text in which this equation is postulated; in 1964 he still claims that it is pertinent to his work and has lost none of its relevance.[88] It is, then, more than possible that this set of oppositions subtends the later reliance upon Lévi-Strauss's nature–culture dualism and that the contention that the feminine is beyond symbolization derives from a biological–genital determinism which is ever-present but rarely enunciated in so many words.

The remarks made in the Seminars of March 1956 are not Lacan's first references to Dora, nor is the reinterpretation of her questions the first slippage to have occurred in relation to her case. Lacan discusses Dora in 'Intervention sur le transfert' (1951), but there are some curious discrepancies between Freud and Lacan. Freud himself pays little attention to Dora's mother, despite the strength of the mother–daughter identification, and contemptuously dismisses her as being a typical representative of 'what might be termed the "housewife's psychosis"'.[89] Lacan marginalizes her still further, reducing her to a 'lateral appendage in the circuit of exchange'.[90] The governess simply disappears from Lacan's account of the case-history. This in itself is a considerable distortion of its narrative and libidinal economy; governesses and maids are often important figures in Freud, and they often play major roles in the case-histories (seduction, the imparting of forbidden knowledge ...). For Lacan, they appear not to exist. Much more important, however, is the manner in which Dora's 'idea that she had been handed over to Herr K. as the price of his tolerating the relations between her father and his wife' is transmuted into an insight into 'the basis of the most elementary of social exchanges'.[91]

In other words, Lacan credits Dora with anticipating Lévi-Strauss's analysis of the elementary structures of kinship. The slippage implies rather more than the conflation of Dora with Lévi-Strauss; whatever else might be said about the anthropologist's analysis of exogamy and of the symbolic exchange of women, it is clearly not an analysis of the perverse wife- and daughter-swapping of which Dora believes herself to be the victim. It is equally clear that Lévi-Strauss's symbolic structures are not a rationale for adultery and do not rest upon the exchange of a daughter for a wife; classically, such structures rest upon the exchange of a daughter for a daughter or a niece for a niece. As with the frequent substitution of 'phallus' for 'penis', what appears to be a neutral recapitulation of Freud proves to be the result of a secondary elaboration on Lacan's part. Dora's fears are perfectly justified; she has unwittingly become the object of a symbolic exchange between Freud, Lacan and Lévi-Strauss. Something very similar happens to St Teresa. Bernini petrifies her into a statue erected *ad maiorem gloriam Dei*; Lacan turns her into an iconic illustration of his theory of *jouissance*. It is also significant that both women are in effect silenced by being caught up in these circuits. To anticipate later developments, it is apparent that neither Dora nor St Teresa knows what she wants or understands the meaning of her questions; Lacan, it is implied, does.

Lacan further specifies Dora's problem as being that of all women:

she has difficulty in accepting herself as the object of male desire. The universalization of her problem must have as its corollary the contention that all women are, like Dora, hysterics. Femininity is being equated with hysteria as well as with determination by the genitals. Lacan himself rarely makes the equation specific, but certain of his followers are less reticent. Montrelay, for instance, suggests that 'feminine discourse' might be better described as 'hysterical discourse', adding by way of explanation that 'All women play upon the uterus.'[92] A double reductionism is at work here: the feminine is reduced to the hysterical, and then to the biological. In historical terms the irony of Montrelay's position is that she comes close to asserting the existence of an innate femininity, in other words to adopting the very views for which Jones and Horney are habitually criticized. Indeed, her entire notion of gender is predicated upon the perception of innate essences. Her description of the experience of childbirth suggests that the gender of a child can be intuitively perceived during labour rather than by empirical observation after the event (or amniocentesis before the event): 'A male child drags you out of the uncertainty all at once. He makes you emerge and reinserts you within the sure, visible order of reality and objects. With a girl, everything remains shadowy.'[93] Whilst the imagery used here is certainly consistent with Freud's light–dark dichotomy, such comments can scarcely contribute to a theory of gender or of gendering that is not reducible to essentialism.

The reduction of the feminine to the genital appears in iconographic form in the fifteenth (Summer 1978) issue of *Ornicar?*, which is largely devoted to the question *Que veut la femme?* (What do women want?). The artwork accompanying a number of the articles features a line drawing of a bare-breasted woman and a playful black cat. This is not merely a further instance of the rather tiresome whimsy that typifies some aspects of *Ornicar?*;[94] in French slang, *le chat* or *la chatte* (for obvious reasons, the feminine form tends to be more common) has precisely the same connotations as the Anglo–American 'pussy'. *Ornicar?* inscribes its discussion of femininity under the sign of pussy. The material published in this issue is far from representing a deviation from Lacan's position with regard to the riddle of the nature of femininity. The 'pussy' motive is itself quite in line with the genital determinism which lies behind the translations of Dora's questions into the universalist 'What is a woman?'. One of the major contributions deals at some length with the 'convulsionaries' of the eighteenth century and derives its themes directly from Lacan's comments on mysticism in *Encore*.[95] It is, in other words, a further contribution to the iconography generated during the earliest stages of Lacan's career, and a return to the cult of convulsive beauty which overdetermined his clinical interest in Aimée and the Papin sisters.

A passage in 'Propos directifs', which has already been shown to be a return to something more – and other – than Freud, further indicates the convergence of a genital determinism and the surrealist cult. In a characteristically dismissive reference to women analysts, Lacan describes them as *les représentantes du sexe*.[96] *Le sexe* is in some contexts the equivalent to the English 'the fair sex', but it is also a standard term meaning 'genitals'. Lacan can, then, be interpreted as saying that women analysts are representatives of their genitals. Lest it be objected that this is a forced or overliteral interpretation, it should be recalled that Lacan himself constantly insists upon the need to read literally, *à la lettre*; there is no reason to exempt his text from his own prescriptions. In the next paragraph Lacan goes on to state that the metaphors used by the representatives of the fair sex (or of their genitals) are in no sense to be preferred to 'what the first comer might offer us by way of less intentional poetry'. 'Less intentional poetry' is either a deliberate reference to or a reminiscence of the title of Eluard's *Poésie involontaire et poésie intentionnelle*, the anthology in which fragments of Aimée's novels were published and which helped to consecrate her as a surrealist heroine.

In the middle of his return to the golden age of the phallic-stage debate Lacan also returns to erotomania, and to a figure he associates with the cult of convulsive beauty. If we adopt Gallop's suggestion as to the translation of words in *Encore* and related texts that begin with the syllable *con*,[97] *beauté convulsive* becomes 'beauty that revolves around the cunt'. The slippages noted in Lacan's discussion of Dora, the frequent but veiled references to convulsive beauty, and the iconography of both *Encore* and *Ornicar?* all combine to suggest that, for Lacan and his disciples, the riddle of femininity is basically a question of pussy. Lacan's peregrinations through surrealism, psychoanalysis and theories of symbolization finally bring him back to the classically sexist reductionism of 'woman as cunt'. As he himself puts it: 'There is nothing to distinguish a woman as being sexed, except of course her *sexe* [sex/ genitals]'. Elsewhere, he muses with an ambivalence of Freud staring at Medusa's head, 'Queen Victoria, there's a woman for you ... when one encounters a toothed vagina of such exceptional size ...'.[98] Lacan's phraseology may at times be more elegant than that of, say, Henry Miller, but the underlying sentiments are not. And when Lacan refers to Hamlet's mother as 'a gaping cunt',[99] his terminology itself is worthy of Miller.

Any claim to the effect that Lacanian psychoanalysis has something to offer feminism must first refute its implicit genital determinism; it must also be measured against what Lacanian psychoanalysis has to say about feminism. Lacan himself has relatively little to say on the subject,

but what he does have to say is not encouraging. His early comments on
family structures do not augur well for later debates. In 1938 he opines
that the origins of our culture lie within 'the paternalist family', and
mourns the decline of 'the paternal imago'.[100] In 1947 he recalls seeing
in the military hospital where he worked in 1940 an 'unforgettable
parade of subjects who had not really awoken from the warmth of the
skirts of their mothers and wives', and remarks that their degeneracy
reflected 'on a collective scale the effects of the degradation of the virile
type'.[101] Such comments come close to expressing the right-wing thesis
that the defeat of 1940 was the result of the effeminate decadence of the
Republic. In 1955 Lacan remarks that there is nothing new about 'the
feminine revolt'; it dates back to Ancient Rome and is the expression of
an imaginary rivalry between the sexes.[102] When he begins to approach
the question of femininity in the 1950s, Simone de Beauvoir's *Le
Deuxième Sexe* (1949) is a major cultural and political point of reference, but Lacan chooses to ignore it. A fleeting reference to Friedan's
The Feminine Mystique aside,[103] *Ecrits* contains no discussion of
contemporary feminism.

The tone of Lacan's discourse is often as revelatory as its content. In
Encore, the text in which he returns to the unanswered question 'What
do women want?', that tone is often one of parody or mockery. In
'Femininity', Freud acknowledges that at least something has been
learned about the developmental process whereby a girl becomes a
woman, 'thanks to the work of our excellent women colleagues'.[104]
Lacan obviously does not concur, and complains that: 'Our colleagues,
the lady analysts, tell us ... not everything about female sexuality.'[105]
Freud's 'excellent women colleagues' have become 'lady analysts'. The
semantic shift from *femme* to *dame*, which has much the same value as
the shift from woman to lady in English, recurs in Lacan's anecdote
about meeting a 'lady' [*dame*] from the local women's movement
[MLF] during his recent visit to Italy. A newspaper has reported him as
saying that women do not exist. Lacan continues: 'She was really ... I
told her ... "Come tomorrow morning, and I will explain what I am
talking about."'[106] Needless to say, tomorrow morning never comes, and
the anecdote is never completed. For Freud, female sexuality was a
mystery because it had not been adequately analysed, because he had
not penetrated far enough into the interior of the dark continent. For
Lacan, its truth – which, he implies, he alone possesses – is to be
deferred until tomorrow morning.

The shift from *femme* to *dame*, which gives the curious collocation
approximating to 'lady feminists', is not the only discursive index of a
paternalist and patronizing stance. In 'L'Etourdit', Deutsch and Horney
are twice referred to as 'Hélène' and 'Karen' respectively;[107] at no point

does Lacan refer to Jones as 'Ernest'. Deutsch is also referred to as *la Deutsch*, a form of appellation sometimes used for a prima donna, but which can also have derogatory overtones in popular usage. It is highly unlikely that any feminist would refer to '*la Beauvoir*'. One of Lacan's followers takes the familiarity of forenames further still, referring simply to 'Melanie' in the title of an article.[108] It would have been a brave man who dared to refer to 'Mrs Klein' in these terms during her lifetime.

The overfamiliar use of forenames and the ironic use of 'lady' are classic instances of everyday sexism, but Lacan can go much further than this. In 1960 he refers to the opposition between clitoral orgasm and vaginal satisfaction as 'fairly trivial';[109] in *Encore* he alludes to women analysts who cannot or will not say anything about *jouissance*, and adds: 'So as best we can, we designate this *jouissance* vaginal, and talk about the rear pole of the opening of the uterus and other suchlike idiocies.'[110] 'Idiocies' is Rose's translation of Lacan's *conneries*, but she has either misjudged his register or is shying away from its implications. Lacan in fact adds *C'est le case de le dire*, thereby deliberately pointing to the words etymological origins in *con*: cunt. The flirtation with obscenity cannot but be deliberate and premeditated; need it be added that Lacan does not refer to phallic *jouissance* as a load of balls or a lot of cock.

The same note of sexist–sexual innuendo persists throughout 'L'Etourdit', where Lacan remarks: 'I will not oblige women to measure by the yardstick of castration the charming sheath they do not elevate to the signifier [*d'auner au chaussoir de la castration la gaine charmante* …]'.[111] The sexual implications of 'sheath' do not need to be stressed, but Lacan is also playing on the popular expression *trouver chaussure à son pied* (to find what one needs and, more specifically, a wife). The next paragraph plays heavily on *chaussure* and *pied*; both these expressions are heavily eroticized in slang. *Prendre pied* means 'to enjoy sexual pleasure', but is certainly amenable to rather more robust translations. Lacan is deliberately – and, it must be said, skilfully – exploiting a semantic field centred on 'cunt' and its cognates; he is indulging in *conneries* of his own.

Certain of Lacan's followers and associates are rather more explicit than their master when it comes to commentating on feminism, but precisely how they understand that term is not always entirely clear. Feminism can take many forms and can mean many things (socialist feminism, radical feminism, separatism …), but for Charles Melman at least, it is all one: a demand for 'the expression of the full and liberated essence of femininity',[112] a definition which some might like to contest on the grounds that such an essence is a social construct. For Dominique Kalfon, the classic female demands for equal rights and for a woman's right to have control over her own body are so many avatars of the little girl's belief that one day she too will grow a penis, 'just like her brother'.[113]

Safouan notes with some interest that most of those who find Freud's discussion of penis envy in 'The Taboo of Virginity' objectionable are women. He has no difficulty in finding an explanation for this: Freud refers in that paper to 'a dream of a newly married woman which was recognizable as a reaction to the loss of her virginity'; the critics protest because their own defloration must have given them plenty to dream about.[114] The authors of a book entitled *Woman as Sex Object* ask why it is that it is men who produce the commonplaces of desire in everything from pornography to fine art. Safouan insists that what they are really asking is: 'Can one speak of the *topoi* of a desire that might be feminine?' He defers the answer to the end of his book: 'Desire is always the same, regardless of sex.'[115] By emending the original question, he is of course deploying one of psychoanalysis's classic defence mechanisms. The answer to a hostile, threatening, or simply difficult question is all too often: 'What you are really saying is ...'. One is reminded of Lemoine-Luccioni's interpolation into her analysand's account of her dream, of the rallying cry 'the phallus, not the penis', but also of the most sinister phrase in the entire vocabulary of Stalinism: 'Objectively, comrade ...'. And *psych et po* did in fact develop a variant on this neo-Stalinist discourse, parrying all objections with the silencing 'Unconsciously, sister ...'.[116]

In her paper on femininity, Aulagnier-Spairani describes how an analysand came to see her after hearing a lecture on 'Orgasm: A Woman's Right'. Oddly enough, the analyst is surprised to learn that the speaker was a woman. In the discussion that follows the presentation of the paper, Perrier refers to the said speaker as 'a genital neurophysiological suffragette', adroitly combining a dismissive anti-feminism with genital determinism.[117] Lemoine-Luccioni picks up a reference in a book co-authored by Marguerite Duras to the fact that certain women have chosen to live in women-only communities. She immediately compares these communities to the *chambrettes provençales* of the nineteenth century (men's houses which no woman was allowed to enter, even [*sic*] to do the housework).[118] All these comments imply that all feminist activity is unconsciously calked on male models and echo *psych et po*'s claims that feminism is yet one more variation of phallocratic discourse and that feminists are women who unconsciously want to become men. When Leclaire asserts that those involved with des femmes are subtly subverting the foundations of the dominant ideologies, one of the ideologies he has in mind is feminism.[119]

The orthodox Lacanian view of the Freud–Jones debate is that Freud was right and the unfortunate Jones was mistaken, but the above statements are uncomfortably redolent of Jones's description of 'The familiar type of women who ceaselessly complain of the unfairness of women's lot and their unjust ill-treatment by men', and who 'retain their interest in men, but set their hearts on being accepted by men as one of themselves.'[120] The women in question are of course immediately recognizable as a sub-species within the genus 'Homosexual Women'. Feminism proclaims that the personal is political. Psychoanalysis – both vulgar and Lacanian – replies that the political is pathological.

The Lacanians may not be so crude as Christopher Lasch, who, in his introduction to Chasseguet-Smirgel's *The Ego Ideal*, equates all feminism with a separatist movement exemplified by the SCUM Manifesto,[121] but they too take a reductionist stance. In a review article dealing with two books on women and language, Kress-Rosen, for example, identifies two major strands within feminism and reduces both to the *topoi* of psychopathology. The first tendency is the 'women's speech' [*parole de femme*] option, the thesis that there is a specifically feminine discourse of which men can know nothing. Its valorization of sexual difference and celebration of the 'imaginary signs' of femininity (the viscous, the humid, and specifically female experiences such as menstruation, pregnancy and childbirth) is, Kress-Rosen argues, reminiscent of Deutsch's views on female masochism. The alternative current is based upon a demand for equality and is motivated by envy. Although the term 'penis envy' itself is not used, it does seem to be hovering in the background, as the whole issue of feminism is held to revolve around the 'phallic problematic'. It is made quite clear that feminism cannot hope to escape the constraints of the politico–pathological.[122]

Lacanians follow the example set by the original participants in the phallic–phase debate, bringing back travellers' tales from the dark continent and consistently invoking psychopathology to deny even the possibility of a sexual politics. In short, they reproduce some of the most basic theses of sexism and heterosexism and thus undermine any stated attempt to produce a theory of the gendering of the subject. Attempts to produce such a theory regularly relapse into the most banal stereotypes. It is probably Lemoine-Luccioni who supplies the supremely bathetic example. In *Partage des femmes*, she elaborates a complex theory which is not dissimilar to that found in some of Irigaray's work. The 'feminine imaginary' is, that is, constructed in terms of doubles and reduplication. A woman has two sexual organs and is of the same sex as the parent who gave birth to her. The instance of reduplication is further determined by pregnancy and parturition; a woman who gives birth is no longer one, but two. This regime of doubles explains the 'well-known fact' that women make poor mathematicians.[123] Living in a world dominated by the figure of the double, they presumably cannot handle the basic concept of unity. Antoinette Fouque of *psych et po*, in the meantime, claims that Lacan helped her not to surrender to 'the feminist illusion.... He made it possible to criticize Sartre and Beauvoir.'[124]

Addressing an EFP seminar in June 1974, Safouan remarks that psychoanalysis began with hysteria and that knowledge or understanding of hysteria will always be the yardstick by which the value of psychoanalysis is judged.[125] His remarks are perfectly in keeping with Lacan's contention that it is the discourse of the hysteric which provokes the emergence of psychoanalytic discourse. In this perspective, psychoanalysis and hysteria are historically and epistemologically inseparable. Yet for Lacan, hysteria centres upon the very questions which neither the hysteric nor the analyst can answer: 'What is a woman? What does it mean to be a woman? What does a woman want?' The riddle of femininity is therefore not simply coeval with psychoanalysis; it is a constituent element thereof, and the entire edifice of psychoanalysis rests upon a question it cannot answer. The focal point of all its scopic–phallic metaphors is a realm of darkness which it cannot penetrate. For Lacan and Safouan, its continued existence depends upon the presence of a constant provocation or frustration to which it can never adequately respond. The structural impasse whereby Freud's desire to penetrate is sustained by the uncannily fascinating sight of the impenetrable remains intact.

   In a short and otherwise rather undistinguished article on *Encore*, Danièle Silvestre perceptively notes that the text is the site of a displacement: the question of female sexuality becomes a question of female *jouissance*.[126] Before going on to discuss the specifics of *jouissance*, surely the most difficult term to translate in the entire Lacanian canon, certain of the effects of the displacement should be examined. By moving from female sexuality to *jouissance* Lacan moves from a realm of darkness to one of startling visibility, from the dark continent to a Baroque church in Rome which houses a statue lit from above. Everything becomes obvious; we have only to go and look at Bernini's statue to know what is happening to St Teresa. Although he normally insists that the medium of psychoanalysis is speech, in *Encore* Lacan moves into the realm of the spectacle and the spectacular. It is, however, women who pay the price for Lacan's illumination.[127] If Freud broke the silence of the *Iconographie photographique de la Salpêtrière* by allowing hysterics to speak, Lacan silences them anew [*encore*] by reformulating Dora's questions and by insisting that St Teresa, like all women, does not know what she is talking about; by making her the silent object of a male gaze.

   The logic of the discursive process at work here is inescapable. Dora's questions are reformulated in such a way as to make femininity centre

on the genitals. Hysteria and femininity are effectively made synonymous, and are made to focus on the cunt. Lacan's displacement of the
question of femininity emphasizes the scopic component of Freud's
desire to penetrate. If there is no final answer to *Was will das Weib?*,
there is an immediately obvious answer to the question *Was will Lacan?*
Quite simply, he wishes to see. But although highly eroticized, Bernini's
statue is of course decorously draped. There is no danger of encountering the petrifying counter-gaze of Medusa when we go to look at it. For
similar reasons, the woman portrayed in *Ornicar?* 15 is not fully naked;
we see only her breasts. The metaphorical cat beside her allows the male
gaze to have the best of both worlds: now you see it, now you don't.
When he gazes at the statue of St Teresa, Lacan, like any good fetishist,
sees only what he wants to see, reassured by the artifice of drapery. The
penetrating gaze sees only so far and carefully avoids looking into the
impenetrable, displacing all to the level of a *jouissance* it can contemplate rather than countenancing the question that cannot be answered.

Lacan's gaze becomes a source of reassurance: you have only to go
and see.... But the overconfidence of that statement is surely a disavowal of his inability to answer the question. As though to make doubly
certain, Lacan tells us to go and see at the very moment when St Teresa
cannot speak. As Leclaire notes, at the moment of orgasm itself, no one
can say 'I'm coming' [*je jouis*]; that statement always relates to a future,
no matter how immediate it may be.[128] The choice of a statue to illustrate *Encore* is very telling. Not only is the saint unable to speak; she is
forever at the point of orgasm. Unable to speak, forever coming, she is
the perfect icon of convulsive beauty. And underlying both the drapery
and the cult of convulsive beauty, the insistence that it is, always was and
always will be a question of cunt. Small wonder that *Ornicar?*'s reflections on femininity are published under the sign of pussy.

Jouissance and the cognate verbal form *jouir* are notoriously
polysemic terms in Lacan, their ambiguity being equalled only by that of
the constantly shifting 'Other'.[129] To complicate matters further, it is
remarkably difficult to pinpoint the precise moment of their incorporation into his discourse or even to begin to trace their derivation and
genealogy. The connotations of the terms shift considerably over the
years, but they never shed their earlier meanings. Their final accept-
ations tend therefore to be the result of a process of semantic-conceptual
accretion, and their meanings are contextual rather than definitional.

The primary meanings of *jouissance* cover the semantic fields of
pleasure and legality, with the core element of enjoyment-possession
allowing a constant oscillation between the two. The term denotes both
the possession-enjoyment of rights, privileges or property, and the
possession-enjoyment of an object capable of procuring pleasure. In

more popular registers it means 'orgasm', with *jouir* as the equivalent of
'to come'. But *jouir* can antiphrastically come to refer to the experience
of exquisite pain which occasions a momentary loss of consciousness;
the 'sweet subtle pain' and 'intolerable joyes' referred to in one of
Richard Crashaw's poems on St Teresa are a perfect example of its
ambiguity at that level.[130]

At the beginning of *Encore*, the entire semantic field is brought into
play by a flurry of rather self-indulgent puns which are presumably
inspired both by the subject of the seminar (the question Freud left
unanswered) and by its institutional setting (it had recently been trans-
ferred to the Faculty of Law). Hence Lacan's punning allusions to the *lit
de justice*, the historical 'bed of justice' of the French kings, and to the
bed of concubinage, the association being fostered by the metonymic
link between 'bed' and 'sexuality' and by the legal–hedonistic connotations of *jouissance*.[131]

Although *jouissance* 'means' orgasm, there is, as Gallop notes,[132]
something curious about its Lacanian acceptation. Orgasms are
normally quantifiable, if potentially multiple, but *jouissance* is always
used in the singular and is inevitably accompanied by the definite article;
there is no such category as *'une' jouissance*. Similarly, *jouir* is an
absolute verb which does not take an object. In so far as it is an existential category, *jouissance* would appear to be one of absolute subjectivity
or interiority were it not that the addition of the preposition *de* produces
further ambiguities by implying an object relation. *Jouissance* can, then,
signify the ecstatic or orgasmic enjoyment of something or someone, and
the expression *la jouissance de la femme* can simultaneously mean 'the
female orgasm' and the 'enjoyment of the woman'.

Given that we do not as yet have the 'Complete Works' of Lacan at
our disposal, it is almost impossible to trace the diachronic development
of the category of *jouissance* with any certainty; it is, however, possible
to identify at least some stages in its probable semantic and conceptual
evolution. Like the phallus, *jouissance* is a relatively late addition to the
canon and does not appear in any of the pre-war texts. No great importance is attached to it in 'Fonction et champ', and in 'La Psychanalyse et
son enseignement' (1957) it refers quite simply to the enjoyment–
possession of a sexual object.[133] That usage appears to derive from
comments made in the Seminars of June 1954 and January 1955; these
apply to Hegel and, more specifically, to the moment in which the slave
is subordinated to the law that states that he must satisfy the desire of
the master by mediating his relationship with the world of things and by
facilitating his enjoyment [*jouissance*] thereof.[134] The reference to Hegel
is further elaborated in 'Subversion du sujet' (1960), and by now *jouissance* has acquired its 'orgasm' connotations from the discussion of

female sexuality in 'Propos directifs'.[135] *Jouissance* is not, then, a category of pure subjectivity, and implies a dialectic of possession and enjoyment of and by another. It has come by 1960 to denote an amalgam of enjoyment and orgasm that is always caught up in a dialectic of desire which defines the subject in terms of the other and of the desire of and for that other.

'Subversion du sujet' also introduces the notion that *jouissance* lies beyond the pleasure principle, and even that the pleasure principle is a barrier or obstacle to *jouissance*.[136] It is probably only in so far as it is literally beyond the pleasure principle that *jouissance* can be related, however indirectly, to Freud. The difficulty of deriving the category from Freud is inadvertently illustrated by Laplanche, who attempts to relate it to Freud's tentative use of the Nirvana principle or the economic tendency to reduce the level of excitation to zero and ultimately to death.[137] Whilst *jouissance* does involve a death drive in that death is the final term of sexuality,[138] and in that *jouissance* itself is an eminently sexual category, Laplanche's suggestion negates the instrumental and possessive implications of Lacan's notion, not to mention its ecstatic connotations; arguably, *jouissance* refers to an *almost* intolerable level of excitation rather than to its reduction or extinction. Laplanche also tends to equate *jouissance* with pleasure,[139] whereas Lacan suggests that they are antithetical. Indeed, he argues in 1973 that *jouissance* cannot be inscribed within the system of energetics which Freud uses to characterize the economy of the pleasure principle.[140] Lacan also metaphorically describes the pleasure principle as a form of 'purring'; *jouissance* goes far beyond that domestic image of feline bliss.[141]

Lacan illustrates 'Subversion du sujet' with a graph of the structures of desire, and one of the vectors relating subject and Other is inscribed with the legend '*Che vuoi?*' ('What do you want?').[142] In terms of the subject–Other dialectic, this means that the question 'What do you want' returns to the subject as a question posed by the Other: 'What do you want of me?' There may, however, be more to this than an illustration of the basic thesis that man's desire is the desire of or for the Other. It is clear from the Seminar on object relations that *Che vuoi* is a quotation from Jacques Cazotte's fantastic tale *Le Diable amoureux* (1772), in which the Devil appears to be hero Alvare and asks him '*Che vuoi?*'.[143] The Devil, that is, personifies a desire which Alvare has yet to recognize as his own. Later developments in the narrative bring us closer to the implications of *jouissance*. The Devil takes on the guise of a woman who falls in love with Alvare, and asks him to give himself to her unreservedly and for ever; to pledge his love, he must kiss her and at the same time declare that he adores her, calling her by her true name of 'Beelzebub'. At this point Alvare is overcome by mortal dread, astonishment, stupor and a fear of annihilation.[144] His unrecognized desire has brought him to the edge of a destructive *jouissance*, from which he finally retreats. He hesitates between the pleasure principle and its beyond, briefly experiencing what Freud calls 'the horror of a pleasure of which he was unaware'.[145]

Alvare's dilemma is well captured by Lacan's rhetorical questions in S XI: 'Who does not know from experience that it is possible not to want to *jouir?* Who does not know from experience, knowing the recoil imposed on everyone, in so far as it involves terrible promises, by the approach of *jouissance* as such.'[146] The alternating identifications of the fetishist also confront him with terrible promises and the horror of pleasure; he identifies either with a phallus which a woman can devour and destroy, or with a woman faced with a destructive penis.[147] *Jouissance*, then, comprises an element of horror, a highly eroticized death drive that makes terrible promises, which goes far beyond the pleasure principle and which can imply possession in both an active and a passive sense. Alvare can possess and enjoy the object of his desire, but only on pain of being diabolically possessed. And in order to *jouir*, the fetishist dices with castration.

Leclaire's general description of *jouissance* in *Psychanalyser* covers most of these facets and is probably clearer than any single reference to the category by Lacan himself: *jouissance* signals

> immmediacy of access to that 'pure difference' which the erotic seeks to find at the extreme point where it borders upon death, and sometimes even in the annulment of the border itself; pleasure is the representation of his access, *jouissance* tempered by the assurance of reversibility into the oscillating and cyclical economy of desire in the strict sense.[148]

As Bataille might have put it, *jouissance* takes us to 'The prostration that follows the final paroxysm, to that "small death" that lies on the edge of orgasm.'[149] For Bataille the erotic is a domain of violence and transgression, a domain adjacent to death itself. It is a realm of transgression in that it poses a challenge to all laws, and in that it is beyond the pleasure principle. Indeed, it might be argued that reading Bataille's fiction is in itself an experience which takes one beyond that principle. Whereas pornography operates with a rhythm of tension and release corresponding to a masturbatory pattern of erection and detumescence, a novella like *Histoire de l'oeil* is an unremitting crescendo of violence and obscenity that cannot be accommodated within the comforting economy of pleasure.[150] It is a textual embodiment of the terrible promises of the erotic and of *jouissance*. Bataille describes the appeal of the erotic thus: 'a desire to die, but at the same time a desire to live with ever-greater intensity at the borderline between possible and impossible. It is a desire to live whilst ceasing to live, or to die without ceasing to live.'[151] He adds that the writer who has best expressed the singular experience of 'dying of not dying' is St Teresa.

Striking as Lacan's use of St Teresa to illustrate his concept of *jouissance* may be, it is not original. She is no stranger to psychoanalytic debates. Breuer dubs her 'the patron saint of hysteria' in *Studies in Hysteria*[152] and her case was discussed at some length by French analysts in the 1940s, with Bonaparte arguing that her transverberation was a violent orgasm which she failed to recognize as such, and Parcheminey contending that all mystical experiences are a hysterical transposition of sexuality.[153] Significantly, Bernini's sculpture is used on the cover of the illustrated edition of Bataille's *L'Erotisme*. Lacan is, then, exploiting a double tradition in *Encore*. He rarely mentions Bataille by name, and does not discuss the earlier analytic discussions of St Teresa. The Bataille–Lacan connection is, however, clearly signalled in the work of some of his associates. Many of the formulations used by Leclaire to describe *jouissance* derive directly from Bataille; the debt is especially evident in the Vincennes seminar referred to earlier.[154] François Perrier is even more explicit, making it perfectly clear that he regards the notion of *jouissance* as deriving from Bataille and from a tradition that leads back to Sade rather than to Freud and arguing that transgression is an essential component of this 'dark Eros'.[155]

The one direct reference to Bataille to be found in *Ecrits* is at the end of Lacan's rereading of Schreber, and is little more than a passing comment on the Senatpräsident's observation that 'God is a whore'.[156] Lacan glosses this illustration of Schreber's theodicy with an allusion to *Madam Edwarda*, a novella first published in 1941 under the pseudonym 'Pierre Angélique'. The fragmentary narrative deals with relations between a first-person narrator and the eponymous Edwarda, an insane prostitute working in a Paris brothel. In the presence of Edwarda, the narrator feels the sense of dread associated with the approach of a divinity; his reactions are those of Cazotte's Alvare when faced with the terrible promises of *jouissance*. It is, however, Edwarda who becomes the icon of *jouissance*. Displaying her genitals – described as 'hairy pink "rags"' and as having the life of 'some repulsive octopus' – she proclaims herself to be God, and then exclaims, with a beatific look on her face, '*Comme j'ai joui*' ('I came, I came').[157] The instance of *jouissance* is illustrated by the image of a woman at the point of orgasm, at the moment of the impossible enunciation. This is the face of God. Although the text contains no overt reference to Bataille, the same association is made in *Encore* when Lacan asks: 'And why not interpret one face of the Other, the God face, as supported by feminine *jouissance*?'[158]

That the representation of *jouissance* should focus upon a woman for both Lacan and Bataille is surely not accidental. It centres upon *le sexe*, upon a linguistic condensation of femininity and the genitals so conspicuously displayed by Edwarda. It could, however, be argued that Bataille 'goes beyond' Lacan by invoking his own image of Medusa's head rather than contemplating Bernini's draped statue. That in itself may be related to the fact that he allows St Teresa to speak in *L'Erotisme*, whereas Lacan's icon of *jouissance* is silent. During his visit to Rome Lacan enjoyed what he calls 'an orgy of churches', and his comment on their Baroque statuary is simply that it is 'an exhibition of bodies evoking *jouissance*'.[159] The iconography of *Encore* – its imaginary – establishes a link between *jouissance*, mystical ecstasy, femininity and hysteria. Whilst it is possible to derive such a link from Freud's observation that the *arc de cercle* contortion which occurs in major hysterical attacks evokes 'a posture of the body that is suitable for sexual intercourse',[160] it should also be recalled that the same contortion becomes part of Dali's iconography of convulsive beauty, and that the related *attitudes passionnelles* are the object of the beatific gazes of Aragon and Breton in 'Le Cinquantenaire de l'hystérie'.

That femininity is for Lacan a construct of the gaze is clear from a discussion of Merleau-Ponty's phenomenology of perception in 1964. Lacan takes a line from Paul Valéry's *La Jeune Parque* to illustrate the moment of reflexive self-consciousness: *je me voyais me voir* (I saw myself see myself). He then asserts that the theme of the poem is femininity; Valéry himself claims that it deals with self-consciousness as such, and makes no mention of gender.[161] Lacan's somewhat forced interpretation thus locates femininity within a scopic field. Initially that field is narcissistic, but it is after redefined in terms of the gaze of the other by a reference to 'the satisfaction of a woman who knows that she is being looked at, on condition that one does not show that one knows she knows'.[162]

Eight years before *Encore*, female *jouissance* is made the object of a male gaze in a formulation which is all too uncomfortably reminiscent of Jones's remarks about lesbian sexuality. In an article which signals an important moment in the feminism–psychoanalysis articulation, Laura Mulvey argues that psychoanalysis can be used to explore the fascination of film. Her main thesis is that narrative film constitutes an economy in which man is the bearer of the look and woman is an image; that the filmic system uses women to connote *to-be-looked-at-ness*.[163] It would be difficult to contest the accuracy of this description of narrative film, but the ease with which Mulvey assumes that psychoanalysis can be appropriated as a political weapon or mobilized to demystify *to-be-looked-at-ness* is more dubious. Psychoanalysis can scarcely challenge the economy of the scopic economy which reduces women to being the object of a gaze, precisely because it constantly reproduces it. Lacan in particular takes *to-be-looked-at-ness* to be an integral part of femininity; that motif is constantly present, from the allusions to the obscurity surrounding the vaginal organ to the rather perverse interpretation of *La Jeune Parque* and the spectacular iconography of St Teresa's *jouissance*. He remains within and promotes the very economy which Mulvey seeks to subvert, just as his discourse reproduces a basic heterosexism and a trivialization of feminism.

The most contentious and provocative assertion to be found in *Encore* and related texts is no doubt the proposition that *la femme n'existe pas*. The use of the definite article here indicates a general category of womanliness or femininity, and is governed by basic grammatical rules; given the differences between the use of articles in French and English, it might be appropriate to render the phrase as 'Woman does not exist'. If Lacan's formula were simply a denial of the existence of an eternal or essential femininity, it would be no more contentious than Simone de Beauvoir's famous dictum to the effect that women are made, not born, but other formulations suggest that this is not the case.

On a number of occasions Lacan makes very general extrapolations on the basis of highly specific statements about femininity, and effectively constructs his own version of the eternal female. In 'La Science et la vérité' he refers fleetingly to Friedan's *The Feminine Mystique*, and remarks that women come into being only through 'the ideals of their sex'.[164] Whilst this might appear to be quite in keeping with his general views on the instability of any identity predicated on the ego, it is gender-specific in that there is no corresponding discussion of male ideals. Friedan's study is a sociological analysis of what might be termed the 'alienated femininity' fostered by a consumer society; Lacan transforms it into a general statement about femininity as such.

Similarly, Joan Rivière's paper on 'Womanliness as a Masquerade' is pressed into service to argue that the belief that femininity is the site of some eternal truth is a lure, that the plenitude promised by the Platonic myth of the androgyne can never be realized. The difficulty is that, for Rivière, 'the masquerade' is a specific defence mechanism: 'women who wish for masculinity may put on a mask of womanliness to avert anxiety and the retribution feared from men.'[165] For Lacan, however, 'the masquerade' becomes the emblem or sign of femininity *qua* femininity; he moves from the partial or restrictive category of 'women who ...' to a totalizing reference to 'the feminine sexual attitude' as such.[166] In both these cases, Lacan generalizes on the basic of specific statements or positions. Friedan and Rivière make statements on specific social or clinical aspects of femininity; Lacan translates their remarks into absolute statements of general import. In other words, his own formulations preclude the possibility of interpreting 'Woman does not exist' as a pro- or proto-feminist thesis that Woman is a social or psychical construct.

'Woman does not exist' is, however, fully consistent with Lacan's many remarks on the relationship or non-relationship between femininity and symbolization. In *Encore*, he describes heterosexual relations in the following terms. 'Man' is no more than a signifier, and it is in so far as he is a signifier that a woman seeks a man. The converse is not true. A man seeks a woman (or Woman) because there is something within her which escapes discourse.[167] The argument is consistent with psychoanalysis's long-standing complaint that there is something about femininity which exceeds its discourse, but it also relates to *Encore*'s thesis that there is and can be no pre-discursive reality. It is because femininity cannot be symbolized that Woman does not exist.

Femininity's alleged resistance to symbolization is ultimately a matter of genital determinism. In the Seminar on the psychoses, Lacan opines that: 'strictly speaking, there can be no symbolization of the female *sexe*; the female *sexe* has the character of an absence, a void or a hole.'[168] A similar assertion is made in *Encore*:

> Don't talk to me about the secondary sexual characteristics of women because, until further notice, it is the sexual characteristics of the mother which predominate in women. There is nothing to distinguish a woman as being sexed, except, of course, her sex/genitals.[169]

The deliberate bracketing out of secondary sexual characteristics is tantamount to the statement that it is all a matter of pussy. The primacy accorded to maternity as the determinant of the feminine is reminiscent of the arguments of the 1938 article on the family, where it is argued that whilst paternity is primarily a matter of symbolism, maternity reveals the incidence of the biological. Masculinity is, then, implicitly equated with symbolism and symbolization, and femininity with a biological maternity and with that which cannot be symbolized: 'there can be no symbolization of the female sex/genitals as such.'[170] Given that symbolism is defined in a priori terms as determined by the phallus and that discursivity or symbolization is adopted as a quasi-ontological category, it is not difficult to conclude that Woman does not exist.

Irigaray noted that Lacan does not challenge Freud's account of the castration complex and merely restates it in other terms. Ultimately, the same has to be said of the riddle of femininity. Freud could not see deeply enough into it, and failed to recognize that his own metaphors constructed femininity as impenetrable. Lacan claims that women cannot or will not speak the truth of their sexuality, and fails to recognize that it is his phallocentric theory of discourse which condemns them to silence or even non-existence.

The Lacanian literature on the dark continent shares many of the weaknesses of earlier essays in the genre. It abounds in travellers' tales and sexist commonplaces, and finally collapses into such banalities as 'There may be a specifically female sexuality of which we can say nothing.'[171] Feminism, and indeed any sexual politics, is constantly trivialized and dismissed as pathological. At both the discursive and the iconographic levels there is a constant reduction of the feminine to the genital, and the old surrealist cult of convulsive beauty is never far away. The one concept which is supposed to help Lacan to go beyond Freud and to produce a theory of the constitution of a gendered subjectivity is the phallus, yet it proves highly unstable and is in itself the site of a constant regression towards the biological. Attempts to back-project that concept on to Freud and to give it his authority rely upon the substitution of one signifier for another and upon reference to faulty translations. The riddle of femininity remains unsolved. The mysterious continent remains impenetrably dark. Indeed, Lacan's theses on the symbiotic relationship between psychoanalysis and hysteria strongly suggest that its impenetrability is a constituent element of psychoanalytic discourse.

7

Jacques-Marie Emile Lacan:
Curriculum Vitae 1901–81

The following *curriculum vitae* does not pretend to be a full biography of Lacan, and is simply an overview of the major events in a long and often tempestuous career. It is restricted to the public domain, and no attempt is made here to record the history of the subject's private life.[1] Nor is a complete bibliography of Lacan provided. The best available biography is that compiled by Joël Dor;[2] although it is now slightly out of date and has some minor omissions, it remains the essential work of reference.

References for all material by Lacan cited or discussed in the body of the text are supplied below, together with reference for translations, when available. The brief remarks as to the content of material not available in translation are indicative rather than comprehensive. No attempt has been made to supply summaries of the Seminars because of their length and because of the very wide range of topics they cover. Bibliographical references are given in chronological order and follow the biographical information given for each year.

1901	Jacques-Marie Emile Lacan born in Paris on 13 April, the eldest child of Emilie and Alfred Lacan, a *représentant de commerce* dealing in soap and oils. The family are prosperous members of the middle bourgeoisie and Lacan is educated at the Collège Stanislas, a well-known Jesuit establishment. Having been declared unfit for military service because he is excessively thin, he studies medicine and then psychiatry in Paris.
1927	Begins his clinical training and then works at Sainte-

Anne, the major psychiatric hospital serving central Paris. He subsequently works under Clérambault at the Infirmerie spéciale près de la Préfecture de Police and at the Hôpital Henri-Rousselle before returning to Sainte-Anne to work under Claude in 1932.

From 1926 onwards Lacan publishes articles on medicine and psychiatry, most of them co-authored, in professional journals.

1931   Awarded his *diplôme de médicine légist*, qualifying him as a forensic psychiatrist.

'Structure des psychoses paranoïaques', *Semaine des Hôpitaux de Paris*, 7 July 1931, pp. 437–45. The paper identifies three types of paranoid psychosis: constitutional paranoia, delusion of interpretation and emotional delusions. The typology owes much to Clérambault, but a notion of structure begins to displace the mental-automatism syndrome as the central category. Although Lacan acknowledges his debt to Clérambault, his 'master' reportedly accuses him of plagiarism.

'Ecrits "inspirés": Schizographie', co-authored with J. Lévi-Valensi and P. Rigault, based on a paper read to the Société Médico-Psychologique on 12 November and published in *Annales Médico-Psychologiques*, December 1931; republished, PP, pp. 365–82. An examination of the writings of 'Marcelle C.', a primary-school teacher interned at the Clinique psychiatrique and diagnosed as suffering from erotomania, paranoid delusions and mental automatism. The paper argues that forms of language can be symptomatic of the evolution and internal mechanisms of psycho-pathological conditions. A parallel is drawn between the writings of 'Marcelle' and the results obtained by the surrealists in their experiments with automatic writing.

1932   Awarded his Doctorat d'état for his thesis, *De La Psychose paranoïaque dans ses rapports avec la personnalité*. Published: Paris, Le François, 1932;

reprinted as *De la Psychose paranoïaque dans ses rapports avec la personnalité, suivi de Premiers écrits sur la paranoïa*, Paris, Seuil, 1975; reprinted, Paris, Seuil, Collection 'Points', 1980, without the appendixes.

Lacan is awarded a *mention très honorable* and a bronze medal for his thesis. It attracts considerable interest in surrealist circles, and Janet comments favourably on it,[3] but it appears to have no impact in psychoanalytic circles. A copy of the thesis is sent to Freud in Vienna; he acknowledges receipt with a postcard, but makes no comment.[4] This appears to be the only instance of direct communication between Freud and Lacan.

Lacan's attitude to his thesis, which deals primarily with 'Aimée', whom he diagnoses as suffering from self-punishment paranoia, is always somewhat ambivalent. In 1933 he asserts that its originality stems from the fact that it represents the first attempt in France at an exhaustive study of the mental phenomenon of paranoid delusions on the basis of an analysis of the 'concrete history' of the subject.[5] He refers to it frequently in later publications, but remarks in 1969 that he would blush to see it reprinted, and in 1980 that it was not without reluctance that he allowed it to be republished.[6]

In 1975 he explained his reluctance by stating that there is no relationship between paranoid psychosis and personality: they are the same thing.[7]

Lacan's translation of Freud, 'Some Neurotic Mechanisms in Jealousy, Paranoia and Homosexuality' (SE XVIII) appears in the third volume of the *Revue Française de Psychanalyse*. His only other published translation – of an article by Heidegger – appears in 1956. A translation of a paper on schizophrenia by Fenichel is announced in 1932 but never appears.

1933   Publishes a sonnet entitled 'Hiatus irrationalis' in *Le Phare de Neuilly*, 3/4; reprinted, *Magazine littéraire*, 121, February 1977, p. 11. This is apparently

Lacan's only venture into poetry; stylistically, the sonnet is somewhat reminiscent of the work of Pierre Jean Jouve.

'Le Problème du style et la conception psychiatrique des formes paranoïaques de l'existence', *Minotaure*, 1, June, pp. 68–9; reprinted, PP, pp. 383–8. This brief paper extends the theses of 'Schizographie' (1931) by arguing that the paranoiac experience and the world-view it generates constitute 'an original syntax'. A certain similarity can be detected between its theses and the theory of critical paranoia elaborated by Salvador Dali at this time.

'Motifs du crime paranoïaque: le crime des soeurs Papin', *Minotaure*, 3/4, pp. 25–8, December 1933; reprinted, PP, pp. 389–98. Based on press reports of the brutal murder of a lawyer's wife and daughter by their servants, Christine and Léa Papin, the paper relates in clinical terms to Lacan's theory of paranoia. More generally, it reveals how close his concerns are to those of the surrealists, who elevated the Papin sisters to the status of heroines.

'Exposé général de nos travaux scientifiques', a résumé of his published work. Although dated '1933', first published as an appendix to *De la Psychose*, and reprinted PP, pp. 399–406.

1934   Becomes a candidate member of the Société Psychanalytique de Paris; his application for full membership is registered on 16 October. During this period, Lacan is in analysis with Rudolph Loewenstein. Precisely when he enters analysis remains a matter for controversy; the analysis is generally accepted as having gone on until approximately 1938. Lacan plays an active part in the life of the SPP, and regularly attends both ordinary scientific meetings and conferences. Most of his contributions to discussions are brief and do not have any great significance.[8] Lacan is also an active member of the *Evolution psychiatrique* group.

1935–6   Brief association with *Recherches philosophiques*, a

yearbook edited by A. Koyré, C. Peuch and A.
Spaier, and one of the first organs of the emerging
phenomenological movement. In a review of Eugène
Minkowski's *Le Temps vécu*, Lacan claims that the
author has effectively reduced phenomenology to a
Bergsonian intuitionism (vol. 5, 1935–36, pp. 424–
31).

1936   Reads a major paper to the Fourteenth Congress of
the International Psychoanalytical Association in
Marienbad on 3 August: 'Le Stade du miroir.
Théorie d'un moment structurant et génétique de la
constitution de la réalité, conçu en relation avec
l'expérience et la doctrine psychanalytique'. Indexed
as 'The Looking-Glass Phase', *International Journal
of Psycho-Analysis*, vol. 18, 1937, p. 78. The paper
remains unpublished; the version included in *Ecrits*
dates from 1949. Lacan states in 1966 that he
omitted to submit the text for publication in the
Conference proceedings.[9] In earlier references to this
paper he recalls that the Viennese group gave it a
fairly warm reception but that Ernest Jones, who
chaired the Congress, interrupted its delivery
because Lacan had overrun his allotted time.[10] Jones
mentions neither the paper nor the incident in his
brief account of the Marienbad Congress.[11] The
Congress is well attended, with 198 participants, but
most discussions centre on organizational matters.[12]
There appears to have been no public discusssion of
Lacan's paper.

After the Congress, Lacan goes on to Berlin: 'Ernst
Kris, as I remember him at the Marienbad Congress,
where the day after my address on the mirror stage, I
took a day off, anxious to get a feeling of the times,
heavy with promises, at the Berlin Olympiad. He
gently objected "*Ça ne se fait pas!*" (in French),
thus showing he had already acquired that taste for
respectability ...'[13] ('*Ça ne se fait pas*': 'It's not
done').

'Au-delà du "Principe de réalité"', dated Marienbad-
Noirmoutier, August–October 1936. Published,
Evolution psychiatrique, 3, 1936, pp. 67–86;

reprinted, *Ecrits*, pp. 73–92. The paper contains an outline of the mirror-stage theory but begins with a critique of associationism, which is described as based upon an empirical theory of knowledge inherited from Locke, and as an idealism that fails to recognize the specific reality of mental phenomena. It is further attacked for its reliance on a 'scholastic psychology whose categories are derived from a traditional philosophical discourse'. It is probable that these criticisms owe something to Politzer's *Critique des fondements de la psychologie* (1929). The Freudian revolution is characterized in terms of its analytic technique (the rules of free association, reformulated by Pichon as the rules of non-omission and non-systematization), which assumes that every facet of mental life is significant. Language is seen as the datum of the analytic experience, and is described in broadly phenomenological terms; before signifying something, language signifies for someone. The analyst's role is to recognize a signifying intentionality of which the analysand remains in ignorance.

1938   Becomes a full member (*Membre titulaire*) of the SPP. Reads a paper on 'De l'Impulsion au complexe' to the SPP on 25 October; résumé published, RFP, vol. 11, 1939, pp. 137–41; reprinted, *Ornicar?*, 31, 1984, pp. 14–19. Lacan briefly introduces the concept of a primordial structural stage in the genesis of the ego: the 'body in pieces' stage, which will be integrated into the theorization of the mirror stage.

'La Famille', *Encyclopédie française*, vol. 8, Henri Wallon, ed.: *La Vie mentale*. This long essay comprises an introduction (L'Institution familiale', 8° 40-3–8° 40-4) and two chapters: 'Le Complexe, facteur concret de la pathologie mentale', 8° 40-5–8° 40-16, and 'Les Complexes familiaux en pathologie', 8° 42-1–8° 42-16. Republished as *Les Complexes familiaux dans la formation de l'individu. Essai d'analyse d'une fonction en psychanalyse*, Paris, Navarin, 1984. The doctoral thesis of 1932 aside, this is Lacan's most substantial and ambitious pre-

war text. The general introduction argues that
'concrete psychology' has to be supplemented by a
reference to ethnography, history, law, etc., and that
psychoanalysis itself has to adapt to the resultant
complex theoretical structure. The chapter on the
complex draws extensively on Lacan's earlier work
and anticipates the themes of 'L'Aggressivité en
psychanalyse' (1948); it also includes a brief account
of the mirror stage in which Lacan's debt to Wallon
is more apparent than in the 1949 paper.[14] The
development of the individual is described in terms
of a 'weaning complex', an 'intrusion complex' and
the Oedipus complex, 'complex' being defined in
terms of an ensemble of reactions ranging from
emotion to behaviour adapted to its object. The
complex reproduces the ambient reality within which
the subject develops in two ways: by representing it
to the extent that it is distinct from earlier stages in
the subject's psychical existence, and by reproducing
the elements it 'fixes' when circumstances require a
greater objectifiction of reality. It is apparent that
this is an early formulation of what will later be
referred to as structure. The main anthropological–
sociological references are to Malinowski, Frazer
and Durkheim. The second chapter on family
complexes brings together Lacan's early findings on
psychosis and a general summary of Freud on the
aetiology and symptomatology of hysteria. Lacan
insists that the view that the ego is a system which
the subject uses to subordinate reality to conscious
perception should be supplemented by a theory of
the imaginary structures of the ego; those structures
are a precondition for human existence. The influence of Politzer is apparent throughout; Lacan
consistently refers to 'concrete psychology' and to
the 'drama of the individual', key terms in the
Critique des fondements de la psychologie. The reference to a 'weaning complex' signal a debt to the
work of René Laforgue,[15] and trace elements of the
work of the 'chauvinist' tendency within the SPP can
also be detected.

A rather ambivalent study of the essay is published

by Edouard Pichon as 'La Famille devant M. Lacan', RFP, 11, 1939, pp. 107–35. This is the first article to be published on Lacan, and marks his recognition by a member of the older generation in the SPP. But although Pichon praises Lacan for his insights, and particularly for his theory of the mirror stage, he also criticizes him for his preciosity and for his use of 'Germanic' jargon. The article is an invaluable guide to the relationship between Lacan and the 'chauvinist' group in the SPP.

Freud, who has been forced to leave Austria, stays briefly at the home of Marie Bonaparte before going on to London. Lacan does not meet him; Miller reports him as having said that he did not attempt to arrange a meeting as it would have meant bowing and scraping to Bonaparte.[16]

1939–45   The SPP is decimated by the war and the Occupation. Many of its members, especially those who are Jewish, flee from France; in 1940, only Françoise Dolto and Jean Leuba are still in Paris. It is impossible to hold meetings, and the Society effectively ceases to exist. Freud's writings are banned; the exemption made for Jewish authors of scientific works is not extended to the founder of psychoanalysis. A small group of psychoanalysts continues to work at Sainte-Anne under the protection of Jean Delay, who keeps them on in the face of German disapproval. The Strasbourg Institut de Psychiatrie transfers to Clermond-Ferrand in 1940; according to its director, Daniel Lagache, it functions as a 'psychoanalytic resistance movement'. Lacan is briefly mobilized and then works at the Val-de-Grâce, the military hospital in Paris. The details of his work remain vague, but the experience was clearly depressing. He speaks of seeing a wretched parade of individuals who had not really awoken from 'the warmth of the skirts of their mothers and wives', and of having found on a collective scale evidence of the degradation of the virile type which he had noted at the end of 'La Famille'.[17] There is still some uncertainty about his subsequent activities, but he is reported to have gone on working in private practice and to have done some teaching. A photograph taken by Brassaï provides evidence that he was in Paris in 1944.[18] During the Occupation Lacan also studies Chinese, and gains a diploma from the Ecole des languages orientales.

Immediately after the war, Lacan states that France's humiliation at the hands of the 'enemies of the human race' discouraged him from writing or publishing anything during the Occupation.[19] He also refers to the feeling of unreality that marked the French experience of the war, adding that the 'fairground ideologies' which were promulgated were similar to the ramblings of senility or the compensatory phantasies of childhood; France fell back on the mechanisms which the neurotic uses as a defence against reality.[20]

Finally, he refers to the Pétainiste era of 'work-fatherland-family and tightened belts' as having been one of penitence (*Travail-Patrie-Famille* was the slogan of the Pétain régime).[21]

1945   The SPP begins to hold informal meetings in Paris; in 1946 its returns to its pre-war practice of holding monthly meetings.

1946   'Le Temps logique et l'assertion de certitude anticipée', written March 1945, published, *Cahiers d'art*, 1940–44, pp. 32–42; reprinted, *Ecrits*, pp. 197–213. One of the earliest indications of Lacan's interest in games theory and mathematical formalization.[22] The paper centres on a logico-mathematical puzzle: a group of prisoners have black and white discs affixed to their backs, and are told that they will be released if they can identify them correctly. As no prisoner can see his own back, he must deduce his own position from what he knows of the position of his fellows. For Lacan, this process signals the logical birth of the 'I' and is a parallel to its psychological birth in the dialectic of self and other. In so far as the experience of the prisoners implies a dialectic between 'the time for understanding' and 'the moment to conclude', it is sometimes read as a paradigm which justifies the practice of 'short sessions' in psychoanalysis.[23]

'Le Nombre treize et la forme logique de la suspicion', *Cahiers d'art*, 1945–46, pp. 389–93; reprinted, *Ornicar?*, 36, Spring 1986, pp. 7–20. A companion piece to 'Le Temps logique', based upon the 'counterfeit coins' puzzle invented by François le Lionnais and brought to Lacan's notice by Raymond Queneau. One of a group of twelve coins is counterfeit, but there is no indication as to whether it is heavier or lighter than the others. It must be identified by weighing the coins, using scales without any standard weights. For Lacan, the puzzle again illustrates the logic of the subject and that of relations between the individual and the set.

'Propos sur la causalité psychique', a paper read to the Journées psychiatriques de Bonneval on 28 September and published in L. Bonnafé *et al.*, *Le Problème de la psycho-genèse des névroses et des psychoses*, Paris, Desclée de Brouwer, 1950, pp. 123–65; reprinted, *Ecrits*, pp. 151–94. After a brief critique of Henri Ey's organicism, which he describes as a continuation of a Cartesian mind–body dualism, Lacan goes on to demonstrate that the problem of madness is inseparable from the problem of language and to develop the themes of his pre-war work, arguing that forms of madness are in effect forms of language. The point is illustrated with a succinct account of the Aimée case. Lacan then describes the mechanisms of identification and the role of the image in terms drawn from Hegel's *Phenomenology*, illustrating them with references to Molière's *Le Misanthrope*. The initial effect of identification is to produce alienation: the subject identifies with the other and therefore experiences himself as other. Once again Lacan refers to Bühler's work on transivitism, as summarized by Wallon. The stages of the history of the subject are described in terms similar to those used in the pre-war texts, but the complexes of 1938 are now referred to as traumatisms. Despite the insistence on the importance of language, the paper contains no specific references to linguistics. It does, however, introduce Merleau-Ponty's *Phénoménologie de la perception* as a major theoretical reference.

In the discussion that follows the paper, Lacan is criticized for having shown that madness is inherent in human nature whilst failing to specify its conditions of existence.[24]

1947   'La Psychiatrique anglaise et la guerre', *Evolution psychiatrique* 1, 1947, pp. 293–318. A report to the *Evolution psychiatrique* group based on a five-week visit to England in the autumn of 1945, and probably the most neglected text in Lacan's entire *oeuvre*. He never refers to it again. Lacan describes Britain's victory as basically the victory of morale; the British people's intrepidity is based upon a truthful relationship with the real, and therefore contrasts greatly with France's experience in 1940. He praises the psychiatric methods used in officer selection and psychological testing; these helped to produce a democratic army. In other words, psychiatry was one of the instruments with which England won the war. Lacan also speaks highly of the group psychology of Bion and Rickman; their study of the task of the group is 'a milestone in the history of psychiatry'.[25] His enthusiasm for group psychology is short-lived, and Rickman's 'two-body psychology' in particular is attacked as a 'phantasy' sheltering the notion of a 'two-ego analysis'.[26]

1948   Lacan discusses the agenda for the forthcoming World Congress on Psychiatry with Melanie Klein and attempts to win her support for his proposal for a discussion on 'The Progress of Psychoanalysis'. At the same time he offers to translate her *Psycho-Analysis of Children*. The project comes to nothing, and Lacan later claims to have lost the German version (by Diatkine) from which he was working. The translation is eventually completed by Françoise Girard and Jean-Baptiste Boulager, who were originally approached by Lacan. Boulager later expressed his early fear that Lacan would take the credit for their work.[27]

'L'Aggressivité en psychanalyse', paper read to the Eleventh Congress of French-Speaking Psycho-analysts, Brussels, May 1948. Published, RFP, 1948, pp. 367–88; reprinted, *Ecrits*, pp. 101–24. Trans-lated, *Ecrits: A Selection*, pp. 8–29.

1949   'Règlement et doctrine de la Commission de l'enseignement', published, RFP, 1949, pp. 426–35; reprinted, *La Scission de 1953*, pp. 29–36. The SPP launches an appeal for funds to set up a Training Institute, and Lacan is largely responsible for drawing up the statutes for its Training Commission. The position they express is clearly based upon Freud's *The Question of Lay Analysis*: whilst medical qualifications are certainly desirable, psychoanalysis cannot be allowed to become the monopoly of doctors of medicine. Lacan stresses the importance of the 'fertile kernel' of the humanities; a conscious knowledge thereof will greatly facilitate the analyst's access to the organization of the un-conscious. At the time it is made clear that the SPP must conform to French law, which does not recog-nize psychoanalysis as a distinct speciality; a lay analyst therefore cannot accept an analysand who has not been referred to him or her by a medically qualified analyst.

'Le Stade du miroir comme formateur de la fonction du je, telle qu'elle nous est révélée dans l'expérience psychanalytique', read to the Fourteenth Inter-national Psychoanalytic Congress, Zurich, on 17 July. Published, RFP, 1949, pp. 449–55; reprinted, *Ecrits*, pp. 93–100. Translated by Jean Roussel, 'The Mirror-Phase as Formative of the Function of the I', preceded by Roussel, 'Introduction to Jacques Lacan', *New Left Review*, 51, September–October 1968, pp. 63–77; as 'The Mirror-Stage, as Form-ative of the I, as Revealed in Psychoanalytic Experi-ence', *Ecrits: A Selection*, pp. 1–7. Author's abstract: 'The Mirror Stage, as shown by Psycho-analytic Experience', IJPA, 30, 1949, p. 203.

1950   'Introduction théorique aux fonctions de la psychanalyse en criminologie', co-authored by Michel
Cénac and read to the Thirteenth Congress of
French-Speaking Psychoanalysts, 29 May. Published,
RFP, 1951, pp. 5–29; reprinted, *Ecrits*, pp. 125–49.
A wide-ranging discussion of criminality, taking
in both anthropological (Malinowski and Mauss)
and psychoanalytic (*Totem and Taboo*, the theory
of the superego) references. It is suggested that the
psychoanalytic dialogue can help to provide access
to the imaginary world of the criminal; it will thus
be possible to identify the neurotic repressions and
the developmental stagnation which constitute the
individual case without dehumanizing the criminal
himself. In view of Lacan's stated opposition to the
'social engineering' associated with ego psychology,
it is perhaps surprising to find him discussing the
reintegration of offenders into the community.
Lacan's account of the discussion that followed the
paper is reprinted as 'Psychanalyse et criminologie',
Ornicar?, 31, Winter 1984, pp. 23–7.

'Intervention au Premier Congrès Mondial de
Psychiatrie'. Published, *Actes du Congrès*, vol. 5,
Paris, Hermann, 1952; reprinted, *Ornicar?*, 30,
Autumn 1984, pp. 7–10. A reply to the papers
presented by Franz Alexander, Anna Freud,
Melanie Klein and Raymond de Saussure. The intervention is of interest in that it includes one of
Lacan's earliest references to structural linguistics.
Invoking the work of Jakobson and Lévi-Strauss,
Lacan insists that psychology cannot explain
language; on the contrary, language determines
psychology. He goes on to attack ego psychology;
the ego is 'the syndic of the most mobile functions
through which man adapts to reality', and has the
power of an illusion or lie; it is a superstructure
imbricated within social alienation.

1951   Attends the Amsterdam Congress of the International Psychoanalytical Association. This is the
last Conference he will attend as a member of the
IPA. Participates in the Symposium on 'Natural

Influences in the Development of Ego and Id', much to the exasperation of Marie Bonaparte, who chairs the session.[28] Lacan is reported to have had private discussions with both Anna Freud and Melanie Klein, but their content remains unknown.[29]

Lacan begins a private seminar on the Dora case in his own home.[30] A seminar on the Rat Man is held in the following year. No record of these seminars has survived; it is probable that the 'Rat Man' seminar provides the basis for 'Le Mythe individuel du névrosé' (1953).

The SPP's Training Commission begins to raise the issue of Lacan's use of 'short sessions' (as opposed to the 'standard analytic hour') in his training analyses. In coming years the issue is to cause major controversies in both the SPP and the IPA, but Lacan's supporters will argue that it is being exploited for political purposes. Lacan defends his technique during an SPP meeting in December and again in June 1952, but there is no extant text which provides a theoretical argument in its favour. 'Le Temps logique' (1945) is sometimes read as a theorization of the short sessions, but in 'Fonction et champ' (1953) Lacan merely puts forward the pragmatic argument that his technique accelerates the process of analysis.[31] Subsequent discussions within the SPP and the IPA suggest that the underlying logic is that if the unconscious itself is timeless, it makes little sense to insist upon 'standard sessions'.

'Intervention sur le transfert'. Paper read to the Fourteenth Congress of French-Speaking Psychoanalysts; published, RFP, 1952 pp. 154–63; reprinted, Ecrits, pp. 215–26. Translated as 'Intervention on Transference', Feminine Sexuality, pp. 61–73.

'Some reflections on the Ego', paper read to the British Psycho-Analytical Society on 2 May; published, IJPA, 34, pp. 11–17. A condensed version of 'Le Stade du miroir', this is the only paper by Lacan to appear in the IJPA.

1952

January   Sacha Nacht proposes that Lacan be elected President of the SPP, but the General Meeting resolves to extend Nacht's own mandate for a further year in view of his organizational abilities. In a letter to Loewenstein, Marie Bonaparte argues that Lacan's election to office would be inadmissible because 'he does analyses on principle in ten minutes'.[32]

June   Lacan defends his use of short sessions in a paper entitled 'La Psychanalyse, dialectique?' It remains unpublished.

17 June   Institut de Psychanalyse de Paris established. Nacht is appointed Director for a period of five years, his mandate being to organize a series of theoretical courses and to ensure that prospective analysts are trained in accordance with the statutes of the SPP; in order to do so, he will work in consultation with the Training Commission. Benassy and Serge Lebovici are appointed Scientific Secretaries. As a number of people will point out in subsequent debates, the appointment of Lebovici is somewhat surprising; in 1949 he was one of the signatories of an article entitled 'Autocritique. La Psychanalyse, idéologie réactionnaire', which appeared in the Parti Communiste Français's journal *La Nouvelle Critique*.[33] The article relies upon the classically Stalinist dichotomy between 'bourgeois' and 'proletarian' science, and comes to the conclusion that psychoanalysis is a mystification and a reactionary ideology. Lebovici's later references (at the IPA's Edinburgh Conference of 1961) to the presence of 'undesirable elements' in the Société Française de Psychanalyse suggest that he learned the lessons of Stalinism well.

November   Nacht's proposed statutes for the Institute are put to a meeting of the SPP. The stated aim is to obtain state recognition of a Diploma in Psychoanalysis which can be awarded only to medically qualified analysts. This arouses considerable hostility, not least from Marie Bonaparte who, despite her biologistic leanings, is a lay analyst. The Nacht proposals are prefaced by a quotation from Manakow and Mourgue to the effect that psychoanalysis, like psychiatry and psychology, is a sub-speciality within the general discipline of neurobiology. Lacan ironically cites this at the beginning of his 'Fonction et champ'.[34]

2 December At an extraordinary meeting of the SPP, Lagache and Bonaparte vote against Nacht. Finding himself in the minority, he offers his resignation but is reappointed President on an interim basis. At the end of the month he does resign and Lacan replaces him as head of the Institute. He accepts the appointment on a temporary basis and states that he will attempt to mediate between the various factions within the SPP.

1953

January Lacan introduces new proposals for the Institute's statutes. They are broadly similar to those drawn up in 1949 and are prefaced by a quotation from Freud's *The Question of Lay Analysis.* Lacan points out the dangers of over-personalized politics and of formalist training methods. He also agrees to respect the convention of the standard session in his training analyses.

20 January Lacan is elected President of the SPP. In a reversal of alliance, Bonaparte, who had originally supported Cénac's candidature, now lends her support to the Nacht group. According to Lacan, she changed her position because the statutes he drafted for the Institute mention neither her name nor her honorary functions. On the other hand, her personal hostility towards him is long-standing; as early as 1945 she described him as 'rather too tinged with paranoia and questionable narcissism'.[35] Lacan's reported comments on Freud's visit to Paris in 1938 indicate that the hostility is mutual. Following Lacan's election to the Presidency, Nacht becomes head of the Institute and a life member of its administrative board. The Nacht statutes are officially adopted.

22 February In a letter to Bonaparte, Loewenstein remarks: 'What you tell me about Lacan is distressing. He has always represented a source of conflict for me ... there is his intellectual worth which I value highly, though I disagree violently with him ... I certainly hope that his hastily analysed (that is to say incompletely analysed) trainees will not be admitted [to the SPP].'[36]

5 March The Institute finally opens. There are immediate objections from analysts in training to the curriculum, to the level of fees, and to the requirement that they will sign an agreement not to describe themselves as psychoanalysts and not to practise analysis until they are authorized to do so by the Training Commission. According to the Nacht statutes, a training analysis consists of an average of two hundred and fifty sessions of forty-five minutes each. After some one hundred and fifty sessions, the candidate will begin three cycles of studies: general theory, clinical psychoanalysis, and psychoanalytic technique. Each cycle will last for one academic year. There are also compulsory courses on general psychiatry (one year), child neuropsychiatry (six months) and paediatrics (six months). Optional courses are also available. Fees are high: 15,000 francs for each of the three cycles; 500, 750 and 1,000 francs respectively for each session of the three compulsory courses. Fees for the training analysis itself are by arrangement with the analyst.

15 May In a letter addressed to both Lacan and Nacht, Jenny Roudinesco expresses the unease felt by many of the analysts in training. She is confused as to the respective roles of the SPP and the new Institute and asks why, having already signed an undertaking not to practise without the authorization of the SPP Training Commission (the only organization which existed when she began her analysis in 1949), she is now required to sign a new undertaking with the Institute.

17 May Fifty-one analysts in training publicly associate themselves with Roudinesco's position and endorse her request for clarification. They postpone any decision as to whether or not to sign the undertaking required of them by the Institute.

2 June During an SPP business meeting, Cénac accuses Lacan of instigating a student revolt. Another of Nacht's supporters claims that if it were not for Lacan, there would be no problems within the SPP. The meeting adjourns until 16 June, when a motion of no-confidence in Lacan is to be debated.

16 June The no-confidence motion is signed by Pasche, Bénassy, Diatkine and Cénac. Lacan resigns and is replaced by Parcheminey, who is elected by reason of seniority. He dies in August and is succeeded by Mâle, appointed on a temporary basis. Lagache, Dolto and Favez-Boutonnier resign from the SPP in protest at the way Lacan has been treated and found the Société Française de Psychanalyse. They are immediately joined by Blanche Reverchon-Jouve, Angelo Hesnard and René Laforgue. It is at their invitation that Lacan resigns his membership of the SPP and joins the SFP. The bureau of the new Society is as follows: President: Lagache; Vice President: Favez-Boutonnier; Secretary: Dolto; Treasurer: Lacan.

17 June In a letter to Loewenstein, Bonaparte states: 'Lacan had promised in March 1951 to cease his practice of short sessions, but he has not kept his promise. Nacht confronted him at a meeting with the students. Lacan said that since he had explained his technique some months ago before the Society, he had been released from his promise, and that moreover he had said that he might change his technique but not that he would do so. Each called the other a liar.'[37]

18 June The SFP issues its first official communiqué, explaining that theoretical differences are being exploited by a group within the SPP which is concerned solely with gaining and retaining power. Psychoanalysis is quite incompatible with the atmosphere prevailing in the SPP. The SFP hopes to be recognized as a competent Society by the IPA at its London Congress in July. The communiqué ends: 'We are fighting for the freedom of science and for Humanism. Humanism is powerless unless it is militant.' As of 23 June, the SFP has thirty-four analysts in training; by July the figure has risen to thirty-nine.

25 June   The SFP sets up a series of study groups co-ordinated by François Perrier.

July   In a memorandum distributed within the SPP, Lagache describes the new Society's stance as democratic and liberal, and the SPP's line as authoritarian.

6 July   Ruth Eissler, Honorary Secretary of the IPA, informs Lacan by letter that his resignation from the SPP (the only body in France recognized as competent by the IPA) implies loss of IPA membership. He will therefore not be allowed to attend the business meeting at the London Conference. He is, however, free to attend the open scientific meetings.

14 July   In an attempt to rally support for the SFP's request for recognition by the IPA, Lacan writes to Perrotti (President of the Italian Psychoanalytic Society), Balint and Loewenstein; he will later write to Hartman too. The letter to Loewenstein gives a long account of Lacan's view of recent events and paints a particularly black picture of Nacht and his associates. Lacan mentions his use of short sessions, but does not provide any detailed explanation of the reasons for the innovation.

18 July   The SFP holds its first scientific meeting, with Lacan speaking on 'The Real, The Symbolic and The Imaginary'. The paper remains unpublished, but some indications as to its likely content can be gleaned from the 9 March 1955 session of the Seminar on the ego. Here, Lacan refers to the imaginary as turning the symbolic into images and turning symbolic discourse into figurative terms, as

in the dream. The symbolic is described as symboliz-
ing the image, as in dream interpretation.[38]

26 July   The Eighteenth Congress of the IPA appoints a
committee to examine the SFP's request for recognition: its members are Kurt Eissler, Phyllis Green-
acre, W. Hoffer, Jeanne Lampl de Groot and D.W.
Winnicott. During the debate in London Loewenstein calls for tolerance and argues that, as the dissidents have been unable to put their case to the
Congress, the proceedings are both abnormal and
unjust. Anna Freud takes the view that the SPP has
made a public issue of the split and has spread the
quarrel outside the psychoanalytic community; it is
therefore too late even to attempt a reconciliation.
Bonaparte argues that the techniques used by the
new group require careful examination, particularly
as one member promised to change his technique,
but failed to do so.

The SFP resolves to hold a meeting in Rome in
September, and times it to coincide with the
Congress of French-Speaking Psychoanalysts. It is
informed that its members will not be allowed to
attend the official Congress.

26–27 September The Rome Congress of the SFP is held at the
Istituto di Psicologia della Università di Roma.

18 November   Lacan begins his first public seminar on Freud's
writings on technique at Sainte-Anne.

'Le Mythe individuel du névrosé, ou Poésie et vérité
dans la névrose', paper read to the Collège philosophique and later described by Lacan as the *initium*
of a structuralist reference to form.[39] Published,
Ornicar? 17/18, 1979, pp. 289–307. Translated
with an introduction by Martha Noel Evans. 'The
Neurotic's Individual Myth', *Psychoanalytic
Quarterly*, 48, 1979, pp. 386–425.

'Fonction et champ de la parole et du langage en
psychanalyse', paper read to the Rome Congress of
the SFP and often referred to as the 'Rome

Discourse'. Published, *La Psychanalyse*, 1, 1956,
pp. 81–166; reprinted with minor revisions and with
an introduction ('Du Sujet enfin en question'),
Ecrits, pp. 229–36. Translated Anthony Wilden,
'The Function of Language in Psychoanalysis', *The
Language of Self*, Baltimore, Johns Hopkins, 1968;
'The Function and Field of Speech and Language in
Psycho-analysis', *Ecrits: A Selection*, pp. 30–113.
Neither translation includes 'Du Sujet ...'

'Actes du Congrès de Rome', interventions from the
floor and Lacan's replies; published, *La Psychanalyse*, 1, pp. 199–255.

S I, 1953–54. *Les Ecrits techniques de Freud*, Paris,
Seuil, 1975; translated with notes by John Forrester,
*The Seminar. Book I. Freud's Papers on Technique,
1953–54*, Cambridge, Cambridge University Press,
forthcoming.

1954

'Introduction au Commentaire de Jean Hyppolite
sur la *"Verneinung"* de Freud', 'Réponse au
Commentaire de Jean Hyppolite sur la *"Verneinung"* de Freud', a discussion of the paper on Freud's
'Negation' (SE XIX) presented to the Seminar by
Hyppolite on 10 February. Published, *La Psychanalyse*, 1, 1956, pp. 17–28, 41–49; reprinted,
Ecrits, pp. 363–80; 381–99. Both the versions given
La Psychanalyse and that in *Ecrits* represent a
reworking and an expansion of the text given in the
transcript of the Seminar itself.[40] Hyppolite's paper is
printed as an appendix to *Ecrits*, pp. 879–87, with
some footnotes by Lacan. Hyppolite's paper is a
detailed reading of 'Negation' and concentrates
initially on the translation problems it poses. He
suggests that *Verneinung* should be translated as
dénégation, rather than as *négation*, in order to bring
out the notion of negative judgement [*déjugement*]
implicit in Freud's paper.[41] He then stresses Freud's
use of *Aufhebung*, relating it to the Hegelian notion
of suppression-supersession: *Verneinung* is a means
of taking repression into account without thereby
lifting it. The instance of negativity is then linked to
the primordial aggression and rivalry to which Lacan

refers in 'Le Stade du miroir'. Lacan's introduction is largely taken up with a discussion of the analysis of resistances, which are defined as an ego phenomenon. Lacan then turns to an exposition of his theory of the ego, demonstrating that analysis of resistances is doomed to failure in that the analyst becomes a support for the subject's alter ego. His response comprises a discussion of the Wolf Man case and a further attack on ego psychology (as represented by Ernst Kris), which is condemned as 'human engineering' and as a psychoanalytic 'New Deal'. This exchange with Hyppolite is an important stage in the elaboration of Lacan's concept of *forclusion*.

S II, 1954–55, *Le Moi dans la théorie de Freud et dans la technique de la psychanalyse*, Paris, Seuil, 1978. Translated, Sylvana Tomaselli, *The Seminar, Book II. The Ego in Freud's Theory and in the Technique of Psycho-Analysis*, with notes by John Forrester, Cambridge University Press, forthcoming.

1955

In his report to the Geneva Congress of the IPA Hartmann announces that the committee appointed to study the SFP's request for recognition has reached the conclusion that 'the Lagache group' should not be recognized as a Competent Society. In the committee's view, its training and teaching capacities are inadequate.

'Variantes de la cure-type', *Encyclopédie médico-chirurgicale*, vol. 3, 1955; the article was not included in the 1960 reprint. Reprinted, *Ecrits*, pp. 323–62, with a brief introductory note and some revisions (signalled by footnotes). A major statement of Lacan's opposition to ego psychology and a restatement of the view that the ego is a narcissistic formation whose structure and function are first established in the mirror stage. Lacan reviews the work of a number of prominent analysts ranging from Anna Freud, who is held to have confused the ego and the subject of discourse,[42] to Balint, whose reference to transference as corresponding to primary love is seen as reducing analysis to the dual relationship of the mirror stage.[43] The increasing tendency to see analysis as a reinforcement of the 'healthy part' of the ego is dismissed as an attempt to induce identification with the ego of the analyst.

'La Séminaire sur "La Lettre volée"', a revised version of the Seminar given on 26 April 1955.[44] Published, *La Psychanalyse*, 2, 1957, pp. 1–44; reprinted with a new introduction and additional matter, *Ecrits*, pp. 11–61. Translated, Jeffrey Mehlman, 'Seminar on "The Purloined Letter"', *Yale French Studies*, 48, 1973, pp. 39–72.

'Psychanalyse et cybernétique, ou De La Nature du langage', lecture to the SFP, 22 June, published, S II, pp. 339–54. Cybernetics is explored both in terms of Lacan's interest in games theory and as a variant on the process of abstraction and formalization which Lacan sees as defining any movement towards scientificity. The formal laws of language and of symbolization, as analysed by Lévi-Strauss, are shown to obey a similar process.

'La Chose freudienne, ou Sens du retour à Freud en psychanalyse', an extended version of a lecture given at the Neuro-Psychiatric Clinic, Vienna, on 7 November 1955. Published, *Evolution psychiatrique*, 1956, pp. 225–52. Revised and reprinted, *Ecrits*, pp. '406–36. Translated, 'The Freudian Thing, Or The Meaning of the Return to Freud in Psychoanalysis', *Ecrits: A Selection*, pp. 114–45.

S III, 1955–56 *Les Psychoses*, Paris, Seuil, 1981.

1956 Translation of Martin Heidegger, 'Logos', *La Psychanalyse*, 1, pp. 59–79. Lacan acknowledges assistance from Mme A. Botond, and states that the translation was approved by Heidegger. The original appeared in *Festschrift für Hans Jantzen*, Berlin 1951.

'Fetishism: The Symbolic, The Real and the Imaginary (in collaboration with Wladmir Granoff), in S. Lorand and M. Balint, eds, *Perversions: Psychodynamics and Therapy*, New York, Random House, 1956.

'Freud dans le siècle', lecture given at the invitation of Jean Delay to mark the centenary of Freud's birth, 16 May 1956. Published, S III, pp. 263–77. A general presentation of Freud, concentrating on *The Interpretation of Dreams* and *The Psychopathology of Everyday Life* and stressing the importance of language to psychoanalysis; in a Freudian perspective, man is a subject trapped within and tortured by language.

'Situation de la psychanalyse et formation du psychanalyste en 1956', *Etudes philosophiques*, 4, October–December 1956, pp. 567–84 (special 'Freud Centenary' issue). The published version is revised; the original exists only in privately published form; reprinted, *Ecrits*, 549–491. A restatement of Lacan's insistence on the need to study the rhetoric of the unconscious; *The Interpretation of Dreams* is said to be Freud's most important work. A sustained attack is made on Hartmann, Kris and Loewenstein. Lacan also gives a satirical and highly entertaining account of the hierarchical organization of the IPA. The paper is closely related to 'La Psychanalyse et son enseignement' (1957).

S IV, 1956–57, 'La Relation d'objet et les structures freudiennes'. Unpublished; authorized summary by J.B. Pontalis, *Bulletin de psychologie*, vol. X, 1956–57: no. 7, pp. 426–30; no. 10, pp. 602–05; no. 12, pp. 742–3; no. 14, pp. 851–4; vol. XI, 1957–58: no. 1, pp. 31–4. In 'Direction de la cure' (1958), Lacan refers to the Seminar thus:'I showed the value of a conception in which child observation is nourished by the most accurate reconsideration of the functioning of mothering in the ego genesis of the object: I mean the notion of the transitional object, introduced by D.W. Winnicott, which is a key-point for the explanation of the genesis of fetishism.'[45]

1957

July   At the Paris Conference of the IPA, Hartmann confirms that the Central Executive would be prepared to study any application for affiliation that might be made by the SFP.

'La Psychanalyse et son enseignement', paper read to the Société française de philosophie on 23 February. Published, *Bulletin de la Société française de philosophie*, 2, 1957, pp. 65–101; reprinted, *Ecrits*, pp. 437–58. The discussion that followed the paper was also published in the *Bulletin*; reprinted as 'Dialogue avec les philosophes français', *Ornicar?* 32, Spring 1985, pp. 7–22. Psychoanalysis is presented as posing a problem for philosophy in that it posits the existence of a subject within the subject, and demonstrates that the ego and the subject are not coterminous. Analysis itself is described as the reconstitution of a symbolic chain based upon three elements: the history of a life lived as a history; subjection to the laws of language; the intersubjective play whereby the truth enters into the real.

'L'Instance de la lettre dans l'inconscient, ou La Raison depuis Freud', lecture given at the Sorbonne on 9 May at the request of the Groupe de philosophie de la Fédération des étudiants ès lettres, published, *La Psychanalyse*, 3, 1957, pp. 47–81; reprinted, *Ecrits*, pp. 493–528. Translated, J. Miel, 'The Insistence of the Letter in the Unconscious', *Yale French Studies*, 36–37, 1966, pp. 112–47; 'The Agency of the Letter in the Unconscious, or Reason since Freud', *Ecrits: A Selection*, pp. 146–78.

'D'Une Question préliminire à tout traitement possible de la psychose', *La Psychanalyse*, 4, 1959, pp. 1–50; reprinted *Ecrits*, pp. 531–83. Translated, 'On A Question Preliminary to Any Possible Treatment of Psychosis', *Ecrits: A Selection*, pp. 179–225.

S V, 1957–58, 'Les Formations de l'inconscient'. Unpublished. Authorized summary by J.B. Pontalis, *Bulletin de Psychologie*, vol. XI, 1957–58, no. 4/5, pp. 293–6; vol. XII, 1958–59, vol. 2/3, pp. 182–92; no. 4, pp. 250–56.

1958   'Jeunesse de Gide, ou La Lettre et le désir', *Critique*, 131, April, pp. 291–315; reprinted, *Ecrits*, pp. 739–

64. Review article on Jean Delay, *La Jeunesse d'André Gide*,[46] with passing comments on Jean Schlumberger, *Madeleine et André Gide*.[47] Delay's study of Gide is a classic and distinguished example of psychobiography; for Lacan, it is a study of the relationship between man and the letter. Lacan also relates Gide's constant adoption of a persona to Freud's comments on the ideal ego.

'La Signification du phallus (*Die Bedeutung des Phallus*)', lecture delivered in German on 9 May at the Max Planck Institute, Munich, at the invitation of Professor Paul Matussek. Published with introductory note, *Ecrits*, pp. 685–95. Translated, 'The Signification of the Phallus', *Ecrits: A Selection*, pp. 281–90; 'The Meaning of the Phallus', *Feminine Sexuality*, pp. 74–85.

'La Direction de la cure et les principes de son pouvoir', Report to the Colloque internationale de Royaumont, 10–13 July, presented at the request of the Société française de philosophie. Published, *La Psychanalyse*, 6, 1961, pp. 149–206; reprinted, *Ecrits*, pp. 585–645. Translated, 'The Direction of the Treatment and the Principles of its Power', *Ecrits: A Selection*, pp. 226–80.

'Remarque sur le rapport de Daniel Lagache: "Psychanalyse et structure de la personnalité"', intervention at the Colloque international de Royaumont; revised Easter 1960 and published, *La Psychanalyse*, 6, 1961, pp. 111–47; reprinted, *Ecrits*, pp. 647–84. In the course of a critical reading of Lagache's report (which also appears in *La Psychanalyse*, 6) Lacan begins to outline a reference to topology by making a distinction between form and structure. Intersubjectivity is described as arising from the subject's relations with signifiers located in a transcendental Other, and not from the symmetrical self–other relation described by Lagache. The paper's discussion of negation and of the structures of the imaginary anticipates the themes of 'Subversion du sujet' (1960).

S VI, 1958–59, 'Le Désir et son interprétation'.

Unpublished; authorized summary by J.B. Pontalis, *Bulletin de psychologie*, vol. XIII, 1959–60; no. 5, pp. 263–72; no. 6, pp. 329–35.

1959

4 July   The SFP requests affiliation to the IPA, and a report on its activities drawn up by Serge Leclaire is submitted for approval.

28 July   At the twenty-first Congress of the IPA (Copenhagen), Gillespie announces that the IPA finds that the SFP's report is inadequate and that a committee has been appointed to investigate further. The committee is headed by P. Turquet; its members are Paula Heimann, Ilse Hellmann and P.J. van de Loeuw. Gillespie adds that in the event of a favourable report from the committee the Central Executive may grant provisional recognition, but that the final decision will rest with the 1961 Edinburgh Conference. It will in fact be two years before the Turquet committee reports.

'A la mémoire d'Ernest Jones: sur sa théorie du symbolisme', dated January–March 1959, *La Psychanalayse*, 7, 1962, pp. 1–20: reprinted, *Ecrits*, pp. 697–717, with a afterword, 'D'un syllabaire après-coup', pp. 717–24. A tribute to Ernest Jones and a critique of his 'Theory of Symbolism',[48] which Lacan describes elsewhere as 'a fundamental paper'.[49] Whilst he gives Jones credit for breaking with the Jungian or hermeneutic notion of symbolism, Lacan criticizes the foundations of his theory and in particular the contention that 'true symbolism' refers to ideas or to the concrete support of the symbol. Symbolism is not founded upon a correspondence between the symbol and the real; the real exists only through the agency of the signifier. Elsewhere, Lacan explains why he concentrates on Jones's theory of symbolism: it is an instructive failure in that it unsuccessfully attempts to relate symbolism to metaphor, and Jones unwittingly provides confirmation of his own theses as to the privileged function of the phallus.[50]

S VI continues. The sessions devoted to *Hamlet* in March–April published as: 'Le Canevas I', *Ornicar?*, 24, Autumn 1981, pp. 7–17; 'Le Canevas II (Fin)', ibid., pp. 18–31; 'III: Le Désir de la mère', *Ornicar?*, 25, Autumn 1982, pp. 13–25; 'IV: II n'y a pas d'autre de l'autre', ibid., pp. 267–36; 'V: L'Objet Ophélie', *Ornicar?*, 26/27, Summer 1983, pp. 7–19; 'VI: Le Désir et le deuil', ibid., pp. 20–32; 'VII: Phallophanie', ibid., pp. 32–44. The last three sections are translated by James Hulbert as 'Desire and the Interpretation of Desire in *Hamlet*', *Yale French Studies*, 55/56, 1977, pp. 11–52.

S VIII, *L'Ethique de la psychanalyse*, Paris, Seuil, 1986. Typescript notes on the *Ethique*, probably dating from 1959–60 with later additions, published as 'Compte rendu avec interpolations du Séminaire de l'Ethique', *Ornicar?*, 28, Spring 1984, pp. 7–18. Lacan appears to have been particularly attached to this Seminar, which is notable for its reading of Sophocles' *Antigone*, and comments that it is the only one he felt inspired to rewrite as an *écrit*.[51]

1960   Lacan's views on the Algerian War are not on record, but the comments he makes in a letter to Winnicott are perhaps indicative of an anti-war position; he mentions with pride that his stepdaughter Laurence Bataille has been arrested because of her political connections, and that a nephew has been sentenced to two months in prison for anti-war activities.[52] Lacan does not, however, sign the *Manifeste des 121*, which called upon conscripts to desert.

Intervention during C. Perelman's paper on 'L'Idée de rationalité et la règle de justice', which was read to the Société française de philosophie on 23 June. Published, *Bulletin de la société française de philosophie*, 1, 1961, pp. 29–33. Rewritten as 'La Métaphore du sujet', *Ecrits*, pp. 889–92. The comments on metaphor are similar to those made in 'L'Instance de la lettre'; Lacan rejects the view that metaphor is based upon analogy and argues that its freshness derives from the heterogeneity of the elements in play.

'Propos directifs pour un congrès sur la sexualité féminine', paper read to an SFP Congress held at the Municipal University, Amsterdam, September 1960. A note states that the paper was written two years before the Congress. Published, *La Psychanalyse*, 7, 1964, pp. 3–14; reprinted, *Ecrits*, pp. 86–98. Translated, 'Guiding Remarks for a Congress on Femine Sexuality', *Feminine Sexuality*, pp. 86–89.

'Subversion du sujet et dialectique du désir dans l'inconscient freudien', paper read to the Royaumont Conference on 'La Dialectique' (organized by Jean Wahl), September 1960. Published, *Ecrits*, pp. 793–827. Translated, 'The Subversion of the Subject and the Dialectic of Desire in the Freudian Unconscious', *Ecrits: A Selection*, pp. 292–325.

'Position de l'inconscient', paper read to a Congress on the unconscious at Bonneval, 31 October–2 November. At the request of Henri Ey, the paper was condensed for publication in Henri Ey, ed., *L'Inconscient*, Paris, Desclée de Brouwer, 1966, pp. 159–70. Full text published with an introductory note, *Ecrits*, pp. 829–50.

S VIII, 1960–61, 'Le Transfert (dans sa disparité subjective)'. Unpublished.

1961   The report of the Turquet committee is submitted to the Central Executive of the IPA, but its findings are not made public. The document is, however, made available to the SFP delegation which travels to Edinburgh for the Twenty-Second Congress.

August   After negotiations with the IPA, the SFP withdraws its application for recognition as a Competent Society. It is offered possible recognition as a Study Group under IPA supervision, and three members (Lagache, Favez-Boutonnier and Leclaire) are offered the status of 'member directly attached to the IPA'.

During the business meeting of the Edinburgh Conference, Gillespie summarizes the requirements to which the SFP must conform. These include strictly defined criteria for training: a training analysis must comprise three or four forty-five-minute sessions per week, and must continue for at least a year before the analyst in training begins to give supervised analyses. The training programme must be extended to include formal lecture courses lasting for one or two years. A training commission must draw up biannual reports on the progress of each student. The SFP cannot be regarded as offering training in child analysis until such time as a new training programme acceptable to the IPA has been drawn up. Training analysis must conform to IPA standards; candidates trained in accordance with other norms must undergo retraining. The SFP must conform to IPA decisions, and no new study groups are to be set up in the provinces until further notice. The full document known as the Edinburgh Requirements consists of nineteen points, almost all of them concerned with training. It is only after it has agreed to the nineteen demands that the SFP delegation learns that a twentieth condition has been inserted into the document; article thirteen specifically states that Lacan and Françoise Dolto must be phased out of the training programme, and that they cannot be permitted to begin new training analyses.

Lebovici addresses the Conference on behalf of the SPP. He claims that the existence of the SFP may lead to the emergence of undesirable elements that could threaten the furture of the international psychoanalytic movement. He expresses the hope that the proposed supervisory committee will encourage the good elements within the SFP and will do all it can to eliminate the bad elements. The SPP is willing to help the committee in its difficult task.

28 September In a letter to the IPA, SFP President Juliette Favez-Boutonnier states that the SFP will conform to the Edinburgh Requirements, but that article thirteen is unacceptable.

'Maurice Merleau-Ponty', *Les Temps modernes*, 184/185, pp. 245–54. Whilst Lacan pays tribute to Merleau-Ponty's work on the phenomenology of perception, he also criticizes it for its reliance upon a Cartesian concept of extension; the corollary of that concept must be a subject which is in fact a module of a universal perception. Phenomenological analysis of perception cannot account for fetishism or for the castration complex, as it lacks the necessary concept of the signifier.

S IX, 1961–2, 'L'Identification'. Unpublished.

1962

2 May   The Bureau of the SFP (Lacan, Dolto, Lagache, Granoff, Perrier, Leclaire and Favez-Boutonnier) privately circulates a report to be presented to the General Meeting of 14 May. Most of the document is taken up with an account of the events leading up to the founding of the SFP and of its dealings with the IPA. The authors express the fear that continued isolation may lead to sclerosis, and note that the request for IPA recognition was intended to prevent this. Most of the Edinburgh Requirements are acceptable in so far as they refer to internationally recognized standards. Article thirteen is inadmissible; the issues it raises should, if necessary, be dealt with internationally and do not concern outside parties.

31 July   In a joint letter to Maxwell Gitelson, President of the IPA, Leclaire and Granoff say that they have heard rumours to the effect that certain parties are attempting to undermine the Study Group status accorded to the SFP at Edinburgh. They point out the the SFP can be re-integrated into the internal community only if it can continue its work in a climate of mutual trust and sympathy.

'Kant avec Sade', *Critique*, 191, April, pp. 291–313. Dated September 1962, and originally written as a preface to Sade's *La Philosophie dans le boudoir* or the fifteen-volume edition of the *Œuvres complètes du Marquis de Sade* published by the Cercle du Livre

Précieux from 1963 onwards. It was in fact published as the 'Postface' to *Justine*, vol. 2, tome III, 1966, pp. 551–77. Reprinted, *Ecrits*, pp. 765–90. A joint reading of Sade, *La Philosophie dans le boudoir* and Kant, *Critique of Practical Reason*, concentrating upon the workings of the universal law and desire in both texts, and related to sections of S VII.

S X, 1962–63, 'L'Angoisse'. Unpublished.

1963

Lacan is appointed *chargé de cours* (part-time lecturer) at the Ecole Pratique des Hautes Etudes and a *directeur de collection* (series editor) at Editions du Seuil. The series he edits will be known as Le Champ freudien.

21 January

A motion adopted by the Bureau of the SFP states that any attempt to force the expulsion of one of its founder members would be discriminatory, and would offend against both the principles of scientific objectivity and the spirit of justice.

19 May

Turquet visits Paris and privately informs members of the SFP of the general tenor of the report he will make to the Twenty-Third Congress of the IPA in Stockholm in September. The SFP members are not shown the document itself; Turquet orally translates sections of it, and Perrier circulates his notes on the contents. For the IPA the main problem is the continued presence of Lacan in the SFP, and the Society's failure to exclude him from the training programme. The prevailing attitude to Freud within the SFP is not acceptable; his works are being studied obsessionally, in the manner of the medieval schoolmen. There is too much concentration on the early texts and too little attention is paid to contemporary psychoanalysis. Turquet expresses doubts as to whether Lacan's pupils have really been analysed, claims that he manipulates transference, and describes his therapeutic work as irresponsible. As a teacher he is a menace, and he must be excluded from the training programme along with Dolto and

André Berge. The SFP's status as a Study Group will be confirmed at Stockholm, but no promises can be made as to the possibility of its definitive recognition as a Competent Society.

2 July   In his opening address to the General Meeting of the SFP, President Serge Leclaire points out that the Society faces two threats. It can either submit to the IPA's demands, or it can break with the international movement. The Bureau successfully moves a three-part motion: the SFP must be organized in such a way as to be able to carry out the tasks defined by its statutes, provide the appropriate conditions for open research, and continue to request affiliation to the IPA whilst re-establishing and developing its contacts with the international psychoanalytic movement.

11 July   Six members of the SFP (Aulagnier, Lang, Laplanche, Lefebvre-Pontalis, Smirnoff and Widlöcher) sign a motion noting that the training commission has not been able to keep the undertakings given to the IPA's consultative committee, and that this has been a major factor in the hardening of the IPA's position. They see no contradiction between allowing Lacan to go on teaching and observing the norms of training analysis. Finally, they point out that if the SFP does not succeed in becoming a true psychoanalytic society, it is in danger of degenerating into an academic 'learned society'.

31 July   During the Stockholm Conference, the Central Executive Committee of the IPA meets the SFP and recommends that its Study Group status should be confirmed, that the advisory committee should continue its work, and that Granoff should be elected a member of the IPA in a personal capacity.

2 August   A memorandum from the IPA congratulates Leclaire and the SPF on their attempts to put the Society's affairs in order, but notes that Lacan still has a voice in training matters, that he has not

observed the Edinburgh Requirements, and that he
has hindered the work of the advisory committee.
Continued sponsorship of the SFP will not be possible unless Lacan is removed from the training
programme by 31 October. All analysts currently in
training with him must undertake a period of training with an approved analyst if they wish to continue.

14 October   Favez-Boutonnier, Lagache, Granoff and Favez put
forward a motion calling for Lacan's name to be
removed from the list of training analysts. The
Bureau is now split into two numerically equal
factions.

16 October   In a letter to members of the SFP, Leclaire states
that he is unwilling to use his casting vote to resolve
the split within the Bureau and proposes that the
entire Bureau should resign in preparation for new
elections at the forthcoming General Meeting.

10 November   Lacan informs Leclaire that he will not be attending
the General Meeting to be held in the afternoon, as
his presence would be tantamount to a request that
the 13 October motion should not be adopted.
During the meeting, Laplanche (speaking on behalf
of himself, Lang, Lefebvre-Pontalis, Smirnoff and
Widlöcher) proposes that the Bureau should resign
and that a provisional commission should be elected
to examine the SFP's problems. A Study Commission should draw up a list of training analysts which
does not include Lacan. A final decision on Lacan's
activities should be deferred until a future general
meeting.

11 November   The Bureau resolves not to adopt the 14 October
motion and to attempt to continue the dialogue
within the SFP. The debate over the problems
associated with training analysis should continue. A
motion to this effect will be put to the General
Meeting called for 19 November.

19 November   The General Meeting rejects the Bureau's motion of

11 November. Leclaire, Dolto and Perrier resign from office.

20 November   Lacan tells those attending his Seminar at Sainte-Anne that in view of recent events, this will be the last time he will be addressing them.

10 December   A general meeting of the SFP elects a new Bureau consisting of Favez-Boutonnier, Berge, Lagache, Granoff, Lang and Anzieu. Leclaire and Perrier are elected to the Study Commission.

11 December   Jean Clavreul circulates a letter to SFP members announcing the formation of a Groupe d'étude psychanalytique (GEP). A circular issued by the SFP describes the GEP as an embryonic psychoanalytic society; its very existence implies a choice between participating in its activities or those of the SFP.

'Le Séminaire des noms-du-père'. Only one session of the Seminar announced for 1963–64 takes place. Fragment published, *L'Excommunication*, pp. 110–11.

1964   Lacan's Seminar on 'The Four Fundamental Concepts of Psychoanalysis' begins at the Ecole Pratique des Hautes Etudes on 15 January. In his opening address, he compares the IPA's decision to pronounce his teachings anathema to the kherem which excommunicated Spinoza from the synagogue in 1656.[53]

14 February   Favez-Boutonnier, now President of the SFP, informs Clavreul that his candidature to become a *membre titulaire* is unacceptable because of his activities in the GEP.

9 June   Favez-Boutonnier informs a general meeting of the SFP of the IPA's decision that it can no longer be regarded as a Study Group because it has failed to comply with the recommendations of the Edinburgh and Stockholm Conferences.

June At a meeting of the GEP, Clavreul describes the group as 'Lacanian'.

21 June Lacan founds the Ecole Freudienne de Paris. According to the *Acte de fondation*, the central aim of the EFP is to restore psychoanalysis to its true function by making a rigorous critique of all the deviations and compromises which threaten its future development. That function is inseparable from the training of analysts who will be able to 'reconquer' psychoanalysis. Membership implies active participation in the work of small study groups. The EFP is organized on the basis of three sections, each of which is divided into three sub-sections: pure psychoanalysis (doctrine, training and supervision), applied psychoanalysis (doctrine of treatment, casuistics, psychiatric information) and a section dedicated to surveying the Freudian field (continuous commentary on the psychoanalytic movement, articulation with related sciences, ethics of psychoanalysis).

July Leclaire and Perrier resign from their positions in the SFP and join the GEP.

The establishment of the Association Psychanalytique de France is announced. It will be recognized as a Study Group by the IPA. Members include Lagache, Anzieu, Granoff, Laplanche and Pontalis.

'Du "*Trieb*" de Freud et du désir du psychanalyste', summary of comments made during a colloquium on technique and casuistics organized by Enrico Castelli at the University of Rome, 7–12 January 1964. Published, *Atti del colloquio internazionale su "Tecnica e casistica"*, Padova, Cedam, 1964, pp. 51–3, 55–60; reprinted, *Ecrits*, pp. 851–4. Brief comments on the distinction between 'instinct' and 'drive' [*Triebe*] and on desire, seen as being instituted by the law prohibiting incest.

S XI, January–June 1964, *Les Quatre Concepts fondamentaux de la psychanalyse*, Paris, Seuil, 1973. Translated, Alan Sheridan, *The Four Fundamental*

Concepts of Psychoanalysis, London, The Hogarth Press and The Institute of Psycho-Analysis, 1977, with a new preface for the English-language edition. (The *postface* dated 1 January 1973 does not appear in the translation. Abstract by Lacan, *Annuaire de l'Ecole Pratique des Hautes Etudes*, 1964–65, pp. 249–51; reprinted, *Ornicar?*, 29, Summer 1984, pp. 7–9. To Lacan's great annoyance, the corrections he added to some of the graphs were not included in the published text. He inscribes the copy given to Jenny Aubry thus: 'Leave this book to your descendants for the bibliographic value it will acquire as an example of the truly exceptional mess a publishing house can make of a manuscript which was the object of the most vigilant care, not to mention the competence of the man whose name follows mine![54]

S XII, 1964–65, 'Problèmes cruciaux pour la psychanalyse'. Unpublished. Abstract by Lacan, *Annuaire de l'Ecole Pratique des Hautes Etudes*, 1965–66, pp. 270–73; reprinted, *Ornicar?*, 29, Summer 1984, pp. 7–9.

1965

19 January   The SFP is dissolved at an extraordinary general meeting. Its assets are equally divided between the APF and the EFP.

28 July   During the business meeting of the Twenty-Fourth Congress of the IPA (Amsterdam), the AFP is recognized as a Competent Society.

'Hommage fait fait à Marguerite Duras, du ravissement de Lol V. Stein', *Cahiers Renaud-Barrault*, 52, December, pp. 7–15; reprinted, *Ornicar?*, 34, Autumn 1985, pp. 7–13. A short tribute to Duras's novel *Le Ravissement de Lol V. Stein*,[55] and Lacan's only real discussion of a novel by a member of the contemporary avant-garde. Lacan's interest focuses on the ambiguity of *ravissement*, which means 'rapture' in both an abstract and a passive sense (being enraptured and being ravished away). The novel appears to have enjoyed something of a vogue in the EFP; Montrelay gives a paper on it to Lacan's Seminar in June, and later teaches courses on it at Vincennes.[56]

'La Science et la vérité', stenographic record of the first session of the 1965–66 Seminar, 1 December. Published, *Cahiers pour l'analyse*, 1, January 1966, pp. 7–30; reprinted, *Ecrits*, pp. 855–77. Perhaps Lacan's most rigorously anti-humanist text, the paper includes a discussion of the cognito and of Lacan's proposed translation of Freud's *Wo Es war, soll ich Werden.* The model of scientificity invoked is derived from Koyré.

S XIII, 1965–66, 'L'Objet de la psychanalyse'. Unpublished. Lacan's abstract published, *Annuaire de l'Ecole Pratique des Hautes Etudes*, 1966–67, pp. 211–12; reprinted, *Ornicar?*, 29, Summer 1984, pp. 12–13.

1966

'Réponses à des étudiants en philosophie sur l'objet de la psychanalyse', 19 February 1966. Published, *Cahiers pour l'analyse*, 3, May–June 1966, pp. 5–13. Brief replies to questions submitted by unidentified philosophy students at ENS on: 1. Consciousness and the subject; 2. Psychoanalysis and society; 3. Psychoanalysis and philosophy; 4. Psychoanalaysis and anthropology.

Ecrits, Paris, Seuil. The text includes a number of pieces written for this edition; all are dated 1966 in the text. Most are introductory comments or afterwords to the various *écrits*; they do not appear in *Ecrits: A Selection.* Includes an *index raisonné* of major concepts and a commentary on the graphs by Jacques-Alain Miller; the commentary first appeared in *Cahiers pour l'analyse*, 2, March–April 1966. Lacan is reportedly reluctant to have these included because of his belief that strict definitions imprison thought.[57] *Ecrits* immediately becomes a best-seller. On 30 November *Le Nouvel Observateur* reports that the initial print-run of 5,000 has sold out with minimal advertising; by the end of the year the text is reprinting. By June 1967, the glossy *Jardin des modes* is recommending *Ecrits* as holiday reading.

'Of Structure as an Inmixing of an Otherness Prerequisite to Any Subject Whatever', paper read to the
Colloquium on 'The Languages of Criticism and the
Sciences of Man', Johns Hopkins University, Baltimore, October 1966, followed by discussion.
Published in Richard Macksey and Eugenio Donato,
eds, *The Structuralist Controversy*, Johns Hopkins
Press, Baltimore and London, 1970 (1972 edn
pp. 186–200). There is no French original.

'Présentation', introduction to Paul Duquenne's
translation of Daniel-Paul Schreber, *Mémoires d'un
névropathe, Cahiers pour l'analyse*, 5, November–
December 1966, pp. 69–72.

'Petit Discours à l'ORTF', radio talk given on
Georges Charbonnier's 'Sciences et techniques'
programme on France-Culture, 2 December 1966.
Published, *Recherches*, 3/4, 1966, pp. 5–9;
reprinted, *Ornicar?*, 35, Winter 1985–86, pp. 7–11.
General comments on the centrality for psychoanalysis of language, the 'bath in which man is
immersed'. Lacan distances himself from the prevailing structuralist movement.

S XIV, 1966–67, 'La Logique du fantasme'.
Unpublished. Lacan's abstract published, *Annuaire
de l'Ecole Pratique des Hautes Etudes*, 1967–68,
pp. 189–94; reprinted, *Ornicar?*, 29, Summer 1984,
pp. 13–18.

1967   'Proposition du 9 octobre 1967 sur le psychanalyste
de l'Ecole', *Scilicet*, 1, 1968, pp. 14–30. The propo-
sition introduces *la passe*, the most controversial of
all the EFP's innovations. The EFP has two grades
of membership: the *passe* is the process whereby the
Analyste Membre de l'Ecole becomes an *Analyste de
l'Ecole*. The distinction is not intended to be hierarchical, but in practice it tends to correspond to a
difference in theoretical commitment and sophistication. Having reached a certain stage in his or her
analysis, the AME may ask to be recognized as an
AE. The request is addressed to two or three *passeurs*, who are themselves in analysis and of similar

standing to the candidate. An account of the on-going analysis is given to the *passeurs*, who communicate what they learn to a jury or committee of two or three senior AEs; Lacan is always a member of the jury. The jury decides whether or not the *passe* has been successful, in other words whether or not the candidate is in a position to use his/her analytic experiences as a basis for research and to continue to the future work of the EFP. In effect, the *passe* marks the transition from analysand to analyst and abolishes the traditional distinction between a personal analysis and a training analysis. In accordance with the principle that 'the analyst authorizes himself', the demand for recognition must emanate from the analysand. Although highly controversial, Lacan's proposition is accepted by a large majority at the General Meeting of the EFP held in January 1969. Lacan himself later describes the *passe* as being an examination of the motives which lead an analysand to propose that he should become an analyst, adding that no one was forced to take part in it.[58]

'Discours de clôture des Journées sur les psychoses chez les enfants', 22 October. Published, *Recherches*, December 1968, pp. 143–52. Closing address to the EFP Congress on child psychosis organized by Maude Mannoni, Paris, 21–22 October. Invited speakers included R.D. Laing and David Cooper; this appears to have been the only formal contact between the EFP and 'anti-psychiatry', though there is in fact little real dialogue between the two parties. Mannoni is one of the few members of the EFP to take a serious interest in Laing. Lacan's closing remarks are mainly of interest because of the link he detects between his *objet petit-a* and Winnicott's transitional object.

'Discours à l'Ecole Freudienne de Paris, 6 December 1967'. Published, *Scilicet*, 2/3, 1970, pp. 9–24, followed pp. 24–29 by a comment dated 1 October 1970. Comments on and defence of the *proposition du 9 octobre*. Lacan stresses that the AME/AE distinction is not based upon a hierarchy of superior-ity; he sees the positions expressed in the *proposition* as an extension of his earlier theses, and as a response to the IPA's hostility to his teachings.

'La Méprise du sujet supposé savoir', address to the Institut français, Naples, 14 December 1967; published, *Scilicet*, 1, 1968, pp. 42–50. Lacan denounces the prevailing trends within psychoanalysis which have effectively abandoned Freud's concept of the unconscious; their failings are typified by their neglect of *Jokes and their Relation to the Unconscious.*

'De Rome 53 à Rome 67: La Psychanalyse. Raison d'un échec', lecture given at the University of Rome, 15 December 1967. Published, *Scilicet*, 1, 1968, pp. 42–50. Lacan once more stresses that the unconscious is isomorphic with discourse, but distances himself from structuralism. The lecture contains one of Lacan's few references to Foucault and a rare allusion to Derrida, whose *différance* is described as an Aphrodite rising out of the foam of Lacan's discourse.

'De la psychanalyse dans ses rapports avec la réalité', address to the Institut français, Milan, 18 December 1967. Published, *Scilicet*, 1, 1968, pp. 51–60. Lacan strongly rejects the view that psychoanalysis is a hermeneutics or a transcendental system of interpretation. The analysand is described as realizing his 'I think' as alienation, as discovering the phantasy is the motor behind psychic reality and that the subject is divided. The title of this address is presumably an allusion to that of Lacan's doctoral thesis of 1932.

S XV, 1967–68, 'L'Acte psychanalytique'. Unpublished. Lacan's abstract published, *Annuaire de l'Ecole Pratique des Hautes Etudes*, 1968–69, pp. 213–20; reprinted, *Ornicar?*, 29, Summer 1984, pp. 18–25.

1968   *Scilicet*, the journal of the EFP, begins publication; seven issues appear between 1968 and 1973. In the introduction to the first issue Lacan explains its curious, if not unique, publishing policy. Only articles by Lacan himself are signed; all other contributions are published anonymously. According to Lacan, the policy is designed to foreground the collective nature of the EFP's work. He compares it to the work of Bourbaki, arguing that the use of a collective signature did not prevent the individuals whose identity it masks from revolutionizing the whole basis of mathematics. Many of the contributors to *Scilicet* have in fact subsequently republished their work under their own names.

During the May Events, Lacan respects the strike call issued by the Syndicat National de l'Enseignement Supérieur and does not officially hold a seminar. Informal discussions are held instead. On 10 May he signs a joint letter expressing solidarity with the student movement.[59] For one account of May by a psychoanalyst which reproduces some of Lacan's comments on the Events, see Maude Mannoni, 'Psychoanalysis and the May Revolution'.[60]

Following the educational reforms introduced after May, a Department of Psychoanalysis opens at the experimental University at Vincennes. Its director is Serge Leclaire, and Jean Clavreul is also closely involved. From the outset, its work is surrounded by controversy. The teaching staff are, for instance, reluctant to award *unités de valeur* (credits) for successful completion of the course. The students demand them. The compromise solution adopted is to award *unités de valeur* to anyone enrolling in the department.

S XVI, 1968–69, 'D'Un Autre à l'autre'. Unpublished.

1969

25 January   The EFP officially adopts Lacan's 'Proposition du 9 octobre 1967'.

26 January   Piera Castoriadis-Aulagnier, François Perrier and Jean-Pierre Valabrega resign from the EFP on the grounds that the training methods it has adopted are incompatible with any rigorous psychoanalytic activity. Their letter of resignation is published, *Scilicet*, 2–3, pp. 41–2.

17 March   Castoriadis-Aulagnier, Perrier and Valabrega officially found the 'Quatrième Groupe – Organisation psychanalytique de langue française'. Certain of their differences with the EFP are set out in the collective document known as the 'Cahier bleu' (1970).[61] They question the assumption that 'being an analyst' and 'being analysed' are problematics that can simply be superimposed upon one another, and argue that it is surely contradictory to ask a student to describe his ongoing analysis to a group of *passeurs* when it would be unethical to ask anyone else in analysis to do so. The process of *la passe* is described as analogous to the university system of qualifying examinations.

Preface to the selection from *Ecrits* published in Seuil's 'Points' collection, dated 14 December 1969, pp. 7–12. A second selection is published in the same collection in 1971.

'L'Impromptu de Vincennes', dated 3 December 1968, published, *Magazine littéraire*, 121, 1977, pp. 21–4. Transcript of a lecture given at Vincennes, memorable mainly for Lacan's altercation with a student who does not know the meaning of 'aphasia'. Four lectures were originally planned, but only two were given. The second, 'Unités de valeur', remains unpublished.

Preface to Anika Rifflet-Lemaire, *Jacques Lacan*, Brussels, Dessart, 1970, pp. 9–20; dated 'Christmas 1969; translated, David Macey, *Jacques Lacan*, London, Routledge & Kegan Paul, 1977, pp. vii–xv. 'Teneur de l'entretien avec J. Lacan', dated 'December 1969', Lemaire, pp. 401–7; translated, 'Appendix: general purport of a conversation with Lacan in December 1969', pp. 249–53.

S XVII, 1969–70; 'L'Envers de la psychanalyse'. Unpublished.

1970   'Allocution prononcée pour la clôture du congrès de l'Ecole Freudienne de Paris le 19 avril 1970, par son directeur', *Scilicet*, 2/3, 1970, pp. 391–9. Comments on the relationship between teaching and the transmission of knowledge; further remarks on the theory of the four discourses elaborated in the unpublished S XVII.

'Radiophonie', transcript of an interview broadcast by Belgian radio on 5, 10, 19 and 26 June 1970; broadcast by the ORTF on 7 June. Published, *Scilicet*, 2/3, 1970, pp. 55–9. Although the broadcast with a discussion of Lacan's debts to – and differences with – Saussure and the Prague circle, it is primarily of interest for its description of the discourses identified in S XVII: the discourse of the Master, that of the University, the discourse of the hysteric and analytic discourse.

'Liminaire', dated 'September 1970', *Scilicet*, 2/3, 1970, pp. 5–6. Introduction to the contents of the journal; Lacan also comments favourably on Montrelay's review of Janine Chasseguet-Smirgel *et al.*, *Recherches psychanalytiques nouvelles sur la sexualité féminine.*[62]

S XVIII, 1970–71; 'D'Un discours qui ne serait pas du semblant'. Unpublished.

1971   'Lituraterre', *Littérature* 3, 1971, pp. 3–10. An unusual text in that Lacan alludes to the contemporary avant-garde (Beckett, Barthes) more openly than usual; includes brief comments on Joyce. Lacan also notes that whilst psychoanalysis is based upon the Oedipus, that does not mean that it has anything to say about Sophocles.

S XIX, 1971–72, '... Ou pire'. Unpublished. Abstract by Lacan, *Annuaire de l'Ecole Pratique des Hautes Etudes*, 1967–73, pp. 287–91; reprinted, *Scilicet*, 5, 1975, pp. 5–10.

1972   'L'Etourdit', paper delivered on the occasion of the fiftieth anniversary of the founding of the Hôpital Henri-Rousselle, 14 July 1972, published, *Scilicet* 4,

1973, pp. 5–52. In many ways a continuation of 'Radiophonie' (1970), and closely related to S XX and *Télévision* (1973). The text is relevant to Lacan's views on female sexuality and to the elaboration of the theory of *lalangue*.

S XX, *Encore*, Paris, Seuil, 1975. Two sections translated as 'God and the *jouissance* of the Woman' and 'A Love Letter', *Feminine Sexuality*, pp. 137–61.

1973

'Postface' to S XI, dated 1 January 1973, pp. 251–4. Not included in the English translation.

'Introduction' to a German edition of *Ecrits*, dated 7 October 1973; reprinted, *Scilicet*, 5, 1975, pp. 11–17. Mainly of interest for Lacan's comments on Heidegger and his theory of language as the house of being.

Télévision. Based on a television broadcast on the ORTF, Christmas 1973; published, Paris, Seuil, 1973. Although he continues to stress the linguistic nature of the unconscious, here and in S XX he begins to use the neologism *linguisterie* to indicate the distance that separates him from academic linguists. Many of the themes of S XX and related texts are restated in schematic form.

S XXI, 1973–74, 'Les Non-Dupes errent'. Unpublished.

1974

The Vincennes Department of Psychoanalysis is reorganized and renamed 'Le Champ freudien', with Lacan as scientific director and Miller as president. All teaching is suspended; anyone wishing to teach a course is required to submit a research proposal to the Scientific Committee (Lacan, Miller, Clavreul and Melman). Irigaray's proposal for a course relating to her *Speculum, de l'autre femme* is rejected, and she is expelled from the EFP.[63] The *matheme* now becomes an essential element in the work of the EFP and in effect the basis for work at Vincennes. Lacan's direct intervention at Vincennes is highly controversial, particularly as he has no legal right to intervene in university affairs.

S XXII, 1974–75, 'RSI'. Published, *Ornicar?*, 2, 1975, pp. 88–105; 3, pp. 96–110; 4, pp. 92–106; 5, pp. 16–66. One session translated, 'Seminar of 21 January 1975'. *Feminine Sexuality*, pp. 162–71.

1975   Republication of *De la Psychose paranoïaque dans ses rapports avec la personnalité*, together with 'Ecrits "Inspirés"', 'Le Problème du style', 'Motifs du crime paranoïaque' and 'Exposé général de nos travaux scientifiques', Paris, Seuil.

American lecture tour. Summaries based on notes, published in *Scilicet*, 6/7, 1976, as follows.

'Yale University, Kanzer Seminar', 24 November 1975, pp. 7–31. General discussion of the interpretation of dreams and other unconscious formations as being centred on verbal material. Lacan also discusses the factors that drew him to psychoanalysis, and describes the 'Aimée' case. Followed by open disscussion.

'Yale University: Entretien avec des étudiants. Résponses à leurs questions', 24 November 1975, pp. 32–7. A very general series of answers to questions, including comments on the opening thesis of *Télévision* (1973): that it is impossible to tell the whole truth because the structure of language always introduces an element of fiction.

'Yale University, Law School Auditorium', 25 November 1975, pp. 38–41. Lacan begins by describing the hysteric as productive of knowledge, but rapidly moves on to a discussion of the properties of Borromenean knots.

'Massachusetts Institute of Technology', 2 December 1975, pp. 53–63. Lacan defines linguistics as that which gives psychoanalysis a hold on science, but adds that psychoanalysis is a practice, not a science. The imbrication of real, symbolic and imaginary is discussed in terms of the topology of knots.

'Sur le Noeud borroméen', *Ornicar?*, 5, 1975, pp. 3–15.

S XXIII, 1975–76, 'Le Sinthome'. Published, *Ornicar?*, 6, pp. 3–20; 7,. pp. 3–18,; 8, 1976, pp. 6–20; 9, 1977, pp. 32–40; 10, 1977, pp. 5–12; 11, 1977, pp. 2–9. Discussion of theory of topology; some discussion of Joyce.

1976   Journées de l'EFP, Paris, October 31–November 2. Three-day discussion of the matheme.

S XXIV, 1976–77, 'L'Insu que sait de l'une bévue s'aile à mourre'. Published, *Ornicar?*, 12/13, 1977, pp. 4–16; 14, 1978, pp. 4–9; 15, 1978, pp. 5–9; 16, 1978, pp. 7–13; 17/18, 1979, pp. 7–23.

1977   S XXV, 1977–78, 'Le Moment de conclure'. One session only published as 'Une pratique de bavardage', *Ornicar?*, 19, Autumn 1979, pp. 5–9. Dated 17 November.

1978   S XXVI, 1978, 79, 'La Topologie et le temps'. Unpublished.

1980   Lacan unilaterally announces the dissolution of the EFP in a letter addressed to members and published in *Le Monde* on 9 January.[64] He asks those who wish to continue working with him to make their intentions known in writing (the term used is un *écrit de candidature*). He receives over one thousand letters within a week. Lacan is immediately challenged on the grounds that the EFP is an association covered by the terms of the 1901 law; its dissolution requires a two-thirds majority at a specially convened general meeting. That majority is finally obtained during the meeting of 27 September.

21 February   Lacan announces the foundation of La Cause freudienne in a letter to those who have expressed their wish to continue with him. He adds that a future letter will tell them what is required of them.

July   Lacan attends an international conference in

Caracas; his opening address is published in *L'Ane*, 1, April–May 1981, pp. 30–31: 'I have come here before launching my *Cause freudienne*. It is up to you to be Lacanians if you wish. I am a Freudian.'

S XXVII, 1980, 'Dissolution'. Published, *Ornicar?*, 20/21, 1980, pp. 9–20; 22/23, 1981, pp. 7–14.

1981   Lacan dies in Paris on 9 September as a result of kidney failure following an operation to remove an intestinal tumour.

Notes

1 The Final State

1. Freud, letter of 28 April 1885 to Martha Bernays, *Letters of Sigmund Freud 1873–1939*, London 1961, p. 152.

2. Paul Roazen, *Brother Animal*, New York 1969.

3. Jeffrey Moussaieff Masson, *The Assault on Truth: Freud's Suppression of the Seduction Theory*, New York 1984; cf. Janet Malcolm, *In The Freud Archives*, London 1984. For an enlightening discussion of both books, see Joel Kovel, 'Sins of the Fathers', *Free Associations*, 1, 1985.

4. Henri F. Ellenberger, *The Discovery of the Unconscious*, New York 1970; Frank J. Sulloway, *Freud, Biologist of the Mind*, London 1980.

5. Steven Marcus, *Freud and the Culture of Psychoanalysis*, London 1984, p. 2.

6. Ellenberger, p. 547.

7. Cited, Claude Dorgeuille, *La Seconde Mort de Jacques Lacan*, Paris 1981, p. 120.

8. Jacques-Alain Miller, *Entretien sur le Séminaire avec François Ansermet*, Paris 1985, p. 66. Lacan gave Laurence Bataille a copy of *Ecrits* bearing the inscription: 'To my faithful Antigone'; cf. Elisabeth Leypold, preface to Laurence Bataille, *L'Ombilic du rêve*, Paris 1987, p. 7.

9. Marcelle Marini, *Lacan*, Paris 1986, p. 103.

10. Sherry Turkle, *Psychoanalytic Politics*, London 1979, p. 86.

11. Catherine Clément, *Vies et légendes de Jacques Lacan*, Paris 1981, p. 30; Stuart Schneiderman, *Jacques Lacan. The Death of an Intellectual Hero*, Cambridge, Mass. and London 1983, p. 164; Elisabeth Roudinesco, *La Bataille de cent ans. Histoire de la psychanalyse en France*, vol. 2: 1925–1985, Paris 1986, p. 161. The second volume of Roudinesco's *Histoire* contains what is in effect the first biography of Lacan and provides a wealth of information. It suffers, however, from the marked absence of the raw material of biography (letters, diaries, private papers) and relies heavily on interviews with individuals who knew or worked with Lacan to supplement material drawn from published sources. It is therefore inevitably a somewhat skeletal biography; we learn almost nothing, for instance, of Lacan's political views. The decision to incorporate it into an encyclopaedic history of French psychoanalysis also results in a certain lack of focus.

12. Reproduced *Magazine littéraire*, 121, February 1977, p. 73.

13. Jean Leuba, 'Report', IJPA, 26, 1945, p. 85.

14. Lacan, 'Acte de Fondation' in Jacques-Alain Miller, ed., *L'Excommunication*, Paris 1977, p. 149.

15. Schneiderman, *Jacques Lacan*, p. 19, emphasis added.

16. Luce Irigaray, 'Misère de la psychanalyse', *Critique* 365, October 1977, p. 885.

17. *Yale French Studies*, 36–7, 1966.

18. Jean Reboul, 'Jacques Lacan et les fondements de la psychanalyse', *Critique*, 187, December 1962; Catherine Backès, 'Lacan ou la porte-parole', *Critique*, 249, February 1968.

19. Republished as Lacan and Wilden, *Speech and Language in Psycho-analysis*, Baltimore and London, 1981.

20. Stuart Schneiderman, ed., *Returning to Freud: Clinical Analysis in the School of Lacan*, New Haven and London 1980; reviewed by M. Masud R. Khan, IJPA, 1982, p. 96.

21. Anika Lemaire, *Jacques Lacan*, London 1977 (first edn, Brussels 1970).

22. Claude Simon, 'La fiction mot à mot', in Jean Ricardou and Françoise van Rossum-Guyon, eds, *Nouveau Roman: Hier, aujourd'hui, vol. 2: Pratiques*, Paris 1972, p. 73. The reference is to 'Propos sur la causalité psychique', E, p. 166.

23. Lacan, 'Kant avec Sade', p. 788; 'Hommage fait à Marguerite Duras', *Cahiers Renaud-Barrault*, 52, 1965.

24. Lacan, 'Lituraterre', *Littérature*, 3, 1971, p. 3.

25. The issue of the appropriation of Lacan by post-structuralist literary theory is not dealt with here. For representative samples, see Juliet Flower MacCannell, *Figuring Lacan: Criticism and the Cultural Unconscious*, London 1986, and Shoshona Felman, *Jacques Lacan and the Adventure of Insight. Psychoanalysis in Contemporary Culture*, Cambridge, Mass. and London 1987.

26. Miller, *Entretien*, p. 17.

27. Ibid.

28. Jean-Pierre Salgas, 'L'Inconscient au tribunal'. *La Quinzaine littéraire*, 454, 1–15, January 1986, p. 7.

29. Jacques-Alain Miller, 'La Propriété des oeuvres de Jacques Lacan', *Le Monde*, 7–8 July 1985, p. 8.

30. 'Jacques Lacan "appartient à" son gendre', *Le Monde*, 15–16 December 1985, p. 16. A full transcript of the December hearing has been published as 'Un Jugement', *Ornicar?*, 35, Winter 1985–86.

31. It is at Miller's insistence that the English translation of S I appears without the introduction prepared for it by John Forrester. The introduction is published as 'The *Seminar* of Jacques Lacan: In Place of an Introduction', *Free Associations*, 10, 1987.

32. ES contains less than half the original material. No criterion for inclusion or exclusion is given; we are simply informed that the selection is Lacan's.

33. Lacan, 'Situation de la psychanalyse et formation du psychanalyste en 1956', E, p. 467; interview with G. Lapouge, *Le Figaro littéraire*, 29 December 1966.

34. Terry Eagleton, *Literary Theory, An Introduction*, Oxford 1983, p. 169; Louis Althusser, 'Freud and Lacan', in *Lenin and Philosophy and Other Essays*, London 1971, p. 188.

35. Lacan, S VII, p. 33.

36. Georges Mounin, 'Quelques Traits du style de Jacques Lacan', *Nouvelle Revue Française*, 193, January 1969, p. 87.

37. Lacan, 'La Chose freudienne', E, p. 436; ES, p. 145.

38. Lacan, S XX, p. 60; dialogue from Godard's *Une Femme est une femme*, cited Jean Collet, *Jean-Luc Godard*, Paris 1963, p. 179.

39. Griselda Pollock, 'Artists, Mythology and Media – Genius, Madness and Art History', *Screen*, vol. 21, no. 3, 1980, p. 58.

40. S XX, p. 60. The reference is to Jean-Luc Nancy and Philippe Lacoue-Labarthe, *Le Titre de la lettre*, Paris 1973.

41. Jacques-Alain Miller, 'Index raisonné des concepts majeurs: Eclaircissement', E, p. 893; ES, p. 326.

42. Ibid., p. 894; p. 327.

43. Freud, *Leonardo da Vinci and a Memory of his Childhood*, SE XI, pp. 83–4.

44. Heinz Hartmann, *Ego Psychology and the Problem of Adaptation*, New York 1958; first published as 'Ich Psychologie und Anpassungsproblem', *Internationale Zeitschrift für Psychoanalyse und Imago*, 1939.

45. Lacan, 'La Psychiatrie anglaise et la guerre', *Evolution psychiatrique*, 1, 1947;

'Introduction théorique aux fonctions de la psychanalyse en criminologie', E, pp. 125–50.

46. 'A Lacanian Psychosis: Interview by Jacques Lacan', in Schneiderman, ed., *Returning to Freud.* The value of this collection is seriously undermined by the quality of the translations. It is difficult indeed to trust a translator who believes that 'In French the word *saint* is feminine' (p. 26, n. 8) and who thinks that *machines à sous* (fruit machines or gambling machines) are 'coin machines' (p. 255).

47. FS, p. 59.

48. Ibid., p. 137.

49. Ibid., p. 75; E, p. 685; ES, p. 281.

50. FS, p. 80; E, p. 690; ES, p. 286: 'it is supposed'.

51. The 1936 paper was entitled 'Le Stade du miroir. Théorie d'un moment structurant et génétique de la réalité, conçu en relation avec l'expérience et la doctrine psychanalytique'; indexed as 'The Looking-Glass Phase', IJPA, 1937, p. 78. Lacan's explanation for its non-appearance in the Congress Proceedings is that he omitted to submit the text for inclusion; 'De Nos Antécédents', E, p. 67, n. 1.

52. 'Le Stade du miroir', E, pp. 98–9; ES, p. 6.

53. Jeffrey Mehlman, 'The Floating Signifier from Lévi-Strauss to Lacan', *Yale French Studies*, 48, 1972, p. 26. 'Radiophonie' is the transcript of a radio interview; full text in *Scilicet*, 2/3, 1970.

54. 'A Lacanian Psychosis'; cf. the anonymous 'Notes prises aux présentations de malades du Dr Lacan à l'hôpital Sainte-Anne, *Scilicet*, 1, 1968.

55. Jacques-Alain Miller, 'Teachings of the Case Presentation', in Schneiderman, ed., *Returning to Freud*, p. 49.

56. 'Editorial', *New Left Review*, 51, September–October 1968, p. 4.

57. 'Healing Words', Dr Lacan's Structuralism', *Times Literary Supplement*, 25 January 1968; 'MMRK', review of *Ecrits*, IJPA, 48, 1967, p. 611.

58. IJPA, 34, 1954, pp. 11–17.

59. Henry H. Hart, *Psychoanalytic Quarterly*, 23, 1954, p. 608.

60. Eight issues of *Theoretical Practice* appeared between January 1971 and January 1973. The presence of Ben Brewster on both editorial boards signals the *Screen–Theoretical Practice*, Lacan–Althusser connection. It should be noted that the translation of Lemaire's *Jacques Lacan* was intended to appear in a planned series of '*Theoretical Practice* books'.

61. 'Editorial', *Screen*, vol. 12, no. 1, Spring 1971, p. 5.

62. Cf. Ben Brewster's review of Macksie and Donato, eds, *The Structuralist Controversy*, 'Structuralism in Film Criticism', ibid., pp. 49–58.

63. Editorial, *Screen*, vol. 13, no. 3, Autumn 1972, p. 2.

64. Edward Buscombe *et al.*, 'Statement: Psychoanalysis and Film', *Screen*, vol. 15, no. 4, Winter 1975–76, p. 19.

65. *m/f*, 8, 1973; translations from *L'Ane*, 2, Summer 1981.

66. FS, p. 138.

67. Ibid., p. 59.

68. Notes by Paul Willemen, *Screen*, vol. 14, nos 1–2, Spring–Summer 1973, p. 235.

69. Althusser, 'Freud and Lacan', p. 191.

70. Louis Althusser, *For Marx*, London 1969, pp. 161–219.

71. 'Freud and Lacan', p. 198. In the later 'La Découverte du docteur Freud', in Léon Chertok, ed, *Dialogue franco–soviétique sur la psychanalyse*, Toulouse 1984, Althusser revises his views and describes Lacan as having elaborated a 'philosophy of psychoanalysis' or even a variation of logical formalism (pp. 86, 87). The status of this text is controversial; Althusser has stated that he did not wish it to be published. See the exchange of letters between Althusser and Chertok, *Le Monde*, 11 May and 25 May 1984.

72. 'La Psychanalyse, idéologie réactionnaire', *La Nouvelle Critique*, June 1949, reprinted in Jacques-Alain Miller, ed., *La Scission de 1953*, Paris 1976.

73. Louis Althusser, 'Ideology and Ideological State Apparatuses', *Lenin and Philosophy*, p. 152.

74. Editorial, *Screen*, vol. 16, no. 1, Spring 1975, p. 6.

75. Colin MacCabe, 'Realism and the Cinema: Notes on Some Brechtian Theses',

Screen, vol. 15, no. 2, Summer 1974, p. 17.

76. J. Laplanche and J.B. Pontalis, *The Language of Psychoanalysis*, London 1973, p. 439.

77. Ben Brewster, Stephen Heath and Colin MacCabe, 'Comment', *Screen*, vol. 16, no. 2, Summer 1975, p. 86, emphasis added.

78. 'Editorial', ibid., p. 5.

79. Rosalind Coward and John Ellis, *Language and Materialism, Developments in Semiology and the Theory of the Subject*, London 1977, p. 93, emphasis added.

80. Ibid., p. 8, emphasis added.

81. Juliet Mitchell, *Psychoanalysis and Feminism*, London 1974, p. 402.

82. Jane Gallop, *Feminism and Psychoanalysis. The Daughter's Seduction*, London 1982, p. 8.

83. Mitchell subsequently – 'Interview' *m/f*, 8, 1983, p. 8 – concedes that there are 'faults' with this attempt to supplement Marxism with psychoanalysis, to add patriarchy to capitalism.

84. *Psychoanalysis and Feminism*, pp. xxi–xxii, 297–8.

85. Undated leaflet; author's collection.

86. Nicole Muchnick, 'Le MLF c'est toi, c'est moi', trans. Elaine Marks, in Elaine Marks and Isabelle de Courtivron, eds, *New French Feminism*, Hassocks 1981, p. 177.

87. Claire Duchen, *Feminism in France. From May 68 to Mitterrand*, London 1986, p. 177.

88. Statement signed 'celles des éditions des femmes, groupe politique et psychanalyse, mouvement de libération des femmes', in Maïté Albistor and Daniel Armoabe, *Histoire du féminisme français*, Paris 1977, p. 477.

89. 'Nouvelles éditions des femmes au MLF', *Tel Quel*, 74, 1974, p. 103.

90. Jill Lewis, '"Women's Liberation Limited" – The French Controversy'. *Spare Rib*, 108, July 1981.

91. *Petit Guide féministe de France et d'ailleurs*, Paris 1982, p. 3.

92. Richard Wollheim, 'Psychoanalysis and Feminism', *New Left Review*, 93, September–October 1975. Wollheim objects to the use of the phrase 'male chauvinism' in a book which takes psychoanalytic theory seriously, and argues in his conclusion (p. 69) that: 'The present assimilation of sexism to, say, class conflict or even racism is just another defence by which men and women alike try to deny themselves knowledge of their counterpart nature.'

93. Lacan Study Group, 'Psychoanalysis and Feminism', *New Left Review*, 93, May–June 1976, p. 108.

94. 'Psychoanalysis and Patriarchal Structures', in *Papers on Patriarchy*, Lewes 1976, p. 8. Cf. Ros Coward, 'Rereading Freud – the Making of the Feminine', *Spare Rib*, 70, May 1978.

95. 'Psychoanalysis and Patriarchal Structures', p. 11; p. 18; no. 8.

96. Laura Mulvey, 'Visual Pleasure and Narrative Cinema', *Screen*, vol. 16, no. 3, Autumn 1975, p. 6.

97. My own minor contribution to the production-reproduction of the final state will be found in a review article devoted to ES and FFC, *Ideology and Consciousness*, 4, Autumn 1978.

98. François Roustang, *Un Destin si funeste*, Paris 1976.

2 Retrospective

1. It is not the intention of this chapter to provide a full history of the early psychoanalytic movement in France, but to outline elements of relevance to Lacan. For more exhaustive accounts, see Victor N. Smirnoff, 'De Vienne à Paris', *Nouvelle Revue de Psychanalyse*, 20, Autumn 1979; Jean-Pierre Mordier, *Les Débuts de la psychanalyse en France 1895–1926*, Paris 1981; Marcel Scheidhauer, 'Freud et le rêve en France, 1900–

1914', *Ornicar?*, 24, Autumn 1981; Elisabeth Roudinesco, *La Bataille de cent ans. Histoire de la psychanalyse en France. vol. 1: 1885–1939*, Paris *1982*, and *vol. 2: 1925–1985*.

2. Freud, letter of 14 June 1907 to Jung, *The Freud/Jung Letters*, London 1974, p. 65.

3. Freud, 'On the History of the Psycho-analytic Movement', SE XIV, pp. 32–3. Freud refers here to E. Régis and A. Hesnard, *La Psychoanalyse des névroses et des psychoses*, Paris 1914.

4. Janet, cited Ellenberger, pp. 817–18. Whether or not Freud knew it, Janet also defended him against hostile criticism during a meeting of the Paris Psychotherapy Society in June 1914. Cf. Ellenberger, p. 821. Given the extent of anti-German feeling at the time, this is a more than honourable stance to have taken.

5. Freud, *An Autobiographical Study*, SE XX, p. 62.

6. Cited, Roudinesco, vol. 1, pp. 283, 284.

7. Cited, ibid., p. 284.

8. A. Hesnard, 1922 preface to Hesnard and Régis, *La Psychoanalyse*: cited, Mordier, p. 107.

9. A. Hesnard, 'L'Etat actuel de la psychoanalyse en France', *Médicine Paris*, 1921, cited, Mordier, p. 159.

10. Hesnard and Régis, *La Psychoanalyse*, cited, Mordier, p. 129, emphasis added.

11. Lacan, 'Jeunesse de Gide', E, p. 748.

12. *Evolution psychiatrique*, 1, 1925, 'Avant propos', cited Mordier, pp. 219–20.

13. Raymond de Saussure, 'Littérature française' (collective review), IJPA, 1, 1920, p. 427.

14. A. Hesnard, 'L'Opinion scientifique française et la psychanalyse', *Le Disque vert*, 1924, p. 18. *Le Disque vert* was a literary journal published in Brussels, with some links with the surrealists in Paris. The special issue devoted to 'Freud et la psychanalyse' in 1924 provides a fascinating cross-section of views.

15. Georges Politzer, 'Note préliminaire sur l' "Aperçu historique du mouvement psychanalytique français" de A. Hesnard et Ed. Pichon, *Revue de psychologie concrète* 1, February 1929, reprinted Politzer, *Ecrits II*, Paris, 1969; A. Hesnard, 'A Propos d'une prétendue crise de la psychanalyse', *Revue de psychologie concrète*, 2 July 1929, in Politzer, *Ecrits II*. The article by Hesnard and Pichon appeared in the first issue of the *Revue*.

16. René Allendy, 'La Libido', *Le Disque vert*, 1924, pp. 77, 85.

17. Charles Blondel, *Introduction à la psychologie collective*, Paris 1928, p. 164.

18. Roland Dalbiez, *La Méthode psychanalytique et la doctrine freudienne*, Paris 1936.

19. Charles Blondel, 'L'Activité mentale selon Freud: moi et libido', *Revue philosophique*, 96, July–December 1923, pp. 110, 119; unsigned review of Régis and Hesnard, *La Psychoanalyse*, *Revue de métaphysique et de morale*, vol. 36, 1929, supplément, July–September, p. 3; A. Burlaud, 'L'Etat actuel de la question freudienne d'après un livre récent', *Revue de métaphysique et de morale*, vol. 49, 1937, p. 764 (review of Dalbiez).

20. Léon Brunschvicg, *La Connaissance de soi*, Paris 1955, pp. 15, 16.

21. Max Eitingon, 'Presidential Address', IJPA, 10, 1929, p. 514.

22. Henri Claude, 'La Méthode psychanalytique', *Le Disque vert*, 1924, pp. 39–40; preface to Dalbiez, *La Méthode psychanalytique*, p. i.

23. Daniel Parodi, 'La Philosophie française de 1918 à 1925', *Revue philosophique*, 100, 1925, p. 364, n.

24. Freud, 'On the History', p. 34, n.

25. On Sokolnicka, see Roudinesco, vol. 1, pp. 286–9, and Marianne Ronvaux, 'André Gide et Eugénie Sokolnicka', *Ornicar?*, 37, Summer 1986. Both authors rely heavily on Edouard Pichon, 'Eugénie Sokolnicka', RFP, 7, 1934. Sokolnicka's major paper is 'Analysis of an Obsessional Neurosis in a child', IJPA, 3, 1922.

26. The original members of the SPP are Bonaparte, Sokolnicka, Allendy, Borel, Codet, Hesnard, Laforgue, Loewenstein, Odier, Parcheminey, Pichon and Saussure.

27. Celia Bertin, *Marie Bonaparte*, London 1983.

28. Marie Bonaparte, *Sexualité de la femme*, Paris 1977.

29. Bertin, pp. 16–161. Cf. Marie Bonaparte, 'Notes on the Analytical Discovery of a Primal Scene', *Psychoanalytic Study of the Child*, 1, 1945.

30. Marie Bonaparte, *Edgar Poe. Sa Vie – son oeuvre*, Paris 1958, vol. 2, pp. 80–83. For an account of Bonaparte as critic, see Elizabeth Wright, *Psychoanalytic Criticism*, London 1984, pp. 38–45.

31. Freud, letter of 11 November 1926 to René Laforgue, *La Correspondence entre Freud et Laforgue 1923–1937*, *Nouvelle Revue de Psychanalyse* 15, Spring 1977, p. 285.

32. J.B. Pontalis, *Après Freud*, Paris 1968, p. 128.

33. Cf. Judith Miller, 'Freud: édition finie ou infinie?', *L'Ane*, 2, Summer 1981, pp. 42–3. Miller ends by taking consolation in the fact that Freud's work will be in the public domain by the end of the century.

34. The surrealists' view of it is discussed in the next chapter. For Janet's comments in *Annales Médico-Psychologiques*, see Denis Hollier, *Le Collège de sociologie*, Paris 1979, p. 200, n. Dalbiez, *La Méthode psychanalytique*, vol. 2, pp. 405–6, speaks of 'this remarkable thesis': 'What seems to me to hold out most promise for the future ... is the use of the psychological method to delineate the domain of validity of psycho-genesis. Psychology thus appears to be able to draw its own frontiers. This idea is borrowed from phenomenology.'

35. All Lacan's known contributions to SPP debates have been republished by Miller as 'Interventions de Jacques Lacan à la Société Psychanalytique de Paris', *Ornicar?*, 31, Winter 1984. Given that it is still necessary to refer to the RFP to understand anything of their content, the value of this act of textual piety is less than self-evident.

36. A second translation – of a paper on schizophrenia by Fenichel – was announced but not published.

37. 'Ecrits "inspirés": Schizographie', *Annales Médico-Psychologiques*, 5, December 1931; reprinted PP, pp. 365–82; 'Le Problème du style et la conception psychiatrique des formes paranoïaques de l'expérience', *Minotaure*, 1, June 1933; PP, pp. 383–8.

38. Cited, Roudinesco, vol. 1, p. 416.

39. Lacan, résumé of 'De L'Impulsion au complexe', followed by summary of discussion by Jean Leuba, RFP, 10, 1938; reprinted, *Ornicar?*, 31; 'La Famille', *Encyclopédie française*, vol. 8; Henri Wallon, ed., *La Vie mentale*.

40. Lacan, 'La Signification du phallus', E, p. 687; ES, p. 283; FS, p. 77.

41. 'Fonction et champ de la parole et du langage en psychanalyse', E, p. 258, n. 2; ES, p. 108, n. 2.

42. Jacques Damourette and Edouard Pichon, *Des Mots à la pensée. Essai de grammaire de la langue française*, 7 vols, Paris 1911–50; vol. 1, pp. 95–6. The Grammar provides the basis for the following articles by Pichon: 'La Grammaire en tant que mode d'exploration de l'inconscient', *Evolution psychiatrique*, 1, 1925; 'Sur la Signification psychologique de la négation en français', *Journal de psychologie normale et pathologique*, March 1928; 'La Personne et la personnalité vues à la lumière de la pensée idiomatique française', RFP, 10, 1938.

43. Edouard Pichon, 'La Famille devant M. Lacan', RFP, 11, 1939.

44. Roudinesco, vol. 1, p. 349.

45. Paul Bercherie, 'The Quadrifocal Oculary: The Epistemology of the Freudian Heritage', *Economy and Society*, vol. 15, no. 1, February 1986, p. 55.

46. Roudinesco, vol. 1, p. 295.

47. René Laforgue, 'Scotomization in Schizophrenia', IJPA, 8, 1927, p. 475.

48. René Laforgue, 'Verdrängung und Scotomization', *Internationale Zeitschrift für ärtzliche Psychoanalyse*, 12, 1926.

49. Laforgue, 'Scotomization', p. 474.

50. Ibid., p. 467.

51. Freud, letter of 7 April 1926 to Marie Bonaparte, in Ernest Jones, *The Life and Work of Sigmund Freud*, London 1955, vol. 3, p. 475.

52. Laforgue, 'Scotomization', p. 473.

53. Freud, letter of 28 October 1925 to René Laforgue, *Correspondence*, pp. 262–4; letter of 18 February 1926, ibid., pp. 277–8.

54. Freud, *Inhibitions, Symptoms and Anxiety*, SE XX, p. 158.

55. Freud, 'Fetishism', SE XXI, pp. 153–4.
56. René Laforgue, 'The Mechanisms of Isolation in Neurosis and their Relation to Schizophrenia', IJPA, 10, 1929, p. 171.
57. Pichon, 'La Famille', p. 107.
58. Ibid., p. 116.
59. Ibid., pp. 107, 108.
60. Emile Boutroux, 'L'Allemagne et la guerre', in *Pages choisies*, Paris 1915, p. 48.
61. Pichon, 'La Famille', p. 113.
62. Ibid., p. 120.
63. Lacan, 'L'Aggressivité en psychanalyse', E, p. 112; ES, p. 18.
64. Pichon, p. 113.
65. Lacan, 'Propos sur la causalité psychique', E, p. 187.
66. 'L'Aggressivité', E, pp. 118, 119; ES, pp. 24–5.
67. Lacan, 'La Famille', 80, pp. 42–4.
68. Pichon, p. 130. The repetitive and punctilious use of M[onsieur] is one of Pichon's more irritating stylistic traits.
69. Pichon, p. 119.
70. Lacan, S III, p. 56.
71. Ibid., p. 117.
72. Freud,'Fetishism', p. 155.
73. Lacan, S III, p. 361.
74. Ibid., p. 171.
75. Lacan, 'D'Une Question préliminaire à tout traitement possible de la psychose', E, p. 575; ES, p. 215.
76. Lacan, 'Réponse au commentaire de Jean Hyppolite sur la "Verneinung" de Freud', E, p. 386 and note 3.
77. 'From the History of an Infantile Neurosis', SE XVII, p. 84.
78. Damourette and Pichon, vol. 1, p. 138.
79. Maurice Grevisse, *Le Bon Usage. Grammaire française, avec des remarques sur la langue française d'aujourd'hui*, eighth edn, Gembloux and Paris 1964.
80. The 'pleonastic' ne is used in temporal expressions such as *avant que je ne me réveille* – 'before I wake up' –. For Lacan (S XI, p. 56) that phrase indicates 'the mode of the presence of the *I am* prior to waking'. Sheridan takes the view that Lacan's discussion of the point is 'strictly untranslatable' because it exemplifies the use of this form of *ne* in French. The passage is therefore reproduced in French, FFC, p. 56, n. 2.
81. Damourette and Pichon, vol. 1, p. 140.
82. Laforgue, 'Scotomization in Schizophrenia', p. 473.
83. Boileau, 'L'Art poétique' (1669–74), in *Oeuvres*, Paris 1957, p. 174.
84. Roudinesco, vol. 1, pp. 384–95. For a complementary and rather more concise account, see Sol Aparicio, 'La Forclusion, préhistoire d'un concept', *Ornicar?*, 28, Spring 1984.
85. François Sauvagnat, 'Une Pierre d'attente. Quelques particularités du premier abord freudien des hallucinations psychotiques'. *Ornicar?*, 36, Spring 1986.
86. Laplanche and Pontalis, p. 166.
87. Roudinesco, vol. 1, p. 386.
88. Ibid., p. 383.
89. Lacan, 'De Nos Antécédents, E, p. 65. In the *curriculum en psychiatrie* which prefaces his theses, Lacan erroneously refers to one 'Georges de Clérambault'. The error has sometimes been reproduced (by, for example, Forrester, 'The *Seminar* of Jacques Lacan', p. 65); for the record, Lacan's master was Gaëtan Gatian de Clérambault.
90. Lacan, S III, p. 183.
91. The question of erotomania is discussed in chapter 6.
92. This translation is used in, for example, 'D'Une Question préliminaire', E, p. 557. A difficulty arises here with the English translation; ES, p. 200, simply has 'repetition compulsion'. The specific connotations of Lacan's terminology are thus lost.
93. In Freud, *Essais de psychanalyse*, Paris 1972. This translation first appeared in 1927.

94. Lacan, S II, p. 79.

95. Lacan, 'Le Séminaire sur "La Lettre volée"', E, p. 11: 'Our research has brought us to the point where we can recognize that repetition automatism [*Wiederholungszwang*] derives its principle from what we have called the insistence of the signifying chain.' Cf. ibid., p. 45.

96. Lacan, S III, p. 14.

97. André Green, 'Passions et destins des passions', *Nouvelle Revue de Psychanalyse*, 21, Spring 1981, pp. 8–9. The following remarks on Clérambault's *automatisme mental* are based upon Dalbiez, *La Méthode psychanalytique*, pp. 511 f.; Paul Bercherie, *Les Fondements de la clinique. Histoire et structure du savoir psychanalytique*, Paris 1980, pp. 251–63; Guy Rosolato, 'Clérambault et les délires passionelles', *Nouvelle Revue de Psychanalyse*, 21.

98. Lacan, PP, p. 209.

99. Lacan, S III, p. 284.

100. Lacan, 'De Nos Antécédents', E, p. 65.

3 Baltimore in the Early Morning

1. Lacan, 'Of Structure ...', in Macksie and Donato, eds, *The Structuralist Controversy*, pp. 186–200.

2. See Hans Richter, *Dada: Art and Anti-art*, London 1965.

3. Lacan, 'Of Structure ...', p. 197.

4. Ibid., p. 189.

5. Lacan, S III, p. 130.

6. James Thrall Sorby collection, Connecticut, reproduced, Dawn Ades, *Dada and Surrealism Reviewed*, London 1978, colour plate 1,10.

7. Former collection of E.F.W. James, reproduced, Dawn Ades, *Dali*, London 1982, plate 101.

8. Aragon, *Le Paysan de Paris*, Paris 1972; André Breton, *Nadja*, Paris 1972; *L'Amour fou*, Paris 1976.

9. Lacan, 'Situation de la psychanalyse et formation du psychanalyste en 1956', E, p. 472.

10. Lacan, 'La Direction de la cure et les principes de son pouvoir', E, pp. 610–11; ES, p. 248. Cf. 'Fonction et champ', E, p. 279; ES, p. 68: 'What is at stake in an analysis is the advent in the subject of that little reality [*ce peu de réalité*] that this desire sustains in him with respect to the symbolic conflicts and imaginary fixations ...'

11. Serge Leclaire, 'Compter avec la psychanalyse', *Cahiers pour l'analyse*, 1, January–February 1966, p. 62; cf. *Psychanalyser*, Paris 1975, p. 19.

12. Lacan, 'De Nos Antécédents', E, p. 65.

13. The theme of *vanitas* and its icons is also discussed in the 1959 Seminar on *Hamlet*; 'Le Désir et le deuil', *Ornicar?*, 26/27, Summer 1983, p. 24: the stakes in the duel are 'precious objects piled up in all their splendour and staked against death. This is what characterizes their presentation as what religious tradition teaches us to call a *vanitas*. This is how all objects and stakes appear in the world of human desire – *objets-a*.'

14. Lacan, S.VII, p. 161.

15. Lacan, S XI, p. 82; FFC, pp. 88–9, translation modified. Sheridan gives 'annihilated' for Lacan's *néantise*, thereby obscuring the reference to *L'Etre et le néant*, which is made all the more obvious in that this session ends with a discussion of Sartre and Merleau-Ponty. 'Nihilation' is the term used by Hazel Barnes in her translation of Sartre, *Being and Nothingness*, London 1957.

16. Elizabeth Cowling, 'An Other Culture', in Ades, *Dada and Surrealism*, p. 460.

17. Lacan, 'Actes du Congrès de Rome', *La Psychanalyse*, 1, 1956, p. 251.

18. Lacan, 'Hiatus Irrationalis', *Le Phare de Neuilly*, 3/4, 1933; reprinted, *Magazine littéraire*, 121, February 1977, p. 11.

19. Lacan, S III, p. 24; 'Propos sur la causalité', E, p. 176.

20. J. Garrabé, 'Prolégomènes à un manifeste de la surpsychiatrie', *Evolution psychi-atrique*, vol. 16, fascicule 1, January–March 1979, p. 23.

21. A minimal bibliography would include Michel Carrouges, *André Breton et les données fondamentales du surréalisme*, Paris 1950; Ferdinand Aliquié, *La Philosophie du surréalisme*, Paris 1956; Patrick Waldberg, *Surrealism*, London 1966; Maurice Nadeau, *The History of Surrealism*, Harmondsworth 1968; Roger Cardinal and Robert Stuart Short, *Surrealism: Permanent Revelation*, London 1970. Ades, *Dada and Surrealism* provides an invaluable survey and documentation.

22. Aragon, *Le Paysan de Paris*, p. 81; Walter Benjamin, 'Surrealism. The Last Snapshot of the European Intelligentsia', in *One-Way Street*, London 1979, p. 236.

23. André Breton, *Anthologie de l'humour noir*, Paris 1970, p. 411, n. 1. Dali appears to have found his new appelation amusing rather than insulting; he is often quoted as saying: 'The only difference between me and the surrealists is that I am a surrealist.'

24. For an early discussion of surrealist sexism, see Xavière Gauthier, *Surréalisme et sexualité*, Paris 1971. Surrealist representations of femininity and of female sexuality continue to be controversial, as is apparent from the arguments over *L'Amour fou: Surrealism and Photography*, an exhibition at London's Hayward Gallery in 1986. In a discussion with Dawn Ades, Helen Carr argues for a basically positive reading of the works shown in 'The Love that Transforms Life', *Women's Review*, 12, October 1986; in response, Louise Parsons (letter, *Women's Review*, 14/15, December 1986–January 1987) criticizes them for their allusions to rape, abuse and murder. The work of Hans Bellmer in particular has always been controversial in this respect.

25. Breton was assigned by the PCF to a cell of gas workers. One of the tasks required of him was the preparation of a report on the situation in Italy; he was told to 'rely on statistical facts (steel production, etc.), and above all, *no ideology*. I could not do it'. 'Second Manifeste du surréalisme', in *Manifestes du surréalisme*, Paris 1972, p. 99. Accounts of relations between the surrealists and the PCF will be found in Nadeau's *History* and in the relevant chapters of Jean-Pierre A. Bernard, *Le Parti Communiste Française et la question littéraire*, 1921–39, Grenoble 1972.

26. Jacques Prévert, *Selections from "Paroles"*, Harmondsworth 1965. Lacan clearly shares the popular enthusiasm for Prévert, and cites his 'Inventaire' (*Selections*, p. 105) to make a point about surrealist symbolism in 'Fonction et champ', E, p. 275; ES, p. 64.

27. Cf. Katia Seus-Walker, 'De la Poésie surréaliste à la poésie de la Résistance', in Université de Reims-Champagne-Ardennes, *La Guerre et la paix dans les lettres françaises de la guerre du Rif à la guerre d'Espagne*, Reims 1983.

28. Lacan refers favourably, if in rather vague terms, to *Viridiana*, S XI, p. 146; FFC, p. 159, and is reported by Buñuel, *My Last Breath*, London 1984, p. 204, to have been one of the few admirers of EL (1952) when it was first released in Paris: 'My only consolation came from Jacques Lacan, who saw the film at a special screening for psychiatrists at the Cinémathèque in Paris and praised certain of its psychological truths.'

29. Marcelin Pleynet, *Painting and System*, Chicago and London 1984.

30. Jean-Louis Houdebine, 'Position politique et idéologique du néo-surréalisme'; Pierre Rottenberg, 'Esquisse cartographique du mouvement: surréalisme'; Guy Scarpetta, 'Limite-frontière du surréalisme'; Jean-Louis Houdebine, 'Méconnaissance de la psychana-lyse dans le discours surréaliste', *Tel Quel*, 46, Summer 1971.

31. Scarpetta, 'Limite-frontière', p. 66.

32. Paul Nizan, 'Notes de lecture', *L'Humanité*, 10 February 1933; René Crevel, 'Notes en vue d'une psycho-dialectique', SASDLR, 5 May 1933.

33. The other reference is made in Nizan's review of SASDLR and *Minotaure* in *Commune*, 1, July 1933, where he remarks that not even the publication of Lacan's 'Le Problème du style' justifies *Minotaure*'s existence.

34. Paul Nizan, 'French Literature Today', *International Literature*, 5, 1934, p. 141. Cf. David Macey, *The Work of Paul Nizan: A Study in the Influence of a Political Viewpoint on Literary Themes and Structures*, unpublished PhD thesis, London 1982.

35. Jean Starobinski, 'Freud, Breton, Myers', in *La Relation Critique*, Paris 1970, pp. 320–41.

36. Breton, 'Manifeste du surréalisme, in *Manifestes*, p. 37.

37. Philippe Audoin, *Breton*, Paris 1970; Anna Balakian, *André Breton*, New York 1971; Marguerite Bonnet, *André Breton: Naissance de l'aventure surréaliste*, Paris 1975.

38. Breton, letter of 25 September 1916 to Théodore Fraenkel, cited, Bonnet, p. 99. 'Twilight states' is an allusion to the nosographic categories of Kraepelin's *Compendium des Psychiatrie*, (1883); twilight states include hypnotic sleep, somnambulism, and certain hysterical and epileptic conditions. For Kraepelin's classification, see Bercherie, *Fondements*, p. 139.

39. Cited, Bonnet, p. 104.

40. Breton, *Manifestes*, p. 34.

41. André Breton, 'L'Entrée des médiums', in *Les Pas perdus*, Paris 1974, pp. 124, 126.

42. Paul Bercherie, *Genèse des concepts freudiens*, Paris 1983, p. 95.

43. Freud, *The Interpretation of Dreams*, SE IV, p. 157. The same point is made in 'A Note on the Prehistory of the Technique of Analysis', SE XVIII, p. 263.

44. Lacan, 'L'Instance de la lettre ou la raison depuis Freud', E, p. 507; ES, p. 157. Lacan also speculates (S VII p. 109) that the description of the plasticity of instincts in the *Introductory Lectures* may have inspired Breton to write *Les Vases communicants*.

45. André Breton, 'Le la', in *Signe ascendant*, Paris 1968, pp. 174–5.

46. André Breton, 'Les Mots sans rides', in *Les Pas perdus*, p. 141.

47. André Breton, *Situation du surréalisme entre les deux guerres*, Paris and Algiers 1945, unnumbered pages.

48. Georges Charbonnier, *Conversations with Lévi-Strauss*, London 1969, p. 92.

49. Los Angeles County Museum, reproduced Uwe M. Schneede, *René Margritte, Life and Work*, New York 1982, ill. 16.

50. René Magritte, 'Les Mots et les images', *La Révolution surréaliste*, 12, March 1929.

51. Jean Clair, 'Le Visible et l'invisible' in *Rétrospective Magritte*, Brussels and Paris 1978.

52. 'Actes du congrès', pp. 299, 251.

53. Jean-Paul Sartre, 'Qu'est-ce que la littérature', in *Situations II*, Paris 1948, pp. 215–16.

54. Two series of *Littérature* (twenty and thirteen issues respectively) appeared between 1919 and 1924. In many ways it marks the transition from Dada to surrealism.

55. Depending on how it is stressed, *Rrose Sélavy* might mean 'Life is rosy' [*Rose, c'est la vie*], 'Eros is life' [Eros, *c'est la vie*] , or even 'Drink to life [*Arrosez la vie*]. For further examples of the work of Duchamp/Sélavy, see Michel Sanouillet and Elmer Peterson, eds, *The Essential Writings of Marcel Duchamp*, London 1975.

56. Lacan, 'Propos sur la causalité', E, p. 166.

57. Michel Leiris, 'Glossaire, j'y serre mes gloses', also in *Les Mots sans mémoire*, Paris 1969. A sheet of the original definitions is reproduced, Ades, *Dada and Surrealism*, p. 192.

58. Michel Leiris, *Biffures*, Paris 1948, p. 12.

59. Lacan, letter to *Le Monde* on the dissolution of the EFP, 11 January 1980.

60. François George, *L'Effet 'yau de poêle*, Paris 1979.

61. E. Chautard, *La Vie étrange de l'argot*, Paris 1931, p. 671.

62. Raymond Queneau, *Chêne et chien*, Paris 1969, p. 91.

63. Lacan, S II, p. 156.

64. Lacan, 'Du Sujet enfin en question', E, p. 233.

65. Raymond Queneau, *Zazie dans le métro*, Paris 1966, p. 91; Lacan, S XX, p. 33.

66. Alexandre Kojève, *Introduction à la lecture de Hegel: Leçons sur la 'Phénoménologie de l'esprit'*, ed. Raymond Queneau, Paris 1947.

67. Jean Lescure, 'Petite Histoire de l'OULIPO', in OULIPO, *La Littérature potentielle*, Paris 1973, pp. 32, 34.

68. Paris 1978. Translated, David Bellos, *Life, a User's Manual*, London 1987.

69. Lacan, 'Le Nombre treize et la forme logique de la suspicion', *Cahiers d'art*, 1945–46, p. 389.

70. Lacan, 'Fonction et champ', E, p. 266, ES, p. 56. Lacan gives the same advice in S II, p. 276, where he remarks that all that is needed to read Plato's *Parmenides* is the average skill of the crossword enthusiast.

71. Lacan, 'Jeunesse de Gide', E, p. 748.

72. Jules Romains, 'Aperçu de la psychanalyse', *Nouvelle Revue Française*, January 1922.

73. André Gide, *Journal 1885–1939*, Paris 1948, p. 729 (entry dated 4 February 1922).

74. Jacques Rivière, 'Quelques Progrès dans l'étude du coeur humain (Freud et Proust)', *Les Cahiers de l'occident*, 4, 1927. The tradition inaugurated by Rivière and the NRF has recently been revived and expanded by Malcolm Bowie, *Freud, Proust and Lacan: Theory as Fiction*, Cambridge 1987. All three authors are introduced (p. 7) as 'portraitists of the mental life'.

75. Lacan, 'Intervention sur le transfert', E, p. 223; FS, p. 69.

76. Albert Thibaudet, 'Réflexion sur la littérature, psychanalyse et critique littéraire', NRF, April 1921; Blanche Reverchon-Jouve and Pierre Jean Jouve, 'Moments d'une analyse', NRF, March 1933; Jean Grenier, review of Bonaparte, *Edgar Poe*, NRF, October 1934; H. le Savoureux, review of Dalbiez, *La Méthode psychanalytique*, NRF, February 1939.

77. Pichon, 'Eugénie Sokolnicka'.

78. Roudinesco, vol. 1, p. 358; Nicolo Geblesco, 'Lacan', in A. Biro and R. Passeron, eds, *Dictionnaire général du surréalisme et de ses environs*, Paris 1982, p. 276.

79. *La Révolution surréaliste*, 3, April 1929, p. 29. The letter is unsigned, and there is still some dispute as to its authorship; it is possible that it was written collectively.

80. Breton, *Nadja*, p. 166.

81. André Breton, 'La Médicine mentale devant le surréalisme', SASDLR, 2, October 1930.

82. René Crevel, 'Notes en vue d'une psycho-dialectique'; 'Le Patriotisme de l'inconscient'. SASDLR, 4, December 1931.

83. Hugh Sykes Davies, 'Biology and Surrealism', *International Bulletin*, 4, September 1936, cited, Ades, *Dada and Surrealism*, p. 348; G.W. Pailthorpe 'The Scientific Aspect of Surrealism', *London Bulletin*, 7, December 1938–January 1939, p. 10. For an overview of British surrealism, see Alexander Robertson *et al.*, *Angels of Anarchy and Machines for Making Clouds: Surrealism in Britain in the Thirties*, Leeds 1986.

84. Freud, letter of 26 December 1932 to André Breton, in Breton, *Les Vases communicants*, Paris 1970, p. 176.

85. Freud, letter of 20 July 1938 to Stefan Zweig, *Letters*, p. 444; Jones, *Life and Work*, vol. 3, p. 251.

86. Max Eastman, cited, Nicolas Powell, *Fuseli: 'The Nightmare'*, London 1973, p. 15.

87. *Delusions and Dreams in Jensen's 'Gradiva'*, SE IX.

88. Salvador Dali, letter of 2 January 1939 to Breton, cited, José Pierre, 'Breton et Dali', in *Salvador Dali: Rétrospective 1920–1980*, Paris 1979, p. 138.

89. Reproduced, Ades, *Dali*, ill. 64.

90. Freud, letter of 20 July 1938 to Zweig.

91. Museum of Modern Art, New York, reproduced, Ades, *Dali*, plate 66.

92. André Breton, *Entretiens*, Paris 1973, pp. 161–2.

93. Cited, Ades, *Dali*, p. 74.

94. Salvador Dali, 'L'Ane pourri', SASDLR, 1, July 1930, pp. 9, 10.

95. Reproduced, Ades, *Dali*, ill. 110.

96. Lacan, 'Le Problème du style', PP, p. 387.

97. Salvador Dali, 'Nouvelles considérations générales sur le méchanisme du phénomène paranoïaque du point de vue surréaliste', cited, José Pierre, 'Breton et Dali', p. 138; cf. Patrice Schmidt, 'De la Psychose paranoïaque dans ses rapports avec Salvador Dali', in *Rétrospective Dali*.

98. Salvador Dali, *La Vie secrète de Salvador Dali*. Paris 1979, pp. 33–4. Dali's account of his meeting with Lacan must be treated with some caution. He mistakenly refers

to his own 'Interprétation paranoïaque-critique de l'image obsédante: "L'Angélus" de Millet', *Minotaure*, 1, as 'Méchanismes internes de l'activité paranoïaque'. He is also mistaken as to the date, claiming that he was thirty-three when he met Lacan and thus implying that they met in 1937, not in 1933 when the article was published.

99. Tate Gallery, London, reproduced Dali, *Ades*, ill. 102.

100. Lacan, S II, p. 138; Paul Claudel, 'Traité de la co-naissance au monde et de soi-même', in *Art poétique*, Paris 1907.

101. Roudinesco, vol. 1, p. 344.

102. Georges Bataille, 'Notice autobiographique', in *Œuvres complètes*, vol. 7, Paris 1976, p. 460.

103. Michel Leiris, *L'Age d'homme*, Paris 1946; J.B. Pontalis, *Après Freud*, p. 320; Claude Lévi-Strauss, *Structural Anthropology*, Harmondsworth 1972, p. 94.

104. Queneau, *Chêne et chien*, pp. 63, 69, 80.

105. Raymond Queneau, 'Conversation avec Georges Ribemont-Desaignes' (1948), in *Bâtons, chiffres et lettres*, Paris 1973, p. 43.

106. Cited, Gaston Ferdière, 'Surréalisme et aliénation mentale', in *Le Surréalisme, Entretiens dirigés par Ferdinand Alquié*, Paris and The Hague 1968, p. 298. Anaïs Nin described her analysis with Allendy in her *Journal 1931–1934*, London 1970. A rather more lurid account figures in her *Henry and June*, New York 1986.

107. Aragon and André Breton, 'Le Cinquantenaire de l'hystérie', *La Révolution surréaliste*, 11, March 1928.

108. André Breton and Paul Eluard, *L'Immaculée Conception*, Paris 1961, pp. 23, 24–5; Breton, *Nadja*, p. 171.

109. Annette Lavers, *Roland Barthes: Structuralism and After*, London 1982, p. 241.

110. Lacan, 'Ecrits "inspirés"', PP, pp. 379–80.

111. Lacan, S III, p. 44.

112. Ibid., pp. 41–2.

113. Ibid., p. 46.

114. Luce Irigaray, 'Communication linguistique et spéculaire', *Cahiers pour l'analyse*, 3, May–June 1966, p. 55.

115. Jean-Pierre Mordier, 'La Psychanalyse tricolore', *L'Ane*, 2, Summer 1981, p. 45.

116. Reproduced, Ades, *Dada and Surrealism*, p. 201.

117. Bercherie, *Genèse*, p. 66. Cf. Freud and Breuer, 'Preliminary communication', SE II, pp. 13–14.

118. Eluard and Breton, 'Le Cinquantenaire'.

119. Conversation with André Parinaud (1952), *Entretiens*, p. 241.

120. Ray's photograph of Oppenheim is reproduced, Waldberg, *Surrealism*, plate 73; three stills from *L'Age d'or*, SASDLR, 1, 1930, reproduced, Ades, *Dada and Surrealism*, p. 258.

121. Reproduced, ibid., p. 283. Dali greatly admired the original 'Cinquantenaire': 'In the *Révolution surréaliste*, Breton and Eluard celebrated the centenary [*sic*] of hysteria, situating it admirably and giving it all its uniquely exemplary significance. The mere sight of these impassioned photographs moved us deeply.' Cited, *Rétrospective Salvador Dali*, p. 212.

122. Collection of Mr and Mrs A. Reynold Morse, reproduced, Whitney Chadwick, *Myth in Surrealist Painting, 1922–1939*, Ann Arbor 1980, plate 47.

123. Galerie Schwartz, Milan, reproduced, Biro and Passeron, *Dictionnaire*, p. 204.

124. Robert Benayoun, *Erotique du surréalisme*, Paris 1964, p. 81.

125. Breton, *L'Amour fou*, p. 12.

126. Ibid., p. 14.

127. As was usual in a case involving a woman, the sentence was commuted to life imprisonment. Nozières was eventually pardoned, married a clerk of the court, and died in 1966.

128. *Violette Nozières*, Brussels 1933. The poems are by Breton, René Char, Eluard, Maurice Henry, E.L.T. Meissens, Benjamin Péret and Guy Rosey; the illustrations by Man

Ray, Dali, Yves Tanguy, Max Ernst, Victor Brauner, Magritte, Marcel Jean, Hans Arp and Alberto Giacometti. The original is now a rare collector's item; full text, with illustrations, reproduced, José Pierre, ed., *Tractes surréalistes et déclarations collectives*, 1922–1964, Paris 1982, vol. 1, pp. 246–62.

129. *Violette Nozières*, pp. 247, 252.

130. Crevel, 'Notes en vue d'une psycho-dialectique', p. 50.

131. André Breton, 'Le Marquis de Sade a regagné l'intérieur du volcan', *Clair de Terre*, Paris 1969, p. 165.

132. SASDLR, 5, May 1933, p. 28. The same issue carries photographs of the sisters before and after the murders; reproduced, Cardinal and Short, *Surrealism*, p. 48.

133. Lacan, 'Motifs du crime,' PP, p. 390.

134. Breton, *Manifestes*, p. 78.

135. Aragon, *La Révolution surréaliste*, 1, December 1924; the photomontage is reproduced, Ades, *Dada and Surrealism*, p. 191.

136. Jean Genet, *Œuvres complètes*, vol. 2, Paris 1951, p. 9.

137. Lacan, 'Propos sur la causalité,' E, p. 168.

138. Villeneuve-les-Avignon, 1942.

139. Cited, Ferdière, *Surréalisme et aliénation mentale*, p. 313.

140. Roudinesco, vol. 2, p. 135. Astonishingly, 'Aimée' was later employed as a housekeeper by Lacan's widowed father. More surprisingly still, she was the mother of Didier Anzieu, who was analysed by Lacan in the early 1950s; he is the source of Roudinesco's information.

141. Lacan fails, for example, to clarify this point when he discusses the Aimée case in a seminar at Yale: 'Yale University, Kanzer Seminar', *Scilicet*, 6/7, 1976, pp. 8–10.

142. See the cover note to the 1980 'Points' edition, and 'Jacques-Marie Emile Lacan: Curriculum Vitae 1901–81'.

143. 'D'Une Question préliminaire', E, p. 576, n. 3; ES, p. 222 n. 6. Lacan adds: 'In fact I had read it all.'

144. Ibid., p. 536; p. 184.

145. Cf. Angelo Hesnard and René Laforgue, 'Les Processus d'auto-punition en psychologie des névroses et des psychoses, en psychologie criminelle et en pathologie générale', RFP, 4, 1930–31; Rudolph Loewenstein, 'D'Un Mécanisme auto-punitif', RFP, 5, 1932.

146. Lacan, PP, p. 256.

147. Ibid., p. 166.

148. Ibid., p. 227.

149. Ibid., p. 228.

150. 'Motifs du crime', ibid., p. 394.

151. Freud, 'Some Neurotic Symptoms in Jealousy, Paranoia and Homosexuality', SE XVIII. The incorporation of the homosexuality motif is a good index of how Lacan begins to move away from Clérambault's 'automatisme' aetiology.

152. Unpublished lecture, Brussels, 26 July 1977, cited, Roudinesco, vol. 1, p. 82.

153. Arguably, the cult of convulsive beauty has outlived Lacan himself. *Ornicar?*, 30, Autumn 1984, contains a study of the *ndop* spirit-possession cult of the Lebou and Wolof peoples of Senegal: Jean-Claude Maleval, 'Les Psychothérapies des hystéries crépusculaires'. Whilst the seriousness of the author's intentions is certainly not in doubt, in some ways the article does represent a throwback to the old surrealist cult. Participation in *ndop* ceremonies is almost always restricted to women, and the photographs of the possessed used here would not be out of place in Dali's *Phénomène de l'ecstase*. Even the title recalls Breton's *états crépusculaires*.

154. Rose, FS, p. 137.

155. *The Life of St Teresa of Avila, By Herself*, Harmondsworth 1957, p. 210.

156. Lacan, S XX, p. 70; FS, p. 147.

157. S XX, p. 9.

158. *The Life of St Teresa*, p. 126.

159. Lacan, 'Fonction et champ', E, p. 249; ES, p. 50. The reference to 'monuments' and 'traditions' is probably an allusion to – or a memory of – the opening sentence of

Totem and Taboo.
    160. Lacan, *Télévision*, Paris 1973, p. 9.

4 Philosophy and Post-Philosophy

    1. Jean-Jacques Lecercle, *Philosophy Through the Looking-Glass*, London 1985, p. 91; Alain Juranville, *Lacan et la philosophie*, Paris 1984.
    2. Freud, 'The Question of a *Weltanschauung*', *New Introductory Lectures on Psychoanalysis*, SE XXII, p. 177.
    3. Freud, *The Future of an Illusion*, SE XXI, p. 177.
    4. *An Autobiographical Study*, p. 59.
    5. Freud, letter of 2 April 1896 to Wilhelm Fliess, *The Complete Letters of Sigmund Freud to Wilhelm Fliess*, ed. Jeffrey Mouusaieff-Masson, Cambridge, Mass. and London 1985, p. 180.
    6. A *Weltanschauung*', p. 159. Cf. Freud's remark to the effect that 'observation alone' is the foundation of science, 'On Narcissism: An Introduction', SE XIV, p. 77 and the opening paragraphs of 'Instincts and their Vicissitudes', SE XXIV, p. 177. A very similar formulation occurs in 'Charcot', SE III, p. 13: 'Charcot never tired of defending the rights of clinical work, which consists in seeing and ordering things, against the encroachments of theoretical medicine.' For a general discussion of the role played by empiricism in Freud's epistemology, cf. Bercherie, 'The Quadrifocal Oculary'.
    7. Freud, *Civilization and its Discontents*, SE XXI, p. 94.
    8. 'A *Weltanschauung*', p. 160.
    9. *The Future of an Illusion*, p. 55. Cf. *The Ego and the Id*, SE XIX, pp. 35–36: 'Psychoanalytic research could not, like a philosophical system, produce a complete and ready-made theoretical structure, but had to find its way towards understanding the intricacies of the mind by making an analytic dissection of both normal and abnormal phenomena.'
    10. 'A *Weltanschauung*', p. 158.
    11. Freud, *Totem and Taboo*, SE XIII, p. 95. The classic example of paranoiac system-building is of course the extraordinary cosmology elaborated by Senatspräsident Schreber.
    12. 'A *Weltanschauung*', p. 166.
    13. *Totem and Taboo*, p. 77.
    14. 'A *Weltanschauung*', p. 171.
    15. 'Instincts and their Vicissitudes', p. 117.
    16. *Inhibitions, Symptoms and Anxiety*, p. 247.
    17. Freud, *Beyond the Pleasure Principle*, SE XVIII, p. 64.
    18. Freud, 'The Unconscious', *New Introductory Lectures*; cf. 'Fixation to Traumas – The Unconscious', *Introductory Lectures on Psycho-analysis*, SE XVI, p. 279: 'The possibility of giving a sense to neurotic symptoms by analytic interpretation is an unshakable proof of the existence – or, if you prefer it, – of the necessity for the hypothesis of unconscious mental processes.'
    19. *Beyond the Pleasure Principle*, p. 7.
    20. Freud, 'Analysis Terminable and Interminable', SE XXIII, p. 225.
    21. Lacan, S III, p. 117.
    22. Sandor Ferenczi, 'Philosophy and Psychoanalysis' (1912), in *Final Contributions to the Problems and Methods of Psychoanalysis*, London 1955, p. 327.
    23. Freud, 'The Claims of Psycho-Analysis to Scientific Interest', SE XIII, p. 179.
    24. *Totem and Taboo*, pp. 1–2.
    25. Freud, *Moses and Monotheism*, SE XXIII, p. 92.
    26. Sulloway, p. 119.
    27. *Totem and Taboo*, p. 1.
    28. Cf. M. Sami-Ali, *De la projection*, Paris 1986, pp. xi–xii.
    29. Janine Chasseguet-Smirgel, *The Ego Ideal*, London 1985, p. 85. In mitigation, it

must be said that this is the best available study of the evolution of the concept of the ideal ego.

30. Jean-Paul Sartre, *Critique de la raison dialectique*, Paris 1960, p. 44.

31. Chasseguet-Smirgel, p. 85.

32. Christopher Lasch, *The Culture of Narcissism*, New York 1979; 'The Freudian Left and Cultural Revolution', *New Left Review*, 129, September–October 1981; *The Minimal Self*, New York 1984. For a highly critical account of the politics informing Lasch's views on narcissism, see Michèle Barrett and Mary McIntosh, 'Narcissism and the Family: A Critique of Lasch', *New Left Review*, 135, September–October 1982.

33. Bercherie, 'The Quadrifocal Oculary', p. 66.

34. Freud, *An Autobiographical Study*, p. 72.

35. Lacan, S XX, p. 32. Here, 'world-view' is quite explicitly made synonymus with 'philosophy'. Elsewhere ('Columbia University', *Scilicet*, 6/7, 1976, p. 47) Lacan insists that he has no world-view whatsoever, because the 'world' is simply a shell housing the 'precious stone' known as man.

36. Lacan, 'compte rendu' of *L'Acte psychanalytique* (Seminar, 1967–68), *Ornicar?*, 29, Summer 1984, p. 19.

37. Lacan, *Télévision*, p. 9.

38. Although the Seminar itself remains unpublished, the concept of the four discourses can be reconstructed on the basis of 'Radiophonie' and sections of S XX. A general account of it is given in Elisabeth Roudinesco, *Pour une politique de la psychanalyse*, Paris 1977, pp. 44–79.

39. G.W.F. Hegel, *The Phenomenology of Mind*, New York 1967, p. 797.

40. Ibid., p. 805.

41. Lacan, S XX, p. 53.

42. Freud, 'Creative Writers and Day-Dreaming', SE IX, p. 150.

43. Lacan, S VII, p. 21.

44. Lacan, 'La Famille', 4° 40–8.

45. Lacan, 'Yale University, Kanzer Seminar', *Scilicet*, 6/7, p. 9.

46. Lacan, 'La Famille', 8° 40–8; S XX, p. 91. The reference is to the *Confessions*, I, viii.

47. Lacan, 'Propos sur la causalité', E, p. 171; 'D'Une Question préliminaire', E, p. 563; ES, p. 205.

48. Lacan, 'Le Temps logique', E, p. 199. Laurence Bataille, *L'Ombilic du rêve*, p. 97. Sartre's reference to 'freedom under the Occupation' appears in 'La République du silence' (1944), *Situations III*, Paris 1949. Lacan's reference to 'four walls' suggests that he may also be thinking of *Huis clos* (1944).

49. Lacan, 'Le Stade du miroir', E, p. 93; ES, p. 1.

50. Cf. Alain Juranville's description of Lacan as an exceptional master in philosophy', 'Psychanalyse et philosophie', *Ornicar?*, 29, Summer 1984, p. 95. Miller's suggestion (*Entretien*, p. 12) that Lacan is in some way to be regarded in the same light as Aristotle is even more disturbing. It is, of course, quite in keeping with the 'myth of the hero'.

51. Lacan, 'Propos sur la causalité', E, p. 159.

52. Lacan, 'La Chose freudienne', E, p. 427; ES, p. 137.

53. Lacan, S II, p. 18.

54. Lacan, 'Aggressivité', E, p. 119; ES, p. 24.

55. Lacan, S II, p. 16.

56. Lacan, 'Fonction et champ', E, p. 281, n. 2; ES, p. 109, n. 55.

57. Lacan, 'Instance de la lettre', E, p. 517; ES, p. 166.

58. S II, p. 252.

59. Paul Bénichou, *Morales du grand siècle*, Paris 1948.

60. Lacan, 'La Chose freudienne', E, pp. 406–7; ES, p. 119.

61. Lacan, S II, p. 19.

62. Jean Paul Sartre, *La Transcendance de l'ego*, Paris 1978, p. 38.

63. Freud, *The Question of Lay Analysis*, SE XX, p. 246.

64. Freud, letter of 5 July 1938 to Schneir, in Jones, *Life and Work*, vol. 3, p. 315.

65. Lacan, 'Situation de la psychanalyse', E, pp. 484, 490.

66. Anna Freud, 'The Ideal Psychoanalytic Institute': A Utopia', in *Problems of Psychoanalytic Technique and Therapy*, London 1972, p. 75.
67. Lacan, 'Règlement et doctrine de la Commission de l'enseignement', *La Scission de 1953*, p. 33; 'La Psychanalyse et son enseignement', E, p. 450.
68. Lacan, 'La Chose freudienne', E, pp. 435–6; ES, pp. 144–5; S II, p. 282.
69. Lacan, 'Règlement et doctrine', p. 33.
70. 'Statuts proposés pour l'Institut de psychanalyse par Sacha Nacht', *La Scission de 1953*, p. 42; Lacan, 'Fonction et champ', E, p. 257; ES, p. 30.
71. Jones, *Life and Work*, vol. 3, p. 315. In the Clarke-Williams case, the court rules that the fact that she worked in an establishment headed by a doctor of medicine was an adequate defence. Cf. Didier Anzieu, 'La Psychanalyse au service de la psychologie', *Nouvelle Revue de psychanalyse*, 20, Autumn 1979, p. 70.
72. Lacan, letter of 14 July 1953 to Loewenstein, *La Scission*, pp. 122–3.
73. 'Règlement et doctrine', p. 32.
74. 'Programme de l'enseignement et de l'activité psychanalytique de la Société Française de Psychanalyse durant les années 1953–54 et 1954–44', *La Psychanalyse*, 1, 1956, p. 289.
75. Lacan, S II, p. 12; S I, p. 88.
76. Jean-Paul Valabrega, 'Aux Sources de la psychanalyse', *Critique*, 108, May 1956, p. 446; Maurice Blanchot, 'Freud', *Nouvelle Revue Française*, September 1956, p. 491, n. 1.
77. When asked by Alquié in 1957 if the affective is structured like a language, Lacan simply replies that he leaves aside the affective, as it is a secondary issue; 'Dialogue avec les philosophes français', *Ornicar?*, 32, Spring 1985, pp. 16, 17. On the question of affect as the missing element in Lacan's return to Freud, see André Green, *Le Discours vivant. La conception psychanalytique de l'affect*, Paris 1973.
78. Lacan, 'La Psychanalyse et son enseignement', E, p. 547. A similar turn of phrase is used in S II, p. 14, where Lacan uses 'dentists' as a 'conventional notation' applying to those who are convinced of the order of the world because they believe that the 'laws of clear reason' are expounded in Descartes's *Discours*. Why dentists rather than, say, chiropodists are singled out for scorn remains a mystery.
79. 'Départment de psychanalyse. Enseignements fondamentaux et enseignements spéciaux du premier semestre', *Ornicar?*, 22/23, Spring 1981, p. 360.
80. Duchen, *Feminism in France*, p. 68.
81. Lacan, 'Position de l'inconscient', E, p. 836.
82. Lacan, review of Eugène Minkowski, *Le Temps vécu*, *Recherches philosophiques*, 5, 1935–36, p. 425.
83. For a caustic account of the teaching of philosophy in schools and colleges, and of the ideological origins of the *classe de philo*, see François Châtelet, *La Philosophie des professeurs*, Paris 1970.
84. Paul Nizan, *Les chiens de garde*, Paris 1932. For Lévi-Strauss's comments on studying philosophy in the 1930s, see his *Tristes Tropiques*, London 1973.
85. Alexandre Koyré, 'Rapport sur l'état des études hegéliennes en France', *Etudes d'histoire de la pensée philosophique*, Paris 1961, pp. 205–30.
86. Sartre, 'Qu'est-ce que la littérature', p. 245.
87. Léon Brunschwicg, *Le Progrès de la conscience dans la philosophie occidentale*, Paris 1953, p. 381.
88. Jean Hyppolite, '*La Phénoménologie* de Hegel et la pensée française contemporaine', in *Figures de la pensée philosophique*, Paris 1961, pp. 205–30.
89. Georges Devereux, 'Aspects de la psychanalyse aux Etats-Unis', *Les Temps modernes*, 12, September 1946.
90. Anzieu, 'La Psychanalyse au service de la psychologie'.
91. Turkle, *Psychoanalytic Politics*, p. 82.
92. Gérard Miller, ed., *Lacan*, Paris 1987. For the advertisements, see *Le Monde*, 27 November 1987, pp. 22–3. Miller's collection is, incidentally, a splendid example of final-statism.
93. Roudinesco, vol. 1, pp. 377–8.

94. Daniel Widlöcher, 'The Self as Illusion', in John Klauber and others, *Illusion and Spontaneity in Psychoanalysis*, London 1987, p. 135. Widlöcher adds (p. 136, n.) that Lacan's theory is 'probably one of the most demonstrable instances' of the 'misunderstanding' so induced.

95. Lacan, S II, p. 77.

96. Ibid., p. 15–16.

97. Michel Foucault, *Folie et déraison. Histoire de la folie à l'âge classique*, Paris 1961; *Les Mots et les choses*, Paris 1966.

98. The most exhaustive account will be found in Hollier, *Le Collège de sociologie*, an excellent anthology of otherwise inaccessible material.

99. Hollier, p. 22.

100. Claude Lévi-Strauss, 'La Sociologie française', in Georges Gurvitch, *La Sociologie du XXᵉ siècle*, Paris 1947, p. 517.

101. Hollier, pp. 188–9.

102. For a brief genealogy of the Bataille–*Critique* 'family', see Anna Boschetti, *Sartre et 'Les Temps modernes'*, Paris 1985, pp. 206–10.

103. Cf. Lacan, S II, p. 193.

104. Alexandre Kojève, *Introduction à la lecture de Hegel.* On Kojève, see Patrick Riley, 'Introduction to the Reading of Alexandre Kojève', *Political Theory*, vol. 9, no. 1, February 1981.

105. The *Grande Encyclopédie* text will be found in Lucien Herr, *Choix d'Écrits II: Ecrits philosophiques et scientifiques*, Paris 1932. Cf. Charles Andler, *La Vie de Lucien Herr*, Paris 1932.

106. Kojève, p. 39.

107. Hollier, p. 164; Roger Caillois, cited, ibid., p. 165.

108. Baillie's translation of Hegel has 'Master' or 'Lord') and 'Bondsman'; for convenience, the terms 'master' and 'slave' are used here.

109. Hegel, *Phenomenology*, pp. 233, 299.

110. Kojève, p. 84.

111. Ibid., p. 169.

112. Ibid, p 11.

113. Lacan, 'Introduction au commentaire', E, p. 374.

114. Lacan, 'L'Etourdit', *Scilicet*, 4, 1973, p. 9.

115. Lacan, 'Au-delà du "Principe de réalité"', E, p. 87.

116. Lacan, 'La Famille', 8° 40–8.

117. Lacan, 'L'Aggressivité', E, p. 121; ES, p. 26; 'Propos sur la causalité', E, p. 172.

118. Lacan, 'Subversion du sujet', E, pp. 794, 804; ES, pp. 293, 302.

119. Lacan, 'Le Stade du miroir', E, p. 98; ES, p. 5. Cf. Henri Wallon, *Les Origines du caractère chez l'enfant*, Paris 1949. Explicit references to Wallon and Bühler gradually disappear from later texts, and their absence contributes to the widespread impression that the mirror stage is an immaculately Lacanian concept. Ironically, Bühler's *Kindheit und Jugend* (Leipzig 1928) is also a significant reference point for the ego psychologists; see Hartmann, *Ego Psychology*, p. 52.

120. Lacan, 'Some Reflections on the Ego', p. 14; 'Le Stade', E, p. 95; ES, p. 3; 'Propos sur la causalité', E, p. 189.

121. Lacan, S I, p. 158; 'Fonction et champ', E, p. 297; ES, p. 84; Cf. S III, p. 108 f.

122. Lacan, 'Propos sur la causalité', E, p. 189.

123. 'Some Reflections on the Ego', p. 14. In this context, it might be noted that when Lacan states ('Réponse au commentaire', E, p. 381) that the 'inexhaustible richness' of Freud's texts predestines them to 'the discipline of commentary', he is reiterating the traditional rationale for the classroom exercise known as *explication de texte*.

124. Juranville, *Lacan et la philosophie.*

125. Jean Wahl, *Vers le concret*, Paris 1932.

126. Paul Nizan, review of D. Mirsky, *Lénine*, *Nouvelle Revue Française*, May 1931, p. 773.

127. Georges Politzer, *Critique des fondements de la psychologie*, Paris 1974. Most of Politzer's contributions to the *Revue de psychologie concrète* will be found in his *Ecrits II*.

For a general account of his work, see G. Lanteri-Laura, 'Nizan et Politzer quarante ans après', *Critique*, August–September 1968.

128. On Sartre and Politzer, see David Archard, *Consciousness and the Unconscious*, London 1985, pp. 38–40. Lacan's final comments on Politzer are made in his preface to Lemaire, pp. ix–x. The most extensive critique of Politzer from a Lacanian stance is that made by Laplanche and Leclaire in their 'L'Inconscient, une étude psychanalytique', in Jean Laplanche, *Problématiques IV: L'Inconscient et le ça*, Paris 1981.

129. Bergson is Politzer's *bête noire*, and is subjected to a searing critique in *La Fin d'une parade philosophique: le bergsonisme*, Paris 1929. Like Nizan's *Les Chiens de garde*, Politzer's pamphlet is an excellent expression of the intellectual revolt of the period.

130. Politzer, *Critique*, p. 70.

131. Ibid., pp. 51–2.

132. Ibid., pp. 232, 233.

133. Lacan, PP, p. 346.

134. Lacan, 'La Famille', 8° 40–10, 8° 42–4.

135. Lacan, 'Réglement et doctrine', p. 33; 'Propos sur la causalité', E, p. 161.

136. Lacan, 'Fonctions ... en criminologie', E, p. 129.

137. Lacan, review of Minkowski, p. 429.

138. Lacan, 'Au delà', E, p. 74.

139. The parallel was first noted by Pontalis in his 1955 essay on Leiris in *Après Freud*, p. 320, n. 2. For a more extensive discussion, see Patrick Vauday, 'Sartre et la psychanalyse sans inconscient', *Ornicar?*, 32, Spring 1985.

140. Sartre, *La Transcendance de l'ego*, p. 63.

141. Ibid., p. 82.

142. Ibid., p. 78.

143. Although Lacan does not allude to Rimbaud in the 1949 paper, he is an important reference in the related Seminar on the ego (S II).

144. Sartre, *La Transcendance*, p. 27; Lacan, S III, p. 276.

145. Vauday, p. 115.

146. Lacan, S I, pp. 240–42.

147. Lacan, 'Le Stade du miroir', E, pp. 94, 97; ES, pp. 2, 4. The use of 'drama' here may be an index of the residual influence of Politzer.

148. Lacan, 'Intervention sur le transfert', E, p. 276; FS, p. 72.

149. Lacan, 'Fonction et champ', E, p. 300; ES, p. 86.

150. Ibid., p. 255; p. 47.

151. Lacan, 'Le mythe individuel du névrosé', *Ornicar?*, 17/18, Spring 1979, pp. 305–6.

152. Martin Heidegger, *Being and Time*, Oxford 1980, p. 373.

153. Jean-Paul Sartre, *L'Etre et le néant*, Paris 1976, p. 162.

154. Ibid., p. 154; Lacan, S I, p. 19.

155. Freud, letter of 12 June 1900 to Fliess, *Complete Letters*, p. 417.

156. Cf. Lacan, S XI, p. 22; FFC, p. 18: 'Thus, for a time at least, I was thought to be obsessed with some kind of philosophy of language, even a Heideggerean one, whereas only a *propaedeutic* reference was involved.'

157. Jean-Paul Sartre, 'Entretien sur l'anthropologie', *Cahiers de philosophie*, 2/3, February 1966, reproduced, Michel Contat and Michel Rybalka, *Les Ecrits de Sartre*, Paris 1970, p. 430.

158. Lacan, S I, pp. 249–50.

159. Lacan, S II, p. 200

160. Lacan, 'Maurice Merleau-Ponty', *Les Temps modernes*, 184/185, 1961, p. 246.

161. Anna Freud, *The Ego and The Mechanisms of Defence*, London 1937. For a detailed account of the elaboration of the second topography, see Bercherie, *Genèse*, pp. 347–80.

162. For a general survey of his work, see Gertrude and Rubin Blanck, *Ego Psychology, Theory and Practice*, New York 1974, and especially chapter 2: 'Psychoanalysis as a Normal Developmental Psychology: Hartmann's Theories and his Work in Collaboration with Kris and Loewenstein'.

163. The most brutal expression of this view is to be found in Lacan's 'Réponses à des étudiants en philosophie', *Cahiers pour l'analyse*, 3, May–June 1966, where ego psychology is denounced as the ideology of a class of *immigrés* who have been forced to adapt to a society in which values are measured on the income-tax scale. This savage hyperbole has more to do with the French anti-Americanism of the mid 1960s than with any history of psychoanalysis.

164. Cf. Anna Freud, *Normality and Pathology in Childhood*, Harmondsworth 1973. For the link between the autonomous ego and Winnicott's 'self', see Jean Laplanche, *Problématiques III: La Sublimation*, Paris 1980, p. 67.

165. Cf. Bruno Bettelheim, *Surviving the Holocaust*, London 1986, p. 106, and especially p. 74: 'If the author should be asked to sum up in one sentence what, during all the time he spent in the camp, was his main problem, he would say: *to safeguard his ego in such a way that, if by any good luck he should regain liberty, he would be approximately the same person he was when deprived of liberty.*'

166. Heinz Hartmann, Ernst Kris and Rudoloph Loewenstein, 'Comments on the formation of Psychic Structure', *Psychoanalytic Study of the Child*, 2, 1946, p. 15.

167. Hartmann, *Ego Psychology*, pp. 8–9, 107.

168. Ibid., p. 8.

169. Heinz Hartmann, 'Comments on the Psychoanalytic Theory of the Ego', *Psychoanalytic Study of the Child*, 5, 1950, p. 77.

170. Sacha Nacht, 'Perspectives ouvertes par le concept des fonctions autonomes du moi'; 'Rôle du moi dans l'épanouissement de l'être humain', in *Guérir avec Freud*, Paris 1971; 'Du Moi et son rôle dans la thérapeutique psychanalytique', RFP, 1948.

171. Cf. Erik K. Erikson, *Childhood and Society*, Harmondsworth 1965, pp. 185–8.

172. Lacan, 'Fonction et champ', E, p. 273; ES, p. 62. The article in question appeared in the IJPA in 1944.

173. Lacan, 'La Chose freudienne', E, p. 403; ES, p. 116; Lacan cites ('I have it from Jung's own mouth') Freud's words to Jung as they arrive in New York: '"They don't realize we're bringing them the plague"'.

174. Hartmann, 'Comments', pp. 94–5.

175. André Green, *Narcissisme de vie, narcissisme de mort*, Paris 1983, p. 141.

176. Freud, 'Analysis Terminable and Interminable', SE XXIII, p. 250.

177. Nacht, 'Rôle du moi', p. 222.

178. Cf. Anna Freud, *Normality*, p. 43: 'So far as the analyst verbalizes and helps in the fight against anxiety, he becomes an auxiliary ego to whom the child clings for protection.'

179. Jean Guillaumin, 'Prise en compte tardive du contre-transfert de fond dans la cure psychanalitique', in Henri Sztulman, ed., *Le Psychanalyste et son patient*, Toulouse 1983, pp. 141–3.

180. *The Ego and the Id*, p. 50, n. 1.

181. Lacan, 'Subversion du sujet', E, pp. 808–9; ES, pp. 306–7; 'Variantes de la cure-type', E, p. 335, n. 1.

182. Lacan, 'Réponses à des étudiants', p. 7.

183. Lacan, S III, pp. 272–3.

184. Lacan, S II, p. 59.

185. Lacan, 'Le Stade du miroir', E, p. 99; ES, p. 6.

186. Lacan, S II, p. 77.

187. Ibid., pp. 11, 179, 188.

188. The subtitle is duly echoed in the anonymous 'La Raison avant Freud', *Scilicet*, 6/7, 1976, an extended review of Cassirer's *Philosophy of Symbolic Forms* which concludes (p. 325), predictably but lamely, that Cassirer's definition of the symbolic relies upon pre-Freudian and *therefore* Kantian notions of reason.

189. Lacan, 'La Psychanalyse et son enseignement', E, p. 437. *Ça parle* is of course a pun on *ça* ('id' and 'it'): Id speaks'.

190. Lacan, 'La Chose freudienne', E, p. 401; ES, p. 114; 'Instance de la lettre', E, p. 516; ES, p. 165; 'Subversion du sujet'; E, p. 796; ES, p. 295.

191. Freud, 'Contribution to a Questionnaire on Reading', SE IX, p. 245; *Leonardo*,

p. 65; *Introductory Lectures*, p. 285.

192. Freud, 'A Difficulty in the Path of Psycho-Analysis', SE XVII, p. 140; 'The Resistances to Psycho-Analysis', SE XIX, p. 271; *New Introductory Lectures*, p. 173.

193. Cf. the discussion of the 'Great Man' theme in *Moses and Monotheism*, pp. 107–11.

194. Freud, *The Interpretation of Dreams*, SE IV, pp. 196–8.

195. Paul-Laurent Assoun, 'Freud, Copernic, Darwin', *Ornicar?*, 22/23, Spring 1981.

196. Freud, *Introductory Lectures*, p. 75; *New Introductory Lectures*, p. 285.

197. Alexandre Koyré, *From the closed World to the Infinite Universe*, Baltimore 1957.

198. Lacan, 'Subversion du sujet', E, p. 795; ES, p. 294.

199. Laplanche and Pontalis, p. 482.

200. Lacan, 'La Direction de la cure', E, p. 627; ES, p. 263.

201. Lacan, 'Subversion du sujet', E, p. 814; ES, p. 311.

202. Lacan, S XI, p. 141; FFC, p. 155.

203. Freud, *The Interpretation of Dreams*, p. 264; Lacan, 'La Direction de la cure', E, p. 625; ES, p. 261.

204. Freud, *The Interpretation of Dreams*, p. 142; Lacan, 'La Direction de la cure', E, p. 625; ES, p. 261. Sheridan goes on to distort the text in an extraordinary way, and has the husband say to the painter: 'Nuts! a slice of the backside of some pretty shit is what you need.' Freud's text reads: 'He was sure the painter would prefer a piece of a pretty girl's behind.' Even allowing for the possibility that Lacan is paraphrasing Freud, 'some pretty shit' is a bizarre translation of '*une belle garce*'.

205. René Descartes, *Les Passions de l'âme*, Paris 1966, p. 110.

206. Lacan, 'Subversion du sujet', E, p. 628; ES, p. 264; Kojève, *Introduction*, p. 169.

207. Sartre, *l'Etre et le néant*, p. 636.

208. Lacan, '*Hamlet* IV: Phallophanie', *Ornicar?*, 26/27, Summer 1983, p. 40.

209. Lacan, 'Remarque sur le rapport de Daniel Lagache', E, p. 667.

210. Lacan, S XI, p. 140; FFC, p. 153.

211. Lacan, 'La Direction de la cure', E, p. 635; ES, p. 270.

212. Lacan, 'La Chose freudienne', E, p. 432; ES, p. 142; Freud, *The Interpretation of Dreams*.

213. Freud, *Introductory Lectures*, p. 313.

214. Freud, *Three Essays on the Theory of Sexuality*, SE VII, p. 135, n. 2. The same point is made in Freud's letter of 19 December 1909 to Jung, *The Freud/Jung Letters*, p. 169.

215. Althusser, 'Freud and Lacan', pp. 191, 195, n.

216. Lacan, *Télévision*, p. 20; Jacques-Alain Miller, 'Encyclopédie', *Ornicar?*, 24, Autumn 1981, p. 36.

217. Lacan, 'Position de l'inconscient', E, p. 837.

218. André Green, 'Une Figure méssianique', *Le Monde*, 11 September 1981.

219. François Perrier, *La Chaussée d'Antin*, Paris 1978, vol. 1, p. 218.

220. Simone de Beauvoir, *Le Deuxième Sexe*, Paris 1981, vol. 1, pp. 287–88; Frantz Fanon, *Black Skins, White Masks*, London 1978, p. 114, n:. 'When one has grasped the mechanism described by Lacan, one can have no further doubt that the real Other for the white man is and will continue to be the black man. And conversely.'

221. The erotic connotations of *jouissance* are discussed in chapter six below.

222. On the links between Lacan and the 'New Philosophers', see Peter Dews,'The "New Philosophers" and the End of Leftism', *Radical Philosophy*, 24, Spring 1980; 'The *Nouvelle Philosophie* and Foucault', *Economy and Society*, vol. 7, no. 2, May 1979. The most relevant survey of the philosophies of desire is that provided in Lecercle, *Philosophy Through the Looking-Glass*.

223. Cf. François Perrier, *Voyages extraordinaires en Translacanie*, Paris 1985, p. 111.

224. Lacan, S XX, p. 40.

225. Lacan, 'Radiophonie', p. 89.
226. Ibid., p. 88.
227. Ibid.
228. Lacan, *Télévision*, p. 36.
229. Lacan, S XI, p. 9; FFC, p. 3.

5 Linguistics or *Linguisterie*?

1. Lacan, 'Règlement et doctrine', p. 36; 'Status proposés', p. 56.
2. Lacan did in fact have discussions with Chomsky in 1975, but a faulty tape-recorder ensured that no transcript survived. Cf. the introductory note to *Scilicet*, 6/7, 1976, p. 5.
3. Lacan, 'Fonction et champ', E, p. 259; ES, p. 50. Semantic evolution is defined here as 'corresponding to the stock of words and acceptations of my own particular vocabulary' and to 'my style of life and to my character'.
4. John Lyons, *Introduction to Theoretical Linguistics*, Cambridge 1968; Oswald Ducrot and Tzvetan Todorov, *Dictionnaire encyclopédique des sciences de la langue*, Paris 1972.
5. For a brief survey of the literature, see the first section of Roland Gori, *Le corps et le signe dans l'acte de parole*, Paris 1978.
6. Lacan, 'A la mémoire d'Ernest Jones: sur sa théorie de symbolisme', E, pp. 697–716.
7. Tzvetan Todorov, *Théories du symbole*, Paris 1985, chapter 8, 'La Rhétorique de Freud'; *Appendice*: 'Freud sur l'énonciation'.
8. Althusser, 'Freud and Lacan', p. 191.
9. Lacan, 'L'Etourdit', *Scilicet*, 4, 1973, pp. 8–9.
10. Lacan, S III, p. 258; 'Fonction et champ', E, pp. 267, 280; ES, pp. 57, 80; 'Situation de la psychanalyse', E, p. 467.
11. Lacan, S III, p. 258.
12. Lacan, S XX, p. 19; Roman Jakobson, 'Two Aspects of Language and Two Types of Aphasic Disturbance', in *Selected Writings*, vol. 2, The Hague 1971, p. 248. Cf. 'Linguistic Types of Aphasia', ibid., p. 314, for the view that metalingual operations represent 'a vital ability to translate one verbal sign into another', and that this ability 'underlies the development and use of language'.
13. Roland Barthes, *Le Degré zéro de l'écriture, suivi de Eléments de sémiologie*, Paris 1970, p. 166. Cf. Octave Mannoni, *Clefs pour l'imaginaire*, Paris 1985, p. 55: 'Linguistics would not be possible if its meta-texts were knit into its texts, if examples and commentaries merged into one.'
14. Lacan, 'Fonction et champ', E, p. 271; ES, p. 61.
15. Ibid.; Freud, *Totem and Taboo*, p. 161.
16. Martin Heidegger, 'The Way to Language', in *On The Way to Language*, New York 1982, p. 119.
17. 'Condensation et déplacement', *Scilicet*, 2/3, 1970, p. 219, n. 3.
18. Lacan, 'Instance de la lettre', E, p. 496, n. 1; ES, p. 176, n. 8.
19. Ibid., p. 498; p. 150.
20. Lacan, 'Subversion du sujet', E, p. 813; ES, p. 311.
21. Lacan, S III, p. 258; 'Subversion', E, p. 816; ES p. 311.
22. Cf. Roland Barthes, 'L'Ancienne Rhétorique', *Communications*, 16, 1970, for the view that rhetoric is a metalanguage with discourse as its object.
23. Lacan, S XX, p. 20.
24. Lacan, 'Une Pratique de bavardage', *Ornicar?*, 19, Autumn 1979, p. 5.
25. 'Au-delà du "Principe de réalite"'. 'Le Stade du miroir', 'L'Aggressivité en psychanalyse'. 'Introduction théorique aux fonctions de la psychanalyse en criminologie', and 'Propos sur la causalité psychique'.
26. Lacan, 'De Nos Antécédents', E, p. 67.

27. In the paper on criminology, Lacan does refer (E, pp. 130, 143) to the *Psychopathology*, but only to note that the 'traces' left behind by criminals are akin to bungled actions and are evidence of a very real psychopathology of everyday life.

28. 'Propos sur la causalité', E, pp. 166–7.

29. 'Fonctions ... en criminologie', E, p. 128.

30. Lacan, 'Au-delà', p. 82.

31. Lacan 'L'Aggressivité', E, p. 102; ES, p. 9.

32. Lacan, ibid., p. 121; p. 26.

33. Jean-Claude Milner, *L'Amour de la langue*, Paris 1978, p. 100.

34. Lacan, 'Fonctions ... en criminologie', E, p. 132.

35. Mounin, 'Quelques Traits du style', p. 89.

36. H. Delacroix, 'Le Langage', in Georges Dumas, ed., *Nouveau Traité de la psychologie: vol. 5. Les Fonctions systématisées de la vie intellectuelle*, Paris 1936.

37. R.L. Wagner, *Introduction à la linguistique française*, Lille and Geneva 1947, p. 21.

38. See, for example, François Rostand, 'Grammaire et affectivité', RFP, 14, 1950.

39. Roudinesco, vol. 2, p. 158.

40. Lacan, 'Intervention au Premier congrès mondial de la psychiatrie', *Ornicar?*, 30, July–September 1984, pp. 7–10. For a general account of the congress, see Roudinesco, vol. 2, pp. 187–90.

41. Lacan, 'La Chose freudienne', E, p. 414; ES, p. 125.

42. Eliane Amado Lévy-Valensi, 'Vérité et langage du dialogue platonicien au dialogue psychanalytique'; Clémence Ramnoux, 'Hadès et le psychanalyse (pour une anamèse de l'homme d'occident)'; Emile Benveniste, 'Remarques sur la fonction du langage dans la découverte freudienne', *La Psychanalyse*, 1, 1956. Benveniste's essay is reprinted in his *Problèmes de linguistique générale*, Paris 1966.

43. On Merleau-Ponty's reading of Saussure, see James Schmidt, *Maurice Merleau-Ponty. Between Phenomenology and Structuralism*, London 1985.

44. Claude Lévi-Strauss, 'Structural Analysis in Linguistics and in Anthropology', in *Structural Anthropology*.

45. Lacan, S I, p. 27 f. Beirnaert became a member of the SFP in 1953 and remained an associate of Lacan's until the dissolution of the EFP in 1980. A selection of his writings will be found in *Aux Frontières de l'acte analytique*, Paris 1987.

46. Lacan, 'L'Instance de la lettre', E, pp. 496–7; ES, p. 148; 'Radiophonie', p. 55, emphasis added.

47. Lacan, 'La Chose freudienne', E, p. 414; ES, p. 125.

48. Cf. 'La Direction de la cure', E, p. 618; ES, p. 255, where Lacan refers to 'the signifier in its double register: the synchronic register of opposition between irreducible elements, and the diachronic register of substitution and combination'.

49. Ferdinand de Saussure, *Cours de linguistique générale*, Paris 1967, p. 156.

50. Lacan, S III, pp. 135, 296.

51. Lacan, 'Instance de la lettre', E, pp. 502–3; ES, p. 154.

52. Perry Anderson, *In The Tracks of Historical Materialism*, London 1983, p. 45.

53. Philippe Sollers, 'Le Marxisme sodomisé par la psychanalyse violée par on ne sait pas quoi', *Tel Quel*, 75, Spring 1985, p. 60, n. 1.

54. Cited, Bernard Doray, *From Taylorism to Fordism*, London 1988, chapter 6, n. 4.

55. Lacan, 'L'Instance de la lettre', E, pp. 502–3; ES, p. 154.

56. Lacan, S III, pp. 297–306.

57. Lacan 'Subversion du sujet', E, p. 805; ES, p. 303, translation modified.

58. Ibid., p. 805; pp. 303–4.

59. Cf. the game of 'Yes means no' described by Mannoni, *Clefs pour l'imaginaire*, p. 71. Mannoni is right to suggest that such games represent a ludic exploitation of the arbitrary nature of the linguistic sign. This does not mean that they produce metaphors.

60. Lacan, cited, Laplanche and Leclaire, p. 300.

61. Lacan, S III, pp. 303–4.

62. Lacan, 'L'Instance de la lettre', E, p. 497; ES, p. 149.

63. Cf. Laplanche, *Problématiques IV*, p. 117, n. 1. For the suggestion that algorithmic procedures may be applicable to the level of Saussure's theory of value, but not at that of the sign itself, see Regnier Pirard, 'Si l'Inconscient est structuré comme un langage ...', *Revue philosophique de Louvain*, 77, 1979, pp. 543–4, and n. 34. Such procedures would imply a much higher level of formalization than that attained by Lacan.

64. Lacan, 'L'Instance de la lettre', E, pp. 499–500;; ES, pp. 151–2. 'Solitary confinement' is a rather curious rendition of *isoloir*, literally an insulator but more commonly used to mean a polling booth.

65. Freud, 'Fragment of an Analysis of a Case of Hysteria', SE VII, p. 99, n. 2.

66. S I, p. 181. The reference is to Melanie Klein, 'The Importance of Symbol Formation in the Development of the Ego', *Contributions to Psycho-Analysis, 1921–1945*, London 1948.

67. Lacan, 'D'Une Question préliminaire', E, p. 498; ES, p. 50.

68. Vincent Descombes, *Objects of All Sorts: A Philosophical Grammar*, Oxford 1986, p. 180.

69. Lacan, 'Le Séminaire sur la "Lettre volée"', E, p. 12.

70. Lacan, S II, p. 232.

71. Saussure, *Cours*, p. 121.

72. Ibid., p. 129.

73. Emile Benveniste,'Coup d'oeil sur le développement de la linguistique', in his *Problèmes*, p. 32.

74. Lacan, S VII, p. 56.

75. Lacan, 'Fonction et champ', E, p. 238; ES, p. 31.

76. Lacan, S XX, p. 69, FS, p. 145, translation modified. The reference is to Oscar Bloch and W. Von Wartburg, *Dictionnaire étymologique de la langue française*, 2 vols, Paris 1932.

77. Lacan, 'L'Instance de la lettre', E, p. 505; ES, p. 156.

78. Ibid., p. 511; p. 160.

79. Jean-François Lyotard, 'The Dream-Work Does Not Think', *Oxford Literary Review*, vol. 6, no. 1, 1983, p. 33, n. 40.

80. Lacan '*Hamlet* V: L'Objet Ophélie', *Ornicar?*, 26/27, Summer 1983, p. 16.

81. For Freud, 'Splitting of the Ego in the Process of Defence' (SE XXIII), the splitting of the ego and the disturbance of its synthetic functions relate to a defence against a powerful but prohibited instinctual demand. Similar points are made in 'Fetishism'. In the 'Outline' of 1938 (SE XXIII) the mechanism is extended to the neuroses, but at no point does Freud imply that splitting is a characteristic of human subjectivity as such.

82. Lacan, 'Position de l'inconscient', E, pp. 842–3.

83. Lacan, 'La Signification du phallus', E, p. 692; ES, p. 287; FS, p. 82.

84. John Forrester, 'Philology and the Phallus', in Colin MacCabe, ed., *The Talking Cure*, London 1981, p. 57.

85. Freud, 'The Antithetical Meaning of Primal Words', SE XI.

86. On Freud and philology, see John Forrester, *Language and the Origins of Psychoanalysis*, London 1980.

87. Freud, *The Interpretation of Dreams*, p. 318, n. 3.

88. Freud, *Introductory Lectures*, p. 180.

89. Beneveniste, 'Remarque sur la fonction du langage', in *Problèmes*, pp. 80–81.

90. Freud, *Leonardo*.

91. Lacan, 'Le Séminaire sur "La Lettre volée"', E, p. 22, n. 1.

92. Lacan, 'Radiophonie', p. 62.

93. Lacan, S I, p. 216.

94. Lacan, 'Le Malentendu', *Ornicar?*, 22/23, Spring 1981, p. 13.

95. Heidegger, *Being and Time*, p. 242.

96. Martin Heidegger, *What Is Philosophy?* New York 1958, p. 45.

97. Lacan, S III, p. 339.

98. Lacan, 'Introduction au commentaire', E, p. 380.

99. Lacan, S I, p. 281.

100. Victor Hugo, *Œuvres poétiques* II, Paris 1967, p. 800.

101. Lacan, 'Fonction et champ', E, p. 272; ES, p. 61. Although Lacan gives Maurice Leenhardt, *Do Kamo*, Paris 1947, as the source for his information, the allusion to 'argonauts' suggests that he is also thinking of Malinowski, *Argonauts of the Western Pacific*, London 1922.

102. For a detailed account of the multiple etymologies in play here, see Wilden, *Speech and language*, pp. 101–2, 118–20.

103. Lacan, S I, p. 242.

104. Lacan, 'Variantes de la cure type', E, p. 351.

105. Lacan, S III, p. 347.

106. Freud, *Jokes and their Relation to the Unconscious*, SE VIII, p. 115.

107. Lacan, 'La Chose freudienne', E, p. 431; ES, p. 141.

108. J.L. Austin, 'Performative Utterances', in *Philosophical Papers*, third edn, Oxford 1979, p. 235.

109. Saussure, *Cours*, p. 30.

110. Ibid., p. 12.

111. Lacan, 'Fonction et champ', E, p. 297; ES, p. 84.

112. Lacan, 'La Chose freudienne', E, p. 414; ES, p. 126.

113. Lacan, 'Fonction et champ', E, p. 274; ES, p. 63.

114. Lacan, 'Fonctions ... en criminologie', E, p. 125.

115. Lacan, 'Fonction et champ', E, p. 291; ES, p. 79.

116. Ibid., p. 279; ES, p. 68. *L'accord de la parole* is an ambiguous phrase, which might also be rendered as 'the granting of speech'.

117. Lacan, S I, p. 61; 'Actes du congrès de Rome', p. 203.

118. Lacan, 'Fonction et champ', E, p. 254; ES, p. 43.

119. Ibid., p. 279; p. 68.

120. Lacan, S I, pp. 125–6.

121. Lacan, 'Fonction et champ', E, p. 254; ES, p. 43, translation modified.

122. Lacan, 'Introduction au commentaire', E, p. 373, n. 1.

123. Heidegger, *Being and Time*, p. 211.

124. Ibid., pp. 104, 214.

125. Ibid., pp. 206, 208.

126. Lacan, 'Fonction et champ', E, pp. 251–2; ES, p. 43.

127. Lacan, 'Intervention sur le transfert', E, p. 216; FS, p. 62.

128. Ibid., pp. 219–20; pp. 65–6.

129. Lacan, 'Variantes de la cure type', E, pp. 351, 354.

130. Lacan, 'Direction de la cure', E, p. 641; ES, p. 275.

131. François Perrier, *La Chaussée d'Antin*, vol. 2, p. 218.

132. Ginette Michaud, *Laborde ... un pari nécessaire*, Paris 1977, p. 78.

133. Lacan, 'Fonction et champ', E, pp. 276–7; ES, p. 66, translation modified.

134. *Tristes Tropiques*, p. 58, translation modified.

135. Ibid., p. 55.

136. Interview with Raymond Bellour in Raymond Bellour and Catherine Clément, eds, *Claude Lévi-Strauss*, Paris 1979, 201–6.

137. Claude Lévi-Strauss, *The Elementary Structures of Kinship*, London 1969, pp. 25, 30.

138. Claude Lévi-Strauss, 'Introduction à l'œuvre de Marcel Mauss', in Mauss, *Sociologie et anthropologie*, Paris 1950, p. xxxiii.

139. Lévi-Strauss, *Structural Anthropology*, p. 65; *Elementary Structures*, p. 464.

140. *Elementary Structures*, p. 220; *Structural Anthropology*, pp. 19–20. Cf. *Elementary Structures*, p. 108: 'As Boas has heavily emphasized ... all types of social phenomena (language, beliefs, techniques and customs) have this in common, that their relationship in the mind is at the level of unconscious thought.'

141. *Structural Anthropology*, p. 203.

142. Freud, 'The Unconscious', SE XIV, p. 186–7.

143. Claude Lévi-Strauss, *The Raw and the Cooked*, London 1970, p. 11 and n. 3. For Paul Ricoeur's remarks, see his 'Structure and Hermeneutics', *The Conflict of Interpretations*, Evanstown 1974.

144. Lacan, 'Position de l'inconscient', E, p. 831.

145. Lacan, 'Fonction et champ', E, p. 259; ES, p. 50; Lévi-Strauss, *Structural Anthropology*, p. 203.

146. Lacan, 'La Famille', 8° 40–12; 'Fonctions ... en criminologie', E, pp. 129–32.

147. Lacan, 'Fonctions', E, p. 128. The Pauline reference is to Romans 7: 8: 'What shall we say then? Is the law sin? God forbid. Nay, I had not known lust, except the law had said, Thou shalt not covet.' For Lacan, the oedipal prohibition of incest demonstrates the 'absolute truth' of St Paul's remarks. Cf. S VII, p. 101.

148. Lacan, SVIII, p. 85.

149. Lacan, 'La Chose freudienne', E, p. 432; Es, Pp. 141–142.

150. Freud, *The Interpretation of Dreams*, SE IV p. 262.

151. Ibid., p. 263, 4:2; 'A Special Type of Choice of Object Made by Men, SE VI, p. 171.

152. Freud, letter of 15 October 1897 to Fliess, *Complete Letters*, p. 272.

153. Jacques-Alain Miller, 'Encyclopédie', *Ornicar?*, 24, Autumn 1981, p. 35.

154. Laplanche, *Problématiques IV*.

155. Lévi-Strauss, *Elementary Structures*, p. 62, emphasis added.

156. Ibid., pp. 61, 481.

157. Cf. Elizabeth Cowie, 'Woman as Sign', *m/f*, 1, 1978.

158. Lévi-Strauss, *Structural Anthropology*, p. 61.

159. Lacan, S III, p. 303.

160. Jean Paulhan, *Les Fleurs de Tarbes*, Paris 1941.

161. Lacan, 'Fonction et champ', E, p. 251; ES, p. 169.

162. Lacan, 'L'Instance de la lettre', E, pp. 511, 521; ES, pp. 160, 169.

163. The aphasia study originally appeared as the second part of Roman Jakobson and Morris Halle, *The Fundamentals of Language*, The Hague 1956. The French translation by A. Adler and N. Ruwet appeared in *Les Temps modernes*, 188, January 1962.

164. Paulhan, *Les Fleurs*, p. 212.

165. Laplanche and Leclaire, 'L'Inconscient', p. 294.

166. Lacan, S III, pp. 250, 259.

167. 'Translator's note', Roman Jakobson, *Essais de linguistique générale*, Paris 1970, p. 66.

168. Barthes, *Eléments de sémiologie*, p. 133; seminar of 1964–65, cited, Jacques Durand, 'Rhétorique et image publicitaire', *Communications*, 15, 1970, p. 72; Laplanche, *Problématiques IV*, p. 139, n. 1.

169. Tzvetan Todorov, 'Synecdoques', *Communications*, 16, 1970, p. 31; *Théories du symbole*, p. 303.

170. Barthes, 'L'Ancienne Rhétorique', p. 216. The example used here is that given in the *Concise OED*.

171. Lacan, 'L'Instance de la lettre', E, p. 505; ES, p. 156; Pierre Fontanier, *Les Figures du discours*, Paris 1968, p. 88. This volume brings together two treatises originally published in 1821 and 1827 respectively.

172. Lyotard, 'The Dream-Work', pp. 18, 20; Gérard Genette, *Figures of Literary Discourse*, New York 1982, p. 124, n. 27.

173. Lacan, S III, p. 247. This is the correct version; in both 'L'Instance', E, p. 506; ES, p. 156; S XI, p. 224; FFC, p. 247, Lacan misquotes the line as *Sa gerbe n'était pas avare ni haineuse.*

174. Lacan, 'L'Instance de la lettre', E, p. 506; ES, p. 156.

175. Victor Hugo, *La Légende des siècles*, Paris 1950, pp. 33–5.

176. Lacan, S XI, p. 224; FFC, p. 247.

177. Lacan, 'La Métaphore du sujet', E, p. 892.

178. Lacan, 'L'Instance de la lettre', E, pp. 503, 515; ES, pp. 157, 164. 'Word to word' is an obvious echo of the 'word by word' formula for metonymy. As Lacan notes, it is also an allusion to *Un Mot pour un autre*, Jean Tardieu's rather slight play of 1950 (in Tardieu, *Théâtre de Chambre*, Paris 1966). The play is not in fact concerned with metaphor, and is an absurdist exploitation of the comic potential of false collocations and unexpected juxtapositions.

179. It is this lack of precision which prompts Mounin ('Quelques Traits du style', pp. 88, 91) to note that Lacan often makes *significant* ('signifier', but also the present participle 'signifying') synonymous with *significatif* ('significant'). Mounin returns to the attack in his *Clefs pour la linguistique*, Paris 1970, p. 13, claiming that Lacan's knowledge of linguistics is dated and superficial and that his reading of Saussure is riddled with errors. For a predictably violent Lacanian reply, see 'Condensation et déplacement', *Scilicet*, 2/3, 1970.

180. Lacan, S III, p. 248.

181. Lacan, 'La Métaphore du sujet', E, p. 890.

182. Lacan, 'Fonction et champ', E, p. 193; ES, p. 81.

183. Lewis Carroll, *Through the Looking Glass*, in Martin Gardner, ed., *The Annotated Alice*, Harmondsworth 1965, p. 269.

184. C. Perelman and L. Olbrechts-Tyteca, *Traité de l'argumentation*, Paris 1958, p. 536. The very title of this treatise points to a vital aspect of rhetoric which Lacan consistently ignores; its function is one of persuasion and argumentation.

185. Cf. Du Marsais, cited, ibid., pp. 534–5: 'The signification specific to a noun is transported, so to speak, to another noun, to which it applies by virtue of a comparison which exists in the mind.' Cf. Fontanier, p. 99: the use of tropes based upon resemblance consists in 'presenting an idea beneath the sign of a more striking or better known idea, its sole connection with the first idea being a certain conformity or analogy'.

186. Lacan, 'La Métaphore du sujet', E, p. 890.

187. Lacan, 'L'Instance de la lettre', E, p. 507; ES, p. 157.

188. Paul Eluard, 'L'Amour la poésie' VII in *Capitale de la douleur*, Paris 1966.

189. Freud, *Introductory Lectures*, pp. 171, 174.

190. Lacan, 'Situation de la psychanalyse', E, p. 466.

191. Lacan, 'Subversion du sujet', E, pp. 799–800; ES, p. 298.

192. For a brief history of the metaphor/metonymy distinction in Jakobson, see J.G. Merquior, *From Prague to Paris*, London 1986, pp. 19–33.

193. Barthes, *Eléments de sémiologie*, pp. 133–4.

194. Claude Lévi-Strauss, *The Savage Mind*, London 1972, pp. 205–8.

195. Jakobson, 'Two Aspects', p. 258.

196. Benveniste, 'Les Niveaux de l'analyse linguistique', in *Problèmes*.

197. Roman Jakobson and Morris Halle, 'Phonology and Phonetics', in Jakobson, *Selected Writings*, vol. 1, The Hague 1962.

198. Lacan, 'Fonction et champ', E, pp. 184–285; ES, p. 73, translation modified.

199. Cf. Barthes, *Eléments de sémiologie*, p. 133: a connoted system is one whose plane of expression is itself constituted by a system of signification.

200. André Martinet, *Elements of General Linguistics*, London 1964, p. 32.

201. André Martinet, 'La Phonologie', in *La Linguistique synchronique: Etudes et recherches*, Paris 1965, p. 69.

202. Lacan, S XX, p. 93.

203. Ibid., p. 108.

204. Roudinesco, vol. 2, p. 564.

205. Lévi-Strauss, *The Savage Mind*, p. 28, n. 1, p. 83.

206. Lacan, 'Le Nombre treize', p. 389. For a simpler version of the coins puzzle, see Martin Gardner, *Mathematical Puzzles and Diversions*, Harmondsworth 1965, pp. 33, 40–41.

207. Lacan, 'Le Nombre treize', p. 389, n. 1.

208. Lacan, 'Le Temps logique', E, p. 208.

209. Lacan, 'Fonction et champ', E, p. 287,; ES, p. 75.

210. Lacan, 'D'Une Question préliminaire, E, p. 548; ES, p. 193.

211. Lacan, S VII, p. 40.

212. Lacan, S I, p. 194; S II, p. 134.

213. Miller, 'Table commentée', E, p. 903; ES, p. 332.

214. Lacan, 'L'Instance de la lettre', E, p. 515; ES, p. 164.

215. Lacan, 'D'Une Question préliminaire', E, p. 557; ES, p. 200.

216. Lacan, 'Radiophonie', p. 68. The criticism is addressed primarily to the use

made of the metaphor formula by Laplanche and Leclaire in their 'L'Inconscient', pp. 301–2. Interpreting Lacan's formula as the algebraic

$$\frac{S}{S} \times \frac{S}{s} \to S' \frac{1}{s} \; (1)$$ they produce the new formula

$$\frac{S}{S} \times \frac{S}{s} \to \frac{\dfrac{S'}{s}}{\dfrac{S}{s}} \; II$$

in which the signifier S 'falls' to the level of a signified, but continues to function as a latent signifier. They argue that their schema accounts for essential elements of repression, of the relationship between the repressed unconscious and the preconscious, and of the structure of the unconscious chain. It can then (p. 309) be mapped on to the clinical structure

$$\frac{S'}{s} \quad Pcs$$

$$\frac{S}{S} \quad Ucs$$

In his Preface to Lemaire, pp. xii–xiii, Lacan attacks this formula for its reliance on the arithmetic proposition $\frac{1}{4} \cdot \frac{4}{16}$ and on the interpretation of the 'bar' as indicating 'Euclidean proportion'. For further discussion of this issue, see Martin Thom, 'The Unconscious Structured as a Language', in MacCabe, ed., *The Talking Cure*.

217. Lacan, 'L'Instance de la lettre', E, p. 515; ES, p. 164.
218. Lacan, 'D'Une Question préliminaire', E, p. 548–9; ES, pp. 153–4. For the original schema, see S II, p. 134.
219. Translator's note, ES, p. xi.
220. Lacan, S XX, p. 100.
221. Lacan, 'L'Instance de la lettre', E, pp. 502–3; ES, pp. 153–4.
222. Lacan, S XX, p. 118.
223. Ibid., p. 115.
224. Lacan, 'L'Etourdit', p. 40.
225. Lacan, 'Subversion du sujet', E, p. 805; ES, p. 303.
226. Lacan, S XX, p. 22.
227. Ibid., pp. 100, 108.
228. Lacan, 'Kant avec Sade', E, p. 774.
229. 'Yale University, Kanzer Seminar', p. 27.
230. Lacan, 'L'Etourdit', p. 9; 'Yale University', p. 26.
231. Ibid.
232. Ibid., pp. 26–30.
233. Lacan, 'L'Etourdit', p. 32; S XX, p. 84.
234. Mannoni, *Clefs pour l'imaginaire*, p. 53.
235. Cited, Turkle, *Psychoanalytic Politics*, p. 182.
236. Descombes, *Objects of All Sorts*, p. 178.
237. Jacques-Alain Miller, 'Théorie de la langue', *Ornicar?*, 1, 1975, cited, Roudinesco, vol. 2, p. 557. Shortly after the Congress, Miller did in fact go into analysis with Charles Melman.
238. Jacques-Alain Miller, 'La Suture (Eléments de la logique du significant)', *Cahiers pour l'analyse*, 1, January–February 1966, p. 38.
239. Jacques-Alain Miller and Jean Clavreul, 'Base nouvelle pour le Département de psychanalyse' (circular issued September 1974), cited, Roudinesco, vol. 2, p. 574.
240. Freud, *New Introductory Lectures*, p. 69.
241. Miller, 'Théorie', cited, Roudinesco, vol. 2, p. 577.
242. Ibid.
243. Lacan, S XX, p. 93.
244. Ibid., p. 126; *Télévision*, p. 21.

245. Ibid., cf. 'A la mémoire d'Ernest Jones', p. 711: 'A minimal composition of the battery of signifiers suffices to install in the signifying chain a duplicity which overlaps with its reduplication of the subject ...'

246. Milner, *L'Amour de la langue*, pp. 22, 104.

247. Lacan, 'Le Sinthôme', *Ornicar?*, 7, June–July 1976, p. 17.

248. Louis Wolfson, *Le Schizo et les langues*, Paris 1970, pp. 41–2. The best account of Wolfson in English is in Lecercle, *Philosophy Through the Looking-Glass*. For a more explicitly psychoanalytic reading, see Gori, *Le Corps et le signe*.

249. Geneviève Morel, 'Point final à une planète infernale', *Ornicar?*, 36, Spring 1986, pp. 88, 89. This issue of *Ornicar?* contains two other articles on Wolfson: Angel Encisco Bergé, 'La Langue maternelle dans la psychose', and Serge André, 'La Pulsion chez le schizophrène'.

6 The Dark Continent

1. Freud, 'Femininity', *New Introductory Lectures*, p. 113.

2. Relevant accounts will be found in Mitchell, *Psychoanalysis and Feminism*; Jacqueline Rose, *Sexuality in the Field of Vision*, London 1986; Mitchell and Rose, 'Introductions' to FS; see also Parveen Adams, 'Representation and Sexuality', *m/f*, 1, 1978; Sara Kofman, *The Enigma of Woman. Woman in Freud's Writings*, Ithaca and London 1985; Janet Sayers, 'Sexual Contradictions: On Freud, Psychoanalysis and Feminism', *Free Associations*, 1, 1985. The anonymous 'La Phase phallique', *Scilicet*, 1, 1968 (trans. 'The Phallic Phase' in FS) gives a good account of the respective positions of Freud and Jones. A dogmatically Lacanian survey of the whole debate can be read in Moustapha Safouan, *La Sexualité féminine dans la doctrine freudienne*, Paris 1976 (one chapter translated in FS).

3. Ernest Jones, 'The Early Development of Female Sexuality', IJPA, 8, 1927, p. 459.

4. Freud, 'Femininity', p. 132; 'The Dissolution of the Oedipus Complex', SE XIX, p. 179.

5. Freud, undated letter to Marie Bonaparte, Jones, *Life and Work*, vol. 2, p. 468.

6. Freud, 'Femininity', p. 116.

7. Hélène Deutsch, 'The Significance of Masochism in the Mental Life of Women', IJPA, 11, 1930, p. 48; 'The Psychology of Women in Relation to the Functions of Reproduction', IJPA, 6, 1925, p. 171.

8. Freud, 'The Psychogenesis of a Case of Female Homosexuality', SE XVIII, p. 171.

9. Freud, The Question of Lay Analysis, SE XX, p. 212.

10. Freud, 'Some Psychical Consequences of the Anatomical Distinction between the Sexes', SE XIX, p. 248.

11. Freud, 'Female Sexuality', SE XXI, p. 241.

12. Ibid., p. 226.

13. Eric Partridge, *A Dictionary of Clichés*, fifth edn, London 1978.

14. Freud, *The Interpretation of Dreams*, pp. 453–4.

15. Cf. Toril Moi, 'Representation of Patriarchy: Sexuality and Epistemology in Freud's Dora', in Charles Bernheimer and Claire Kahane, eds, *In Dora's Case*, London 1985, p. 198: 'Freud's epistemology is clearly phallocentric. The male is the bearer of knowledge; he alone has the power to penetrate woman and text: woman's role is to let herself be penetrated by such truth.'

16. Freud, 'On Transformations of Instinct as Exemplified in Anal Erotism', SE XVII, p. 129; 'Femininity', p. 135.

17. Safouan, *La Sexualité féminine*, p. 38.

18. Lacan, S III, p. 223.

19. Lacan, 'Propos directifs', E, p. 727; FS, p. 89.

20. Lacan, 'Discours de clôture des journées sur les psychoses chez l'enfant', *Recherches*, December 1968, p. 151.

21. Serge Leclaire, *Démasquer le réel*, Paris 1983, p. 21, n. 9.
22. Deutsch, 'The Significance of Masochism', pp. 59–60; 'The Psychology of Women', p. 413.
23. 'A.E. Narjani' (Marie Bonaparte), 'Considérations médicales sur les cause anatomiques de la frigidité chez la femme', *Bruxelles médical*, April 1924, cited, Bertin, *Marie Bonaparte*, p. 141; cf. pp. 142, 171–2.
24. Marie Bonaparte, *Sexualité de la femme*, pp. 242–5, and n.
25. Ibid., pp. 127–8.
26. Freud, 'Femininity', p. 132.
27. Freud, 'Medusa's Head', SE XVIII; Lacan, S II, p. 196.
28. Eugénie Lemoine-Luccioni, *Partage des femmes*, Paris 1982, pp. 11, 70.
29. Ibid., pp. 57, 93.
30. Piera Aulagnier-Spairani, 'La Fémininite', in Aulagnier–Spairani *et al.*, *Le Désir et la perversion*, Paris 1981, p. 66; pp. 71–2, n. 1.
31. Jones, 'The Early Development', p. 468; Lacan, 'Propos directifs', E, p. 735; ES, p. 97.
32. Aulagnier-Spairani, p. 71.
33. Lacan, 'La Famille', 8° 40–7; Karen Horney, 'The Flight from Womanhood: The Masculinity Complex in Woman, As Viewed by Men and Women', in *Feminine Psychology*, New York 1973, p. 60.
34. Lacan, 'La Signification du phallus', E, p. 687, FS, p. 77; ES, p. 283.
35. Lacan, 'Propos directifs', E, p. 733; FS, p. 94.
36. Freud, 'Psycho-Analytic Notes on an Autobiographical Account of a Case of Paranoia (*Dementia Paranoides*)' SE XII, pp. 63–4.
37. Georges de Morsier, L'Erotomanie', *Annales de psychologie*, 20, 1927.
38. Lacan, 'Yale University, Kanzer Seminar', p. 9.
39. Gaëtan Gatian de Clérambault, 'Erotomanie', *Bulletin de la Société clinique de médicine mentale*, December 1920; 'Délires passionnelles; érotomanie, revendication, jalousie', *Bulletin*, February 1921, reprinted, *Ornicar?*, 32, Spring 1932; 'Dépit érotomanique après possession', *Bulletin*, June 1921; 'Erotomanie pure, érotomanie associée', *Bulletin*, July 1921, reprinted, *Nouvelle Revue de Psychanalyse*, 21, Spring 1981, preceded by André Green, 'Clérambault et les délires passionnelles'.
40. Lacan, S III, pp. 53–4, 61.
41. François Perrier, 'De l'érotomanie', in Aulagnier-Spairani *et al.*, *Le Désir et la perversion*, pp. 137–8.
42. Aulagnier-Spairani, p. 76.
43. Lemoine-Luccioni, p. 93.
44. Perrier, pp. 150–51.
45. Freud, 'The Taboo of Virginity', SE XII, p. 204; *Leonardo*, p. 125.
46. A. Hesnard, 'Glossaire', in Freud, *Essais de psychanalyse*, Paris 1972, p. 276.
47. Phyllis Grosskurth, *Melanie Klein*, London 1985, p. 391.
48. Lacan, 'Some Reflections on the Ego', p. 13.
49. Lacan, 'Fonction et champ', E, p. 317 n.; ES, p. 112, n. 108; cf. Wilden, p. 151.
50. Leclaire, *Démasquer le réel*, p. 69.
51. Lacan, S II, p. 315.
52. Lacan, S III, pp. 200, 257.
53. Ibid., pp. 358–9.
54. Lacan, S II, p. 315; 'La Signification du phallus', E, p. 692; ES, p. 288; FS, p. 82.
55. Lacan, 'D'Une Question Préliminaire', E, p. 543; ES, p. 189.
56. Otto Fenichel, 'The Symbolic Equation: "Girl = Phallus"', *Psychoanalytic Quarterly*, 28, 1949.
57. Lacan, 'D'Une Question préliminaire', E, p. 565, n. 1; ES, p. 224, n. 25.
58. Sheridan adds to the confusion by rendering *elle* as 'she', and thus suggesting that it is 'the girl' sho suggests the theme of the paper; the pronoun in fact refers to *la parité* (the equation) and should be rendered as *it*.
59. Cited, Wilden, p. 187.

60. Lacan, 'La Signification du phallus', E, p. 688; ES, p. 282; FS, p. 76.
61. Ibid., cf. Klein, 'The Importance of Symbol Formation'.
62. Luce Irigaray, *Ce Sexe qui n'en est pas un*, Paris 1977, p. 78.
63. Nicole Kress-Rosen, 'Hélène Deutsch, une théorie de la femme', *Ornicar?*, 15, Summer 1978, p. 46.
64. Kress-Rosen, p. 46, citing Freud (trans. Anne Berman), *Nouvelles Conférences sur la psychanalyse*, Paris 1971, p. 168 (first edn 1936); Freud, *Neue Folge der Vorlesungen zur Erführung in dies Psycholanalyse*, Frankfurt am Main 1978, p. 104. The German text cited conforms to that of the *Gessammelte Werke*.
65. Freud, *Nouvelles Conférences*; *Nueue Folge*, p. 103.
66. For a cogent discussion of the SE translation, see Bruno Bettelheim, *Freud and Man's Soul*, London 1983.
67. Safouan, *La Sexualité féminine*, p. 11; FS, p. 124.
68. Lacan, S XX, p. 68.
69. Serge Leclaire, *Psychanalyser*, Paris 1975, p. 163.
70. Leclaire, *Demasquer le réel*, p. 97.
71. Serge Leclaire, *On Tue un enfant*, Paris 1981, p. 32.
72. Juan David Nasio, 'Métaphore et phallus', in Leclaire, *Démasquer le réel*, pp. 101–17.
73. Lemoine-Luccioni, pp. 9, 45, 71.
74. Ibid., p. 23.
75. Jane Gallop, *Feminism and Psychoanalysis*, p. 95.
76. Anonymous review of Karen Horney, *La Psychologie de la femme*, Scilicet, 5, 1975, pp. 153–9; Frederic Jameson, 'Imaginary and Symbolic in Lacan', *Yale French Studies*, 55/56, 1977, pp. 352–3 and n. 14.
77. Freud, 'Negation', pp. 235.
78. Maude Mannoni, *Le Premier Rendez-vous avec le psychanalyste*, Paris 1965; *L'Enfant, sa 'maladie' et les autres*, Paris 1971; *Le Cas Dominique*, Paris 1971.
79. Lacan, 'L'Instance de la lettre', E, p. 522; ES, p. 170.
80. Jacques Derrida, 'La Facteur de la vérité', *Poétique*, 21, 1975.
81. Catherine Baliteau, 'La Fin d'une parade misogyne: la psychanalyse lacanienne', *Les Temps modernes*, 348, July 1975, p. 1952. The title alludes to Politzer's *Fin d'une parade philosophique*.
82. Lacan, 'Fonction et champ', E, p. 271; ES, p. 61.
83. Ernest Jones, 'The Phallic Phase', IJPA, 14, 1933, p. 33.
84. Lacan, S III, p. 197.
85. Freud, 'Fragment of an Analysis of a Case of Hysteria', SE VIII, p. 97.
86. Lacan, S III, p. 192.
87. Lacan, 'La Famille', 8° 40–3.
88. Lacan, S XI, p. 8; FFC, p. 3.
89. Freud, 'Fragment', p. 20.
90. Lacan, 'Intervention sur le transfert', E, p. 219; FS, p. 69.
91. Ibid., p. 222; p. 68.
92. Michèle Montrelay, *L'Ombre et le nom*, Paris 1977, p. 28.
93. Ibid., p. 139.
94. The journal's very title is an index of its tendency towards whimsicality; it derives from *mais, où, est, donc, ni, car*, the list of conjunctions drilled into generation after generation of French schoolchildren. Hence the rather facile advertisement: 'Mais où es donc *Ornicar?*', followed by a list of bookshops ('So where is *Ornicar?*, Where can I get it?').
95. Gérard Wajeman, 'La Convulsion de Saint-Médard', *Ornicar?*, 15.
96. Lacan, 'Propos directifs', E, p. 728; FS, p. 89: 'The representatives of the female sex'.
97. Gallop, p. 29.
98. Lacan, S XX, . 13; Seminar of 11 February 1975, cited Stephen Heath, 'Difference', *Screen*, vol. 19, no. 3, Autumn 1978, p. 61.
99. Lacan, '*Hamlet* III: Le Désir de la mère', *Ornicar?*, 25, Autumn 1982, p. 23.
100. Lacan, 'La Famille', 8° 42–8; 8° 40–16.

101. Lacan, 'La Psychiatrie anglaise', pp. 304–5.

102. Lacan, S II, p. 305.

103. Lacan, 'Position de l'inconscient', E, p. 728.

104. Freud, 'Femininity', p. 116.

105. Lacan, S XX, p. 54.

106. Ibid.

107. Lacan, 'L'Etourdit', pp. 20, 21.

108. Eric Laurent, 'Ce que savait Melanie', *Ornicar?*, 24, Autumn 1981.

109. Lacan, 'Propos directifs', E, p. 727; FS, p. 89.

110. Lacan, S XX,; p. FS, p. 146.

111. Lacan, 'L'Etourdit', p. 21.

112. Charles Melman, 'Que veut une femme?', *Ornicar?*, 15, p. 31.

113. Dominique Kalfon, 'Ma Mère est une femme', *Ornicar?*, 25, Autumn 1981, p. 68.

114. Freud, 'The Taboo of Virginity', p. 205; Safouan, *La Sexualité féminine*, p. 131, n. 1.

115. Ibid., pp. 25, 157. The reference is to Thomas B. Hess and Linda Nochlin, eds, *Woman as Sex Object*, London 1973.

116. 'Cathy', 'La Naissance d'une secte', *Libération*, 1 June 1977, reprinted, Association du mouvement pour les luttes féministes, *Chroniques d'une imposture: Du Mouvement de libération des femmes à une marque commerciale*, Paris 1981, unnumbered pages.

117. Aulagnier-Spairani *et al.*, *Le Désir et la perversion*, pp. 58, 59, 84.

118. Lemoine-Luccioni, p. 92. The reference is to Marguerite Duras and Xavière Gauthier, *Les Parleuses*, Paris 1977. Lemoine-Luccioni gives the publisher as des femmes; it is in fact Minuit, and des femmes have never published anything by Duras. Given the importance of light–darkness metaphors in the debate on femininity, the substitution of *des femmes* (women) for *minuit* (midnight) is very intriguing. For an exploration of the many slips and inconsistencies in Lemoine-Luccioni, see Gallop, pp. 92–112.

119. Leclaire, in *Des femmes en mouvement hebdo 1*, cited, Marie-Jo Dhavernas, 'Des Divans profonds comme des tombeaux', in *Chroniques d'une imposture*.

120. Jones, 'The Early Development', p. 467.

121. Lasch, 'Introduction' to Chasseguet-Smirgel, *The Ego Ideal*, p. xiii.

122. Nicole Kress-Rosen, 'Sociolinguistique féminine', *Ornicar?*, 19, Autumn 1979. The texts under discussion are Robin Lakoff, *Language and Woman's Place*, New York 1975, and Marina Yaguello, *Les Mots et les femmes*, Paris 1978. *Parole de femme* is a reference to Annie Leclerc, *Parole de femme*, Paris 1974. For a political critique of Leclerc, see Christine Delphy, 'Proto-feminism and Anti-Feminism', 'The Main Enemy', *Explorations in Feminism*, 3, n.d.

123. Lemoine-Luccioni, p. 80.

124. Cited, Roudinesco, vol. 2, p. 430.

125. Moustapha Safouan, *Etudes sur l'Oedipe*, Paris 1974, p. 206.

126. Danièle Silvestre, 'Chercher la femme', *Ornicar?*, 25, Autumn 1982, p. 61.

127. Dora and St Teresa are not the only women to have been silenced by Lacan. Following the publication of *Speculum, de l'autre femme* in 1974, Luce Irigary was expelled from the EFP and the courses she taught at Vincennes were suspended. She comments in an interview entitled 'Women's Exile', *Ideology and Consciousness*, 1, May 1977, p. 71: 'The meaning of this expulsion is clear; only men may say what female pleasure consists of. Women are not allowed to speak.' In 1979 Lacan refused to allow Montrelay to use EFP premises for a proposed seminar on male sexuality: 'Her opponents accused her all along of being a feminist at heart rather than an analyst'; Monique David-Menard, 'Lacanians Against Lacan', *Socialtext*, 6, Fall 1982, p. 89. Cf. Nicolas Francion, 'Almanach de la Dissolution', *L'Ane*, 1, April–May 1982, p. 24.

128. Leclaire, *Psychanalyser*, p. 132.

129. For a discussion of the translation problems the terms pose, see Jane Gallop, 'Beyond the *Jouissance* Principle', *Representations*, 7, Summer 1984. It transpires, rather late in the debate, that *jouissance* is in fact given in the OED.

130. Richard Crashaw, 'In Memory of the Vertuous and Learned Lady Madre de

Teresa that sought an early Martyrdome', *The Poems of Richard Crashaw*, ed. L.C. Martin, Oxford 1957, p. 134.

131. Lacan, S XX, pp. 9–18.

132. Gallop, *Feminism and Psychoanalysis*, p. 30.

133. Lacan, 'La Psychanalyse et son enseignement', E, p. 452.

134. Lacan, S I, p. 248; S II, p. 92. Cf. Hegel, *The Phenomenology*, pp. 234–6.

135. Lacan, 'Propos directifs', E, p. 727; FS, p. 89.

136. Lacan, 'Subversion du sujet', E, p. 821; ES, p. 319.

137. Jean Laplanche, *Vie et mort en psychanalyse*, Paris 1977, p. 157 f.; on the Nirvana principle, see Freud, *Beyond the Pleasure Principle*; 'The Economic Problem of Masochism', SE XIX.

138. Lacan, S XI, p. 162; FFC, p. 177.

139. Laplanche, *Vie et mort*, p. 161.

140. Lacan, *Télévision*, p. 35.

141. Lacan, S XVII, 'L'Envers de la psychanalyse' (unpublished), cited, Juranville, *Lacan et la philosophie*, p. 172.

142. Lacan, 'Subversion du sujet', E, p. 815; ES, p. 313.

143. Lacan, 'La Relation d'objet et les structures freudiennes', summary by Pontalis, *Bulletin de psychologie*, vol. 10 no. 12, 15 May 1957, p. 743. In the seminar on *Hamlet*, *Ornicar?*, 26/27, Summer 1983, p. 9, the *Che vuoi?* motif is used to illustrate the constitution of subjectivity in the other.

144. Jacques Cazotte, *Le Diable amoureux*, Paris 1981, p. 113.

145. Freud, 'Notes upon a Case of Obsessional Neurosis', SE X, pp. 167–8.

146. Lacan, S XI, p. 212; FFC, p. 234, translation modified.

147. Lacan, 'La Relation d'objet', p. 743.

148. Leclaire, *Psychanalyser*, p. 145.

149. Georges Bataille, *L'Erotisme*, Paris 1965, p. 100.

150. Georges Bataille, *Histoire de l'oeil*, in *Oeuvres complètes*, vol. 1, Paris 1971.

151. Bataille, *L'Erotisme*, p. 262.

152. Freud and Breuer, *Studies in Hysteria*, SE II, p. 232.

153. Marie Bonaparte, 'De l'Essentielle Ambivalence d'Eros', RFP, 12, 1948; Georges Parcheminey, cited Bataille, *L'Erotisme*, p. 247.

154. Leclaire, *Démasquer le réel*, especially p. 78.

155. François Perrier, 'Démoisation', in *La Chaussée d'Antin*, vol. 2, Paris 1978, pp. 163–78.

156. Lacan, 'D'Une Question préliminaire', E, p. 583 and n. 1; ES, p. 225 and n. 40.

157. Georges Bataille, *Madame Edwarda*, in *Oeuvres complétes* vol. 3, Paris 1971, pp. 20–21.

158. Lacan, S XX, p. 71; FS, p. 147.

159. Lacan, S XX, p. 102.

160. Freud, 'Some General Remarks on Hysterical Attacks', SE IX, p. 230.

161. Lacan, S XI, pp. 71, 76; FFC, pp. 74, 80; Paul Valéry, letter of 1917 to Albert Morel, *Œuvres*, vol. 1, Paris 1959, p. 1621.

162. Lacan, S XI, p. 71; FFC, p. 75.

163. Mulvey, 'Visual Pleasure and Narrative Cinema', p. 11.

164. Lacan, 'La Science et la vérite', E, p. 832.

165. Joan Rivière, 'Womanliness as Masquerade', IJPA, 10, 1929, p. 303.

166. Lacan, S XI, p. 176; FFC, p. 193.

167. Lacan, S XX, p. 34.

168. Lacan, S III, pp. 198–9.

169. Lacan, S XX, p. 13.

170. Lacan, S III, p. 198.

171. Danièle Silvestre, 'Chercher la femme', *Ornicar?*, 25, 1982, p. 58.

7 Jacques-Marie Emile Lacan: *Curriculum Vitae* 1901–81

1. Primary sources are as follows: *International Journal of Psycho-Analysis: Revue Française de psychanalyse; La Psychanalyse; Scilicet; Ornicar?*; Jacques-Alain Miller, ed., *La Scission de 1953*, and *L'Excommunication*; Sherry Turkle, *Psychoanalytic Politics*; Elisabeth Roudinesco, *La Bataille de cent ans*, vols 1 and 2. To avoid overloading the text, specific references have not been provided for information drawn from these sources; all such information is readily traceable. Indeed, given the overlap between the various accounts, detailed references would result in confusion rather than enlightenment. Detailed references for other sources are given in notes.

2. Joël Dor, *Bibliographie des travaux de Jacques Lacan*, Paris 1983.

3. Denis Hollier, *Le Collège de sociologie*, p. 200, n.

4. Postcard dated 8 January 1933, reproduced as cover illustration to *Ornicar?*, 29, Summer 1984.

5. Lacan, 'Exposé général de nos travaux scientifiques', PP, p. 401.

6. Lacan, preface to selection from *Ecrits*, Seuil, Collection 'Points' 1969, p. 9; cover note to 'Points' edition of PP.

7. Lacan, 'Le Sinthôme', *Ornicar?*, 7, June–July 1976, p. 7.

8. 'Interventions de Lacan à la Société Psychanalytique de Paris', *Ornicar?*, 31, Autumn 1984.

9. Lacan, 'De Nos Antécédents', E, p. 67, n. 1.

10. Lacan, 'Propos sur la causalité psychique', E, pp. 184–5; cf. 'A la mémoire de Ernest Jones', E, p. 697.

11. Jones, *Life and Work*, vol. 3, p. 223.

12. Uwe Henrick Peters, *Anna Freud. A Life Devoted to Children*, London 1985, p. 144.

13. Lacan, 'La Direction de la cure', E, p. 600; ES, p. 239.

14. Cf. Henri Wallon, *Les Origines du caractère*.

15. René Laforgue, 'Scotomization in Schizophrenia'.

16. Miller, *Entretien*, pp. 63–4.

17. Lacan, 'La Psychiatrie anglaise', pp. 302, 304–5.

18. Reproduced, *Magazine littéraire*, 121, February 1977, p. 73. The photograph was taken on the occasion of a private performance of Picasso's *Le Désir attrapé par la queue* at the home of Michel Leiris. Cf. Simone de Beauvoir, *Mémoires d'une jeune fille rangée*, Paris 1975, pp. 651–2.

19. Lacan, 'Propos sur la causalité psychique', E, p. 151.

20. Lacan, 'La Psychiatrie anglaise', p. 293.

21. Lacan, S VII, p. 135.

22. On Lacan's interest in and use of games theory, see Nathalie Charraud, 'La Psychanalyse et la théorie des jeux', *Ornicar?*, 24, Autumn 1981.

23. Cf. Laurence Bataille, 'D'Une Pratique', in *L'Ombilic du rêve*.

24. Juliette Boutonnier, 'A Propos du *Problème de la psychogénèse des névroses et des psychoses*', *Evolution Psychiatrique*, 1951, p. 362.

25. W.R. Bion and John Rickman, 'Intra-Group Tensions in Therapy. Their Study as the Task of the Group', *The Lancet*, 27 November 1943; cf. Bion, 'Psychiatry at a Time of Crisis', *British Journal of Medical Psychiatry*, 21, 1948.

26. Lacan, 'La Chose freudienne', E, p. 429; ES, p. 139. See John Rickman, 'The Factor of Number in Individual and Group Dynamics', *Selected Contributions to Psycho-analysis*, London 1957.

27. Grosskurth, *Melanie Klein*, pp. 376–7, 389–90.

28. Bertin, *Marie Bonaparte*, p. 236.

29. Peters, *Anna Freud*, p. 188.

30. Lacan, 'De Nos Antécédents', E, p. 71.

31. Lacan, 'Fonction et champ', E, pp. 315–16; ES, pp. 100–101.

32. Marie Bonaparte, letter of 14 January 1952 to Rudolph Loewenstein, cited, Bertin, p. 222.

33. On *La Nouvelle Critique*'s political style at this time, see Maxime Rodinson, 'Self-Criticism', in *Cult, Ghetto, State*, London 1983; Pascal Delwit and Jean-Michel Dewaele, 'The Stalinists of Anti-Communism', *Socialist Register*, 1984.
34. Lacan, 'Fonction et champ', E, p. 237; ES, p. 31.
35. Marie Bonaparte, letter of 2 July 1945 to Loewenstein, cited, Bertin, p. 222.
36. Cited, ibid., p. 245.
37. Cited, ibid., pp. 245–6.
38. Lacan, S II, pp. 183–4.
39. Lacan, 'De Nos Antécédents', E, p. 72, n. 1.
40. Lacan, S I, pp. 63–74.
41. On the translation problems involved in Freud's 'Negation', see Laplanche and Pontalis, *The Language*, pp. 261–2.
42. The primary reference is to Anna Freud, *The Ego and the Mechanisms of Defence*.
43. The primary reference is to Michael Balint, *Primary Love and Psychoanalytic Technique*, London 1952.
44. Lacan, S II, pp. 225–40.
45. Lacan, 'Direction de la cure', E, p. 612; ES, p. 250.
46. Paris 1956.
47. Paris 1956.
48. Ernest Jones, 'The Theory of Symbolism', *British Journal of Psychology*, 9, 1916.
49. Lacan, 'Fontion et champ' E, p. 294; ES, p. 82.
50. Lacan, letter of 5 August 1960 to D.W. Winnicott, *Ornicar?*, 33, Summer 1985, p. 8.
51. Lacan, S XX, p. 50.
52. Lacan, letter to Winnicott, p. 10.
53. Lacan, S XI, p. 9; FFC, p. 3.
54. Cited, Roudinesco, vol. 2, p. 571.
55. Paris, 1964.
56. Montrelay, *L'Ombre et le nom*, pp. 9–23.
57. Anzieu, 'La Psychanalyse au service de la psychologie', p. 67.
58. Lacan's choice of terminology is curious, and has never really been explained. *La passe* can mean 'pass' or 'passage', whilst the verbal phrase *être en passe de...* is equivalent to 'to be on the way to [doing something]'. *Une passe* is also a 'trick', in the prostitution sense. A *passeur* is a ferryman, but also a smuggler, whilst *un passant* is a passer-by. For a very negative first-hand account of *la passe*, see Jeanne Fauvret-Saada, 'Excusez-moi, je ne faisais que passer', *Les Temps modernes*, 371, June 1977; she describes the experience as being akin to being put through a food-grinder. A much more positive account will be found in Schneiderman, *Jacques Lacan*.
59. Full text reproduced, Contat and Rybalka, *Les Ecrits de Sartre*, p. 463.
60. In Charles Posner, ed., *Reflections on the Revolution in France: 1968*, Harmondsworth 1970.
61. In François Perrier, *La Chaussée d'Antin/Antienne*, pp. 181–7.
62. Paris, 1964; Michèle Montrelay, 'Recherches sur la fémininité', in *L'Ombre et le nom*, pp. 55–82; trans. Parveen Adams, 'Inquiry into Femininity', *m/f*, 1, 1978.
63. Cf. 'Women's Exile Interview with Luce Irigaray', *Ideology and Consciousness*, 1, May 1978. See also M. Nguyen, 'Les Exclues du Département de psychanalyse de Vincennes', *Les Temps modernes*, 342, January 1975; Gilles Deleuze and Jean-François Lyotard, 'A Propos du Département de psychanalyse', ibid.
64. For day-to-day accounts of the events leading up to and following the dissolution, see Dorgeuille, *La Seconde Mort de Jacques Lacan*, and Nicolas Francion, 'Almanach de la dissolution 1980–81', *L'Ane*, 1, April–May 1981.

Bibliography

For works by Lacan, see 'Jacques-Marie Emile Lacan: *Curriculum Vitae 1901–81*. Where relevant, the date of the first publication is given in parentheses immediately after the author's name; in the case of Freud, the date given is that of composition.

Adams, Parveen, 'Representation and Sexuality', *m/f*, 1978.
Ades, Dawn, *Dada and Surrealism Reviewed*, London: Arts Council of Great Britain, 1978.
—— *Dali*, London: Thames & Hudson, 1982.
Allendy, René, 'La Libido', *Le Disque vert*, 1924.
Alquié, Ferdinand, 'Le Surréalisme et la psychanalyse', *La Table ronde*, 108, 1956.
—— *La Philosophie du surréalisme*, Paris: Flammarion, 1956.
—— ed., *Le Surréalisme, Entretiens dirigés par Ferdinand Aliquié*, Paris and The Hague: Mouton, 1968.
Althusser, Louis, *For Marx*, trans. Ben Brewster, Harmondsworth: Penguin, 1969.
—— *Lenin and Philosophy and Other Essays*, trans. Ben Brewster, London: New Left Books, 1971.
—— 'La Découverte du Docteur Freud', in Léon Chertok, ed., *Dialogue franco-soviétique sur la psychanalyse*, Toulouse: Privat, 1984.
Anderson, Perry, *In the Tracks of Historical Materialism*, London: Verso, 1983.
Andler, Charles, *La Vie de Lucien Herr*, Paris: Rieder, 1932.
André, Serge, 'La Pulsion chez le schizophrène', *Ornicar?*, 36, Spring 1983.
Ane, 'Dossier – The Mother in the Unconscious', trans. Ben Brewster, *m/f*, 8, 1983.
Anzieu, Didier, 'La Psychanalyse au service de la psychologie', *Nouvelle Revue de Psychanalyse*, 20, Autumn 1979.
Aparicio, Sol, 'La Forclusion, préhistoire d'un concept, *Ornicar?*, 28, Spring 1984.
Aragon, Louis, (1926) *Le Paysan de Paris*, Paris: Folio, 1972.

—— and Breton, André, 'Le Cinquantenaire de l'hystérie', *La Révolution surréaliste*, 11, March 1928.

Archard, David, *Consciousness and the Unconscious*, London: Hutchinson, 1985.

Assoun, Paul-Laurent, 'Freud, Copernic, Darwin', *Ornicar?*, 22/23, Spring 1981.

Audoin, Philippe, *Breton*, Paris: Gallimard, 'Pour une bibliothèque idéale', 1970.

Aulagnier-Spairani, Piera, *et al.*, *Le Désir et la perversion*, Paris: Seuil, 'Points', 1981.

Austin, J.L., *Philosophical Papers*, third edn, Oxford: The Clarendon Press, 1971.

Backès, Catherine, 'Lacan ou la porte-parole', *Critique*, 249, February 1968.

Balakian, Anna, *André Breton*, New York: Oxford University Press, 1971.

Balint, Michael, *Primary Love and Psychoanalytic Technique*, London: The Hogarth Press and The Institute of Psycho-Analysis, 1959.

Baliteau, Catherine, 'La Fin d'une parade misogyne: la psychanalyse lacanienne', *Les Temps modernes*, 348, July 1975.

Bär, Eugen, 'The Language of the Unconscious According to Lacan', *Semiotica*, 3, 1971.

Barrett, Michèle and McIntosh, Mary, 'Narcissism and the Family: A Critique of Lasch', *New Left Review*, 135, September–October 1982.

Barthes, Roland, *Le Degré zéro de l'écriture, suivi de Eléments de sémiologie*, Paris: Gonthier, 1970.

—— 'L'Ancienne Rhétorique', *Communications*, 16, 1970.

Bataille, Georges, *L'Erotisme*, Paris: UGE/10/18, 1965.

—— *Œuvres complètes*, vol. 1, Paris: Gallimard, 1971.

—— *Œuvres complètes*, vol. 3, Paris: Gallimard, 1971.

—— *Œuvres complètes*, vol. 7, Paris: Gallimard, 1976.

Bataille, Laurence, *L'Ombilic du rêve. D'Une Pratique de la psychanalyse*, Paris: Seuil, 1987.

Beauvoir, Simone de, (1949) *Le Deuxième Sexe*, Paris: Gallimard, 'Idées', 1981.

—— *Mémoires d'une jeune fille rangée*, Paris: Folio, 1975.

Beirnaert, Louis, *Aux Frontières de l'acte analytique. La Bible, Saint Ignace, Freud et Lacan*, Paris: Seuil, 1987.

Bellour, Raymond and Clément, Catherine, eds, *Claude Lévi-Strauss*, Paris: Gallimard, 'Idées', 1979.

Benayoun, Robert, *Erotique du surréalisme*, Paris: Pauvert, 1964.

Bénichou, Paul, *Morales du grand siècle*, Paris: Gallimard, 1948.

Benjamin, Walter, *One-Way Street*, London: New Left Books, 1979.

Benveniste, Emile, *Problèmes de linguistique générale*, Paris: Gallimard, 1966.

Benvenuto, Bice and Kennedy, Roger, *The Works of Jacques Lacan*, London: Free Association Books, 1986.

Bercherie, Paul, *Les Fondements de la clinique. Histoire et structure du savoir psychiatrique*, Paris: Navarin, 1980.

—— *Genèse des concepts freudiens*, Paris: Navarin, 1983.

—— 'The Quadrifocal Oculary: The Epistemology of the Freudian Heritage', trans. David Macey, *Economy and Society*, vol. 15, no. 1, February 1986.

Bergé, Angel Encisco, 'La Langue maternelle dans la psychose', *Ornicar?*, 36, Spring 1986.

Bernard, J.-P, A., *Le Parti Communiste Français et la question littéraire (1921–1939)*, Grenoble: Presses Universitaires de Grenoble, 1972.

Bernheimer, Charles and Kahane, Claire, eds., *In Dora's Case. Freud, Hysteria, Feminism*, London: Virago, 1985.

Bertin, Celia, *Marie Bonaparte: A Life*, London: Quartet, 1983.

Bettelheim, Bruno, *Freud and Man's Soul*, London: Chatto, 1983.

—— *Surviving the Holocaust*, London: Flamingo, 1986.

Bion, W.R., 'Psychiatry at a Time of Crisis', *British Journal of Medical Psychology*, 21, 1948.

—— and Rickman, John, 'Intra-Group Tensions in Therapy. Their Study as the Task of the Group', *The Lancet*, 27 November 1943.

Biro, A., and Passeron, R., *Dictionnaire général du surréalisme et de ses environs*, Paris: PUF, 1982.

Blanchot, Maurice, 'Freud', *Nouvelle Revue Française*, September 1956.

Blanck, Gertrude and Blanck, Rubin, *Ego Psychology: Theory and Practice*, New York: Columbia University Press, 1974.

Bloch, Oscar, avec la collaboration de W. Von Wartburg, *Dictionnaire étymologique de la langue française*, Paris: PUF, 1932, 2 vols.

Blondel, Charles, 'L'Activité mentale selon Freud: moi et libido', *Revue philosophique*, 96, July–December 1923.

—— *Introduction à la psychologie collective*, Paris: Librairie Armand Colin, 1928.

Boileau, *Œuvres*, Paris: Garnier, 1957.

Bonaparte, Marie, 'Le Cas de Mme. Lefebvre', RFP, 1, 1927.

—— (1933) *Edgar Poe, Sa Vie - son œuvre. Etude analytique*, Paris: PUF, *Study of the Child*, 1, 1945.

—— 'De l'Essentielle Ambivalence d'Eros', RFP, 12, 1948.

—— (1933) *Edgar Poe, Sa Vie - son oeuvre. Etude analytique*, Paris: PUF, 1958, 3 vols.

—— *Sexualité de la femme*, Paris: UGE 10/18, 1977.

Bonnafé, Lucien, *et al.*, 'La Psychanalyse, idéologie réactionnaire', *La Nouvelle Critique*, June 1949.

Bonnet, Marguerite, *André Breton: Naissance de l'aventure surréaliste*, Paris: Librairie José Corti, 1975.

Boschetti, Anna, *Sartre et 'Les Temps modernes'*, Paris: Minuit, 1985.

Boutonnier, Juliette, 'A Propos du *Problème de la psychogenèse des névroses et des psychoses'*, *Evolution psychiatrique*, 1951.

Boutroux, Emile, *Pages choisies*, Paris: Larousse, 1915.

Bowie, Malcolm, *Freud, Proust and Lacan: Theory as Fiction*, Cambridge: Cambridge University Press, 1987.

Breton, André, (1924) *Les Pas perdus*, Paris: Gallimard, 'Idées', 1974

—— (1924/1929–30) *Manifestes du surréalisme*, Paris: Gallimard, 'Idées', 1972

—— (1928) *Nadja*, Paris: Folio, 1972

—— 'La Médicine mentale devant le surréalisme', *Surréalisme au Service de la Révolution*, 2, October 1930.

—— (1932) *Les Vases communicants*, Paris: Gallimard, 'Idées', 1970.

—— (1937) *L'Amour fou*, Paris: Folio, 1976.

—— (1940) *Anthologie de l'humour noir*, Paris: Livre de Poche, 1970.

—— *Situation du surréalisme entre les deux guerres*, Paris and Algiers: Fontaine, 1945.

—— (1952) *Entretiens*, Paris: Gallimard, 'Idées', 1973.

—— *Signe ascendant*, Paris: Gallimard, 'Poésie', 1968.

—— and Eluard, Paul, (1930) *L'Immaculée Conception*, Paris: Seghers, 1961.

—— and Soupault, Philippe, (1920) *Les Champs magnétiques*, Paris: Gallimard, 'Poésie', 1971.

Brewster, Ben, 'Structuralism in Film Criticism', *Screen*, vol. 12, no. 1, Spring 1971.

—— , Stephen Heath and Colin MacCabe, 'Comment', *Screen*, vol. 16, no. 2, Summer 1975.

Brunschwicg, Léon, *Le Progrès de la conscience dans la philosophie occidentale*, Paris: PUF, 1953.

—— *La Connaissance de soi*, Paris: PUF, 1955.

Buñuel, Luis, *My Last Breath*, trans. Abigail Israel, London: Jonathan Cape, 1984.

Buscombe, Edward, *et al.*, 'Statement: Psychoanalysis and Film', *Screen*, vol. 16, n. 4, 1975–76.

Cardinal, Roger and Short, Robert Stuart, *Surrealism: Permanent Revelation*, London: Studio Vista, 1970.

Carr, Helen, 'The Love that Transforms Life and Gives it Meaning', *Women's Review*, 12, October 1986.

Carroll, Lewis, *The Annotated Alice*, Martin Gardner, ed., Harmondsworth: Penguin, 1965.

Carrouges, Michel, *André Breton et les données fondamentales du surréalisme*, Paris: Gallimard, 1950.

Cazotte, Jacques, *Le Diable amoureux*, Paris: Folio, 1981.

Certeau, Michel de, *Heterologies: Discourse on the Other*, Manchester: Manchester University Press.

Chadwick, Whitney, *Myth in Surrealist Painting, 1922–1939*, Ann Arbor: UMI Research Press, 1980.

Charbonnier, Georges, *Conversations with Lévi-Strauss*, trans. John and Dorothy Weightman, London: Jonathan Cape, 1966.

Charraud, Nicole, 'La Psychanalyse et la théorie des jeux', *Ornicar?*, 24, Autumn 1981.

Chasseguet-Smirgel, Janine, 'Freud and Female Sexuality. The Consideration of Some Blind Spots in the Exploration of the "Dark Continent"', IJPA, 57, 1976.

—— *The Ego Ideal*, trans. Paul Barrows, London: Free Association Books, 1985.

—— *et al.*, *La Sexualité féminine. Recherches psychanalytiques nouvelles*, Paris: Payot, 1964.

Châtelet, François, *La Philosophie des professeurs*, Paris: Grasset, 1970.

Chautard, E., *La Vie étrange de l'argot*, Paris: Denöel et Steele, 1931.

Chroniques d'une imposture: Du Mouvement de libération des femmes à une marque commerciale, Paris: Association du Mouvement pour les luttes féministes, 1981.

Claude Henri, 'La Méthode psychanalytique', *Le Disque vert*, 1924.

Claudel, Paul, *Art Poétique*, Paris: Mercure de France, 1907.

Clément, Catherine, *Vies et légendes de Jacques Lacan*, Paris: Grasset, 1981.

—— *The Weary Sons of Freud*, trans. Nicole Ball, London: Verso, 1987.

Clérambault, Gaëtan Gatian de, 'Erotomanie', *Bulletin de la Société clinique de médicine mentale*, December 1920.

—— 'Delires passionelles; érotomanie, revendication, jalousie', *Bulletin de la Société clinique de médicine mentale*, February 1921.

—— 'Dépit érotomanique après possession', *Bulletin de la Société clinique de médicine mentale*, June 1921.

—— 'Erotomanie pure, érotomanie associée', *Bulletin de la Société clinique de médicine mentale*, July 1921, reprinted, *Nouvelle Revue de Psychanalyse*, 21, Spring 1980.

'Condensation et déplacement', *Scilicet*, 2/3, 1970.

Contat, Michel and Rybalka, Michel, *Les Ecrits de Sartre*, Paris: Gallimard, 1970.

Coward, Rosalind, 'Lacan and Signification: An Introduction', *Edinburgh 76 Magazine*.

—— 'Rereading Freud – The Making of the Feminine', *Spare Rib*, 70, May 1978.

—— Lipschitz, Sue and Cowie, Elizabeth, 'Psychoanalysis and Patriarchy', in *Papers on Patriarchy*, Lewes: Women's Publishing Collective, 1976.

—— and Ellis, John, *Language and Materialism. Developments in Semiology and the Theory of the Subject*, London: Routledge & Kegan Paul, 1977.

Cowie, Elizabeth, 'Woman as Sign', *m/f*, 1, 1978.

Crashaw, Richard, *The Poems of Richard Crashaw*, ed. L.C. Martin, Oxford: Oxford University Press, 1957.

Crevel, René, 'Le Patriotisme de l'inconscient', *Le Surréalisme au Service de la Révolution*, 4, December 1931.

—— 'Notes en vue d'une psycho-dialectique', *Le Surréalisme au Service de la Révolution*, 5, May 1933.

Dalbiez, Roland, *La Méthode psychanalytique et la doctrine freudienne* (préface de Henri Claude), Paris: Desclée de Brouwer, 1936.

Dali, Salvador, 'L'Ane pourri', *Le Surréalisme au Service de la Révolution*, 1, July 1930.

—— 'Interpretation de l'image obsédante. *L'Angélus* de Millet', *Minotaure*, 1, February 1933.

—— (1952) *La Vie secrète de Salvador Dali*, Paris: Gallimard, 'Idées', 1979.

Damourette, Jacques and Pichon, Edouard, *Des Mots à la pensée. Essai de grammaire de la langue française*, Paris: D'Artrey, 1911–50, 7 vols.

David-Menard, Monique, 'Lacanians Against Lacan', trans. Brian Masurani, *Socialtext*, 6, Fall 1982.

Davies, Howard, *Sartre and 'Les Temps modernes'*, Cambridge: Cambridge University Press, 1987.

Davies, Hugh Sykes, 'Biology and Surrealism', *International Bulletin*, 4, September 1936.

Deleuze, Gilles and Lyotard, Jean-François, 'A Propos du Département de psychanalyse', *Les Temps modernes*, 342, January 1975.

Delphy, Christine, 'The Main Enemy', trans. Diana Leonard Barker, *Explorations in Feminism*, 3, n.d.

Delwit, Pascal and Dewaele, Jean-Michel. 'The Stalinists of Anti-Communism', trans. David Macey, *Socialist Register*, 1984.

Derrida, Jacques, *L'Ecriture et la différence*, Paris: Seuil, 1967.

—— 'Le Facteur de la vérité', *Poétique*, 21, 1975.

Descartes, René (1649), *Les Passions de l'âme*, Paris: Librairie philosophique J. Vrin, 1966.

Descombes, Vincent, *Modern French Philosophy*, trans. Lorna Scott-Fox and Jeremy Harding, Cambridge: Cambridge University Press, 1980.

—— *Objects of All Sorts: A Philosophical Grammar*, trans. Lorna Scott-Fox and Jeremy Harding, Oxford: Basil Blackwell, 1986.

Deutsch, Hélène, 'The Psychology of Women in Relation to the Function of Reproduction', IJPA, 6, 1925.

—— 'The Significance of Masochism in the Mental Life of Women', IJPA, 11, 1930.

Devereux, Georges, 'Aspects de la psychanalyse aux Etats-Unis', *Les Temps modernes*, 12, September 1946.

Dews, Peter, 'The *Nouvelle Philosophie* and Foucault', *Economy and Society*, vol. 8, n. 2, May 1979.

—— 'The "New Philosophers" and the End of Leftism', *Radical Philosophy*, 24, Spring 1980.

Dolto, Françoise, *Psychanalyse et pédiatrie*, Paris: Seuil, 'Points', 1971.

—— *Le Cas Dominique*, Paris; Seuil, 'Points', 1971.

Dor, Joël, *Bibliographie des travaux des Jacques Lacan*, Paris: Inter Editions, 1983.

Doray, Bernard, *From Taylorism to Fordism*, trans. David Macey, London: Free Association Books, 1988.

Dorgeuille, Claude, *La Seconde Mort de Jacques Lacan. Histoire d'une crise: Octobre 1980–Juin 1981*, Paris: Actualité freudienne.

Duchen, Claire, *Feminism in France, From May 68 to Mitterrand*, London: Routledge & Kegan Paul, 1986.

Ducrot, Oswald and Todorov, Tzvetan, *Dictionnaire encyclopédique des sciences de la langue*, Paris: Seuil, 1972.

Dumas, Georges, ed., *Nouveau Traité de psychologie*, Paris: Librairie Félix Alcan, 1936.

Durand, Jacques, 'Rhétorique et image publicitaire', *Communications*, 15, 1970.

Duras, Marguerite, *Le Ravissement de Lol V. Stein*, Paris: Gallimard, 1964.

—— and Gauthier, Xavière, *Les Parleuses*, Paris: Minuit, 1977.

Eagleton, Terry, *Literary Theory, An Introduction*, Oxford: Basil Blackwell, 1983.

Ellenberger, Henri, F., *The Discovery of the Unconscious. The History and Evolution of Dynamic Psychiatry*, New York: Basic Books, 1970.

Eluard, Paul, ed., *Poésie involontaire et poésie intentionnelle*, Villeneuve-les-Avignon, 1942.

—— *Capitale de la douleur*, Paris: Gallimard, 'Poésie', 1966.

Erikson, Erik, K., *Childhood and Society*, Harmondsworth: Pelican, 1965.

Fanon, Frantz, *Black Skins, White Masks*, trans. Charles Lam Markham, London: Paladin, 1970.

Fauvret-Saada, Jeanne, 'Excusez-moi, je ne faisais que passer', *Les Temps modernes*, 371, June 1977.

Felman, Shoshona, *Jacques Lacan and the Adventure of Insight, Psychoanalysis in Contemporary Culture*, Cambridge, Mass. and London: Harvard University Press, 1987.

Fenichel, Otto, 'The Symbolic Equation: "Girl = Phallus"', *Psychoanalytic Quarterly*, 28, 1949.

Ferenczi, Sandor, *Final Contributions to the Problems and Methods of Psycho-analysis*, London, The Hogarth Press and the Institute of Psycho-Analaysis, 1955.

Fontanier, Pierre, *Les Figures du discours*, Paris: Flammarion, 'Champs', 1968.

Forrester, John, *Language and the Origins of Psychoanalysis*, London: Macmillan, 1981.

—— 'The *Seminar* of Jacques Lacan: In Place of an Introduction', *Free Associations*, 10, 1987.

Foucault, Michel, *Folie et déraison. Histoire de la folie à l'âge classique*, Paris: Librairie Plon, 1961.

—— *Les Mots et les choses*, Paris: Gallimard, 1966.

Freud, Anna, *The Ego and the Mechanisms of Defence*, New York: International Universities Press, 1936.

—— *Problems of Psychoanalytic Technique and Therapy*, London: The Hogarth Press and The Institute of Psycho-Analysis, 1972.

—— *Normality and Pathology in Childhood*, Harmondsworth: Penguin, 1973.

Freud, Sigmund, *The Standard Edition of the Complete Psychological Works of Sigmund Freud*, ed. James Strachey, London: The Hogarth Press and The Institute of Psycho-Analysis, 1953–74, 24 vols.

—— (1893) 'Charcot', SE III.

—— (1900) *The Interpretation of Dreams*, SE IV–V.

—— (1901) *The Psychopathlogy of Everyday Life*, SE VI.

—— (1905) *Jokes and their Relation to the Unconscious*, SE VII.

—— (1905) *Three Essays on the Theory of Sexuality*, SE VII.

—— (1905) 'Fragment of an Analysis of a Case of Hysteria', SE VII.

—— (1906) 'Contribution to a Questionnaire on Reading', SE IX.

—— (1907) Delusions and Dreams in Jensen's 'Gradiva', SE IX.

—— (1907) 'Creative Writers and Day-Dreaming', SE IX.

—— (1908) 'On The Sexual Theories of Children', SE IX.

—— (1909) 'Some General Remarks on Hysterical Attacks', SE IX.

—— (1909) 'Analysis of a Phobia in a Five-Year-Old Boy', SE X.

—— (1909) 'Notes upon a Case of Obsessional Neurosis', SE X.

—— (1910) *Leonardo da Vinci and a Memory of his Childhood*, SE XI.
—— (1910) 'The Antithetical Meaning of Primal Words', SE XI.
—— (1910) 'A Special Type of Choice of Object Made by Men', SE XI.
—— (1911) 'Psycho-Analaytic Notes on an Autobiographical Account of a Case of Paranoia (Dementia Paranoides)', SE XII.
—— (1912) 'On The Universal Tendency to Debasement in the Sphere of Love', SE XI.
—— (1912–13) *Totem and Taboo*, SE XIII.
—— (1914) 'On Narcissism: An Introduction', SE XIII.
—— (1914) 'On the History of the Psycho-Analytic Movement', SE XIV.
—— (1915) 'Instincts and their Vicissitudes', SE XIV.
—— (1915) 'The Unconscious', SE XIV.
—— (1916–17) *Introductory Lectures on Psycho-Analysis*, SE XV–XVI.
—— (1917) 'A Difficulty in the Path of Psycho-Analaysis', SE XVII.
—— (1917) 'On Transformations of Instinct as Exemplified in Anal Erotism', SE XVII.
—— (1918) 'The Taboo of Virginity', SE XVII.
—— (1918) 'From the History of an Infantile Neurosis', SE XVII.
—— (1919) 'The Uncanny', SE XVII.
—— (1920) 'The Psychogenesis of a Case of Female Homosexuality', SE XVIII.
—— (1920) 'A Note on the Prehistory of the Technique of Analysis', SE XVIII.
—— (1920) *Beyond the Pleasure Principle*, SE XVIII.
—— (1921) *Group Psychology and the Analysis of the Ego*, SE XVIII.
—— (1922) 'Medusa's Head', SE XVIII.
—— (1922) 'Some Neurotic Mechanisms in Jealousy, Paranoia and Homosexuality', S XVIII.
—— (1923) 'Two Encyclopaedia Articles', SE XVIII.
—— (1923) 'Neurosis and Psychosis', SE XIX.
—— (1923) *The Ego and the Id*, SE XIX.
—— (1923) 'The Infantile Genital Organization', SE XIX.
—— (1924) 'The Dissolution of the Oedipus Complex', SE XIX.
—— (1924) 'The Economic Problem of Masochism', SE XIX.
—— (1924) 'The Loss of Reality in Neurosis and Psychosis', SE XIX.
—— (1924) *An Autobiographical Study*, SE XX.
—— (1925) 'The Resistances to Psycho-Analysis', SE XIX.
—— (1925) 'Negation', SE XIX.
—— (1925) 'Some Psychical Consequences of the Anatomical Distinction between the Sexes', SE XIX.
—— (1925) *Inhibitions, Symptoms and Anxiety*, SE XX.
—— (1926) *The Question of Lay Analysis*, SE XX.
—— (1927) 'Fetishism', SE XXI.
—— (1927) *The Future of an Illusion*, SE XXI.
—— (1928) 'Dostoievsky and Parricide', SE XXI.
—— (1930) *Civilization and its Discontents*, SE XXI.
—— (1931) 'Female Sexuality', SE XXI.

—— (1933) *New Introductory Lectures on Psycho-Analysis*, SE XXII.

—— (1937) 'Analysis Terminable and Interminable', SE XVIII.

—— (1937–39) *Moses and Monotheism*, SE XXIII.

—— (1938) 'Splitting of the Ego in the Process of Defence', SE XXIII.

—— (1938) *An Outline of Psycho-Analysis*, SE XXIII.

—— and Breuer, Joseph, (1893–95) *Studies in Hysteria*, SE II.

—— *Letters of Sigmund Freud 1873–1939*, selected and edited by Ernest L. Freud, trans. Tania and James Stern, London: The Hogarth Press, 1961.

—— *The Freud/Jung Letters*, ed. William McGuire, trans. Ralph Mannheim and R.F.C. Hall, London: The Hogarth Press and Routledge & Kegan Paul, 1974.

—— *La Correspondance entre Freud et Laforgue 1923–1937*, preceded by André Bourguignon, *Nouvelle Revue de Psychanalyse*, 15, Spring 1977.

—— *The Complete Letters of Sigmund Freud to Wilhelm Fliess, 1887–1904*, trans. Jeffrey Moussaieff-Masson, Cambridge, Mass. and London: Harvard University Press, 1985.

—— *Neue Folge der Vorlesungen zur Einführung in die Psychoanalyse*, Frankfurt am Main: Fischer Taschenbuch Verlag, 1969.

—— *Drei Abhandlugen zur sexualtheorie und verwondte schriften*, Frankfurt am Main: Fischer Taschenbuch Verlag, 1984.

—— *Nouvelles Conférences sur la psychanalyse*, trans. Anne Berman, Paris: Gallimard, 'Idées', 1971.

—— *Essais de psychanalyse*, trans. S. Jankélévitch, Paris: Payot, 1972.

Gablik, Suzi, *Magritte*, London: Thames & Hudson, 1970.

Gallop, Jane, *Feminism and Psychoanalysis. The Daughter's Seduction*, London: Macmillan, 1982.

—— 'Beyond the *Jouissance* Principle', *Representations*, 7, Summer 1984.

—— *Reading Lacan*, Ithaca and London: Cornell University Press, 1985.

Gardner, Martin, *Mathemtical Puzzles and Diversions*, Harmondsworth: Pelican, 1965.

Garrabé, Jean 'Prolégomènes à un manifeste de la surpsychiatrie', *Evolution psychiatrique*, January–March 1979.

Gauthier, Xavière, *Surréalisme et sexualité*, Paris: Gallimard, 'Idées', 1970.

Genet, Jean, *Œuvres complètes*, vol. 2, Paris: Gallimard, 1951.

Genette, Gérard, *Figures of Literary Discourse*, trans. Alan Sheridan, New York: Columbia University Press, 1982.

George François, *L'Effet 'yau de poêle*, Paris: Hachette, 1979.

Gide, André, *Journal 1885–1939*, Paris: Bibliothèque de la pléiade, 1948.

Gori, Roland, *Le Corps et le signe dans l'acte de parole*, Paris: Dunod, 1978.

Green, André, 'L'Inconscient freudien et la psychanalyse française contemporaine', *Les Temps modernes*, 195, August 1962.

—— *Le Discours vivant. La Conception psychanalytique de l'affect*, Paris: PUF, 1973.

—— 'Psychanalyse, Langage, L'Ancien et le nouveau', *Critique*, 381, 1979.

—— 'Une Figure messianique', *Le Monde*, 11 September 1981.

—— *Narcissisme de vie, narcissisme de mort*, Paris: Minuit, 1983.

Grevisse, Maurice, *Le Bon Usage. Grammaire française, avec des remarques sur la langue française d'aujourd'hui*, eighth edn, Gembloux and Paris: Duclos and Hatier, 1964.

Grosskurth, Phyllis, *Melanie Klein*, London: Hodder & Stoughton, 1985.

Groupe 'mu', *Rhétorique générale*, Paris: Seuil, 1970.

Hartmann, Heinz, 'Comments on the Psychoanalytic Theory of the Ego', *Psycho-analytic Study of the Child*, 5, 1950.

—— *Ego Psychology and the Problem of Adaptation*, trans. David Rapoport, New York, International Universities Press, 1958.

——, Kris, Ernst and Loewenstein, Rudolph, 'Comments on the formation of Psychic Structure', *Psychoanalytic Study of the Child*, 2, 1946.

—— 'Healing Words: Dr Lacan's Structuralism', *Times Literary Supplement*, 25 January 1968.

Heath, Stephen, *'Difference'*, *Screen*, vol. 19, no. 3, Autumn 1978.

Hegel, G.W.F., *The Phenomenology of Mind*, trans. J.B. Baillie, New York: Harper Torchbooks, 1967.

Heidegger, Martin, 'Logos', trans. Jacques Lacan, *La Psychanalyse*, 1, 1956.

—— *What Is Philosophy?*, trans. William L. Klubach and Jean T. Wilde, New York: Vision Press, 1958.

—— *On The Way to Language*, trans. Peter D. Hertz, New York: Harper & Row, 1982.

—— *Being and Time*, trans. John MacQuarrie and Edward Robinson, Oxford: Basil Blackwell, 1980.

Herr, Lucien, *Choix d'Ecrits II: Ecrits philosophiques et scientifiques*, Paris: Rieder, 1932.

Hesnard, Angelo, 'L'Opinion scientifique française et la psychanalyse', *Le Disque vert*, 1924.

—— 'A Propos d'une prétendue "crise" de la psychanalyse', *Revue de psychologie concrète*, 2, July 1928, reprinted Politzer, *Ecrits* 2.

—— and Laforgue, René, 'Les Processus d'auto-punition en psychologie des névroses et des psychoses, en psychologie criminelle et en pathologie générale', RFP, 4, 1930–31.

Hess, Thomas B. and Nochlin, Linda, *Woman as Sex Object*, London: Allen Lane, 1973.

Hibbard, Howard, *Bernini*, Harmondsworth: Pelican, 1965.

Hollier, Denis, *Le Collège de sociologie*, Paris: Gallimard, 'Idées', 1979.

Horney, Karen, *Feminine Psychology*, New York: Norton, 1973.

Houdebine, Jean-Louis, 'Méconnaissance de la psychanalyse dans le discours surréaliste', *Tel Quel*, 46, Summer 1971.

—— 'Position politique et idéologique du néo-surréalisme', *Tel Quel*, 46, Summer 1971.

Hugo, Victor, *La Légende des siècles*, Paris: Bibliothèque de la pléiade, 1950.

—— *Oeuvres poétiques* II, Paris: Bibliothèque de la pléiade, 1967.

Hyppolite, Jean, *Figures de la pensée philosophique*, Paris: PUF, 1961.

Irigaray, Luce, 'Communication linguistique et spéculaire', *Cahiers pour l'analyse*, 3, May–June 1966.

—— *Speculum, de l'autre femme*, Paris: Minuit, 1974.

—— *Ce Sexe qui n'en est pas un*, Paris: Minuit, 1977.

—— 'Women's Exile. Interview with Luce Irigaray', trans. Couze Venn, *Ideology and Consciousness*, 1, May 1977.
—— 'Misère de la psychanalyse', *Critique*, 365, October 1977.
Jakobson, Roman, *Selected Writings*, vol. 1, The Hague: Mouton, 1962.
—— *Essais de linguistique générale*, Paris: Seuil, 'Points', 1970.
—— *Selected Writings*, vol. 2, The Hague: Mouton, 1971.
Jameson, Frederic, 'Imaginary and Symbolic in Lacan', *Yale French Studies*, 55/56, 1977.
Jones, Ernest, 'The Theory of Symbolism', *British Journal of Psychology*, 9, 1916.
—— 'The Early Development of Female Sexuality', IJPA, 8, 1927.
—— 'The Phallic Phase', IJPA, 14, 1933.
—— 'Early Female Sexualist', IJPA, 16, 1935.
—— *The Life and Work of Sigmund Freud*, London: The Hogarth Press and The Institute of Psycho-Analysis, 1955, 3 vols.
Juranville, Alain, *Lacan et la philosophie*, Paris: PUF, 1984.
—— 'Psychanalyse et philosophie', *Ornicar?*, 29, Summer 1984.
Kalfon, Dominique, 'Ma Mère est une femme', *Ornicar?*, 25, Autumn 1981.
Klauber, John and others, *Illusion and Spontaneity in Psychoanalysis*, London: Free Association Books, 1987.
Klein, Melanie, *Contributions to Psycho-Analysis, 1921–1945*, London: The Hogarth Press and The Institute of Psycho-Analysis, 1948.
—— *Love, Guilt, Reparation, and Other Works*, London: The Hogarth Press and the Institute of Psycho-Analysis, 1975.
Kofman, Sarah, *The Enigma of Woman. Woman in Freud's Writing*, trans. Catherine Porter, Ithaca and London: Cornell University Press, 1985.
Kovel, Joel, 'Sins of the Fathers', *Free Associations*, 1, 1985.
Koyré, Alexandre, *From The Closed World to the Infinite Universe*, Baltimore: Johns Hopkins Press.
Kress-Rosen, Nicole, 'Hélène Deutsch, une théorie de la femme', *Ornicar?*, 15, Summer 1978.
—— 'Sociolinguistique féminine', *Ornicar?*, 19, Autumn 1979.
Kris, Ernst, 'Ego Psychology and Interpretation to Psychoanalytic Therapy', *Psychoanalytic Quarterly*, 20, 1951.
Lacan Study Group, 'Psychoanalysis and Feminism', *New Left Review*, 96, May–June 1976.
Ladimer, Bethany, 'Madness and the Irrational in the Work of André Breton', *Feminist Studies*, vol. 6, no. 1, 1980.
Laffal, Julius, 'Freud's Theory of Language', *Psychoanalytic Quarterly*, 33, 1964.
Laforgue, René, 'Verdrängung und Scotomization', *Internationale Zeitschrift für ärtzliche Psychoanalyse*, 12, 1926.
—— 'Scotomization in Schizophrenia', IJPA, 8, 1927.
—— 'The Mechanisms of Isolation in Neurosis and their Relation to Schizophrenia', IJPA, 10, 1929.
—— 'On The Eroticization of Anxiety', IJPA, 11, 1930.
Lakoff, Robin, *Language and Woman's Place*, New York: Harper & Row, 1975.

Lanteri-Laura, G., 'Nizan et Politzer quarante ans après', *Critique*, August–September 1968.

Laplanche, Jean, *Vie et mort en psychanalyse*, Paris: Flammarion, 'Champs', 1977.

—— *Problématiques II: Castration et symbolisations*, Paris: PUF, 1980.

—— *Problématiques III: La Sublimation*, Paris: PUF, 1980.

—— *Problématiques IV: L'Inconscient et le ça*, Paris: PUF, 1981.

—— and Leclaire, Serge, 'L'Inconscient, une étude psychanalytique', in Laplanche, *Problématiques IV*.

—— and Pontalis, J.B., *The Language of Psychoanalysis*, trans. Donald Nicholson-Smith, London: The Hogarth Press and The Institute of Psycho-Analysis, 1973.

La Rochefoucauld, *Maximes et réflexions*, Paris: Livre de Poche, 1966.

Lasch, Christopher, *The Culture of Narcissism*, New York: Norton, 1979.

—— 'The Freudian Left and Cultural Revolution', *New Left Review*, 129, September–October 1981.

—— *The Minimal Self*, New York: Norton, 1984.

Laurent, Alexandre, 'Freud et Politzer', *Europe*, 429, March 1974.

Laurent, Eric, 'Ce que savait Melanie', *Ornicar?*, 24, Autumn 1981.

Lautréamont, Comte de (ps. Isidore Ducasse), *Œuvres complètes*, Paris: Livre de Poche, 1968.

Lavers, Annette, 'Some Aspects of Language in the Work of Jacques Lacan', *Semiotica*, 3, 1971.

—— *Roland Barthes: Structuralism and After*, London: Methuen, 1982.

—— 'Sartre and Freud', *French Studies*, vol. 41, no. 3, July 1987.

Lecercle, Jean-Jacques, *Philosophy Through the Looking-Glass*, London: Hutchinson, 1985.

Leclaire, Serge, 'L'Incurable psychanalyse', *La Table ronde*, 108, 1956.

—— 'Compter avec la psychanalyse', *Cahiers pour l'analyse*, 1, January–February 1966.

—— 'Les Eléments en jeu dans une psychanalyse', *Cahiers pour l'analyse*, 5, November–December 1966.

—— *Psychanalyser*, Paris: Seuil, 'Points', 1975.

—— (1975) *On Tue un enfant*, Paris: Seuil, 'Points', 1981.

—— *Démasquer le réel*, Paris: Seuil, 'Points', 1983.

Leclerc, Annie, *Parole de femme*, Paris: Grasset, 1974.

Leiris, Michel, *L'Age d'homme*, Paris: Gallimard, 1946.

—— *Biffures*, Paris: Gallimard, 1948.

—— *Les Mots sans mémoire*, Paris: Gallimard, 1969.

Lemaire, Anika, *Jacques Lacan*, trans. David Macey, London: Routledge & Kegan Paul, 1977.

Lemoine-Luccioni, Eugénie, *Partage des femmes*, Paris: Seuil, 'Points', 1982.

Lévi-Strauss, Claude, 'La Sociologie française', in Georges Gurvitch, *La Sociologie au XXᵉ siècle*, Paris: PUF, 1947.

—— (1955) *Tristes Tropiques*, trans. John and Dorothy Weightman, London: Jonathan Cape, 1973.

—— (1949) *The Elementary Structures of Kinship*, trans. James Harle Bell,

John Richard von Sturmer and Rodney Needham, London: Eyre & Spottis-
woode, 1969.

—— (1958) *Structural Anthropology*, trans. Claire Jacobson and Brooke
Grundfest Schoepf, Harmondsworth: Penguin, 1972.

—— (1962) *The Savage Mind*, London: Weidenfeld & Nicolson, 1972.

—— (1964) *The Raw and the Cooked*, trans. John and Dorothy Weightman,
London: Harper & Row, 1973.

Lèvy-Valensi, Eliane Amado, 'Vérité et langage, du dialogue platonicien au
dialogue psychanalytique', *La Psychanalyse*, 1, 1956.

Lewis, Jill, '"Women's Liberation Limited" – The French Controversy', *Spare
Rib*, 108, July 1981.

Loewenstein, Rudolph, 'D'Un Méchanisme auto-punitif ', RFP, 5, 1932.

—— 'Some Remarks on the Role of Speech in Psychoanalytic Technique',
IJPA, 37, 1956.

Louvain, François, 'Jacques Lacan et le président Schreber', *Magazine littéraire*,
99, April 1975.

Lyons, John, *Introduction to Theoretical Linguistics*, Cambridge: Cambridge
University Press, 1968.

Lyotard, Jean-François, 'The Dream-Work Does Not Think', trans. Mary Lydon,
Oxford Literary Review, vol. 6, no. 1, 1983.

MacCabe, Colin, 'Realism and the Cinema: Notes on Some Brechtian Theses',
Screen, vol. 15, no. 2, Summer 1974.

—— ed., *The Talking Cure. Essays in Psychoanalysis and Language*, London:
Macmillan, 1981.

Macey, David, 'Review Article: Jacques Lacan', *Ideology and Consciousness*, 4,
Autumn 1978,

—— *The Work of Paul Nizan: A Study in the Influence of a Political Viewpoint
on Literary Themes and Structures*, unpublished PhD thesis, London, 1982.

—— 'Fragments of an analysis: Lacan in Context', *Radical Philosophy*, 35,
Autumn 1983.

—— 'Review Article: Lacan et la philosophie', *Economy and Society*, vol. 14,
no. 2, May 1985.

Macksie, Richard and Donato, Eugenio, eds, *The Structuralist Controversy*,
Baltimore and London: The Johns Hopkins Press, 1972.

Magritte, René, 'Les Mots et les images', *La Révolution surréaliste*, 12, March
1929.

Malcolm, Janet, *In the Freud Archives*, London: Jonathan Cape, 1984.

Maleval, Jean-Claude, 'Les Psychothérapies des hystéries crépusculaires', *Ornicar?*, 30, Autumn 1984.

Malinowski, Bronislaw, *Argonauts of the Western Pacific*, London: Routledge &
Kegan Paul, 1922.

Mannoni, Maude, *Le Premier Rendez-vous avec le psychanalyste*, Paris: Denoël/
Gonthier, 1965.

—— *L'Enfant, sa 'maladie' et les autres*, Paris: Seuil, 1967.

Mannoni, Octave, *Clefs pour l'imaginaire, ou l'autre scène*, Paris: Seuil, 'Points',
1985.

Marcus, Steven, *Freud and the Culture of Psychoanalysis*, London: Allen &
Unwin, 1984.

Marini, Marcelle, *Lacan*, Paris: Belfond, 1986.

Marks, Elaine and Courtivron, Isabelle de, eds, *New French Feminisms*, Hassocks: Harvester, 1981.

Martinet, André, *Elements of General Lingistics*, trans. Elisabeth Palmer, London: Faber & Faber, 1964.

—— *La Linguistique synchronique: Etudes et recherches*, Paris: PUF, 1965.

Masson, Jeffrey Moussaieff, *The Assault on Truth: Freud's Suppression of the Seduction Theory*, New York: Farrar, Strauss & Giroux, 1984.

Maurice, Christine, 'L'Etendue. Notes sur quelques photographies d'hystériques', *Ornicar?*, 22/23, 1981.

Mauss, Marcel, *Sociologie et anthropologie*, Paris: PUF, 1950.

Mehlman, Jeffrey, 'The Floating Signifier from Lévi-Strauss to Lacan', *Yale French Studies*, 48, 1972.

Melman, Charles, 'Que veut une femme?' *Ornicar?*, 15, Summer 1978.

Merquior, J.G., *From Prague to Paris. A Critique of Structuralist and Poststructuralist Thought*, London: Verso, 1986.

Michaud, Ginette, *Laborde ... un pari nécessaire. De la notion d'institution à la psychothérapie institutionnelle*, Paris: Gauthier-Villars, 1978.

Miller, Gérard, ed., *Lacan*, Paris: Bordas, 1987.

Miller Jacques-Alain, 'La Suture (Eléments de la logique du signifiant)', *Cahiers pour l'analyse*, 1, January–February 1966.

—— 'Action de la structure', *Cahiers pour l'analyse*, 9, Summer 1968.

—— 'El Piropo', *Ornicar?*, 22/23, Spring 1981.

—— 'Encyclopédie', *Ornicar?*, 24, Autumn 1981.

—— *Entretien sur le Séminaire avec François Ansermet*, Paris: Navarin, 1985.

—— ed., *La Scission de 1953. La Communauté psychanalytique en France I.* Supplément au numéro 7 d'*Ornicar?*, 1976.

—— ed., *L'Excommunication. La Communauté psychanalytique en France II*, Supplément au numéro 8 d'*Ornicar?*, 1977.

Miller, Judith, 'Freud: édition finie ou infinie?', *L'Ane*, 2, Summer 1981.

Milner, Jean-Claude, *L'Amour de la langue*, Paris: Seuil, 1978,

Mitchell, Juliet, *Psychoanalysis and Feminism*, London: Allen Lane, 1974.

—— 'Interview', *m/f*, 8, 1983.

—— *Women: The Longest Revolution. Essays in Feminism, Literature and Psychoanalysis*, London: Virago, 1985.

Montag, Warren, 'Marxism and Psychoanalysis: The Impossible Encounter', *Minnesota Review*, Fall 1984.

Montrelay, Michèle, *L'Ombre et le nom*, Paris: Minuit, 1977.

Mordier, Jean-Pierre, *Les Débuts de la psychanalyse en France 1895–1926*, Paris: Maspero, 1981.

—— 'La Psychanalyse tricolore', *L'Ane*, 2, Summer 1981.

Morel, Geneviève, 'Point final à une planète infernale', *Ornicar?*, 36, Spring 1986.

Morsier, Georges de, 'L'Erotomanie', *Annales de psychologie*, 20, 1927.

Mounin, Georges, 'Quelques Traits du style de Jacques Lacan', *Nouvelle Revue Française*, 193, January 1969.

—— *Clefs pour la linguistique*, Paris: Seghers, 1970.

Mulvey, Laura, 'Visual Pleasure and Narrative Cinema', *Screen*, vol. 16, no. 3, Autumn 1975.

Nacht, Sacha, 'Du Moi et son rôle dans la thérapeutique psychanalytique', RFP, 1948.

—— *Guérir avec Freud*, Paris: Payot, 1971.

Nadeau, Maurice, *The History of Surrealism* trans. Richard Howard, Harmondsworth: Pelican, 1968.

Nancy, Jean-Luc and Lacoue-Labarthe, Philippe, *Le Titre de la lettre*, Paris: Editions Galilée, 1973.

Nassif, Jacques, 'Freud et la science', *Cahiers pour l'analyse*, 9, Summer 1968.

New Left Review, 'Editorial', 51, September–October 1968.

Nguyen, M., 'Les Exclues de Département de psychanalyse de Vincennes', *Les Temps modernes*, 341, January 1975.

Nin, Anaïs, *The Journal of Anaïs Nin 1931–34*, London: Peter Owen, 1970.

—— *Henry and June*, New York: Harcourt Brace Jovanovich, 1986.

Nizan, Paul, *Les Chiens de garde*, Paris: Rieder, 1932.

—— 'D. Mirsky, Lénine', *Nouvelle Revue Française*, May 1931.

—— 'Notes de lecture', *L'Humanité*, 10 February 1933.

—— 'French Literature Today', *International Literature*, 5, 1934.

'Notes prises aux présentations de malades du Dr Lacan à l'hôpital Sainte-Anne', *Scilicet*, 1, 1968.

OULIPO, *La Littérature potentielle*, Paris: Gallimard, 'Idées', 1973.

Pailthorpe, G.W., 'The Scientific Aspect of Surrealism', *London Bulletin*, 7, December 1938–January 1938.

Partridge, Eric, *A Dictionary of Clichés*, London: Routledge & Kegan Paul, 1978.

Paulhan, Jean, *Les Fleurs de Tarbes, ou la terreur dans les lettres*, Paris: Gallimard, 1941.

Perec, Georges, *La Vie, mode d'emploi*, Paris: Hachette, 1978.

Perelman, C. and Olbrechts-Tyteca, L., *Traité de l'argumentation*, Paris: PUF, 1958.

Perrier, François, *La Chaussée d'Antin/Antienne*, Paris: UGE 10/18, 1978.

—— *La Chaussée d'Antin*, 2, Paris UGE 10/18, 1978,

—— *Voyages extraordinares en Translacanie*, Paris: Lieu commun, 1985.

Peters, Uwe Henrick, Anna Freud. A Life Dedicated to Children, London: Weidenfield & Nicolson, 1985.

Petit Guide Féministe de France et d'ailleurs, Paris, Carabosses, 1982.

'Phase phallique', *Scilicet*, 1, 1968.

Pichon, Edouard, 'La Grammaire en tant que mode d'exploration de l'inconscient', *Evolution psychiatrique*, 1, 1925.

—— 'Sur la signification psychologique de la négation en français', *Journal de psychologie normale et pathologique*, March 1928.

—— 'Eugénie Sokolnicka', RFP, 7, 1934.

—— 'La Reálité devant M. Laforgue', RFP, 10, 1938.

—— 'La Personne et la personnalité vues à la lumière de la pensée idiomatique française', RFP, 10, 1938.

—— 'La Famille devant M. Lacan', RFP, 11, 1939.

Pierre, José, ed., *Tractes surréalistes et déclarations collectives 1922–1964*, vol. 1, Paris: Eric Losfeld Editeur, 1982.

Pirard, Regnier, 'Si l'Inconscient est structuré comme un langage …', *Revue philosophique de Louvain*, 77, 1979,

Pleynet, Marcelin, *Painting and System*, trans. Sima N. Godfrey, Chicago and London: University of Chicago Press, 1984.

Politzer, Georges, (1928) *Critique des fondements de la psychologie*, Paris: PUF, 1974.

—— *La Fin d'une parade philosophique: le bergsonisme*, Paris: Rieder 1929.

—— *Ecrits II. Les Fondements de la psychologie*, Paris: Editions sociales, 1969.

Pollock, Griselda, 'Artists, Mythology and Media – Genius, Madness and Art History', *Screen*, vol. 21, no. 3, 1980.

Pontalis, J.B., 'La Lecture de Freud', *Les Temps modernes*, 195, August 1962.

—— *Après Freud*, Paris: Gallimard, 'Idées', 1968.

—— *L'Amour des commencements*, Paris: Gallimard, 1986.

Posner, Charles, ed., *Reflections on the Revolution in France: 1968*, Harmondsworth: Pelican, 1970.

Powell, Nicolas, *Fuseli: 'The Nightmare'*, London: Allen Lane, 1973.

Prévert, Jacques, *Selections from 'Paroles'*, trans. Lawrence Ferlinghetati, Harmondsworth: Penguin, 1965.

Queneau, Raymond, (1952) *Chêne et chien*, Paris: Gallimard, 'Poésie', 1969.

—— (1959) *Zazie dans le métro*. Paris: Livre de Poche, 1966.

—— *Bâtons, chiffres et lettres*, Paris: Gallimard, 'Idées', 1973.

'Raison avant Freud', *Scilicet*, 6/7, 1976.

Ramnoux, Clémence, 'Hadès et le psychanalyste (pour une anamnèse de l'homme de l'occident)', *La Psychanalyse*, 1, 1956.

Reboul, Jacques, 'Jacques Lacan et les fondements de la psychanalyse', *Critique*, 187, December 1962.

Rétrospective Magritte, Brussels and Paris: Palais des beaux-arts, Musée national d'Art moderne and Centre national d'Art et de culture Georges Pompidou, 1978–79.

Reverchon-Jouve, Blanche, and Jouve, Pierre Jean, 'Moments d'une psychanalyse', *Nouvelle Revue Française*, 134, 1934.

Rey, Alain, 'Le Schizolexe', *Critique*, 279/280, August–September 1970.

Richter, Hans, *Dada: Art and Anti-Art*, trans. David Britt, London: Thames & Hudson, 1965.

Ricoeur, Paul, *Freud and Philosophy: An Essay on Interpretation*, trans. Denis Savage, New Haven and London: Yale University Press, 1970.

—— *The Conflict of Interpretations*, trans. K. McLaughlin, Evanston 1974.

Riley, Patrick, 'Introduction to the Reading of Alexandre Kojève', *Political Theory*, vol. 9, no. 1, February 1981.

Rivière, Jacques, 'Quelques Progrès dans l'étude du coeur humain (Freud et Proust)', *Les Cahiers de l'occident*, 4, 1927.

Rivière, Joan, 'Womanliness as Masquerade', IJPA, 10, 1929.

Roazen, Paul, *Brother Animal. The Story of Freud and Tausk*, New York: Arnold A. Knopf, 1969.

—— *Freud and his Followers*, New York: Arnold A. Knopf, 1975.

Robertson, Alexander, *et al.*, *Angels of Anarchy and Machines for Making Clouds: Surrealism in Britain in the Thirties*, Leeds: Leeds City Galleries, 1986.

Rodinson, Maxime, *Cult, Ghetto, State*, trans. Jon Rothschild, London: Al Saqui Books, 1983.

Ronvaux, Marianne, 'André Gide et Eugénie Sokolnicka', *Ornicar?*, 37, Summer 1986.

Rose, Jacqueline, *Sexuality in the Field of Vision*, London: Verso, 1986.

Rosen, Victor, H., 'Sign Phenomena and Their Relationship to Unconscious Meaning', IJPA, 50, 1969.

Rosolato, Guy, *Essais sur le symbolique*, Paris: Gallimard, 1969.

—— 'Symbol Formation', IJPA, 59, 1978.

—— 'L'Analyse des résistances', *Nouvelle Revue Psychanalyse*, 20, Autumn 1979.

—— 'Clérambault et les délires passionnelles', *Nouvelle Revue de Psychanalyse*, 21, Spring 1980.

Rottenberg, Pierre, 'Esquisse cartographique du mouvement: surréalisme', *Tel Quel*, 46, Summer 1971.

Roudinesco, Elisabeth, *Pour une politique de la psychanalyse*, Paris: Maspero, 1977.

—— *La Bataille de cent ans. Histoire de la psychanalyse en France, vol. 1: 1885–1939*, Paris: Ramsay, 1982.

—— *La Bataille de cent ans. Histoire de la psychanalyse en France, vol. 2: 1925–1985*, Paris: Seuil, 1986.

Roustang, François, *Un Destin si funeste*, Paris: Minuit, 1976.

Safouan, Moustapha, *Le Structuralisme en psychanalyse*, Paris: Seuil, 'Points', 1973.

—— *Etudes sur l'Oedipe*, Paris: Seuil, 1974.

—— *La Sexualité féminine dans la doctrine féminine*, Paris: Seuil, 1976.

Salgas, Jean-Pierre, 'L'Inconscient au tribunal', *La Quinzaine littéraire*, 454, 1–15 January 1986.

Salvador Dali: Rétrospective 1920–1980, Paris: Centre Georges Pompidou, Musée national d'Art moderne, 1979–80.

Sami-Ali, M., *De la projection, Une Etude psychanalytique*, Paris: Dunod, 1986.

Sanouillet, Michel and Petersen, Elmer, eds, *The Essential Writings of Marcel Duchamp*, London: Thames & Hudson, 1975.

Sartre, Jean-Paul, (1936) *La Transcendance de l'ego. Esquisse d'une description phénoménologique*, Paris: Librairie philosophique J. Vrin, 1978.

—— (1943) *L'Etre et le néant*, Paris: Gallimard 'Tel', 1976.

—— *Situations II*, Paris: Gallimard, 1948.

—— *Situations III*, Paris: Gallimard, 1949.

—— *Critique de la raison dialectique*, Paris: Gallimard, 1960.

Saussure, Ferdinand de, (1915) *Cours de linguistique générale*, Paris: Payot, 1967.

Saussure, Raymond de, 'Littérature française', IJPA, 1, 1920.

Sauvagnat, François, 'Une Pierre d'attente. Quelques particularités du premier abord freudien des hallucinations psychotiques', *Ornicar?*, 36, Spring 1986.

Sayers, Janet, 'Sexual Contradictions: On Freud, Psychoanalysis and Feminism', *Free Associations*, 1, 1985.

Scarpetta, Guy, 'Limite-frontière du surréalisme', *Tel Quel*, 46, Summer 1971.

Schneede, Uwe, A., *René Margritte: Life and Work*, trans. Walter Jaffe, New York: Barron's, 1982.

Schneidhauer, Marcel, 'Freud et le rêve en France, 1900–1914', *Ornicar?*, 24, Autumn 1981.

Schmidt, James, *Maurice Merleau-Ponty. Between Phenomenology and Structuralism*, London: Macmillan, 1985.

Schneiderman, Stuart, ed. and trans., *Returning to Freud: Clinical Analysis in the School of Lacan*, New Haven and London: Yale University Press, 1980.

—— 'Entretien', *Ornicar?*, 24, Autumn 1981.

—— *Jacques Lacan. The Death of an Intellectual Hero*, Cambridge, Mass. and London: Harvard University Press, 1983.

Screen, 'Editorial', vol. 12, no. 1, Spring 1971.

—— 'Editorial', vol. 13, no. 2, Autumn 1972.

—— 'Editorial', vol. 16, no. 2, Summer 1975.

Silvestre, Danièle, 'Chercher la femme', *Ornicar?*, 25, Autumn 1982.

Simon, Claude, 'La Fiction mot à mot', in Jean Ricardou and Françoise van Rossum-Guyon, eds, *Nouveau Roman: Hier, aujourd'hui, vol. 2: Pratiques*, Paris: UGE 10/18, 1972.

Smirnoff, Victor N., 'De Vienne à Paris, *Nouvelle Revue de Psychanalyse*, 20, Autumn 1979.

Sokolnicka, Eugenia, 'Analysis of an Obsessional Neurosis', IJPA, 3, 1922.

Starobinski, Jean, *La Relation critique*, Paris: Gallimard, 1970.

Sulloway, Frank, J., *Freud, Biologist of the Mind*, London: Fontana, 1980.

Sztulman, Henri, ed., *Le Psychanalyste et son patient*, Toulouse: Privat, 1983.

Tardieu, Jean, *Théâtre de chambre*, Paris: Gallimard, 1966.

Teresa of Avila, *The Life of Saint Teresa, By Herself*, trans. J.M. Cohen, Harmondsworth: Penguin, 1957.

Thibaudet, Albert, 'Réflexion sur la littérature, psychanalyse et critique littéraire', *Nouvelle Revue Française*, January 1922.

Todorov, Tzvetan, 'Synecdoques', *Communications*, 16, 1970.

—— *Théories du symbole*, Paris: Seuil, 'Points', 1985.

Turkle, Sherry, *Psychoanalytic Politics. Jacques Lacan and Freud's French Revolution*, London: Burnett Books in association with André Deutsch, 1979.

Université de Reims-Champage-Ardennes, *La Guerre et la paix dans les lettres françaises de la guerre du Rif à la guerre d'Espagne*, Reims 1983.

Valabrega, Jean-Paul, 'Aux Sources de la psychanalyse', *Critique*, 108, May 1956.

Valéry, Paul, *Œuvres* I, Paris: Bibliothèque de la pléiade, 1959.

Vauday, Patrick, 'Sartre et la psychanalyse sans inconscient', *Ornicar?*, 32, Spring 1985.

Wagner, R.L., *Introduction à la linguistique française*, Lille and Geneva: Librairie Girard and Librairie Droz, 1947.

Wahl, Jean, *Le Malheur de la conscience dans la philosophie de Hegel*, Paris,

Rieder, 1929.

—— *Vers le Concret*, Paris: Urin, 1932.

Waldberg, Patrick, *Surrealism*, London: Thames & Hudson, 1966.

Wallon, Henri, *Les Origines du caractère chez l'enfant*, Paris: PUF, 1949.

Wilden, Anthony, *System and Structure. Essays in Communication and Exchange*, London: Tavistock, 1980.

Wolfson, Louis, *Le Schizo et les langues*, Paris: Gallimard, 1970.

Wollheim, Richard, 'Psychoanalysis and Feminism', *New Left Review*, 93, September–October 1975.

—— 'The Cabinet of Dr Lacan', *New York Review of Books*, 25 January 1979.

Wright, Elizabeth, *Psychoanalytic Criticism: Theory in Practice*, London: Methuen, 1984.

Yaguello, Marina, *Les Mots et les femmes*, Paris: Payot, 1978.

Index

The name of Jacques Lacan has been omitted from this index